Libra.

From Behind a Closed Door

Michael Mallin (centre) and Countess Markievicz after
surrendering St Stephen's Green

RTÉ CASHMAN COLLECTION

From Behind a Closed Door

Secret Court Martial Records
of the 1916 Easter Rising

BRIAN BARTON

THE
BLACKSTAFF
PRESS

BELFAST

To Valerie, Deirdre and Allen

First published in 2002 by Blackstaff Press Limited
Wildflower Way, Apollo Road, Belfast BT12 6TA

Printed in Northern Ireland by W & G Baird Limited

A CIP catalogue record of this book is available from the British Library

ISBN 0-85640-697-x

www.blackstaffpress.com

Contents

Acknowledgements

I wish to thank the trustees, archivists and staffs of the following institutions for their invaluable assistance in the conduct of my research: the Allen Library, North Richmond Street, Dublin; the Bodleian Library, Oxford; the British Library, London; the Imperial War Museum, London; Kilmainham Gaol and Museum, Dublin; the Military Archives, Dublin; the National Archives, Dublin; the National Museum of Ireland, Dublin; the National Library of Ireland, Dublin; the Public Record Office, London; the Manuscripts Department, Trinity College, Dublin; the Archives Department, University College, Dublin; and the Linen Hall Library, Belfast. Every effort has been made to trace the copyright holders of the various primary sources used: in the instances where this search has not been successful, I offer most genuine apologies.

Sincere thanks are also due to those who provided photographs and the other material used to illustrate the text: at the Allen Library, especially Arran O'Reilly; at the National Museum, Kildare Street and Collins Barracks, Michael Kenny; at Kilmainham Gaol and Museum, Niamh O'Sullivan; at the *Belfast Telegraph*, Walter McAuley and at Radio Telefís Éireann, Aimee Kerr. Sister Louise, Daughters of Charity, Dublin, most graciously provided me with information regarding the photograph reproduced on page forty-eight. I am indebted also to the Bodleian Library; and to the Public Record Office, London, for granting permission to publish documents which are held there in facsimile form. In addition, I am extremely grateful to Tara O'Reilly, Dublin, who expertly reproduced many of the photographs in preparation for publication.

Finally, I wish to acknowledge the extent of my indebtedness to several individuals whose help and advice were crucial to the completion of this book. The support given by Dr Michael Foy was invaluable. He offered advice regarding the primary sources used and provided some of them; his knowledge of the material available relating to the Easter Rising is exhaustive, and his understanding of the tumultuous events during this period in Ireland's history is uniquely comprehensive. Dr Gerard Oram also most generously provided me with detailed information on the nature of courts martial proceedings in the British army during the First World War; he is an acknowledged authority in this field. I wish also to express my sincere gratitude to my publisher, Blackstaff Press; the expertise and encouragement given by the staff there was vital in shaping the present volume. In particular, I would like to thank my editor, Bronagh McVeigh, and Wendy Dunbar who designed the book. I am also profoundly grateful to Margaret Lamont, who typed the manuscript, for her forbearance, promptitude and efficiency, and to my wife, Valerie, for undertaking the laborious task of typing up the footnotes and for painstakingly proof reading the entire typescript.

BRIAN BARTON
BELFAST, APRIL 2002

View of the GPO and of the west side of lower Sackville Street,
after the Rising had ended, taken from the top of Nelson's Column

Introduction

The Easter Rising was conceived, planned and guided to fruition by the Irish Revolutionary Brotherhood (IRB); a small, underground organisation which had been formed in 1858. Its members drew their inspiration from Wolfe Tone and the 1798 rebellion, and the litany of subsequent unsuccessful Irish insurrections which had occurred over the one hundred years that followed. The IRB's last attempted rising had been a fiasco. On the night of 4 and 5 March 1867, several hundred poorly armed rebels had marched to the outskirts of Dublin in the snow and cold without any clear military objective. They were quickly rounded up, defeated by informers, bad weather, a well-prepared government, a disciplined army and their own inadequate planning. Subsequently, the IRB constitution was amended, to state: 'The IRB will await a decision of the Irish nation as expressed by a majority of the Irish people as to the fit hour of inaugurating a war against England.'[1]

Within the Brotherhood in 1914, the truly dynamic element was a militant minority, some of whom had committed themselves to a rising within weeks of the outbreak of the First World War. They were acting on the old republican adage often repeated in wartime: 'England's difficulty is Ireland's opportunity.' Twelve months later, on the initiative of Thomas Clarke, this group formed the IRB Military Council. It was eventually composed of seven members: Thomas Clarke, Sean MacDermott, Patrick Pearse, Eamonn Ceannt, Joseph Plunkett, James Connolly and Thomas MacDonagh. They were aided by a body of Irish-American extremists, called in

Clan na Gael: a movement founded in 1869, with over twenty-five thousand members in 1914 and committed to the same objectives. The organisation provided financial, logistical and moral support and was virtually the only channel of contact between the Irish insurgents and England's enemy, Germany.[2]

The IRB was too small a body – just two thousand members in 1911 – and its militant members too covert by habit and instinct to openly precipitate a large-scale rising. The Military Council hoped to use the Irish Volunteers (IVF) as a strike force in their planned rebellion. The Irish Volunteers had been launched on 25 November 1913 on the initiative of more moderate nationalists who had been impressed by the successful organisation and political impact of the Ulster Volunteer Force and who aimed to form a paramilitary counterbalance to it. The IVF had one hundred and eighty thousand members by the autumn of 1914 but formally split following an appeal made by John Redmond, the Irish nationalist leader, in a speech at Woodenbridge, County Wicklow, on 24 September that year. He had encouraged its members to enlist in British forces and to fight in the European war. The more extreme rump of two to three thousand men, which included most of the rank and file members from Dublin as well as most of the officers in the force, had strongly opposed this initiative, and retained the original name, IVF. (Redmond's supporters went on to establish the National Volunteers.) The IRB attempted to gain the support of the Irish Volunteers through a process of covert infiltration and deceit. A number of the leaders of the Irish Volunteers, notably Eoin MacNeill, were opposed to a wartime rebellion on grounds of principle. He strongly supported the IRB's constitution – that rebellion could only be justified if it had some prospect of military success and enjoyed a significant measure of support from within the Irish people and he firmly believed that this was the wrong time. However, the Military Council did form an alliance with the socialist, James Connolly. He was leader of the Irish Transport and General Workers Union (ITGWU) and commanded the Irish Citizen Army (ICA), whose members numbered about two hundred. Liberty Hall was the headquarters of both organisations. Initially, the ICA was established to protect workers in clashes with the police during the Dublin lockout of 1913, but when the First World War broke out Connolly hoped to deploy it in a rebellion aimed at establishing an independent, thirty-two county, workers' republic in Ireland. In mid-January 1916, he made common cause with the IRB Military Council after it had disclosed to him its own secret plans for insurrection.

The seven members of the Military Council differed widely in temperament and also in their ultimate objectives; the others did not share Connolly's vision of a socialist republic. Nor were they uniformly devout; Clarke, Connolly and MacDonagh had to a greater or lesser extent abandoned their religious beliefs and practices. But apart from the veteran, Thomas Clarke, who was of an earlier generation, they were all of similar age. Each could be described as middle-class. All were writers and propagandists as well as active revolutionaries. Most vitally, they were all suffused with a boundless energy, borne of a passionate desire to achieve the goal of Irish independence, and were unshakeable in their conviction that it could only be achieved by force. By early 1916, the attainment of this objective had come to give meaning to their lives. On 17 April 1916 the seven approved, and later signed, the draft of the Proclamation of the Irish Republic which was to be declared on the first day of the Rising. It announced the formation of a provisional government in Ireland, formed of the Military Council members themselves. The Proclamation, which was found by troops still on the printing press at Liberty Hall after the Rising, stated: 'in the name of God and of dead generations ... Ireland, through us, strikes for her freedom ... she strikes in full confidence of victory'. Its text has the paced composition of an orator such as Pearse; he probably wrote most of it. Its inflated language and sentiments reflect the passion behind it.

Irish Volunteers parading through the streets prior to the rebellion

ALLEN LIBRARY

The dogmatic and elitist claim that through this small, self-appointed group of revolutionaries the people of Ireland were being summoned into violent action, sprang from the authors' overpowering conviction that they spoke for the country's deepest self and that freedom was essential for Ireland's well-being as a nation.

The Rising was the product of the men and movements which preceded it. From the 1890s onward a new nationalism had emerged in Ireland – a more radical, uncompromising spirit. It found expression in the emergence of new cultural movements, for example, the Gaelic Athletic Association and Gaelic League, and in a number of political initiatives – the birth of the Sinn Féin party and the revitalisation of the IRB, as well as developments in the labour movement. The roots of this new nationalism are complex. One factor was disillusionment with the constitutional nationalism of the Irish Parliamentary Party – its continuing failure to achieve self-government, and its factional divisions after the fall of Parnell. Some came to regard its leaders as a remote, privileged elite, out of touch with Irish life, devoid of new ideas, and with apparently little interest in Ireland's culture, its economy or the deprived state of its working class. Equally, the centenary of the Wolfe Tone rebellion in 1898 reminded a new generation of an old faith, whilst the Boer War (1899–1902), helped dispel the assumption that British troops were invincible. The establishment of new cultural bodies gave a stimulus to the formation of more militant political organisations. Membership of these bodies often affected the outlook of those who joined them and they were drawn towards enrolment in more militant nationalist movements. In addition, prior to the outbreak of war, Britain's delay in granting Ireland Home Rule and the militancy of Ulster unionists in their opposition to it, helped confirm the drift towards support for physical force, certainly amongst a minority in Ireland.

For the more militant, the outbreak of war seemed a uniquely opportune moment for an insurrection – England and her empire were fully stretched, and throughout Europe men were dying for their country. Members of the Military Council were also at least partially influenced by the idea of a 'blood sacrifice'. They shared the view that the success of an insurrection could not be gauged solely in military terms; its suppression and their own deaths would not mean that the enterprise had failed or had not been justified. The Military Council members were convinced that Ireland's national spirit – its sense of itself as a distinct nation with a right to independence – was fading. This seemed to have been further demonstrated when the conflict began, by the initial burst of recruitment to the crown forces. The council feared that if Britain did grant Ireland limited self-government, the Irish people would come to accept permanent inclusion within the United Kingdom, and the English Crown as head of state. The members considered this future could be avoided through a rising; through their death and martyrdom, militant Irish nationalism would be revived and the republican tradition preserved. Ultimately, this would enable their successors to wage a successful war against British rule and thus achieve full national independence. Even MacNeill partially accepted this justification, stating: 'if we came to the conclusion that at least the vital principle of nationality was to be saved by laying down our lives then we should make that sacrifice without hesitation'.[3] The rebel leaders also hoped to prove, through their willingness to die, that Ireland had a right to freedom.

Thomas Clarke and Sean MacDermott with John Daly, an ardent republican and friend of both men

ALLEN LIBRARY

For romantic nationalists – Pearse, MacDonagh and Plunkett – the idea of blood sacrifice had additional appeal. For Pearse, especially, religion and nationalism fused; he acted as he did partly in conscious emulation of Christ's sacrifice on the cross; in following His example, he would redeem the Irish nation. Pearse was also influenced by the widespread, contemporary mystical belief in the regenerative importance for mankind of blood spilt on the battlefield.

The wealth of sources now available gives a clearer insight than was possible hitherto into the Military Council's motivation and plans. As a consequence, the traditional blood sacrifice interpretation of the Rising – with its assumption that the leaders from its inception regarded it as a doomed military enterprise – is now open to serious challenge. This approach is misleading in that it focuses too much on the attitude and role of those romantic nationalists within the Military Council and, in particular, on Pearse. But with regard to the inception, planning and preparation of the insurrection the driving force, above all others, was Thomas Clarke, aided by and mentor to the much younger Sean MacDermott. Both were archetypal republican figures – hard-headed, practical, ruthless, manipulative, earthy realists who were exclusively committed to the use of force as the sole means of achieving what was in their view the only worthy nationalist objective, the complete eradication of British rule in Ireland. At the moment of surrender, when defeat was certain and with it the slaughter of the rebels, the members of the provisional government decided to negotiate with the British authorities. They did so apparently after discussion between themselves; their aim was to agree terms under which they would be executed but the rank and file Volunteers would be permitted to go free. Thus, in practice, their blood sacrifice, rather than redeem Ireland, served a much more immediate purpose – that of preserving the lives of their followers.

Powerful evidence for this is provided by the detailed plans drawn up by Joseph Plunkett and Roger Casement, the rebels' self-appointed envoys in Germany. The plans are contained in the thirty-two page *Ireland Report*,[4] which they jointly submitted to the German High Command in May 1915. The report clearly reveals the scale of the military operations which the leadership was anticipating and the full extent of their ambitions. Military victory for the insurgents was to be achieved through a rising in Dublin, which it was hoped would be supported by massive foreign aid. The report requested that twelve thousand German troops should land at Limerick, and that they should bring with them and distribute forty thousand rifles to help arm and activate the Volunteers in Munster and Connaught. This composite force, led by German Army officers, was then to sweep eastwards in support of the insurrection in the capital. The planned outcome was that British units in Ireland would be isolated and crushed and that the episode would culminate in a victory march in Dublin along Sackville Street (affectionately referred to at the time as O'Connell Street and officially known as such today), accompanied by the strains of 'A Nation Once Again' and 'Deutschland Uber Alles'. The newly established rebel-led government was then to ally itself with Germany in the Great War, joining Turkey and Bulgaria. Though these plans were subsequently modified, the essential ingredients remained the same – a rebel rising in the capital and the landing of German troops to arm, join, and facilitate rebel armies across Ireland to the prospect of absolute victory. In April 1916, the Military Council requested that a U-Boat be positioned off the east coast of Ireland to block the arrival of reinforcements from Britain.

During the protracted, covert negotiations the German government rejected all the insurgents' proposals to send either submarines or troops; this was regarded as too hazardous given the strength of the Royal Navy. But it did eventually agree to provide arms – twenty thousand captured Russian rifles (1905 pattern) and one million rounds of ammunition and explosives. Germany hoped that an Irish rebellion would tie-up substantial British forces (the rebels estimated as many as half a million), impress its allies by illustrating its capacity to provide vital assistance despite the Royal Navy's blockade and expose the alleged shallowness of Britain's claims to be fighting for the rights of small nations. Eventually, on 9 April 1916, the munitions were dispatched aboard a 1,200 ton ship, the *Aud*. Already, in September 1915, the rebels had decided that consignments of imported arms should be landed at Fenit Pier, a secluded location in County Kerry with good rail links to Limerick and Galway. Arrangements were also made to land Casement on the west coast of Ireland ostensibly to prepare for the shipment; he left Germany with two members of his Irish Brigade on a U-boat on 15 April.

By the spring of 1916 the Military Council's preparations for a rising had proceeded apace. Leadership positions within the IVF were infiltrated both in Dublin and elsewhere with considerable success and its rank and file members trained in street-fighting techniques: amongst some at least expectations were growing that an insurrection was imminent. By January 1916, the Military Council had indeed set the date for a rising – initially Good Friday, 21 April 1916, later changed to Easter Sunday, 23 April. Their revolutionary intentions were to be masked behind publicly advertised and apparently routine Volunteer manoeuvres arranged for that day. Of necessity, on Wednesday, 19 April 1916, the IVF's commandants were given details of the plans for insurrection, despite the obvious risk of information leaking to those of its members who were opposed to it, or to the British authorities. Disaster threatened when Eoin MacNeill received confirmation of their intentions from Patrick Pearse in the early hours of Friday, 21 April. After initial hesitation, he issued a last minute countermand order cancelling the now publicised IVF manoeuvres for Easter Sunday, by placing a notice to this effect in that morning's edition of the *Sunday Independent*. He also dispatched trusted staff into the provinces as well as throughout Dublin to deliver this instruction by hand. Afterwards MacNeill maintained 'that the postponement of the Rising to Monday, served as a first class "ruse de guerre"'.[5] In confusion and despair, the seven Military Council members met at Liberty Hall at 9 a.m. on 23 April for four hours to consider their options. They decided by majority vote to proceed with what forces they could muster at noon next day, Easter Monday. Clarke alone dissented; he opposed any post-ponement. Meanwhile, that afternoon, the ICA held a route march which passed so close to Dublin Castle that the sentry slammed the gates closed and summoned all the guards on duty. On their return to Liberty Hall, Connolly in his last public speech urged the men no longer to think of themselves as Citizen Army members or Volunteers, but as all now belonging to the Irish Republican Army.[6]

British intelligence 'failed hopelessly' in its sur-veillance of the preparations for a rising.[7] Dublin Castle, the British seat of government in Ireland, lay virtually unprotected on Easter Monday morning. Volunteer manoeuvres were so common that there seemed to be 'no more reason to apprehend an armed rebellion than when similar mobilisations [had been] carried out';[8] over six thousand Volunteers had marched throughout Ireland on the previous St Patrick's Day. The two officials with greatest responsibility for Irish governance, the age-ing Chief Secretary, Augustine Birrell and his Under Secretary, Sir Matthew Nathan, were both commit-ted to the Liberal government's policy of granting Ireland Home Rule; neither had any expectation that an insurrection was imminent. Birrell was indolent, inert, some-what withdrawn and resided mainly in London where he attended cabinet meetings and parliamentary sessions. Over previous months, he had apparently stated repeatedly, 'I don't take these people seri-ously. I laugh at the whole thing.' His approach was characterised by an unimpressed contemporary as 'give peace in our time, O Lord'.[9] Nathan, his key adviser and the major determinant of Dublin Castle's response, was of German-Jewish origin, fifty two years old, assiduously hard-working and had hitherto enjoyed a consistently successful administrative career. He had a growing feeling that 'everything is not quite right',[10] but nonetheless, on Saturday 22 April, he wrote reassuringly to his superior: 'I see no indications of a rising.'[11]

Order issued to the Volunteers in his company by Sean Heuston, during the afternoon of Sunday, 23 April 1916. It was found by soldiers after the Rising in one of Heuston's report pads and produced as evidence by the prosecution during his court martial.

PRO LONDON

This profound misjudgment, which would end Nathan's career in Ireland and lead to Birrell's replacement, was due in part to the distractions of war. Against its background, Birrell and his officials had been mainly concerned over previous months to contain, and not to provoke, Irish extremists. Moderate Irish nationalist leaders, who exercised considerable influence, argued that any repressive measures 'would advertise [extremists] and increase difficulty'.[12] In addition, the insurrection leaders had laid their plans and preparations with unusual caution and skill. They also enjoyed considerable good fortune and were helped by the sheer incompetence of the British administration. From February 1916, Sir Neville Chamberlain, the Inspector General of the Royal Irish Constabulary (RIC), had warned Dublin Castle of the increasing strength of the Volunteers, their accumulation of arms and the growing evidence that a rising was being planned with German support. His reports were ignored. Also, the exchange of messages between the rebel leadership and the German government, in particular those passing through its embassy in New York, had routinely been intercepted by British naval intelligence. Hence, from March 1916, the plans for a rising, the arrangement to import arms and Casement's involvement, were known to senior British naval and military personnel. The ship containing German munitions, the *Aud*, was probably monitored as it passed along the Connaught and Munster coast. Certainly, police and troops in the south and west were placed on alert; both the ship and Casement were captured on Friday, 21 April. But fearing leaks, full knowledge of such sensitive information was restricted mainly to the service chiefs. It was certainly not communicated to either Birrell or Nathan.[13]

Nonetheless, by the eve of the Rising, Dublin Castle officials had themselves begun to receive more ominous and graphic reports of the real intentions of Irish extremists, mainly from two paid informers in Dublin, code-named Chalk and Granite. Though their reports were inconsistent, in March they did warn: 'Things look as if they are coming to a crisis.'[14] Nathan, who stored the reports in a safe in his office, had as a consequence decided, by Saturday 22 April, to intern a list of suspects. However, he felt no sense of urgency having meanwhile received word that the arms shipment had been captured and Casement arrested. Nathan was further reassured when

Liberty Hall 16

To the man in charge in Camp. Fredrick St. I want all you men to report to me at Liberty Hall by 11 a.m. Today Monday. with full equipment

Seanmac Diarmada

24/4/16

Instruction sent out by Sean MacDermott, from Liberty Hall, urgently summoning Volunteers early on the first morning of the Rising, Easter Monday, 24 April 1916. It was found in one of Sean Heuston's report pads by troops searching the Mendicity Institution and later produced as evidence by the prosecution at MacDermott's court martial.

PRO LONDON

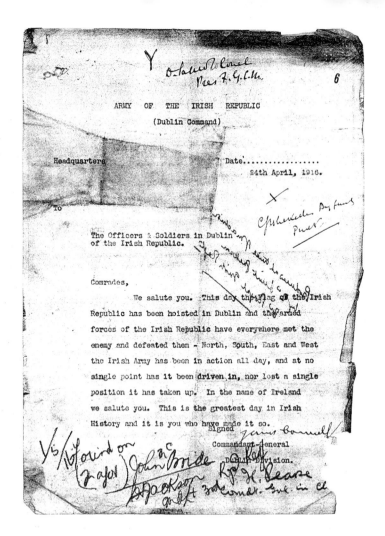

Stirring message issued by Connolly to the Volunteers on the first day of the Rising, 24 April 1916. A copy of the document was found on Major John MacBride when he was searched by soldiers at Richmond Barracks after the surrender; it was later used in evidence by the prosecution during Connolly's trial.

PRO LONDON

MacNeill's published countermand was noticed in the *Sunday Independent*. The planned arrests were also delayed by the need to receive written authorisation from London before such action could be taken and by a justifiable reluctance to proceed over the Easter period whilst so many people were on holiday in Dublin. Furthermore, though the Inspector General of the RIC was increasingly concerned at the activities of the Volunteers, he had advised in March that they were incapable of making 'even a brief stand against a small body of troops'.[15]

On Easter Monday morning in Dublin, the city's four Volunteer battalions and Irish Citizen Army members assembled at various pre-arranged meeting points. Liberty Hall was the most significant; it was by now a veritable armoury and had for days been placed under constant armed guard by the rebels. At just before noon the units marched towards a number of key buildings which they subsequently occupied. These had been selected to command the main routes into the city and because of their strategic position in relation to the main British military barracks and their value in disrupting telephone and telegraph systems. They included the General Post Office (GPO); at the time Special Branch estimated that eighteen Sinn Féiners worked there and the Irish postal system had for long been regarded by some as a 'disaffected service'.[16] The Four Courts, Jacob's Biscuit Factory, Boland's Bakery, the South Dublin Union, St Stephen's Green and later the College of Surgeons were also seized. Given the advantage of surprise, all of these premises were occupied virtually without opposition. The insurgents then immediately set about making them defensible – sandbagging windows, loopholing walls, seizing adjacent properties as outposts and erecting barricades.

Owing to the confusion caused by MacNeill's countermand order, the numbers mobilised were considerably lower than anticipated, forcing the abandonment of some of the original plans, most notably the intention to occupy the grounds of Trinity College. The capture of Dublin Castle had been considered by the leaders well before the Rising but rejected as they believed they would never have sufficient men to hold such an extensive complex of buildings. The General Post Office served as rebellion headquarters and as the seat of the provisional government. Five of its members served there: Clarke, Patrick Pearse, Connolly, MacDermott and Plunkett. Pearse was designated President (Clarke had refused the post), and also Commandant-General of the army, and Connolly was appointed Vice-President and Commandant of the forces in Dublin. It was Pearse therefore who had the honour of reading the Proclamation from the step in front of the GPO at 12:45 p.m. on Easter Monday; it was received with a muted response by bewildered onlookers. Hundreds of copies were then posted throughout the city and distributed to the other rebel strongholds. Meanwhile, because telephone communication had been disrupted, a British army officer in civilian clothes had had to cycle to Kingston Wireless Telegraph Station to transmit a message at 12:30 p.m. It began: 'Armed Sinn Fein rising in Dublin today ... Troops called out.'[17] It was received at 3:23 p.m. by the Admiralty who then advised the War Office.

The British military onslaught which the rebels anxiously anticipated and prepared for was not at once forthcoming. When the Rising began, the Dublin Castle authorities had just four hundred troops available to confront roughly one thousand insurgents. Their immediate priorities were to mobilise mass reinforcements, to

Overleaf:
Letter written by Sarah Hughes to the military authorities in Dublin, dated 19 July 1916. The letter vividly describes the circumstances in which her husband, Michael, was allegedly killed by British troops during the fighting in North King Street, in the course of the Rising.

PRO LONDON

172, North King Street,
Dublin.
July 19th, 1916.

Honourable Sir,

I beg leave to state my case.

I am the wife of Michael Hughes, whom was shot
in North King Street, by the Military, on the 29th of
April.

To state my case accurately on the 29th of April,
the Military called to my door, and I myself (Sarah Hughes)
opened the door and admitted 11 armed men   I told them
we were no Sinn Feiners here, I also showed my War
Certificate, there was, myself, and husband, and three
children of mine.

I had 18 Refugees, namely, Walsh, his wife and
four children, one old man aged 84 years, a blind man and
his son aged 16 years, Mrs O'Neill and her son, all these
people had to leave their homes as they were sent from
their Homes by the Sinn Feiners, and I took them in and
gave them shelter.

When the Military entered my premises, they
first thoroughly searched the shop, they then came, into
my kitchen, they looked around there, and then proceed
upstairs. We were all in the back Drawing room to
escape the heavy firing, as the Sinn Feiners were firing
from the distillery.

One of the soldiers that entered my place a
Corporal and a Sergeant they searched my Husband also
the man Walsh, one of the soldiers said give those Irish
pigs an ounce of lead.

In the early part of that morning I gave my
Husband Michael Hughes, all the Jewellry I possessed, to
keep for me as every minute I expected a raid on my shop
                                                    and

gather information on rebel strength, location and arms levels and
to identify and protect vital strategic positions – not least the Castle
itself. However, as the week progressed the fighting in some areas at
least did become intense and was characterised by prolonged, hand-
to-hand street battles in which no holds were barred. In these
circumstances, lapses in military discipline were, perhaps, inevitable.
Matthew Nathan himself accepted that on occasion the troops exercised 'summary justice'.[18] On Wednesday, official orders were issued
instructing soldiers to shoot first any individual suspected of being

and private premises, I was only one week moved into this house. The Military put all women and children down to the cellars, including myself.

I heard the man Walsh saying what are you doing that for. I understood they were taking the men prisoners and handcuffing them, let any human being think over it, one man taking into the Drawing room and shot dead. My poor Husband brought to the top of the House, and instantly shot dead for no crime at all, it was murder and cool blooded murder, there is no other word for it.

During my time in the cellar, I heard some person moaning, as if they were in pain. I went up and there found a Sergeant lying wounded in my Hall, the firing was fierce and I asked his comrades to go upstairs and take down the Sofa into the kitchen. I helped the Soldiers to take him in, and I done all I possibly could to alleviate his pain until the Doctor came, little did I think at the time that the Father of my three children was cold and dead. When the Doctor came, to attend this wounded soldier, namely Sergeant Bancks, he asked me how many people I had in my house, I told him 18 people, the Doctor asked me to bring the old man a cup of tea, I done so, the Guard on the door asked me would I give him a cup of tea, which I did.

I then looked into the Drawing room to see was there much damage done, I saw a man lying dead on my Fender. I asked no questions as I was very much afraid of the Military. I recognised the man dead to be Walsh, I went down to the cellar, and asked Mrs. Walsh what kind of socks her Husband wore, she said the Colour was between a green and brown, I said thank God the man

I

a rebel, uniformed or otherwise, who was armed and not surrendering. In parts of the city 'free fire zones' operated; any civilian visible on the streets was assumed to be one of the enemy and was treated accordingly. On Thursday morning, troops 'warned people' in the Amiens Street area to disperse, and 'those who refused to leave were fired on'.[19] Rebels made substantiated allegations later of indiscriminate shooting into houses from armoured cars.

Subsequent allegations of British military brutality centred mainly on events in the Four Courts area of Dublin. It was widely

I saw had grey Military Socks on him.

I did not want to frighten this woman, as she was every day expecting her baby to be born.

In the afternoon a took a gastly feeling over me, and I asked the Sergeant would he allow me to go upstairs as I had a presiment over me that there was something wrong with my Husband, he told me he had no Authority to allow me to go. He then sent for the Officer, the Officer came, and I told him I had a feeling over me that my Husband was dead, the Officer asked me to leave it until morning. I said I could not exist until morning, he then told me there was two men shot in the House, one shot through the brain, (and to use his own words not a very nice sight to look at), I said I only wanted to see the man on the top of the house, he accompanied me up, and there I found my Husband dead, shot through the brain, murdered in cool blood for no crime.

I made no outcry, or never murmured, I walked back, and made no complaint. My sight went and the power of speech failed me, the Soldiers in the early part of the day told me he was in the detention Barracks and then to find him dead in his own home. I sent on my statement to Sir Jno. Maxwell and he graciously sent me on a reply, saying he would have my case fully inquired into. The Military took my Jewellry, also money to the amount of £80. Honourable Sir, I am only a woman trying to live out of a small business, any little saving I had, I invested in the War loan, and since this trouble arose, I had to withdraw it. Honourable Sir, I respectfully ask you to consider my case, my means and support is gone, I have three children to provide for the eldest 11 years and the youngest two years. I am only a delicate woman and my Husband saw after the business, I am now left with the

believed amongst local civilians that soldiers had killed fifteen innocent and unarmed men in a block of roughly ten houses in North King Street in the course of a series of fierce, house-to-house gun-battles lasting almost two days, from 28 to 29 April. Within nationalist Ireland the episode came to be regarded as a 'massacre', a 'cold-blooded calculated atrocity', 'an atrocious crime',[20] in which innocent bystanders were murdered by troops, supervised by officers, in some cases after the immediate danger had passed. At the subsequent coroner's enquiry, Lieutenant Colonel H. Taylor, the officer in

the charge of three orphans, boys,   Honourable Sir, my
husband belonged to no society what so ever,   Honourable
Sir, I ask you to take my case into your kind consideration,
and if you will condescend to read my statement and in the
interest of Justice, you cannot fail to deal with my case.

    I now place my case in your Honour, and Sense
of Justice, that you will see Justice done to me and my
orphans.

               I have the Honour to remain

                  Your Humble Servant,

                    (Sd.) Sarah Hughes.

command of the unit involved, claimed that: 'no persons were attacked by the troops other than those who were assisting the rebels, and found with arms in their possession'; the jury found the military explanation 'unsatisfactory'.[21] A later military court of enquiry concluded that: 'it was unlikely that any persons were shot or killed unless the men had reason to think that they had been fired on, whether they were mistaken or not'. On this occasion, however, Taylor conceded in reference to some of the deaths: 'I think it very possible that these men might have been shot or killed [by the soldiers] at sight'.[22] The court's presiding officer, Brigadier E.W.S.K. Maconchy, stated: 'some men were possibly wrongly shot because they were found with arms on them in houses from which the troops had been fired at'.[23] The General Officer Commanding troops, Ireland, Major General Sir John Maxwell, conceded publicly that, 'possibly some unfortunate incidents which we should regret now may have occurred'. He also admitted that perhaps some of the troops, in the heat of battle, 'saw red'.[24] Privately, he confessed to his wife that he was, 'bothered to death with these cases where soldiers are accused of having murdered innocent civilians in cold blood. I fear there have been some cases of this.'[25] He informed Field Marshal Lord Kitchener: 'It must be borne in mind ... there was a lot of house-to-house fighting going on, wild rumours in circulation ... a good deal of "jumpiness". With young soldiers and under the circumstances I wonder there was not more.'[26] His official explanation of the deaths was that they had occurred 'during rebellion and active armed resistance to His Majesty's troops in the execution of their duty'.[27] By implication the rebels were ultimately responsible.

Referring to the incident in the Commons, the Prime Minister Herbert Asquith, accepted that: 'There could be little doubt that some men who were not taking an actual part in the fighting were in the course of the struggle killed by both rebels and soldiers'.[28] He also indicated that it had not been possible to identify and charge those responsible. A detailed memorandum relating to the episode prepared for the premier and written in late May 1916 by Sir Edward Troup, Permanent Secretary at the Home Office, was much less circumspect. It refers to an order given by Brigadier-General William Lowe, who was in command of overall operations at the time. It stated that 'no hesitation was to be shown in dealing with these rebels; that by their action they had placed themselves outside the law, and that they were not to be made prisoners'. As a direct result of this, in Troup's opinion, 'it is not unlikely that the soldiers did not accurately distinguish between refusing to make prisoners and shooting immediately prisoners whom they had made'. Troup considered Lowe's instruction to be 'the root of the mischief ... This [order] in itself may have been justifiable but it should have been made clear that it did not mean that an unarmed rebel might be shot after he had been taken prisoner, still less could it mean that a person taken on mere suspicion could be shot without trial.' He strongly advised the Prime Minister against publishing the evidence taken by the enquiries, stressing that 'there are many points that could be used for the purpose of hostile propaganda'. It was his opinion that: 'Nothing but harm could come of any public inquiry that would draw further attention to the matter'.[29]

The best known civilian victim of Easter week was Francis Sheehy-Skeffington, a pacifist. On 25 April, he had organised a poorly attended meeting in Dublin at 5 p.m. to discuss looting and relief measures for the city's poor. Afterwards he was arrested and next morning shot by firing squad without trial in Portobello Barracks. The British army officer responsible for giving the order was Captain J.C. Bowen-Colthurst. The impact of the episode on Irish opinion was again magnified due to the attempt made by the authorities to cover up the murder. The incident caused much bitterness, particularly in County Cork. In June, the captain's house, six miles from Macroom, had to be placed 'under constant protection by [RIC] patrols',[30] and eventually troops had to be moved into the area to restore order. The captain's farm was also boycotted by the local community. The Volunteers themselves considered that those troops who were from Irish backgrounds were the most bitter in their reaction to the Rising.

As for the rebels, their part in the fighting was somewhat less chivalrous than has frequently been depicted; they quickly came to be regarded as 'heroes, martyrs and clean fighters'. There is, of course, ample evidence that they generally treated their prisoners (mainly soldiers and policemen) well. They seemed to show considerable courtesy to the owners of the private properties which they occupied, causing little malicious damage, and they were polite to the occupants of the vehicles they commandeered for the purpose of erecting barricades. Their efforts to stop looting and to distribute food within their battalion districts and also their overall sobriety, were commented on with genuine admiration by many civilians. But more dubious actions and behavioural lapses on the part of the rebels did take place. With justification, Sir John Maxwell complained: 'Great capital is made out of these [the deaths in North King Street] but the cold-blooded shooting of soldiers, police and civilians by the rebels in passed over in silence.'[31] At the start of the Rising, several policemen and soldiers who were still unaware that it had begun, were shot dead by the insurgents in cold blood. Within hours, the unarmed Dublin Metropolitan Police were withdrawn from the streets after two of its members had been gunned down and killed in separate incidents at around noon on Easter Monday. Eyewitnesses observed that the shooting by Volunteers was sometimes indiscriminate; this they surmised was in order to assert their authority and overawe the public, and also because of the youth, nervousness and, in some cases, the arrogance of their members. Police files contain numerous detailed reports of civilians shot and, on occasion, fatally wounded if they attempted to resist the occupation of their shops and homes or the seizing of their vehicles on the street or if they failed to respond promptly to instructions. It is beyond doubt that dum-dum bullets were used by the rebels, their noses shaped so as to inflict more terrible injuries. Pat Rankin, a member of the GPO garrison, recalls nervously discarding some of the bullets by dropping them at his feet while standing near Nelson's Column after the surrender.[32] Evidence of the existence of such bullets is also provided by post-mortem reports on a number of the fatally wounded, and by the content of arms caches uncovered by troops during later house-to-house searches. A St John's Ambulance Brigade officer graphically describes Volunteers breaching a locally arranged ceasefire near the Four Courts at Church Street on Easter Saturday evening.[33] Allegations were made by both sides that the other failed to respect Red Cross personnel or property and that they used civilians for cover.

Pearse's decision to surrender on Saturday was taken partly because he had just witnessed the death of one civilian bystander, who had been riddled with bullets, and had seen a group of women shot at during the fighting in Moore Street. Of the 450 who died in Easter week, over 250 were civilians. This was partly because much of the fighting occurred in or near densely populated areas; one-third of Dublin's population lived in insanitary slums adjacent to the main streets in which most of the rebel strongholds were located. The number of fatalities was inflated by the insatiable curiosity of the citizens of Dublin and their apparently fatalistic acceptance of the dangers involved in watching the spectacle. One lady commented that although she 'saw terrible sights, [she] felt drawn towards it'. Another stated enthusiastically when it began, 'I shall see and hear the revolution.' One eyewitness explained '[you] could not stay in the house, but must be out either to see what was going on or to talk to the neighbours'. Near the GPO on Wednesday, Dick Humphries noted: 'An over inquisitive crowd is standing at D'Olier Street and O'Connell Bridge, right between the firing parties. They appear quite unconcerned.' He added that they seemed to regard it as 'a sham battle for their amusement'.[34] Doctors later reported cases of fear-induced hysteria. Some civilians unwisely wore green clothing and so unwittingly became targets themselves. More elderly individuals might enter contested areas oblivious of the danger to themselves or unable to react to it with sufficient speed. Others took unavoidable risks, courageously serving the needs of those actively participating

Two uniformed nurses after the Rising, standing adjacent to the ruins of the Dublin Bread Company, a restaurant on the lower east side of Sackville Street; it had been occupied by the rebels, 24–26 April.

RTÉ MURTAGH COLLECTION

in the fighting or those who were merely caught up in it – priests, medical personnel and ambulance drivers in particular.

Apart from the physical dangers to themselves, during Easter week civilians progressively suffered increasing levels of dislocation and disruption. Houses caught within the fighting zones had to be vacated and much property was destroyed or damaged. The transport system in Dublin collapsed. The rebels cut off gas supplies so as to reduce the risk of fire in their fortified strongholds, mail went undelivered, most newspapers ceased publication and telephone and telegraph services were disrupted. Many offices and businesses closed – the Post Office (thus benefits could not be claimed) and also corporation premises, civil service departments, numerous shops, banks, theatres and cinemas. Essentials became scarce and expensive – coal, milk and above all, bread. Most bakeries and retailers closed and the closure of the distribution system hit supplies of flour and meal. The problem was aggravated by panic buying and the requisitioning of food both by troops and rebels. But apart from these privations, the Rising was also an immensely exciting, dramatic and compelling spectacle, vividly described by its citizen observers as well as by participants. On Thursday at the GPO, Joseph Plunkett exulted: 'It is the first time this has happened since Moscow. The first time a capital city has burned since 1812!'[35] The Rising provided unprecedented opportunities for looting. This began soon after noon on Easter Monday and was facilitated by the withdrawal of the 1,100 Dublin Metropolitain Police members (DMP) from the streets. The looting soon reached epidemic proportions, far beyond the capacity of either the troops or the insurgents to prevent or contain. The reappearance of the police on 30 April occasioned some derision; Douglas Hyde records two old men shouting at members of the force in pursuit of a looter 'to accelerate their pace ... "Houl that fellow! Houl that fellow!"'[36]

The civilian population was by no means uniformly hostile to the Rising even during Easter week. Nonetheless, some had 'thought Ireland was the only safe place to be at present, so remote from battle'[37] and inevitably anger was expressed at the number of fatalities and the scale of destruction and distress the Rising caused. Its timing was also criticised, when the country was prosperous and Home Rule seemed imminent. In the context of war it outraged those with relatives in military service, by whom it was regarded as an act of treachery; 85,000 Irishmen had enlisted by the end of 1915 and over 16,300 from Dublin itself (though some 2,200 young men had by then emigrated from Ireland for fear that conscription would be introduced). Thus, during the fighting in the Four Courts area several people were arrested by the rebels as spies. Here, as elsewhere, some of the Volunteers recorded bitter confrontations with local priests. At the College of Surgeons, the mood of the crowds who witnessed the Volunteers' surrender was one of ferocious hostility; the insurgents were profoundly relieved when a British troop cordon was hurriedly set up in Grafton Street to restrain the sullen mob at bayonet point. There were similar scenes when the insurgents emerged from Jacob's factory and again when their defeated battalions marched under military guard to Richmond Barracks amidst the jeers and taunts of furious spectators.

But to concentrate exclusively on such episodes would give a misleading impression of public attitudes. The route to Richmond Barracks led through areas of acute deprivation in which a significant proportion of the indigenous catholic poor had family members fighting on the Western Front, whilst the sympathies of any local protestant artisans lay wholly with the authorities. However in some battalion areas the surrendering rebels were greeted with genuine enthusiasm. At Boland's Bakery, de Valera was consumed with emotion at the spontaneous warmth of the civilian response; he remarked: 'If only you had come out to help us ... you would not behold us like this.'[38] Ceannt's Volunteers were likewise heartened by the friendly reception they received from spectators after they had vacated the South Dublin Union.

With justification several rebels believed that sympathy for their cause had grown as the week progressed. One diarist noted that by Thursday, 'the ancient racial hatred of England [had begun] to revive'.[39] Even those observers who were initially hostile had to concede that, by and large, the Volunteers had fought a clean fight, with undoubted courage, palpable conviction and evident concern for the distress caused to the civilian population by their actions. With their motley collection of rifles and revolvers they had held out for a week against the resources of an empire, which was able and willing to deploy apparently limitless numbers of troops equipped with machine-guns, heavy artillery, incendiary shells, armoured cars and even a gunship. Eamonn Ceannt's brother, Michael, who was not a republican, observed, 'Lord, if we thought they had the least chance wouldn't we all be in it';[40] certainly the authorities fully shared this impression and were later to act upon it.

John Clarke, owner of a small shop who lived near the Four Courts, wrote after witnessing its surrender: 'This ends the last attempt for poor old Ireland. What noble fellows! The cream of the land. None of your corner-boy class.'[41] In the Four Courts area, police had recorded over previous months a measurable growth in political extremism, and soldiers serving near there were acutely aware of the hostility of some civilians during the fighting. Several of the medical staff at Richmond Hospital nearby gave the rebels vital support – informing them of troop movements as well as helping them man their casualty posts, tending those more gravely wounded in the hospital itself and assisting all of those recuperating in their wards to escape after the surrender. Though some in religious orders had been hostile, many local priests and nuns were also supportive, providing not only the comforts of religion but also food, accommodation, information on the disposition of British forces, concealing weapons and likewise assisting some to evade capture at the end. They thus earned the enduring gratitude of some of the rebels. Paddy Holohan paid particular tribute to the Capuchin Fathers, Church Street, 'for the part they played in succouring the wounded and amid constant danger in bringing the consolations of religion to the dying all through the week'. He affirmed that 'it began an association between the Volunteers and the Capuchins which lasted throughout the trying years of the Black and Tan war'.[42] When the rising was over and the insurgents were being escorted from the Rotunda to Richmond Barracks, Oscar Traynor later recalled how 'outside the gates of the ... Barracks, I saw a Capuchin priest who as we were entering ... kept saying, with tears in his eyes, "Misneach" [Courage] which was completely unintelligible to the enemy forces'.[43]

Father Albert, one of the Capuchin priests from Church Street Friary, Dublin; he visited a number of the rebel prisoners in Kilmainham prison prior to their execution

ALLEN LIBRARY

Despite their initial lapses in intelligence, overall the British authorities responded competently to the Rising. Mass military reinforcements began to be drafted into Dublin on Easter Monday afternoon. The first to arrive came from the Curragh, followed by

others from Belfast, Athlone and Templemore. A further ten thousand were already en route from England. By early on Friday, 28 April, rebel numbers had risen to about 1,550 but they were confronted by between eighteen and twenty thousand troops, with still more in transit, their arrival imminent. Information was also quickly gathered on rebel strength and positions. Vital locations in the city were speedily identified and defended, including the docks, railway stations, telephone exchange, munitions sites and the grounds of Dublin Castle and Trinity College. On Tuesday, the military forged an axis running east–west, from Kingsbridge to the Customs House, effectively splitting the insurgent forces in two, providing a safe line of advance for troops and facilitating their communications. Progressively a cordon was placed around the city, using the readily defensible line of the Royal and Grand canals; it was completed by Friday. By Wednesday, the most strategically significant rebel-held outposts had been taken, including the City Hall, the Mendicity Institution and Liberty Hall, which despite its appearance was actually unoccupied. From Thursday, the General Post Office was entirely cut off from the other strongholds and preparations were being made similarly to isolate the Four Courts. The subsequent ferocious artillery attack on the GPO induced the rebel leaders there first to evacuate, and hours later to accept the only terms the British were prepared to offer – unconditional surrender. Their decision was then made known to all the commandants and garrisons still fighting in the capital and in the provinces. It was accepted, often reluctantly, amidst scenes of heartbreak, anguish, bitterness and also disbelief as some units had been doing more than hold their own against the troops and were convinced that they could have held out for weeks.

During the fighting, the military made several costly tactical errors, most notably at Mount Street Bridge on Wednesday, 26 April. There, the Sherwood Foresters, who had disembarked at Dun Laoghaire early that morning, made successive frontal assaults without artillery support on a select group of determined, disciplined, well-armed Volunteers occupying strongly fortified and barricaded outposts. The attack succeeded but only after a gun-battle lasting from midday to dusk and at the loss of 234 men dead or wounded, only five Volunteers were killed. A hard lesson had been learnt. Thus, two days later, after the Sherwoods had encircled the GPO, they did not attempt to repeat the mass infantry attack which the rebels were then anticipating. Instead they deluged the entrenched insurgent positions with incendiary shells to incinerate and destroy them, drive their occupants out and force them to capitulate. The strategy was effective. The cost was the destruction of much of Sackville Street where the conflagrations caused £1 million in damage to property and £750,000 in lost stock. As elsewhere in the city most of the fires were caused by British tactics, the rest by Volunteers strengthening their defences or by the casual violence of looters. Military losses were minimal and in total only nine members of the GPO garrison died during the fighting in Easter week. Nonetheless, afterwards, one contemporary who was unsympathetic to the rebels observed: 'People are all saying. Oh, our beautiful city! Look how the military have destroyed it. The English will have to pay for this.'[44]

Owing to the capture of the *Aud*, Casement's arrest and the confusion caused by MacNeill's countermanding order, the Rising was almost exclusively confined to Dublin. Cork failed to mobilise. In Limerick, local Volunteer leaders met and conferred but decided not to act. In Galway, one thousand men assembled on Easter Monday, seized several RIC stations and then abandoned their activities on receiving news of Dublin's capitulation. At Wexford, the rebels took over the town of Enniscorthy on Wednesday, 26 April; they only surrendered after two of their officers were permitted to meet Pearse in person and receive instructions direct from him. The most significant action outside the capital occurred ten miles north of it when Volunteers, led by Thomas Ashe and the highly effective Richard Mulcahy, attacked several police barracks. In the course of a tense gun-battle at Ashbourne on Friday, 28 April, two Volunteers and between eight and fifteen members of the RIC died. There were no plans for Ulster to play any part in the Rising as the Military Council had feared setting off a sectarian war in the province.

According to official estimates, the death toll from the Rising rose to 450 persons killed, 2,614 wounded and 9 missing, almost all losses occurring in the city of Dublin. The military had 17 officers killed and 46 wounded; 99 other ranks killed, 322 wounded and 9 missing. In Maxwell's view: 'We have lost a good few men ... but considering the number of bullets flying about, not excessive.'[45] The RIC had 13 men killed and 22 wounded; the DMP had 3 killed and 7 wounded. Government figures combined civilian and insurgent casualties, giving a total of 318 killed and 2,217 wounded. It is widely accepted that 64 rebels died; two of these losses occurred at

Boland's Bakery when one of the rebels became mentally unhinged and shot dead a comrade; he was then fatally wounded by one of his own officers. The Volunteer casualties were low partly because in Dublin they were the defending force and they fought with discipline and skill. Also, in the end, under instructions from Pearse and Connolly, they surrendered their strongholds rather than fight to the last man in an uneven contest against superior numbers of troops, armed with artillery and machine-guns. After the insurgents had been forced to evacuate the GPO and were facing inevitable defeat, a majority of their leaders then agreed to negotiate with British officers. They hoped to strike a deal – namely that they themselves would be executed and that their death and sacrifice would enable the rank and file to go free and fight more successfully another day. Thus their blood sacrifice was not a strategy carefully devised months in advance, but a gambit hastily concocted as the Rising disintegrated. It was designed not to redeem Ireland, but to perform the eminently practical task of saving the lives of their men.

The tactical errors made by British troops inflated their otherwise modest losses. The engagement at Mount Street Bridge proved the most costly, but at North King Street ignorance of the exact location of rebel strongholds in the area contributed to high casualty levels for the South Staffordshire regiment. During gun-battles there on the Friday and Saturday of Easter week, 16 soldiers died and 31 were wounded. But the military leadership learnt from these mistakes. It was a considerable achievement to suppress the insurrection inside one week as the military force comprised mainly of young inexperienced troops, most with no knowledge of Dublin (some unaware at first that they were even in Ireland!), no training in street-fighting and often operating in improvised, scratch units. Three-quarters of the Sherwood Foresters fighting at Mount Street Bridge had less than three months military service. Men drawn from twenty-four different regiments were based at Portobello Barracks during the Rising and this disparate composition was probably replicated at the other main military bases in the city. After the surrender 'a benefit mass was celebrated' in the Provost's dining room at Trinity College, for the motley range of troops that had gathered there; his daughter notes that it was probably 'the first time that mass had been said' at the university.[46]

There can be no doubt that the response of Asquith's cabinet to the Rising contributed measurably to the further alienation of Irish public opinion. Acting against advice from its leading public servants in Dublin Castle, the Cabinet introduced nationwide martial law on Wednesday, 26 April. This decision resulted from its concern at 'some disquieting features ... indicating the spread of the rebellious movement ... particularly in the west'. Next day, Major General Sir John Maxwell was appointed General Officer Commanding British troops, Ireland, and thus also head of the country's civil administration: the 'Irish administrators' were informed that they must 'place themselves at his disposal and carry out his instructions'.[47] For the next six months he played a decisive role in determining British government policy in Ireland. His ardent conviction from the outset was that militant nationalism must now be crushed; he believed that the preceding years of laxity and indecision had merely served to undermine respect for law and order. He never doubted that the leaders of the insurrection should be court-martialled and those most prominent executed. But he was also concerned that those who had surrendered with them, along with their suspected supporters, should be arrested and their arms seized in a nationwide sweep by British troops, supported by the Irish police force and intelligence services. At the end of Easter week, military personnel were dispatched in large numbers into the provinces, focusing especially on those areas which had shown any indication of active sympathy towards the insurgents. The most dramatic incident that occurred in the course of these operations was on 2 May, when an RIC party called at Bawnard House, Castlelyons, County Cork, intending to arrest two prominent, local dissidents, Thomas and

David Kent. A gun-battle ensued after which both men and another brother, William, were placed under arrest, charged with taking part in 'armed rebellion' and subsequently court-martialled.[48] Thomas was found guilty and sentenced to death.

In Dublin, for several weeks after the Rising, districts were cordoned off, numerous pickets posted on the streets, the ports kept under close surveillance and houses searched for known extremists and for arms. Meanwhile, preparations were being made to court martial those suspected of being the leaders of the insurrection. Rumour had been rife amongst the Dublin rebels during and after the surrender of their various garrisons on Saturday and Sunday, 29–30 April as to what would become of them. They were all subsequently escorted to Richmond Barracks in the course of Sunday, the last arriving at about 8 p.m. where the selection procedure for the trials was to take place. On arrival, they were crammed into billets with a few buckets to serve as latrines. Robert Holland, who served at Marrowbone Lane, recalls: 'The door was locked and we had hardly room to sit down. We were in this room all night. Everyone seemed to be in serious thought, and no one wanted to converse as we were practically jammed tight together. Someone suggested that if one side of the room tightened, the other half might get room to sit down and rest for a while. This was done.'[49] In sombre mood some speculated that they might be transported to the Western Front to be used as cannon fodder, or expelled to some remote British colony or perhaps all summarily executed. Next day, 1 May, they were paraded in the barrack square, where soldiers took

Liberty Hall shortly after the Rising. It was the headquarters of the Irish Citizen Army and the Irish Transport and General Workers' Union, and had been James Connolly's power base.

ALLEN LIBRARY

note of their names, addresses and occupations on sheets of paper; in a few cases the troops were relatives of the men held captive. Next, they were ordered into a wooden gymnasium hall, searched, and instructed to sit in rows of ten facing a partition constructed of clear glass panes and wooden panels. They were soon aware that behind it DMP Special Branch detectives were standing, watching them, whilst scrutinising the lists. After twenty minutes the detectives entered the hall 'like a flock of carrion crows', walked amongst the prisoners and, over a period of two hours, identified those thought to have played the most prominent role in the Rising. They were ordered to stand to one side – MacDonagh, Ceannt, MacBride ... and a numbered list was drawn up of those to be tried.

Those selected at the gymnasium were afterwards packed in parties of forty into separate rooms of the barracks, mostly unfurnished, except for stinking slop pails. Piaras Beaslai recalls that for some at least: 'There was a preliminary investigation for all the accused prisoners, where British officers and soldiers, held during the fight by the Volunteers, gave evidence of identification and of bearing arms against those charged. Some of these witnesses were vindictive; others generous, many refusing to recognise and identify.' Beaslai referred specifically to a Royal Army Medical Corps officer who 'said briefly he knew nothing about combatants, his job had been to care for British and Volunteer wounded impartially, and he had done that'. Beaslai added: 'Some of the "G men" openly offered chances to Volunteers they knew to escape, or hustled them out of sight of their more officious colleagues.'[50] After what Maxwell described as 'an unavoidable delay',[51] the court martial proceedings began in the afternoon of 2 May; Richmond Barracks was deemed to be a suitable location as it was capable of accommodating large numbers of prisoners and was convenient to Maxwell's residence at the Royal Hospital, Kilmainham. A number of trials including those of MacBride, MacDonagh and Clarke had been due to be heard on the previous day. During the first sessions of court hearings, six rebels faced charges in two adjacent rooms at Richmond Barracks. In one, Patrick Pearse's case was followed by Thomas MacDonagh and Thomas Clarke, in the other Piaras Beaslai, then Joseph MacGuinness and Eamonn Duggan. Occasionally, the other Volunteers, caught glimpses of a 'leader or officer ... being escorted from one building to another ... brought out singly between four soldiers and an NCO'.[52] Jack Plunkett described the courtrooms as 'crowded ... very small. With quite a lot of office equipment and the witnesses had to sidle in an out.'[53] Beaslai confirms this description, stating that 'the small room was suffocating with the crowd of witnesses, detectives, guards, three officers of the court-martial and the prosecutor'. He also records his impression that 'the attitude of the officers of the court-martial towards the prisoners, however, was exceedingly courteous'.[54]

On 28 October 1916, the Judge Advocate General's Office stated that in Dublin, 'There have been held in connection with the Rebellion in Ireland',[55] 161 Field General Courts Martial on civilians and one on a Non-Commissioned Officer and 22 General Courts Martial on civilians (including Eoin MacNeill). There were also General Courts Martial on an officer (Captain J.C. Bowen-Colthurst for the murder of Sheehy-Skeffington and two other civilians), a warrant officer (Sergeant R. Flood for the murders of Lieutenant A. Lucas and W. J. Rice) and a private (H. J. Wyatt for the murder of R. Glaister). In addition, four civilians were tried by Field General Courts Martial outside the capital – two in Cork (Thomas and William Kent) and two in Enniscorthy (R. Donaghue and T. Doyle). Thus, a total of 187 civilians, including one woman, Countess Constance Markievicz, were in due course tried by military court. The General Court Martial was the highest form of military court. In these, a judge advocate presided and was assisted by thirteen officers; it was normally reserved for serving officers. From the viewpoint of the authorities, the Field General Court Martial had the advantage .of being easier to convene as the panel was reduced to just three officers; there was no requirement that any of them be legally trained, but the most senior had to hold the substantive rank of captain or above. A death sentence required the unanimous verdict of all three judges. It could not be carried out, however, until it had been confirmed by the appropriate commander-in-chief – in May 1916 it was Generals Haig or French on the Western Front, General Maxwell in Ireland. The jurisdiction of this type of military court extended beyond the British Army. It was applied, for example, to civilians in Egypt as well as Ireland, and in the trials of dominion and colonial soldiers and of German and

Turkish POWs (usually accused of killing British troops). A number of foreign nationals and suspected spies living in Britain were also tried under its procedures on espionage charges; several were subsequently executed in the Tower of London.[56]

The power to try by courts martial those not subject to military law after the Rising in Ireland, derived from the government's emergency powers, specifically the Defence of the Realm Regulations, section 56. The charges were made under Regulation 50 ('doing an act ... prejudicial to the public safety or the defence of the realm ... for the purpose of assisting the enemy'), and Regulation 42 ('attempting to cause mutiny, sedition or dissatisfaction ... among the civil population'). The British Government's proclamation of martial law, dated 26 April, 1916, suspended in Ireland the right of a civilian to be tried by a civil court with a jury, but rather by court martial. The courts martial operated according to the provisions of ('by virtue of and subject to') the Army Act.[57]

Sir John Maxwell decided that the cases consequent on the insurrection should be heard in camera (in other words, not open to the public), a ruling supported at the time by the Irish Law Lords. This was justified subsequently on the grounds that the prisoners were being held at a 'critical period', when 'an act of rebellion was in the process of being quelled', which had required the introduction of martial law.[58] Nonetheless, the Law Officers of the Crown later gave the legal opinion that it had been illegal not to permit public access. In their judgement, dated 30 January 1917, they stated 'There does not seem to be any legal justification for the holding of a court martial in camera.' Sir Reginald Brade, Secretary of the Army Council, was fully in agreement, stating 'There appears to be nothing in the Army Act, or the rules of procedure, to justify the holding of a court martial in camera ... the power to sit in camera is only given to civil courts.'[59] On three occasions in 1916 (1 June, 10 July and 24 October), Sir Herbert Asquith, responding to requests from Irish nationalist MPs in the Commons that the court martial proceedings be published, had indicated that he was prepared to do so. On the last instance, he had stated unequivocally, in reply to a query by John Dillon, 'I will arrange for this to be done.' At the time the Prime Minister himself considered that 'the pledge was too definite to be got out of'.[60] His government fell in December 1916, and his commitment was then in no way binding on any succeeding administration.

In early 1917, both Brade and the then Adjutant General, General Sir Neville Macready, wrote minutes in which they put forward powerful arguments to the government against publishing the court martial proceedings. It was suggested that to do so would imply that it had never been justified to hold the trials in camera, and would therefore be 'a grave reflection on the discretion of Sir John Maxwell'. It was claimed that if it was done, the lives of members of the courts, even of Sir John himself and his staff, might well be placed in jeopardy. It was also argued that at the time of the trials the witnesses had come forward in good faith, and had given evidence openly and freely. They might not have done so if it had not been for the distinct understanding that the proceedings were in camera, and that they could not be identified in future and so lay themselves open to 'any danger of life and limb' which their testimony would otherwise entail. In these circumstances, public disclosure might therefore be regarded as a 'breach of faith' towards them and 'a contempt of court'. In addition, the potential long-term significance of publication was highlighted. It was asserted that in future 'it would in all probability be impossible to obtain evidence in support of charges, and military courts and authority would become as impotent as the civil courts in Ireland'. As a consequence 'the difficulties of a successful and hasty suppression of rebellion ... would be greatly increased and the interests of justice would be defeated if it were realised that the evidence given in camera would in all probability be given publicly'. It was also considered that, 'the position of any General, who in the future may be required to cope with another rising would be rendered almost impossible if he had to keep in view the possibility of his actions forming the subject of enquiry or comment [for example, his confirmation of death sentences].' The Adjutant General stated: 'I doubt that any general officer would consent to undertake the repression of rebellion without the assurance that in all cases where he might deem it necessary to administer justice in secrecy that such secrecy should be maintained.' Maxwell himself considered that 'publication would be not only a grave indiscretion, but also a distinct breach of faith with those who took the decision that the courts martial were to be held in camera'.[61]

When asked for their judgement on the legal position regarding publication, the Law Officers stated that, under Section 124 of the Army Act, 'the only person who ... is entitled to obtain a copy of the proceedings is the person tried', and therefore, 'if the accused person is dead, no copy can be supplied'. They argued strongly that giving the public access to the court documents could only be justified on grounds of national or public expediency; it was 'a question of policy alone'.[62] In these circumstances, however, there was one vital consideration which was bound ultimately to determine the response of politicians – the inadequacy of the evidence that had been produced in the courts martial of those who had been found guilty, sentenced to death and executed. Sir Reginald Brade advised on 9 January, 1917: 'I have read the proceedings in each of the latter cases [those executed] very carefully, and while I can safely say that the evidence taken as a whole is conclusive of their guilt, there are one or two cases in which the evidence is extremely thin.' The Adjutant General on 10 January clearly felt even greater unease. He stated:

> As I have reason to believe that in certain cases the evidence was not too strong, the inevitable results of publication would be that a certain section of the Irish community will urge that the sole reason for the trials in camera was that the authorities intended to execute certain of the Sinn Féiners whether there was evidence or not. This is an argument which in my humble judgement would be extremely difficult to meet successfully if as I think the evidence in some of the cases was far from conclusive.[63]

Not surprisingly when, shortly after the Rising, solicitors acting for the families of those executed urged the government to make the records available to them, it was to no avail. Precedent had hardly been encouraging; court martial papers relating to the 1798 rebellion were closed to the public and were to remain so for two hundred years.[64]

To be court-martialled by British military authorities and executed by firing squad was no new experience for Irishmen at Easter 1916. Out of 2,916 traceable death sentences passed by court martial on British army personnel during the First World War, 221 were Irish soldiers. Though they constituted just 2 per cent of those enlisted in the force, they were the recipients of 8 per cent of all the death sentences imposed. According to one authority, these uniquely disproportionate figures stemmed from a belief, endemic within the British officer class that, 'the Irish needed firm, even harsh handling. The Easter Rising ... merely confirmed the British in their preconceived idea, concerns and fears about Irish unreliability.'[65]

Of the 187 civilians who were accused court-martialled after the Rising, eleven were acquitted. Of the remainder, the courts martial registers contain details of eighty-eight sentences of 'death by being shot'. This is contradicted by the *Catholic Bulletin*, published in August 1917, which cites a figure of ninety-seven. However, *The Sinn Féin Rebellion Handbook*, produced in the same year, records the names of those so convicted and corresponds very closely to the registers, but its list is incomplete (it contains eighty-seven names, omitting Peter Slattery who was tried on 5 May; his sentence was commuted to eight years penal servitude). Certainly, Maxwell confirmed the death sentence in fifteen cases. The official British government record of the trials involving these fifteen rebels was released to the public for the first time in 1999, and is reproduced in this volume. The transcripts of proceedings appear to be comprehensive, true and accurate; at the time each page was verified and signed by the President of the court and even minor textual changes and amendments were checked and initialled by him. The records are, however, inconsistent regarding dates, but as far as can be determined the trials of those listed below took place as follows:

2 May	Patrick Pearse, Thomas MacDonagh and Thomas Clarke
3 May	Edward Daly, William Pearse, Michael O'Hanrahan and Joseph Plunkett
3–4 May	Eamonn Ceannt
4 May	John MacBride, Sean Heuston, Con Colbert, and Thomas Kent
5 May	Michael Mallin
9 May	James Connolly and Sean MacDermott

Their sequence appears to have followed the number allocated to each of them after the selection procedure had been completed at Richmond Barracks on 1 May – with the exception of James Connolly. The numbering suggests no obvious sequence – Daly was allotted number twenty-one, the lowest apart from Patrick Pearse (who was number one); William Pearse was number twenty-seven, whilst Connolly and MacDermott were ninety and ninety-one respectively. They were the highest numbered of the rebels to be executed and therefore the last.

All but two of the cases were heard at Richmond Barracks. The exceptions were James Connolly who, owing to his injuries, was tried, propped up in his bed at the Red Cross Hospital in Dublin Castle, and Thomas Kent who faced charges at the Detention Barracks in Cork city, twenty-five miles from where his alleged offenses were committed. Between 2 and 4 May, Brigadier-General Charles Blackader of the 177th Infantry Brigade presided at seven of the fourteen cases held in Dublin (Patrick Pearse, Clarke, MacDonagh, Daly, O'Hanrahan, MacBride and Ceannt). He was then in his mid-forties and had seen service with the Leicester Regiment in the Boer War and had later acted as aide de camp (ADC) to the King. He was described by Elizabeth, Countess of Fingall, with whom he dined occasionally in 1916 at Killeen Castle, County Meath, as a 'charming, sympathetic person, half-French, very emotional, and terribly affected by the work he had to do'.[66] In June he was transferred to the Western Front, becoming a divisional commander, but was demoted on health grounds after contracting rabies from his dog in May 1918. Though his health was broken, he took up duties again in Ireland as Commander, Southern District, in March 1919 and died in April 1921.

From 3 to 5 May, Brigadier Maconchy of the 178th Brigade, Sherwood Foresters, presided over the trials of four of the rebel leaders (Plunkett, Heuston, Mallin and William Pearse). He was more sanguine than Blackader but found the role similarly stressful and was replaced on 5 May by Colonel D. Sapte, who presided over the cases of Colbert, Connolly and MacDermott. Maconchy was born at Rathmore, County Longford, was in his mid-fifties, and had seen extensive service in India. In unpublished memoirs, he wrote

> On the 3rd I was appointed President of one of the two ...
> courts martial ... although I protested to Sir John Maxwell
> as I was an Irishman. We tried a very large number. There
> could be no doubt on the evidence before us of the only
> sentence permissible, but of course it rested with the
> confirming officer to decide as to the carrying out of the
> sentence and it is possible that referral was also made to the
> cabinet in London. We could only recommend certain cases

for mercy. When called on for their defence they [the rebels] generally only convicted themselves out of their own mouths, and in many cases I refused to put down what they said as it only made their case worse. During the trial of one of the ring-leaders, his whole attitude seemed so strange to me that I asked him if he would mind telling me quite apart from his trial what he was fighting for. He drew himself up and said: 'I was fighting to defend the rights of the people of Ireland.' I then asked him if anyone was attacking these rights and he said: 'No, but they might have been.' This seemed a strange excuse for shooting down innocent citizens in the streets, but I presume that it is the fashion in all rebellions against constitutional authority. He then made a strong plea for the Irish National Volunteers [sic] as they were called whom he said had been kept in ignorance of the purpose for which they had been called out. This was a fact which was evident from the testimony of the men themselves. I was much relieved when an officer of the Judge Advocates Department was sent over to take my place.[67]

At a few hours notice, William G. Wylie was appointed as prosecution counsel. He recalls:

I was just preparing to go to bed when an orderly arrived on a motor bicycle and said I was wanted at GHQ ...[There] I was shown into a room and found a brass hat seated at a desk. It was General Byrne who had just arrived from England as Assistant Adjutant General. He said: 'Are you Wylie?' 'Yes, Sir.' 'Well, you will prosecute at the courts martial on the prisoners. Start tomorrow morning [2 May] at 9 a.m. at Richmond Barracks.' 'What charge Sir?' 'That is for you. Make out your charge sheets, and notify the accused'.[68]

Wylie was born in Dublin, the son of a presbyterian clergyman from Ulster, and brought up in Coleraine. He was called to the Irish Bar in 1905 and appointed King's Counsel in 1914. In 1924 he became a judge of the High Court of the Irish Free State. He had helped in suppressing the Rising as a member of the Officer Training Corps in Trinity College Dublin, and indeed had taken the surrender of some of those he was to prosecute. On the morning of his appointment as prosecutor, 1 May, he had 'walked down Sackville Street'. He wrote later 'such a sight as it was. Dead horses, wrecked cars and tramcars, broken glass and shop goods of all kinds scattered over the streets. The GPO and the houses round it were blackened and still smouldering ruins. When you know a town well, I think destruction of that kind seems much worse. Such frightful and unnecessary waste and loss. It cured me of wars particularly of civil wars.'[69]

Wylie felt considerable sympathy for the accused. He was convinced, possibly by Pearse's testimony in court (his first case as prosecutor) that 'the majority ... did not know when marching out on Easter Monday morning that there was to be a rebellion. This I am satisfied was true.'[70] He voiced strong disapproval of the speed and secrecy of the proceedings, believing that the trials should have taken place in public. He recalls, in unpublished memoirs written in the 1930s: 'I used to go out and ask them had they any defence or were there any witnesses which they wished to be called. In fact it was unfair to try them without giving them an opportunity to defend themselves.' He proposed that the accused be allowed access to defence counsel. This suggestion was firmly rejected at Dublin Castle by James Campbell, then Irish Attorney General and later Chairman of the Irish Free State Senate. Campbell had recommended Wylie's appointment, and bluntly informed Wylie that: 'he would not be satisfied until 40 [rebels] were shot'. Wylie claims that Campbell then told him that 'in addition to prosecuting [the rebels], I would defend them to the best of my ability and bring out every damn thing in their favour'.[71] Wylie was not without influence; throughout the trials he dined regularly with Maxwell at his headquarters in the Royal Hospital at Kilmainham, and the General Officer Commanding (GOC) 'always cross-examined me for a few hours or so after dinner about the courts martial'.[72] Wylie did succeed, after MacDonagh's trial on 2 May, in ensuring that defendants were permitted to call witnesses if they so wished. John MacBride expressed fulsome gratitude to Wylie for the consideration he had shown him during his court martial.

The right of the accused in Field General Courts Martial to call witnesses and cross-examine those who were called for the prosecution was at the discretion of the court, but was rarely, if ever, denied. To have legal representation, however, was extremely rare – no lawyers were allowed – but serving soldiers were permitted to have a 'prisoner's friend', usually a subaltern, to help them present their defence. It was unusual for this right to be exercised. The official records are both indispensable and unique, as they provide the only definitive record of the court martial proceedings, hitherto the subject of much speculation and propaganda. They contain the precise text of the charges faced, the pleas entered by the accused in response, the evidence produced by the crown, the testimony of the witnesses called by both the prosecution and the defence, and the statements, if any, which the rebels made to the court. All faced the same central charge, which in most, if not all cases, was handed to them in advance of the trial. It stated that they 'did an act, to wit, did take part in an armed rebellion and in the waging of war against his Majesty, the King, such act being of such a nature as to be calculated to be prejudical [sic] to the defence of the realm, being done with the intention, and for the purpose of assisting the enemy'. In fourteen of the fifteen cases the plea from the dock was one of not guilty. William Pearse was the exception; he alone pleaded guilty.[73] Ned Daly, in an illuminating comment afterwards, explained to his sister that he had 'protested strongly against the part of the charge about "assisting the enemy", that all he did ... was for Ireland, his own land'.[74] When one defendant (not one of those executed) attempted to plead guilty exclusively to the section that he did 'take part in an armed rebellion', he was advised that this was inadmissible on legal grounds.[75] In several cases, an additional charge was included stating that the accused, 'did attempt to cause disaffection among the civil population of His Majesty'. Interestingly, no reference to the charge having been put to the prisoner is actually recorded in any of the court proceedings. Moreover, apart from a few instances (at Joseph Plunkett's trial and at Thomas Kent's trial) the court proceedings do not record either that witnesses had been sworn-in; this laxity is surprising given that this was done routinely at Field General Courts Martial on the Western Front.

The defendants also faced broadly similar types of evidence. Typically, the witnesses for the prosecution were military officers captured during Easter week, who could give eyewitness testimony regarding the actions and role of individual rebels during the fighting. On occasion, other servicemen were called who had observed the rebels' surrender, and could recall the rank that the accused had then stated, and whether it appeared at the time as though they were in command of the others being taken captive. Police officers, and on one occasion a prison warden, were also produced to provide information on the defendant's past record of involvement in extreme nationalist organisations. Not surprisingly, given the haste of the proceedings, the deficiencies in Dublin Castle's intelligence and the numbers accused, the evidence provided by the Crown was in a number of instances entirely circumstantial, misleading and inaccurate. This was especially so in the trials of the five rebels who fought at the North Dublin Union, Marrowbone Lane and Jacob's Biscuit Factory and who surrendered at St Patrick's Park on 30 April – MacDonagh, MacBride, Ceannt, Colbert and O'Hanrahan. In all of these cases apart from MacBride's, prosecution counsel called just one witness, Major J.A. Armstrong, the Officer Commanding British troops deployed at the park at the time when almost four hundred rebels surrendered. In each case, predictably, Armstrong knew virtually nothing about the accused and in some instances was unable even to inform the court which garrison they had served with, let alone what their specific role had been in the Rising.[76] Similarly, in the trials of the six Volunteers belonging to the GPO garrison, the prosecution relied heavily on the testimony of a single witness, Lieutenant King, a British officer who had been held captive there (he appeared at the trials of Patrick and William Pearse, Clarke and Connolly). In two instances, in order to speed up progress, multiple trials were held; both William Pearse and Sean Heuston appeared before the judges alongside three other defendants who were charged with the same offenses. Thomas Kent's trial was distinctive. Three local RIC members involved in the gun-battle at his home in County Cork were called, as well as two of the soldiers afterwards summoned by the police to supervise his family's surrender.[77] In addition, at many of the trials documentary evidence was submitted – most of it recovered in later searches of the premises occupied by the insurgents during Easter week. It included copies of dispatches allegedly sent and received by the accused, letters written, notes and jottings.

During the court hearings little reference was made to the Proclamation. Wylie explains that:

> During MacDonagh's trial, Blackader asked me wasn't there
> a proclamation of a republic which was signed by
> MacDonagh amongst others, and why did I not draw their
> attention to it. I said that I understood that there was such a

document ... I had a copy in my pocket, but I was not in a
position to prove it. The General asked why not. I said that
a document with certain names at the end of it was not
proof of any of the alleged signatories unless I could get the
original and prove the accused's signature to it ... I must ask
the court to obliterate all knowledge of it from their
minds.[78]

Though not adverted to by Wylie in the trials, apart from when
cross-examining at Ceannt's and Plunkett's trials, the Proclamation
certainly influenced Maxwell when deciding whether or not to
confirm the death sentences of the court in the cases of each of its
seven signatories.

Jack Plunkett, the brother of Joseph, later described his overall
impression of the court martial procedure. He wrote:

The general [who presided] had about two feet of service
ribbon on his chest. He did not seem to enjoy his job. The
charges were read out. The court seemed to regard its duties
as clerical ones and it was very interesting to observe the
peculiar detached attitude the members displayed not only
to persons but to facts also. So long as the maximum of
evidence against a prisoner was recorded the truth of it
seemed of very minor importance.[79]

The rules of evidence in courts martial were of course the same as
in civil trials; nonetheless, to an extent the courts martial in wartime
always had some of the characteristics of show trials. Whether the
accused was a civilian, or a soldier at the front, they tended to be a
legitimising veneer, with the outcome a foregone conclusion. After
the Rising, Maxwell wrote to Asquith to justify the instances in
which he had confirmed the death penalty on the rebel leaders; he
did so by citing evidence against the defendants culled from his
intelligence sources, rather than that which was actually produced
by the prosecution in court. This material had not therefore been
subject to cross-examination.

Whilst in prison during their Field General Courts Martial, the
rebels were permitted to correspond and to have visitors. This was a
concession to their unique status as civilians being tried by military
court – wartime conscientious objectors in British prisons were
treated similarly. The issue did not normally arise at the Front, as

serving soldiers were only held captive very briefly for the period of their trial; afterwards they were hurriedly returned to their units to await the outcome.

There is an unnerving unpredictability in relation to the death sentences which the GOC confirmed. The fifteen men executed included of course the seven signatories of the Proclamation, three of the four Volunteer commandants in Dublin (Ceannt and MacDonagh were also signatories) and also the officers commanding at two important outposts (Mallin at the College of Surgeons and Colbert at Jameson's Distillery) at both of which severe fighting had occurred. But the pattern otherwise appears random and haphazard. De Valera escaped the death penalty though he was one of the city's four commandants. So also did all of the members of his battallion at Boland's Bakery, though British forces sustained by far their heaviest casualties in this command area. Of those who did face the firing squad, one had served at the College of Surgeons, two at the Four Courts (including the Mendicity Institution), two at the South Dublin Union and its outposts, three at Jacob's and six at the GPO. James Connolly was clearly correct in his observation: 'the enemy feels that in this building is to be found the heart and inspiration of our great movement'. Jacob's was virtually inactive throughout Easter week. That three of its Volunteers should have faced the firing squad probably reflects the influence of Armstrong's testimony, and the fact that British troops were fired upon whilst they waited for the battalions serving in this area to come to the surrender point, on 30 April. Looking outside Dublin, that Thomas Kent should have lost his life for his part in the skirmish at Bawnard

Prisoners being marched along Eden Quay in Dublin under military escort, prior to deportation to internment camps in England
NATIONAL MUSEUM OF IRELAND

House, yet none of the Volunteers involved at the Battle of Ashbourne did so, is difficult to account for on any logical grounds. Of those in Dublin shot for their role in the Rising, the cases of William Pearse, Heuston and MacBride are certainly amongst the most difficult to justify; other Volunteers had played a much more prominent role in Easter week.

Above all, the official courts martial records provide an invaluable insight into the minds of the rebel leaders at the defining moment in their lives. Though several in their evidence distorted the truth in a bid to escape the firing squad, all but one of the seven men who signed the Proclamation approached death without remorse, proud of their achievements, still imbued with a deep conviction of the rightness of their cause, the legitimacy of their actions and entirely reconciled to their fate. Within the republican tradition, death by shooting was regarded as an honourable end. Wolfe Tone had requested at his trial (10 November 1798) that he should die a soldier's death – by firing squad; when he was informed that he was to hang, he cut his throat rather than face the ignominy of the gallows. In one regard Eamonn Ceannt was the exception in 1916. Whilst awaiting execution at Kilmainham, he regretted bitterly the leadership's decision to surrender; he was convinced that they ought to have fought on to the bitter end. It was an error of judgement which he hoped future generations of Irishmen would not repeat. James Connolly wrote in February 1916: 'But deep in the heart of Ireland has sunk the sense of the degradation wrought upon its people – so deep and so humiliating that no agency less powerful than the red tide of war on Irish soil will ever … enable the Irish race to recover its self-respect … without the shedding of blood there is no Redemption.'[80] After the Rising, Thomas Clarke assured his wife that: 'we have struck the first successful blow for freedom. The next blow, which we have no doubt Ireland will strike, will win through. In this belief we die happy.'[81] Undoubtedly, the executions and deportations in its aftermath fuelled popular hostility towards Britain, and increased sympathy for the use of force to achieve independence as well as support for an independent Irish republic. A cause is hallowed by those who die for it. Bulmer Hobson's verdict on the insurrection was that: 'it would have been completely disastrous to this country had it not been saved by the subsequent mishandling of the situation by the English government'.[8]

Sir John Maxwell

On Wednesday, 26 April 1916, the British Cabinet decided to declare martial law throughout Ireland. Next day, Major Sir John Maxwell was appointed Commander-in-Chief troops, Ireland. As such he was the main architect of the British government's response to the Rising and has been charged with having 'lost Ireland for the British'.[1] In part he was appointed commander-in-chief because he was immediately available, having been discharged from his duties in Egypt in March 1916 and having only just recovered from recent illness. But he was also thought to have the relevant military experience and expertise and the necessary political skills. His name was suggested by the influential Secretary of State for War, Field Marshal Lord Kitchener, with whom Maxwell said himself he had 'been associated for the best part of [his] life'.[2] According to Maxwell's biographer, Kitchener was aware of Maxwell's 'insight into and sympathy with racial characteristics, his fearlessness as to assuming responsibility, and his strong common sense ... Imperturbable good humour marked him out as a man to deal and deal promptly ... with danger for Ireland and ... the conduct of the war.'[3] Major General Sir Lovick Friend, the incumbent commander-in-chief prior to Easter week, had disqualified himself. Despite receiving secret intelligence regarding a possible insurrection, he was on leave on Easter Monday and had permitted 'officers of the Irish command ... to attend a race meeting' who were then reportedly taken hostage by the rebels.[4] This was the subject of an army council inquiry. General Sir Ian Hamilton was considered for the post but was thought by

General Sir John Grenfell Maxwell, who was appointed Commander-in-Chief, British troops in Ireland, on 27 April 1916. It was said of him that he 'lost Ireland for the British'.

Asquith to be too intimately associated with the recent doomed Dardenelles campaign in which many Irishmen had died; the campaign was to mark the end of his active military career. Asquith wrote: 'There is a good deal of bitterness in Ireland about Suvla, etc. to which Redmond gave expression in the House this afternoon. It is very desirable to send a competent man who so far as Ireland is concerned has no past record.'[5] Maxwell had from the outset regarded the attack on Turkey as a doomed enterprise and had advised that it be 'left severely alone'.[6] Thus sensitivity to Irish sensibilities as well as chance and influential contacts, helped determine Westminster's choice.

The task of suppressing the Rising was not far from completion when Maxwell arrived in Dublin to assume command at 2.30 a.m. on Friday, 28 April. On the previous day, the 177th Brigade had arrived at Kingstown. By then, Lowe had a firm grip on the city; vital strategic locations had been reinforced and the rebel positions and their relative importance were known. He had sufficient troops and materials to deal with the rebels in any order he wished, despite some military dispersal to Athlone and Limerick. An inner cordon was constructed around the GPO, so isolating the headquarters of the insurgents; this objective had been successfully achieved by 5 p.m. Soon after his arrival Maxwell wrote to his wife, 'from the sea, it looked as if the entire city of Dublin was in flames ... When we got to North Wall ... bullets were flying about, the crackle of musketry and machine gun fire breaking out every other minute ... But,' he continued, 'from all that I can gather the nerve centre of the movement is in Dublin and in that part which we have surrounded. ... I think the signs are that the rebels have had enough.'[7] Maxwell had at his disposal eighteen to twenty thousand troops in the capital, with substantially more due to arrive within the next forty-eight hours. Having consulted his commanding officers, he decided to isolate further the 'infected patches'.[8] Brigadier-General William Lowe was ordered to close in on Sackville Street and the artillery bombardment of the area from Trinity College and Ballsbridge was intensified, eventually forcing the rebels to evacuate from their headquarters. At the same time, the construction of a military cordon around the Four Courts was begun, and the existing one around the north side was extended southwards, so encircling the city, using the line of the Grand Canal.

Maxwell wrote later, 'When it became known that the rebels

In order to present the further slaughter of unarmed people, and in the hope of saving the lives of our followers now surrounded and hopelessly outnumbered, the members of the Provisional Government present at Headquarters have agreed to an unconditional surrender, and the commanders of all units of the Republican forces will order their followers to lay down their arms.

P. H. Pearse

29th April 1916

4.45 p.m.

Pearse's handwritten surrender order. It was subsequently typed up at British military headquarters in Dublin, signed by Pearse and copies then made which were brought to the Commandants of the various rebel garrisons.
NATIONAL MUSEUM OF IRELAND

wished to surrender, the officers used every endeavour to prevent further bloodshed.'[9] After interviewing Pearse at military headquarters on Saturday, 29 April, the rebel leader wrote and signed the order to the commandants of the various districts in the city and the country to lay down their arms. Later that afternoon, an eyewitness watched the GPO/Moore Street garrison surrender, and observed:

> Sackville Street presented a bizarre appearance ... The only signs of life were firemen working furiously to check the conflagration. Suddenly from out of a side street marched the first detachment of the rebels, headed by a large white flag. Down the street they came in fours, arms carried at the slope, and marching like trained soldiers. They halted, according to instruction, one hundred yards from the troops, laid down their arms and stepped back on to the pavement. The arms were of various kinds, but all of them were formidable. Hardly had the first detachment been dealt with when a second and third marched in similar fashion.[10]

On 29 and 30 April, emissaries – mainly Capuchin priests and nurse Elizabeth O'Farrell ('a very pretty girl and very pale'[11]), brought Pearse's order of surrender to the other rebel garrisons in the city.

Brigadier-General William Lowe (centre) and his ADC (his son, John) receive Patrick Pearse's surrender. The figure mostly hidden by Pearse is nurse Elizabeth O'Farrell.
NATIONAL MUSEUM OF IRELAND

By Sunday, Maxwell considered that 'the rebellion ... [was] ... practically crushed ... Rebels surrendering freely ...' But he stressed that 'every precaution is being taken'. He feared that there might be 'one or two Sidney Street affairs, as some of these fellows are fairly desperate'. An order was sent out suspending any further movement of troops to Ireland, though units already embarked were to proceed to their destination. Until Thursday 4 May the GOC continued to report sniping in Dublin, but nonetheless, clearing-up work was continuing at Irishtown, on the south side of the Liffey, and that the city was 'reverting to normal conditions'. Throughout this process, Maxwell insisted that 'all surrenders must be absolutely unconditional'.[12] This had been the consistent approach of the Irish administration from the beginning of the Rising. Early in Easter Week, the Mayor of Dublin had suggested that Dublin Castle officials ascertain Friend's attitude to a deputation of citizens acting as intermediaries and holding a conference with Sinn Féin. Nathan rejected the offer out of hand. On 29 April, the Irish Attorney-General expressed the view that it was vital no terms other than unconditional surrender should be offered or accepted from anyone who had taken part in armed rebellion.[13] Brigadier-General Lowe's note to Pearse, written when he first heard that the rebels wished to discuss terms (it is dated 1:40 p.m., 29 April) was unambiguous. It stated: 'A woman [nurse O'Farrell] has come in and tells me you wish to negotiate with me. I am prepared to receive you in Britain Street at the north end of Moore Street, provided that you surrender unconditionally. You will proceed up Moore Street, accompanied only by the woman who brings you this note under a white flag.' When Pearse replied, hoping to open negotiations, Lowe responded again emphatically (at just after 2 p.m.): 'I have received your letter. Nothing can be considered until you surrender unconditionally or you surrender to me. I will take steps to give everyone under your orders sufficient time to surrender before I recommence hostilities which I have temporarily suspended.'[14] This response was no doubt partly prompted by the widespread presumption of strong German involvement in the Rising. Field Marshal Lord French, Commander-in-Chief Home Forces, considered that the rebels' intention had been to prevent British army reinforcements being sent as back-up to the military in France. A memorandum considered by Cabinet, argued that the Rising was a calculated military response after the palpable failure of the enemy attack on Verdun on the Western Front.

When appointed GOC, Maxwell had been given full authority to restore order, put down the rebellion and punish its participants. Kitchener advised Lord French: 'His Majesty's Government desire that ... [he] ... will take all such measures as may in his opinion be necessary for the prompt suppression of insurrection in Ireland and be accorded ... a free hand in the movement of all troops now in Ireland or ... placed under his command hereafter and also ... [with regard to] ... such measures as may seem to him adviseable under the proclamation.'[15] At the time, Nathan, Birrell and their Irish legal advisers registered their strong disapproval of these measures. After they had met together at Dublin Castle, on 28 April, the Chief Secretary telegrammed Asquith protesting: 'All of us are strongly of the opinion that for the moment the imminent proclamation of martial law for the whole of Ireland is most undesirable. First, all useful powers already exist under DORA [the government's emergency powers] ... Secondly, we anticipate grave possibility of bad effects produced if martial law is extended to the very large areas which at present show no signs of disturbance ... Please consider this immediately.'[16]

This intervention prompted much Cabinet discussion later that afternoon, Lloyd George expressing fears that Ireland might be 'set ablaze by the inconsiderate actions of some subordinate officer'. General Sir C.F.N. Macready, whose opinion was sought, considered it 'better to risk overstepping authority than to delay action'. Still concerned by continuing military reports of rebel activity in the west of Ireland, ministers agreed to persist with 'universal martial law' but to restrict Maxwell's authority to delegate his powers to subordinate officers. Asquith also informed his colleagues that 'in accordance with what he believed were the feelings of the House of Commons, he had sent a letter to Sir John Maxwell to the effect that he was not to use extreme measures except in case of emergency'.[17] In practice Maxwell's powers were ill-defined and much less than he had hoped on the basis of the verbal assurances he had been given. Though empowered to 'deal with a state of rebellion' and responsible for the preservation of law and order, he had no right to interfere in civil matters. All goverment departments continued to report to officials at Dublin Castle and they to the Home Secretary. Maxwell noted ruefully that: 'the RIC and the police are not directly under my orders, they take their instructions from and report to the Under-Secretary'; they were not even 'under any obligation ... to report to [me]'.[18] Moreover, he felt that the government had no real commitment to martial law. By early June, he expressed concern that he might be 'chucked over any day'.[19]

Inevitably, Maxwell's relations with the Irish officials were somewhat strained. After meeting Birrel and Lord Wimborne (Sir Ivor C. Guest, the Lord Lieutenant) for the first time on 28 April, he noted: 'They do not altogether appreciate being under my orders but I told them I did not mean to interfere unless it was absolutely necessary and hoped they would do all I asked them to do.' It was after this meeting that the Chief Secretary had telegramed Asquith expressing strong opposition to all-Ireland martial law. After a further meeting with Birrel the GOC wrote: 'He's not as bad as I thought but like so many politicians he does not put into effect what he preaches.' Shortly after his arrival in Dublin, Maxwell had predicted, accurately: 'I do not think that Birrel will be in Ireland much more.'[20] On 30 April, the Chief Secretary had left himself 'in Asquith's hands', stating: 'You will I am sure let me know as quickly as possible what you want me to do. Of course I cannot go on.'[21] Next day a cipher arrived at the Viceregal Lodge stating that his resignation had been accepted. Birrell later confessed to the House: 'I made an untrue estimate of the possibility of a disturbance of the kind which has occurred in Dublin and of the mode of warfare which has been pursued, of the desperate folly displayed by the leaders and their dupes.'[22] His dreams of being Ireland's last Chief Secretary lay in ruins. He observed, 'All this shatters me ... the thing that has happened swallows up the things that might have happened had I acted differently.' On 3 May, Birrell telegraphed Nathan stating simply: 'P.M. thinks you must share my fate.'[23] The Under Secretary resigned that day, expressing apologies and regrets for the inaccuracy of his advice. He left Ireland days later, never to return, as he said, 'not to see the land, I had hoped and failed to help', and privately 'very much cut up about the rebellion'.[24]

Predictably, serving soldiers who commented on the Rising in their correspondence, naturally condemned it and favoured strongly repressive measures, though doubting they would be forthcoming. Captain H. Peel, writing to his wife on 27 April, commented: 'The daily papers make me pace with rage. Is there no one in England with any guts at all? This little Irish affair will wake them up. I suppose they will shamble and slither and compromise through

it ... Lord, what a pack of invertebrate monkeys they are! ... I wish
they would send me to kill some of them [the rebels].'[25] J.W.
Roworth, travelling on the Fishguard train to Ireland noted: 'It was
easy to see that all the British troops who had like me joined Irish
regiments were upset by the Rising.'[26] A soldier who had served in
Dublin observed on 1 May: 'I do not for a moment believe that with
a firm and determined government, resolved to
win the war we would have been treated to this
humiliating affair in Ireland.' He predicted that the
rebels would be 'made recipients of bounties in
return for keeping the peace. They well know that
the fate that they justly deserve will not be meted
out to them.'[27]

NO REST FOR THAT BRUTE MAXWELL!

Though he largely shared these views, and was
soon characterised as a 'bloody butcher' throughout
nationalist Ireland, Maxwell's own attitudes were
more complex than is often assumed. He hated the
'state and genuflexion' associated with high office.[28]
William Wylie said of him: 'he made a great impression on me as a most able administrator. I don't
know if he was a great soldier, but he was certainly a clever man, broad-minded and open to argument.'[29] Maxwell regarded the recent progressive
collapse of law and order in Ireland as having been
rooted in the British government's weak and ineffectual response to northern unionist militancy
before the war. In his opinion, ministers 'winked at Ulster breaking
the law ... wait and see. Well, we waited and now see the result, viz.
rebellion and loss of life.' He also quoted with enthusiasm comments
which he attributed to a 'charming old priest', Dr W.J. Walsh,
(Catholic Archbishop of Dublin 1885–1921) – 'the government is as
much to blame as any Sinn Féiners for allowing it to get to such a
pitch'.[30] These views were largely confirmed by the Royal
Commission of Inquiry into the origins of the Rising, appointed by
Asquith. It concluded that its 'main cause ... was an unchecked
growth of lawlessness and the fact that Ireland for several years
had been administered on the principle that it was safer and more
expedient to leave the law in abeyance if collision with
any faction could thereby be avoided'.[31] In addition, Maxwell
forthrightly condemned the callous neglect of Ireland's absentee

Propagandist postcard
probably produced in
late 1916. Maxwell's
headquarters at the
Royal Hospital,
Kilmainham, were
within earshot of the
executions of the rebel
leaders, which were
being carried out at
Kilmainham Gaol, a
few hundred yards
away.
KILMAINHAM GAOL
AND MUSEUM

Daughters of Charity of St Vincent de Paul, North William Street, Dublin, distribute bread to people in need towards the end of Easter week. The slim figure standing sideways in the centre of the photograph is Sister Margaret Collins, the aunt of Michael Collins.

NATIONAL MUSEUM OF IRELAND

landlords and considered it to be a root cause both of rural poverty and of political disaffection. He regarded the squalor of Dublin's slums as 'a disgrace to the British race' [32] and, like Pearse, a standing indictment of British rule (twenty-six thousand families, almost one-third of the city's population lived in decayed slum tenements). He personally gave £200 to the St Vincent de Paul Society after the Rising to help relieve distress. From the moment of his arrival in the city, he was determined that his decisions should illustrate a responsiveness to moderate Irish opinion. But he was also convinced that they must give no sustenance to any impression that the recent violence had won concessions or was being rewarded.

At root, Maxwell bore no real affection for Ireland and fully shared the prejudices of the English officer class. He thought Dublin 'cold and cheerless', its 'poverty and improvidence appalling'. As for its people, 'the majority', he stated, 'seem to be on the verge of madness which finds its outlet in poetry and emotional traits'. He considered that their 'temperament makes them easy to lead or mislead … like spoiled children'. In his opinion, they were easy prey to venal politicians, unscrupulous priests and political manipulation by foreign states. He described militant nationalism as being 'worked for what its worth by Germany' not only within Ireland itself but in the United States as well. He found Ireland from the outset 'very difficult and tiresome to govern', its political difficulties apparantly insoluble. His view was that this was because 'Ireland seems to live entirely in its past, brooding over its wrongs and never looking to the future'. He doubted that the Irish would ever 'settle down to any sort of government, adding that 'the only thing all Irishmen are united on is a keen desire to get everything they can out of the British'.[33]

From the outset, Maxwell was determined to crush revolutionary nationalism in Ireland, a function which in his opinion the previous civil government had conspicuously failed to perform, and to punish those involved in the Rising. He believed that its leading participants should be court-martialled and those who had organised it, executed. He also considered that 'Ireland would remain a danger spot as long as these [extreme nationalist] secret societies exist and people are armed'.[34] He thus favoured the arrest of 'all dangerous Sinn Féiners, including those who have taken an active part in the movement although not in the present rebellion', to be carried out by columns of troops assisted by police, combing the countryside.[35] In reaching these opinions he was influenced by the considerable death and destruction caused by the Rising, despite its brevity, and by the involvement in it of England's wartime enemy, Germany. (Accurate casualty figures were not available to him at the time. On or about 10 May, Asquith estimated their total number as: military 521, of which 124 killed; civilians 794, of which 180 killed; total 1315, of which 304 killed). Moreover, the GOC was convinced by police reports that Ireland had 'narrowly missed the most serious rebellion' and that this would surely have occurred but for the

PUBLIC NOTICE

POLITICAL MEETINGS, PARADES, OR PROCESSIONS

I, GENERAL SIR JOHN GRENFELL MAXWELL, K.C.B., K.C.M.G., C.V.O., D.S.O., Commanding-in-Chief His Majesty's Forces in Ireland, hereby Order that no Parade, Procession, or Political Meeting, or organized Football, Athletic, or Hurling Meeting, shall take place anywhere in Ireland without the written authority, previously obtained, of the Local County Inspector of Royal Irish Constabulary, or, in Dublin City, of the Chief Commissioner of the Dublin Metropolitan Police.

J. G. MAXWELL,
*General, Commanding-in-Chief,
The Forces in Ireland.*

HEADQUARTERS, IRISH COMMAND,
11th May, 1916.
(261.) Wt. 557/G. 88. 5,000, 5, '16. FALCONER, DUBLIN.

Orders issued after the Rising by General Sir John Maxwell. He was exercising the powers granted to him, under martial law, by the British cabinet on 27 April 1916.

PRO LONDON

seizure of the *Aud* and Casement's arrest.[36] After analysing submissions by Special Branch officers in the provinces, the Inspector General (Sir Neville Chamberlain) had reported that if the arms and ammunition had been landed successfully 'the volunteers outside Dublin would not have held back'.[37] Furthermore, Maxwell considered that retribution was justified partly to deter further acts of extremism and partly to underline the gravity with which the recent insurrection was regarded by the British government. He anticipated that his actions were likely to generate opprobrium in Ireland, though he did not foresee its intensity, and was saddened by the extent to which he became its object.

Maxwell disregarded those who advised against his intended course of action. When Lord Monteagle suggested that the royal prerogative of clemency be exercised, Maxwell replied dismissively:

> Open rebellion occurred at a time when the Empire is engaged in a desperate war involving the safety of the Realm ... Supposing that the bulk of them believed that they were called out for manoeuvres only. Does that exonerate them for keeping out when they saw what was? ... I think not. When Dublin is still smouldering and the blood of the victims of this mad rebellion is hardly dry is this the moment for clemency to win the rank and file?[38]

Ivor Price, a British Intelligence Officer in Ireland, informed Eoin MacNeill after his arrest that there would be 'a clean sweep of disloyalty in Ireland this time'. MacNeill had gone to see Maxwell when the Rising was over because he considered that 'the government would use military force in other parts of the country in such a way that resistance would be inevitable'. He had sought the meeting with him therefore in order 'to have an opportunity of preventing further bloodshed' and so that if his efforts failed, 'the responsibility for the consequences would be clearly fixed'.[39] Likewise, in discussion with Maxwell in 30 April, both the nationalist M.P. John Dillon, and Nathan, 'strongly argued against the execution of unknown men'. Dillon also expressed concern at the danger of arresting innocent men. He left Maxwell with a deep sense of unease and, reporting back to Redmond later, he quoted the GOC as saying that 'after he had finished with Dublin, he would deal with the country'.[40] In the commons (27 April), Redmond initially expressed his 'feeling of detestation and horror' at the Rising. But he later pleaded with the government 'from the bottom of my heart and with all my earnestness, not to show undue hardship or severity to the great masses of those who are implicated', and to show a 'spirit of leniency' (3 May). In due course (11 May), Dillon criticised the government's handling of the insurrection much more forcefully and controversially. He stated that the executions were 'letting loose a river of blood ... between the two races who, after three hundred years of hatred and of strife, we had nearly succeeded in bringing together'. He also indicated that he was 'proud of these men ... Their conduct was beyond reproach as fighting men. I admit they were wrong ... but they fought a clean fight, and they fought with superb bravery and skill'. He added: 'It is not murderers who are being executed; it is insurgents who have fought a clean fight, a brave fight, however misguided, and it would be a damned good thing for you if your soldiers were able to put up as good a fight as these men in Dublin'. The nationalist leaders received a measure of support from the Ulster unionist leader, Sir Edward Carson. While he urged the necessity to 'put down these rebels now and for ever more' (27 April), he too warned six days later, 'It will be a matter requiring the greatest wisdom and the greatest coolness, may I say, in dealing with these men, and all I can say to the executive is, whatever is done, let it be done not in a moment of temporary excitement but with due deliberation in regard both to the past and to the future'.[41]

> **PUBLIC NOTICE.**
> **PASSENGERS**
> **LEAVING IRELAND**
>
> I, GENERAL SIR JOHN GRENFELL MAXWELL, K.C.B., K.C.M.G., C.V.O., D.S.O., Commanding in Chief His Majesty's Forces in Ireland, hereby Order that no person shall embark as a passenger on board any vessel except at one of the following ports, viz: Dublin (North Wall), Kingstown, Belfast, and Greenore. Each passenger must produce satisfactory credentials or proofs of identity to the Military Embarkation Officer or Police Authorities at the place of intended embarkation and give valid reasons for the intended journey.
>
> **J. G. MAXWELL,**
> GENERAL,
> COMMANDING-IN-CHIEF,
> THE FORCES IN IRELAND.
> HEADQUARTERS, IRISH COMMAND.
> 2nd May, 1916.
>
> Powell Press, Printers, 22 Parliament Street, Dublin.

Orders issued after the Rising by General Sir John Maxwell
PRO LONDON

Apart from those thought sufficiently culpable as to merit a court martial, the Volunteers who surrendered in Dublin were transported almost immediately to England. By 3 p.m. on 30 April, 707 people had been taken into custody. In the course of the day the total rose to around 1,000 as Pearse's order was brought to the various garrisons in the city; that evening 489 were placed on board a ship at the North Wall. By 3 May, 500 had been removed from Richmond Barracks and lodged in Knutsford Detention Barracks in England; a further 289 were sent to Stafford. Meanwhile, the arrest of fugitive rebels continued; numerous pickets were posted, a tight street cordon was maintained, quaysides were closely monitored and passengers could only leave Ireland from Dublin, Kingstown, Belfast

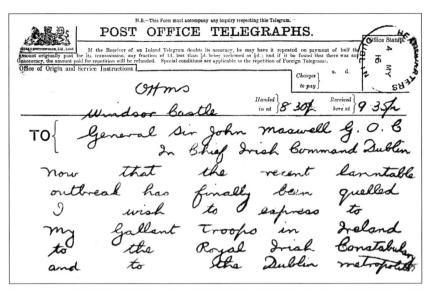

POST OFFICE TELEGRAPHS.

N.B.—This Form must accompany any inquiry respecting this Telegram.

Windsor Castle

TO General Sir John Maxwell G. O. C. In Chief Irish Command Dublin

now that the recent lamntable outbreak has finally been quelled I wish to express to my gallant troops in Ireland to the Royal Irish Constabuly and to the Dublin metropolit

---

POST OFFICE TELEGRAPHS.

N.B.—This Form must accompany any inquiry respecting this Telegram.

Windsor Castle

TO (2) Genl sir John Maxwell

Police my deep sense of the wholehearted devotion to duty and spirit of selfsacrifice with which throughout they have acted George R I.

Congratulatory telegram sent by King George V to General Sir John Maxwell on 4 May 1916, after the Rising had 'finally been quelled'

PRO LONDON

and Greenore (one of Nathan's last acts had been to recruit port-watchers). The path to Richmond Barracks, and from there to the North Wall and thence to internment camps in Britain became an exceedingly well-beaten one by the insurgents from the end of Easter week.[42]

As normality returned to the capital, military columns were being dispatched to the provinces, reinforcing the troops already there and concentrating on those areas which had shown recent signs of dissatisfaction, radiating out from Limerick, Cork, Kilkenny, Athlone and Waterford. Their purpose was partly to detain any dispersed rebel bands still at large. But primarily, acting under Defence of the Realm Regulation 14B, Lowe was instructed by Headquarters, Irish Command (under orders dated 3 May), to arrest 'dangerous Sinn

Feiners' who 'supported the movement throughout the country', even though they had not been active in the Rising. The GOC's instructions, however, had specified that: 'Care should be taken that those known to be strong Nationalists should not be confused with Sinn Féinners and in cases of doubt the dividing line between the two should be generously in favour of the Nationalists.'[43] He reinforced this on 5 May, stating: '[I] wish to impress on you the importance of arresting only dangerous Sinn Féiners. The object being to secure leaders of the movement and those who are known to have taken part in the rising or have arms with the intention of taking part in the rebellion against his Majesty's government.'[44] The columns set to their task zealously and in close co-operation with the local police, supported by intelligence personnel from Dublin. Those arrested were then dispatched under escort to Dublin. Any suspect resisting arrest could be court-martialled 'on the spot' under the authority of the local officer commanding. The troops also sought to compel the surrender of weapons. The RIC Inspector General, Sir Neville Chamberlain, had stated on Easter Saturday that they were powerless when outnumbered by large bodies of armed Volunteers. On 2 May, Maxwell issued a proclamation stating: 'All members of the Irish Volunteer Sinn Fein organisation or the Citizen Army shall forthwith surrender all arms, ammunition and explosives ... to the nearest Military Authority ... or Police Barracks. Any member ... found in possession of ...' [these] ... after 6 May 1916, will be severely dealt with.'[45]

Whilst fulfilling these duties the troops carried out demonstration route marches in a conscious bid to overawe the civilian population. Villagers witnessed a military procession which might consist of an artillery battery of eighteen-pound guns, a squadron of cavalry, and a large body of infantry equipped with rifles and sabres. Their intentions, one soldier commented, was to 'make the rebels furiously to think'. More often, their observers appear to have been most 'genuinely disturbed' by the garrisons' field canteens, which they mistakenly identified as 'poison gas machines'.[46] During lulls the soldiers trained for the Western Front, practising musketry and the artillery barrage, and conducting mock battles in especially constructed trenches.

From the correspondence of the soldiers involved, their experience of provincial Ireland left a deep impression. Some enjoyed the novelty and variety of army life there – censoring local mail and counteracting cattle-drivers, as well as digging up fields and gardens in search of arms and hunting down suspected rebels. One soldier-wrote home describing with delight how he had been stopping traffic on a bridge 'like a London policeman'.[47] The soldiers were struck by the 'glorious scenery' in areas such as Wicklow or Killarney and more frequently by the leisurely pace of life in rural Ireland. One wrote: 'old women with shawls over their heads driving donkey carts form a good proportion of the traffic. The driving is very slovenly, and carts and traps get all over the road.'[48]

The soldiers' own perceptions of local feeling regarding their presence in an area varied. Some reports were positive. When the 59th Division went to Galway it found 'people sullen at first', but by the time they were leaving, 'the long causeway over which the railway runs into ... [the city] ...was packed with cheering crowds bidding us farewell'.[49] At Clonmel, four hundred troops were able to find accommodation in homes within the town and one noted that when they first arrived in Enniscorthy, though the rebels had fled, 'most of the men got drunk on the hospitality of the town'.[50] Other units felt less welcome. Those based in Cork, generally thought it 'full of Sinn Féiners.' They complained of people being 'very unfriendly', of 'hard looks and occasional hard words', and of not therefore being allowed to leave the camp; some were 'cheered up' by the thought of transfer to the Western Front.[51] One soldier who had relatives living in the area commented on their 'rabid hatred of England' and that they would do anything to help Germany win the war.[52] Other soldiers in Limerick, wrote of the 'mixed feelings towards us, the population is half and half, rebel and loyalists', and thus having to 'go about in twos and threes, ... keep to main streets, ... [and] ... carry swords in their belts'.[53]

The units claimed variable degrees of success in their pursuit of the rebels in their locality. In the area of Fermoy and Tralee, the 177th Brigade found much evidence of 'Sinn Féin' influence, 'shown by the fact that in most of the villages all of the able-bodied men took to the hills. All movements of the troops were heralded by a series of signal fires in the hills lit by the various fugitives, presumably to warn others.'[54] One soldier expressed his frustration in Macroom, writing: 'It had 600 rebels with rifles last night, tonight they will be snug up in to the mountains.'[55] Elsewhere, more subtle tactics were adopted. In Athlone, for example, the Sherwood Foresters reported 'completely successful' operations through

conducting searches in the early morning, 'the inhabitants apparently not dreaming of its likelihood' then. Their official history
explains: 'The policy pursued by the column comprised of a sudden
encircling of disloyal areas by the cavalry, all egress being blocked,
while the infantry systematically drives the enclosed area section by
section, sending all suspects to police examination posts whose position had been determined beforehand.' One platoon member
recalls: 'We would surround a house, demand all occupants to come
out ... then we searched. On several occasions, the men would try
to escape from the back of the house as soon as the officer knocked
the front door ... Often [we] search rooms with occupants in bed.'[56]

Brigadier-General Lowe gauged the mop-up operations after the
Rising to be a complete success: this conclusion was based on
observation of the troops under his own command, and also he
claimed, on conversations he conducted with local priests as well as
police. He informed Maxwell that the work of the flying columns
had been 'excellently carried out' and that the role of the RIC had
been invaluable; it had shown a 'ready co-operation' with the troops
and 'great gallantry and devotion to duty'. Overall, Lowe concluded
that military personnel 'had met with no resistance or difficulty in
... arresting prominent and dangerous Sinn Feiners.' He considered
that the 'swift arrests and punishment of Rebels had a most benefi-
cial effect and thoroughly frightened' their supporters. In his opinion, the presence of the soldiers had had 'an excellent morale effect
on the country, troops not having been seen for some time past and
in some cases never. People [had] felt England could not spare them
for Ireland.' He therefore suggested that if the troops could be kept
there 'permanently or temporarily ... [it] ... would very materially
help recruiting and would counter-balance the influences and
ascendancy of Sinn Fein and parties hostile to the government.'[57]

Even Lowe, however, conceded that despite Maxwell's proclamation, the security operation had only limited success in locating
arms, one of its primary objectives; to do so, he suggested, would
require house-to-house searches which were likely to 'exasperate
the populace'.[58] The GOC, likewise, expressed his frustration that 'as
few weapons had been surrendered'. He informed the Cabinet that
it was 'impossible to estimate the number of arms of various kinds
... still concealed in Ireland but the great bulk ... were known to be
in possession of the Ulster and National Volunteers'.[59] According to
the Inspector General of the RIC, during the period when the

columns of troops were traversing the countryside, 1,244 rifles, 1,262 shotguns and 309 revolvers had either been seized or handed over. Just before the Rising the total Irish Volunteer stockpile was believed to be 1,886 rifles, 1,654 shotguns and 925 revolvers: though substantial, it was a fraction of the 53,000 rifles then believed to be held by the Ulster Volunteer Force or the 9,000 thought to be in National Volunteer hands.[60]

The security forces did, however, succeed in making numerous arrests – in total 3,430 men and 79 women, most of them detained between 1 and 23 May. These were clearly substantial numbers in relation to the scale of the outbreak. Despite Lowe's positive assessment, increasing government concern was felt at this scale and at its impact on Irish public opinion – especially as so many had clearly not been involved in the Rising and were from areas that had been quiescent throughout. It was feared that the effect would be merely to spread disaffection into the provinces. It seemed evident that the troops were being overzealous and paying insufficient attention to the instruction from headquarters to take care in distinguishing between members of Sinn Féin and more moderate nationalists. From the outset, Herbert Samuel, Secretary of State for Home Affairs, had also expressed acute anxiety at the legality of detaining so many merely on suspicion. He stated that 'it was not clear what vital answer there would be if a writ of *Habeas Corpus* was applied for in respect of any of them', adding, 'things cannot go on as they are indefinitely'.[61] During a brief, damage-limitation visit to Ireland, Asquith called at Richmond Barracks on 13 May with the GOC, and saw about three or four hundred of the prisoners. He was impressed by them, describing them as 'very good looking fellows, with lovely eyes'. But he noted that they were 'mostly from remote parts of the country' and he was convinced that 'there were a lot who had much better have been left at home'. He indicated that these should be combed out – 'only send to England those against whom there is a real case'.[62]

Maxwell fully shared the Prime Minister's concern. He too observed that 'It is very difficult to differentiate between Sinn Feiners and Redmondites. It is merely a question of degree.'[63] He

PUBLIC NOTICE.

ARMS & AMMUNITION.

I, GENERAL SIR JOHN GRENFELL MAXWELL, K.C.B., K.C.M.G., C.V.O., D.S.O., Commanding in Chief His Majesty's Forces in Ireland, hereby Order that all members of the Irish Volunteer Sinn Fein Organization, or of the Citizen Army, shall forthwith surrender all arms, ammunition and explosives, in their possession to the nearest Military Authority or the nearest Police Barracks.

Any member of either of these organizations found in possession of any arms, ammunition, or explosives, after 6th May, 1916, will be severely dealt with.

J. G. MAXWELL,

GENERAL,
COMMANDING-IN-CHIEF,
THE FORCES IN IRELAND

HEADQUARTERS, IRISH COMMAND,
2nd May, 1916.

Powell Press, Printers, 22 Parliament Street, Dublin.

Orders issued after the Rising by General Sir John Maxwell
PRO LONDON

considered that moderate nationalists were abandoning the Home Rule party because it was 'becoming too constitutional and self-seeking'. In correspondence between 12 and 16 May, he professed himself 'anxious to release without delay any innocent person who may have been inadvertently arrested', and to provide them 'with opportunities to prove their innocence', while 'only retaining for further enquiry ... more responsible persons ... who appear to have been connected with the rebellion'.[64] He wrote to Redmond: 'I wish to reassure you that no one realises more than myself the necessity for releasing all innocent persons in the interests of the pacification of the country'.[65] By 8 May, he had already released all but twelve of the seventy-four women arrested in Dublin, 'without prejudice, cautioning them as to good behaviour'.[66] Just after the Rising, he had dispatched William Wylie to interview the remaining women prisoners in Kilmainham Gaol and empowered him to

conduct the selection procedure. Maxwell appears to have been delighted that so many were freed. He told Wylie that he didn't know what to do with 'all these silly little girls,' and he was sure that 'the right thing to do was to send them home'.[67] Countess Markievicz reportedly told her sister that 'she thought ... [the female prisoners] ... must have played a very deep game, for all those who mattered were released a day or two after they were arrested'.[68]

On 14 May, the troops were issued with new and more specific orders – to arrest only 'men against whom there is evidence to try by court martial on charge of having taken part in the rebellion' or

Soldiers and rebel prisoners standing in one of the British military barracks in Dublin. The figure in civilian clothes on the right may be Major John MacBride.

ALLEN LIBRARY

'those known to be inciting others to retain arms or to resist authority and whose continued presence in a neighbourhood is considered
likely to lead to bloodshed'.[69] Those arrested on any other grounds
were to be released. Maxwell informed Kitchener that in issuing his
instructions he had been 'careful ... to impress on all concerned ...
that we are dealing with Sinn Feiners and Citizen Army only and
that only the dangerous ones known to the police should be arrested'.[70] After investigation 1,424 men were freed. In addition, those
who had already been interned in England (1,836 men and five
women) were empowered to appeal their cases before a newly constituted Irish Advisory Committee; it paralleled an already existing
body in London, and was chaired by Lord Justice Sankey. By 23
May, the Deputy Inspector General reported that it was dealing with
150 cases daily, and was 'combing out ... the innocents ... with
vigour'.[71] On its recommendation, 1,272 out of 1,841 applicants
were released by 9 August – those who it considered had been kept
in ignorance by the organisers of their intention to convert a route
march into a rebellion.

No doubt there genuinely were such cases. A letter, written on 5
May by a prisoner who had been deported and was being detained
in Stafford, was intercepted by the authorities; it must have broadly
confirmed their impression that some Volunteers had been duped. A
copy of it was typed up and sent to Asquith; it stated:

> We were no doubt deceived and taken by surprise by our
> leaders. I have not yet met one member of the rank and file
> who was aware that the Republic was to be proclaimed. Of
> course we expected trouble from the military if there was an
> attempt to disarm the country, that was the policy of
> McNeill [sic] ... and everyone was with him ... It can be
> plainly seen that Connolly and Clarke and the extreme men
> on our [IRB Supreme] Council got control of the movement
> and rushed matters ... The yarn about 20,000 Germans
> landing put great spirit into our lads. They feared nothing but
> God and really thought that Ireland's hour had come ... John
> Dillon was here today but did not interview the men. A
> couple managed to get a few words with him. He said that
> we may be sent to an internment camp until the Home Rule
> matter is settled. He gave us great praise for the great fight
> that we made ... they all blame McNeill for his letter in the

paper on Easter Sunday. Of course it prevented about 1,000 of the Dublin lads from turning out.[72]

Similar evidence comes from other sources. When W.T. Cosgrave – he had fought at the South Dublin Union and became President of the Dáil government in August 1922 – was being court-martialled, Wylie records asking him 'if he had any defence and he said that he had "never heard of the rebellion until he was in the middle of it"'. 'He assured me,' Wylie continues, 'that when he marched out on Easter Monday he thought he was merely going out for a route march.'[73] Some of the leading figures in both the IVF and the IRB were kept in total ignorance of the plans for a rising until the action began or was at least imminent, including Denis McCullough, The O'Rahilly, and Diarmuid Lynch who was a confidente of MacDermott. Oscar Traynor first received confirmation of the true purpose of the Easter Sunday manouvers on Easter Saturday; he was astonished to hear at the same time that there were divisions within the volunteer leadership on the issue, and that some of those who were opposed were likely to be arrested by those who favoured an insurrection.[74]

The bulk of all the releases took place between 8 and 30 May. Indeed, they proceeded with such haste that by early September, the RIC leadership was expressing concern that the whole process had been too casual, so allowing the genuinely seditious to be freed; it urged therefore that further cases should be referred to the RIC Inspector General or the Police Commissioner of the DMP. Amongst those detained at Richmond Barracks during May 1916 was Bernard O'Rourke from County Monaghan. Though he was not court-martialled and was held only briefly, his daily private correspondence provides an insight into both the attitudes of the prisoners there, and their living conditions. Writing to his wife, he informed her that a friend, 'McMahon of Ardee, [had] got three years imprisonment'. He added: 'The fellows here are quite jealous of him as they look on it as a great honour to get so much. In fact any man who doesn't get some time is in the eyes of all the prisoners here a disgrace.'

As for the prisoners' conditions at Richmond Barracks, O'Rourke noted that: 'The first few days we were here the food and accommodation were very bad'; they were given 'bully beef and dog biscuits and had to sleep on the floor'. But thereafter, according to

To/

    A.D. of S.& T.

        Irish Command.

Sir,

      I have the honour to submit attached Supply account of Sinn
Fein Prisoners for period 14/5/1916. to 15/6/1916, for you inspection. It will be found on auditing that the bread, sugar, vegetables,
cheese, and milk, are over-drawn over and above the special rate of
issue laid down in attached letter of authority.

      Re Vegetables :- I would like to point out that since the
majority of the prisoners were larely from the peasantry with whom
bread and potatoes are the staple food, I considered that to allow
them the extra when asked for would not be outside me province.
More over, I was given to understand both personally from the
Officer in charge of Prisoners, and from the attached letter, that
everything possible was to be done regardless of expense, to avoid
complaints on the part of prisoners.

      When it was brought to my notice that the vegetable rations
were insufficient, and certain of the prisoners wanted more bread, I
increased the rations as I saw fit. The over-draft of sugar corresponds with the increased ration of teas, vude Medical Authority
attached. Extra Milk drawn over and above the ration needed for tea,
was used to meet the extra teas for escorts, milk diets and milk
puddings. The fish and tinned salmon was issued in lieu of meat
and bacon on fast days in deference to the religious convictions of
the Prisoners, under the authority of the Officer in charge of
Prisoners. The other items outside the rations were similarly
authorised as coming under the heading :- "Prisoners Comforts",
(Vide,P.M.'s letter).

      I would like to point out that coal, jam, margarine and
tea, were under-drawn for the total period.

      Would it be possible to put the value, in money, so
saved to the public, against the over drafts in the other direction.

      The above report has been submitted to the D.A.G.,

Undated note by
military officer
G.W. Rushton,
(written probably in
late June 1916)
outlining the dietary
preferences of the
Irish prisoners
arrested after the
Rising

PRO LONDON

his letters, their circumstances had improved dramatically. They had been given seats, tables, cutlery, towels and blankets; they received newspapers, had organised concerts and had 'got the light on to 10 o'clock'. He described how a priest said mass 'out in the open space opposite our windows and all the prisoners can see it from their rooms'. They had hot meals and were 'giving leftovers to the English soldiers'. He described his fellow inmates as 'the finest men alive' and indicated that all were in the 'best of spirits'. He concluded that they were 'better off than at the Gresham [Hotel] ... I have never spent a more enjoyable holiday in my life ... over 1,000 prisoners in this block and I didn't meet any of them but said they never had such an holiday in their life'.[75] With good reason they hoped to avoid being transferred to detention camps in England. Most of the men still interned in Britain were brought to Frongoch camp, which held at peak one thousand internees in July 1916, and 540 by October. There they claimed that they were kept in rat-infested grain lofts, never intended for human habitation, with totally inadequate sanitary facilities and that illness was rampant, including consumption, scabies and skin diseases. The War Office reported that their stocks of bread and potatoes became overdrawn 'since the majority ... were largely from the peasantry with whom ... [these] ... are the staple food'.[76] Most were released by Christmas, and the remainder under a general amnesty in July 1917, timed to coincide with the opening of the Irish Convention.

Meanwhile, the trials of the 186 men and one woman held in Ireland for court martial continued apace throughout May with still as many as twenty-seven cases being heard on the 15th. In some instances the judgements of the courts were followed by a delay lasting several days whilst Maxwell, as Commander-in-Chief, reviewed the evidence and made the final decision – whether to 'confirm the findings and sentence' from which there was no appeal or, 'make a recommendation to mercy' and commute the judgement to a period of penal servitude. Sections of the Irish press expressed strong views on the issue. In its first editorial after the Rising, the pro-Union *Irish Times* advised: 'All the elements of disaffection have shown their hand. The state has struck, but its work has not finished ... In the verdict of history, weakness today would be even more criminal than the indifference of the last few months. Sedition must be rooted out of Ireland once and for all. The rapine and bloodshed of the past week must be finished with a severity, which will make any repetition of them impossible for generations to come.'[77] The *Irish Independent*, voice of catholic business interests, declared on 4 May: 'no terms of denunciation that pen could indict would be too strong to apply to those responsible for the insane and criminal rising of last week.' In an editorial six days later, it stated: 'Let the worst of the ring leaders be singled out and dealt with as they deserved.'

Maxwell himself, never doubted that the rebel leaders should be executed. He explained to his wife: 'some must suffer for their crimes'.[78] Of the six Volunteers court-martialled on 2 May, three received the death sentence; Maxwell confirmed it that same day and they were notified (the sentence was promulgated) soon afterwards. They were executed the next morning. On 3 May, twenty-two Volunteers were tried, and twenty sentenced to death; Maxwell approved the verdict in four cases. All four were informed within hours and faced the firing squad at dawn next day. On 4 May, thirty-five men were tried as was Countess Markievicz, but most were not immmediately informed of their fate. Maxwell states that 'owing to my sudden departure for England, I was only able to deal with' three cases (he had been summoned to attend a Cabinet meeting in London, held on 5 May).[79] Whether by accident or design – perhaps because of his role in the South African War, John MacBride was one of those processed; Maxwell endorsed the court's judgement of death, and he was executed early on 5 May.

After the GOC returned, he confirmed the death sentences on Colbert, Heuston and Ceannt on 6 May. They were informed the next day and executed on 8 May. Meanwhile, Thomas Kent was tried in Cork on 4 May and his sentence was confirmed on the 6 May. Probably because of distance he was not informed until 8 May and was executed the following day. With James Connolly and Sean

A casual note made by Asquith, in which he recorded that 'Con. [Connolly] & McD [MacDermott]' were to be executed. Asquith has also jotted down the number of casualties resulting from the Rising

BODLEIAN LIBRARY, UNIVERSITY OF OXFORD

MacDermott, a delay was caused for different reasons. Both were tried on 9 May and received death sentences which Maxwell confirmed the same day. But initially their 'execution was suspended on the Prime Minister's orders'; there was a growing apprehension about the numbers being executed and a real concern about the effect on Irish opinion.[80] However, both were eventually executed on 12 May. On 10 May, the GOC wrote to Asquith to defend and explain his actions. He stated:

> In view of the gravity of the rebellion and its connection with German intrigue and propaganda and in view of the great loss of life and destruction of property resulting therefrom, the General Officer Commanding in Chief, Irish Command, has found it imperative to inflict the most severe sentences on the known organizers of this detestable Rising and on those Commanders who took an active part in the actual fighting which occurred. It is hoped that these examples will be sufficient to act as a deterrent to intrigues and to bring home to them that the murder of His Majesty's subjects or other acts calculated to imperil the safety of the realm will not be tolerated.[81]

Note, dated 12 May 1916, by Major C. Harold Heathcote, the Officer in Charge of Prisoners at Richmond Barracks, confirming that the death sentences on both Connolly and MacDermott had been carried out

PRO LONDON

Apart from Thomas Kent, the death sentences on all of those condemned was carried out at Kilmainham Gaol. It had been built over a century before and although it had catered for common convicts, the 'Irish Bastille' was closely linked with defeated and incarcerated Irish rebels. Its inmates had included Henry Joy McCracken, one of the leaders of the 1798 rebellion, and Robert Emmet in 1803. The five Invincibles, who had killed the Chief Secretary for Ireland in 1882, were also executed in Kilmainham. The gaol had ceased to operate as a convict prison in 1911 and had been taken over by the army for use as a detention barracks for military prisoners. Micheal

Kent recalls arriving there to see his brother, Eamonn. He writes: '[We were] admitted, handed up our letters, names registered, lanterns procured and then down the dark corridors into the bowels of this hellish abode ... and up to the iron grill and door of one of the endless cells. Great God to think poor Ned is locked and barred in that saddened tomb!'[82] Jack Plunkett described it as 'old, condemned ... [It] had not been in use for many years and was lamentably lacking in the most basic amenities.'[83] This is attested to by the friends and family of other prisoners who recall the almost total lack of furniture in the cells, sacks or ground sheets on the floor, buckets for waste in the corner, the eerie light from candles or naked gas flames and walls once whitewashed, looking grey and dirty. The former stonebreaker's yard was used as the place to carry out the executions in 1916.

The procedures to be adopted in relation to the death sentences were hastily improvised. On 2 May, Brigadier J. Young, Headquarters, Irish Command, summarised them in a minute sent to Major General A.E. Sandbach, the GOC troops, Dublin. He had been prompted to write the minute 'in case there should be a large number of executions tomorrow' but considered that 'owing to the delay in the court's proceedings it is not likely that there will be more than four', and thus the scale of both firing and burying parties would be reduced. It specified:

> In the event of any of the Sinn Fein prisoners being condemned to death today, they will be segregated (so far as circumstances permit) and asked whether they want to see relatives or friends or chaplains; and these persons will be sent for as required by the prisoners. A number of motor cars will be stationed at Richmond Barracks for this purpose, and more may be asked for from HQ, Irish Command, as necessary. The whole of the visitors and friends are to be taken back to their homes before 3:30 a.m. the next day, at which time the first firing party will parade.

The first man to be shot will be brought out at 3:45 a.m. facing the firing party officer, and 12 men at 10 paces distant. [It was light then as daylight saving did not come into operation in Ireland until 21 May 1916 and GMT was not introduced until 1917]. The rifles of the firing party will be loaded by other men behind their backs, 1 rifle with a blank cartridge, and eleven with ball, and the firing party will be told that this is the arrangement, and no man is to know which rifle in loaded with [a] blank. There will be 4 Firing Parties, who will fire in turn.[84]

Artist's impression of the executions, which was sold as a postcard and produced probably in late 1916; though propagandist in purpose, the image is historically accurate
KILMAINHAM GAOL AND MUSEUM

Father Augustine, while accompanying John MacBride to the execution yard, records that 'the firing party [was] already waiting with loaded rifles. Six now kneel and behind them six stand. He faced them about 50 feet from the guns, 2 or 3 feet from the wall ... a silent signal, a loud volley and the body collapses in a heap.'[85] On some occasions at least – at the executions of Sean Heuston and Eamonn Ceannt – a soapbox was brought out and the prisoner asked to sit on it, rather than stand before the firing squad.

Accounts of the final minutes of the condemned men are not entirely consistent, but that provided by Father Albert when with Sean Heuston, is vivid and probably typical. He writes: 'We walked out [of the cell] together, down to the end of the large open space from which a corridor runs to the jail yard [the place of execution]. Here his hands were tied behind his back, a cloth place over his eyes and a small piece of white paper, about 4 inches or 5 square, pinned to his coat over his heart.' They then proceeded past the firing squad waiting for Michael Mallin to a second yard where there was 'another group of military armed with rifles'.[86] This procedure was probably thought advisable because the condemned man did not enter the execution yard restrained, and it thus reduced the likelihood of him seeing the firing party, panicking and putting up strong physical resistance.

Young's memorandum also outlined the course to be followed after the execution. It stated:

> After each prisoner has been shot, a Medical Officer will certify that he is dead, and his body will be immediately removed to an ambulance, with a label pinned on his breast giving his name. When the ambulance is full, it will be sent to Arbour Hill Detention Barracks, entering by the gate at the Garrison Chapel. The party then will put the bodies close along side one another in the grave (now being dug), cover them quickly with quicklime (ordered) and commence filling in the grave. One of the officers with his party is to keep a note of the position of each body in the grave, taking the name from the label. A priest will attend for the funeral service.[87]

From the outset, Maxwell was insistent that the bodies of those executed should not be released to their families. Peceptively, when justifying this decision, he explained: 'Irish sentimentality will turn these graves into martyrs' shrines to which annual processions will be made.'[88] Hence, the executed rebels were to be buried in quicklime and without coffins. At Kilmainham, a rumour circulated, recorded by Eoin MacNeill, that a grave fifty feet long, twelve feet deep and eighteen feet wide had been dug at Arbour Hill – big enough to hold between two to three hundred bodies.

In addition to the documents relating to the courts martial of each rebel, the whole execution procedure generated a substantial volume of paperwork. An officer was to 'promulgate the findings and sentence and enter the fact on a form, date it and sign it'. At the prison, 'the sentence was to be carried out by the Assistant Provost Marshall and a certificate rendered by him' containing details regarding time and place. A medical officer was to be 'present at the execution to certify death before disposal of body', again completing the relevant form. Finally, a 'certificate of burial' had to be completed by the officer in command of the burial party at Arbour Hill, on which the position of the grave of each condemned man was to be clearly indicated.[89] Given the number of cases, a single

The G.O.C in C has confirmed the sentence of death in the following cases:-

P.H.Pearse (at Kilmainham)

Thomas MacDonagh. (at either Richmond Bks or Kilmainham).

Thomas J Clarke.   "   "   "   "

The instructions contained in my P1 of today as regards execution of sentence should therefore be carried out tomorrow morning as arranged.   On receipt of this letter an Officer should be detailed to proceed to Richmond Bks & to Kilmainham gaol where the prisoners now are and this officer should promulgate the finding and sentence to the prisoners forthwith and enter the fact of promulgation on page 60 3 of the proceedings with the date and his signature.   The prisoners should be kept in separate rooms and under observation during the night.   The sentence should be carried out under your Provost Marshal and a certificate should be rendered by him that this has been done, together with a certificate of death from the medical officer.

The proceedings after the promulgation should be returned to Gen'l Hd Qrs,Park Gate.

Dublin

2nd May 1916.

Brig: Gen:

D.A.G.

form was often used at each stage, on which the relevant details for several prisoners were recorded rather than one being produced for each of them. Whilst the forms seem brutal in their coldness and formality, those officers who completed them were not necessarily so. A number of the certificates of death – including those for Pearse, MacDonagh and Clarke – were completed by Captain H.V. Stanley RAMC. Father Aloysius, who met him while tending to the spiritual needs of the prisoners, said of him:

> I must here stop to pay tribute to Captain Stanley. All through these days, and I had many occasions to meet him, he showed himself a kind hearted and Christian man. In religion as well as politics differing, he respected the convictions and admired the courage of the men, and was anxious to do any service he could for them in keeping with his duty. Connolly himself told me that Stanley had been extremely kind to him. Wherever he is today may God reward his good nature and his human feelings for those who were in sore need of it.[90]

The hastily produced British army memorandum, dated 2 May 1916, which contains detailed and graphic instructions on how the executions of the rebels were to be conducted

PRO LONDON

Whilst these arrangements were being finalised and circulated, the first court martial verdicts were being pronounced and in the cases of Patrick Pearse, Thomas MacDonagh and Thomas Clarke, the GOC confirmed the death sentence. Officers were dispatched to inform the three rebels at Kilmainham where they had been brought during the evening of 2 May, and kept in separate cells and under observation during the night. The executions were conducted under the direction of Major Harold Heathcote, the Assistant Provost Marshal and officer in charge of prisoners. They took place, broadly as Young had instructed, between 3:30 – 4:00 a.m. on 3 May. The firing squad was provided by 59th Division; its official history states that: 'All met their fate bravely.'[91] The bodies were then taken to Arbour Hill for burial. But clearly the procedures did not run entirely smoothly. The officer in command, Brigadier Maconchy, recalls: 'Last night on the 2 May I received orders to have three of the ringleaders shot at dawn. The instuctions were in great detail but on going carefully through them nowhere could I see

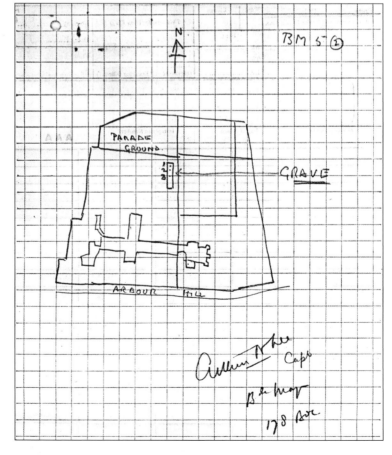

Drawing by an officer indicating the positions of the rebels' bodies after burial on 3 May at Arbour Hill Detention Barracks. Patrick Pearse was number 1, MacDonagh number 2 and Clarke number 3.

PRO LONDON

anybody's signature on the orders and therefore refused to carry them out unless they were signed by someone having authority to do so. This was eventually done and the orders carried out.'[92] Also,

for whatever reason, no labels were affixed to the three bodies. In addition, though motor cars had been dispatched to convey two Capuchin priests and Pearse's mother and MacDonagh's wife to the prison, they came back without the women. This was not mainly due to pressures of time. Father Aloysuis explains: 'sniping from the roofs of the houses was so bad that when we got as far as Charlemont Bridge the soldiers thought it advisable to abandon their plans and return'. The priest was also upset by the fact that while at Kilmainham, some time before the executions, 'orders were given that all ... should leave ... and that the orders referred to me, too'. He returned to the prison later that morning to lodge a formal complaint, stating that 'in every civilised community the clergy were permitted to remain with the prisoner and administer the last rites of the church. I had not been permitted to remain to administer Extreme Unction, as I was not permitted to be present at the execution.'[93] As a result of his protest the procedures were changed immediately.

Most, if not all, of the dreaded letters, dispatched to summon the relatives of the rebels to the prison, prior to their execution, were signed by Major W.S. Lennon, the Commandant at Kilmainham. He was himself a Dubliner, in his mid-thirties, who had served for twelve years in the RIC, becoming District Inspector, and had enlisted in the Royal Dublin Fusiliers in 1914. He was wounded at Suvla Bay, 15 August 1915, losing the use of his right arm and thus forced to return home on leave several weeks later. On 8 April 1916, the Army Medical Board had declared him 'fit for service at home';

Drawing indicating the positions of the bodies of the four rebels executed on 4 May 1916 and buried at Arbour Hill Detention Barracks

thus, when the Rising began he was summoned to report for duty
and given the post of commandant at the gaol which he held until
August 1916.[94] Despite strict proceedures maladministration continued to occur from time to time. A most regretable instance of this
was when the family of Michael O'Hanrahan, one of the prisoners
awaiting execution, was summoned to Kilmainham to see him; the
official letter stated erroneously that he wished to meet them 'before
his departure to England'.[95] In fact, no deportees, even those whose
death sentence was commuted to penal service for life, were given
the opportunity to meet family or friends before leaving.

The experience of being summoned to the gaol was in itself traumatic. Michael Kent recorded receiving the request, on 7 May, to go
to the prison to see his brother. He wrote: 'I was at home tonight
with my boots off ... when a knock came to the front door and an
official envelope was handed in to me on His Majesty's Service ... A
few lines from the governor of Kilmainham to say my brother
Eamonn wished to see me. I never in my whole life experienced my
heart sinking right down to my boots till that night. I knew it was
all up with poor Ned.' The journey itself was stressful. Kent continues: '[I] was shown into the waiting motor car by a policeman, the
driver being a soldier ... The car was stopped every quarter of a mile
or so by sentries in the middle of the road, their rifles pointing and
bayonets fixed ... The last two days and nights and today, it has rained
without ceasing.'[96] According to other accounts, when challenged at
check-points the cryptic response from the driver was 'King's
Messenger!'

James Connolly's wife and his daughter, Nora, were among the
last relatives to be called on such an errand, though in their case
their destination was the Red Cross Hospital at Dublin Castle,
rather than Kilmainham. Nora later recalled her last meeting with
her father, early in the morning of 12 May. In the course of their
conversation, she records: 'I told him that it had been in the paper
there was to be no more shootings and that it had been stated in the
House of Commons. He said: "England's promises, Nora, you and I
know what they mean".'[97] In fact, Maxwell had been coming under
growing pressure from Westminster to call a halt to the executions,
particularly after the death sentences carried out in the early
morning of 8 May. Next day, the day of Connolly's trial, he had
complained to his wife: 'Now that the rebellion is over ... the government is getting cold feet and afraid. They are at me every

moment not to overdo the death sentences.' But he added: 'I never intended to.'[98]

On 8 May, Maxwell had received a letter from Lord Wimborne, the Lord Lieutenant in Ireland; his criticism of the GOC was phrased in the strongest possible terms. He wrote:

> I hope you will not take exception to me expressing my views to you on the subject of military executions in connection with the recent disturbance. No one in Ireland outside of a few experts will believe that I am without influence in settling the cases of capital sentences or admit that I have no responsibility in the matter. I am therefore bound to express my opinion and to take all means at my disposal to ensure them being considered. After our conversation last night I was I must admit dismayed to learn that three comparatively unknown insurgents were executed that morning [in fact four had been shot - Ceannt, Mallin, Colbert and Heuston, though perhaps he considered that the punishment was deserved in Ceannt's case as he was one of the four Volunteer commmandants in the city]. In popular estimation if these men are to be shot nearly a hundred others are liable to the same penalty with it will be held in many cases more justification. I know that you do not mean to create this impression but I am bound to tell you that it exists and is capable of producing disastrous consequences. I have felt it my duty to communicate these facts and my opinion of their effects to the Prime Minister and I must respectfully urge you in the most serious manner that public opinion will not support either here or in England further executions of any save one of two very prominent and deeply implicated suspects and that a statement from you of a reasoning character is urgently needed to allay the feeling aroused by this morning's action and to define the limits of your contemplated policy.[99]

In a scrawled note, probably also written on 8 May after the execution of the four 'unknown insurgents', Asquith stated that there was a 'grave danger of general and bitter' reaction at what appeared to be 'periodical' acts of 'vengence' on the part of the military authorities in Ireland, and that a 'reassuring statement was needed without delay'.[100]

That Asquith's government harboured from the outset reservations about martial law is evident from it's instruction to Maxwell just after his appointment, that he was 'not to use extreme measures except in cases of emergency'.[101] The Prime Minister came under immediate and mounting pressure to prevent any executions. When Dillon met Asquith two days later, he concluded that Asquith had 'not the least conception of the situation he had to face in Ireland'. The nationalist MP at once wrote to his party leader, John Redmond, stating: 'You should strongly urge on the government the extreme unwisdom of any wholesale executions of prisoners.' He suggested: 'the wisest course is to execute no one' in view of the likely impact on public opinion.[102] Such sentiments had the support of Matthew Nathan. Though Birrell thought the leaders of the Rising should be given short shrift he too was concerned about the likely consequences.

After the first executions had taken place, Asquith indicated that he was a 'little surprised and perturbed by the drastic action of shooting so many rebel leaders'. He instructed that the GOC be reminded that it would cause a 'revulsion of feeling in Britain and lay up a store of future trouble in Ireland'.[103] After eight rebels had been shot, Maxwell was asked to report to the 5 May Cabinet meeting. He outlined then the position in Dublin and Ireland and disclosed that he had accepted the court's 'recommendation to mercy' in the case of Countess Markievicz. The implementation of the death sentence was clearly discussed; after the meeting, Asquith informed the King that the GOC had been instructed 'not to allow the capital sentence to be carried out in the case of any woman [Markievicz was the only woman to be court-martialled]. It was agreed to leave to his discretion the dealing with particular cases subject to a general instruction that death should not be inflicted except upon ringleaders and proven murderers and that it was desirable to bring the executions to a close as soon as possible.'[104]

On 9 May, Maxwell confirmed the court's verdict on Connolly and MacDermott and informed Asquith, stating that 'Connolly having been reported fit to be tried, was tried and sentenced to death. This I confirmed. MacDermott also tried, convicted and sentenced to death, confirmed. They will be shot at dawn on morning of May 11.'[105] The Prime Minister, who crossed over to Dublin on the night of 11 May, intervened personally to suspend its implementation.

Earlier, during the afternoon, Kitchener had telegrammed Maxwell to say: 'Unless you have heard anything to the contrary from Mr Asquith you may carry out tomorrow the extreme sentence of death on MacDermott and Connolly.'[106] Clearly the GOC heard nothing: a scrawled note in Asquith's private papers, probably written on 11 May, merely records: 'Con and McD to be exd'.[107] It would have been difficult to have argued in either case that they did not fall within the Cabinet injunction that only ringleaders of the Rising could be executed or Wimborne's stipulation that the death sentence should only be applied to 'very prominent and deeply implicated suspects'. Maxwell himself regarded them as 'the worst of the lot'.[108]

Aware of the mounting pressures on the GOC from nationalist politicians and the liberal press, some 760 influential persons signed a memorial, in Dublin and Cork, between 12 and 15 May, protesting against 'any interference with ... [his] ... discretion' whilst martial law was in operation. On 12 May, HRH Princess Louise wrote to Kitchener, stating that: 'Maxwell has done only what is just and good in Ireland. He must have full military powers for there is a much deeper led plot than one imagines it to be ... [the Rising] ... must be put down with a strong hand ... [or] ... it will spread to England. Another German hope.'[109] Maxwell also sought to defend his own policies, though perhaps less publicly than Wimborne had had in mind. On 9 May, he wrote to Asquith to reassure him that 'I have confirmed no death sentence, unless I have been convinced by the evidence that the convict was either a leader of the movement or a commander of rebels, who were engaged in shooting down His Majesty's troops or subjects.' He also sent him a list of casualties sustained by the security forces during the Rising (for press release), pointing out that though those for the rebels were unknown, 'from the nature of things compared with others ... [they] ... must be insignificant'.[110] Two days later, in support of this assertion, he sent both the Prime Minister and Wimborne a memorandum, entitled 'a short history of rebels on whom it has been necessary to inflict the supreme penalty'.[111] He also dispatched a copy to Kitchener, describing it as 'a precis of the antecedents of all the executed rebels', and informed him: 'I do not consider that in any of these cases there were any extenuating circumstances. I weighed everything before I confirmed the courts.' Writing to his wife, he described the task of making the decision on each of the accused as a 'horrible onus'.[112]

In part, this document summarised any hard evidence presented by the prosecution in their respective courts martial; Maxwell's heavy black markings at salient points on the text of the official record of the proceedings provide clear evidence that he had thoroughly examined them. But it also relied heavily on Special Branch files on the defendants and as such, provides an insight into the quality of British intelligence at the time; as Maxwell himself noted: 'naturally we have to depend largely on police reports'.[113] The main factors which determined Maxwell's judgement when deciding whether or not to confirm the death sentences imposed by the courts were the accused's past record of involvement in extreme nationalist organisations, their rank in rebel forces during the Rising and the intensity of the fighting and scale of British casualties in their garrison area. The existence of the Proclamation also influenced him in the cases of each of its seven signatories. To the GOC, it provided evidence not only of leadership in the insurrection, but of having been one of those to declare an independent Irish Republic, of membership of the provisional government 'hereby constituted' and, perhaps above all, of collaboration with Ireland's 'gallant allies' abroad. Maxwell was of course blissfully unaware that the seven rebel leaders also shared membership of the IRB Military Council, the body which had planned and executed the Rising.[114]

The content of Maxwell's short history underlines in particular, the good fortune of Eamonn de Valera and Countess Markievicz in escaping the death penalty. De Valera was less high profile than some of the other leaders during the years preceding the insurrection. This fact is reflected in the sparse content of his MI5 file for the period around 1916. Knowledge of him seems to have been limited to his name appearing in Connolly's notebook of addresses which was uncovered in a house search after the Rising; a reference to him in a document discovered on The O'Rahilly's body; and his appearance in a group photograph unearthed in a raid on Thomas Clarke's property. Nonetheless, he had been a leading figure in the Irish Volunteers and during Easter week he had served as Commandant at Boland's Bakery. The three other officers of the same rank in the city were each executed – Thomas MacDonagh, Eamonn Ceannt and Ned Daly. The gun-battle at Mount Street Bridge, in the course of which almost half of all military casualties were sustained, took place within de Valera's area of command. In fact, a later, undated British intelligence report referred to him (inaccurately) as having 'shown a greater genius for tactics than any other rebel leader'.[115]

De Valera was charged with 'armed rebellion and waging war against His Majesty the King' and sentenced to death.[116] It was no doubt to his advantage that he was court-martialled as late as 8 May, when government pressure on the GOC was mounting – though

MacDermott and Connolly did not face trial until the following day. Representations by the United States Consul in Dublin that he was an American citizen may have helped. It is, however, evident from a report, dated August 1916, by the Governor of Dartmoor Prison, where he was then being held, that neither the authorities nor the prisoner himself knew with certainty his national identity. The report states: 'The prisoner gives New York as his place of birth. He states that he has asked his mother to find out whether his father – who was a Spaniard – became an American citizen. If so, he (prisoner) claims to be such. If not, he is Spanish. He further states that he did not become a British citizen, but he would have become an Irish citizen if that had been possible.'[117] The Governor was almost certainly responding to an approach made by the US Embassy on behalf of the American State Department, on 28 June 1916, to the War Office. The Embassy was clearly unsure of de Valera's nationality; it stated that he was 'understood to be an American citizen', but requested that 'enquiry ... be made of him

On Sunday 30 April 1916, just after the surrender, Eamonn de Valera (marked X) leads the Boland's Bakery garrison under military escort, along the Northumberland Road.

ALLEN LIBRARY

through the camp officials as to whether he claims to be an American citizen'.[118]

William Wylie records having a conversation with the GOC when the courts-martial were in session which he considers may have helped determine de Valera's fate. He recalls that Maxwell asked him who was next on the list for trial and he replied, 'somebody called de Valera, sir'. 'Who is he?' queried Maxwell, 'I haven't heard of him before.' 'He was in command of Boland's Bakery in the Ringsend area,' Wylie responded. 'I wonder would he be likely to make trouble in the future?' Maxwell continued. The prosecution counsel proffered the opinion: 'I wouldn't think so, sir. I don't think he's important enough. From what I can hear he's not one of the leaders.' Wylie concludes, 'I don't think it is an exaggeration to say that on that conversation in Richmond Barracks a considerable part of subsequent Irish history depended. If I had answered differently, if I had told Maxwell that de Valera was important, he would certainly have gone the way of the others ... there would have been no split at the time of the Treaty ... no civil war.'[119]

However improbable it may seem that the GOC would not have been aware of the defendant's prominent role in the Rising and the scale of British casualties in his area of command, notably at Mount Steet Bridge, nonetheless he did commute de Valera's sentence to penal servitude for life. Whilst at Dartmoor, de Valera sought to keep mentally active. He asked for writing materials so that he could 'continue certain researches in Higher Applied Mathematics on which I was engaged prior to my conviction', including 'problems in conformal representation', 'line complexes' and 'modern electrical theories – Relativity, etc'.[120]

De Valera also displayed features which were to charactarise his public career over the next fifty years – an assumption of the role of leader, a powerful patriarchal instinct and a deep-rooted inflexibility in political outlook. This is evident from a memorandum by F. Battiscondie, the Deputy Medical Officer at Dartmoor, dated 20 October 1916, written after de Valera had gone on a short hunger strike. It states:

> Prisoner's demeanour in hospital is civil and pleasant, but he
> maintains the attitude of: 1. A father to his children with
> reference to the other Irish prisoners [sixty-five were held
> in the prison], eg. says it hurts him to hear the others

ordered about by the warders etc etc ... 2. Insisting that he
is a prisoner-of-war like the Belgians, and should be treated
in exactly the same the same way that the Belgians have
been threated by the Germans all thro' this war – his own
words. 3. He threatens also that if he is again placed under
punishment he will repeat his hunger strike. Forcible
feeding he will consider as causing an injury to his health
and that will be sufficient grounds for him to refuse all food
in future ... It would be war to the bitter end.

Battiscondie concludes his report:

I consider prisoner to be of a determined and fanatical
temperament and I fully believe he will carry out his threats
re hunger striking ... Prisoner looks upon everything from
the political point of view, and believes apparently that
every man, woman and child of English origin is imbued
with hatred for Ireland and is constantly endeavouring to
injure her ... He accused the medical staff of grossly ill-
treating the whole Irish faction but would give no
particulars.[121]

The case of Countess Constance Markievicz was unique; she
escaped the firing squad exclusively because of her gender.
Markievicz, who was in her mid-forties in 1916, had been well-
known to British intelligence long before the Rising. The British
were aware of her role in establishing Fianna (a youth organisation
to train boys for participation in a war of liberation), her presidency of Cumann na mBan, her involvement in the suffragette movement and the Dublin lockout in 1913, and two years later in organising and training the Citizen Army. In August 1910, she had been
convicted of assaulting a policeman and for referring to King
George V as the 'greatest scoundrel in Europe'.[122] A later intelligence report described her as belonging by then to the 'inner circle
of the murder gang'.[123] Like de Valera in 1916, the authorities were

uncertain of her nationality, though she was the daughter of a well-known, landed Sligo family. In response to police enquiries regarding her husband, the Polish Consul reported that 'there was no such person as Count Markievicz but he knew a man called Danui Markievicx [sic] ... a play-writer living in Warsaw, ... [who] ... before the European war was a Russian'. Apparently, when traced, he refused to give details of 'his marriage abroad and his Polish nationality could not be established'.[124] Without clarification, the Countess could not therefore be recognised as a Polish citizen, or be expelled there if she had committed an offence punishable by expulsion.

Whilst in Aylesbury prison in September 1916, Markievicz was overheard telling her sister that when Connolly disappeared in mid-January (he had been kidnapped by the IRB Military Council) 'and it was feared that he did not intend to come back ... if he had not returned, ... [she] ... was quite ready and would have started the revolution herself'.[125] She certainly played a leading role in the Rising as second-in-command to Michael Mallin at St Stephen's Green. Both in Ireland and abroad the exploits of the 'Larkinite rebel countess' dominated press reports of the insurrection, dwarfing those of more significant encounters. In Dublin, there were few places where she had not allegedly been sighted during Easter week; a British intelligence profile compiled years later stated erroneously that she 'was in the attack on Dublin Castle, [and] fought in the City

Hall ...'[126] These depictions had a basis in fact; she had undoubtedly been active in an actual fighting capacity throughout the week. It was widely believed at the time and has been authoritatively asserted since, that she shot at and may have killed members of the security forces during the fighting; in speeches made after her release from prison she herself claimed with pride to have 'fired the second shot, wounding a policeman'.[127] Her defiant but calculated gesture at the surrender – kissing her revolver before handing it over to the British officer, was the most celebrated moment of the entire insurrection. The officer she had surrendered to was Captain Henry de Courcy Wheeler, who was also of Anglo-Irish background (his family had held estates in Kildare since the seventeenth century), and was related to her by marriage; he had married her cousin. On the march under military escort to Richmond Barracks afterwards, she claimed to have discussed with her associates the manner of their deaths at the hands of the British authorities, whether they would be 'shot or hung'. This may have been mere bravura, but she had good reason to harbour genuine fears of summary execution. Certainly the British military authorities were anxious to detain her. After the provisional government agreed to surrender to the British OC on Saturday afternoon, 29 April, Brigadier-General Lowe immediately asked Pearse where Markievicz was. According to Elizabeth O'Farrell, he stated: 'I understand you have the Countess Markievicz down there ... I know she is down there ... I know she is in the area.' Pearse replied: 'Well, she is not with me, Sir.'[128]

Markievicz was tried on 4 May, Brigadier-General Blackader presiding. Prosecution counsel called two witnesses. One, a seventeen-year-old page-boy at the Shelbourne Hotel, alleged that he had seen her giving orders and shooting in the direction of the University Club in St Stephen's Green. The other was Captain Henry de Courcy Wheeler. Wylie later recorded his colourful impressions of the trial. He stated:

> We quite expected she would make a scene and throw
> things at the court. In fact I saw the General getting out his
> revolver and putting it on the table beside him. He did not
> have trouble as she curled up completely. 'I am only a
> woman. You can't shoot a woman. You must not shoot a
> woman.' She never stopped moaning the whole time she
> was in court. She had been in command of the St Stephen's

Green contingent and according to her report had been full of fight but she crumpled up at the court martial. I think we all felt slightly disgusted as she had been preaching rebellion to a lot of silly boys, death and glory, die for your country, etc, and yet she was literally crawling. I won't say any more. It revolts me still.[129]

This account clearly circulated widely in Dublin at the time. Miss Mahaffy, daughter of the Provost at Trinity College, recorded: 'At the trial [Markievicz] utterly broke down, cried and sobbed and tried to incite pity in General Blackader. It was a terrible scene.' She referred to 'the evidence of a little boy … who saw her shoot a policeman … [the Countess] could not frighten or confuse the child who remained clear'.[130]

In fact the official record of Markievicz's trial shows that she acted bravely and with charactaristic defiance throughout; beneath her aristocratic hauteur, her undoubted theatricality and her considerable capacity for embroidering her own exploits, she did possess both courage and flair. She pleaded not guilty to the charge that she 'did … take part in an armed rebellion … for the purpose of assisting the enemy', but guilty to having attempted 'to cause disaffection among the civilian population of His Majesty'. There is not the slightest suggestion in the proceedings that she tried to overawe the first prosecution witness, the page-boy from the Shelbourne Hotel, during her cross-examination. De Courcy Wheeler in his evidence noted that she had readily volunteered her rank at the time of the surrender and had been determined to march with the others to Richmond Barracks, rejecting his offer of motor transport (he had made the suggestion because a crowd of hostile byestanders had gathered around the Green). When speaking in her own defence, she retracted nothing, stating simply: 'I went out to fight for Ireland's freedom and it doesn't matter what happens to me. I did what I thought was right and I stand by it.'[131] Wylie's wilful and scurrilous distortion of her response at her trial is difficult to interpret. It may reflect a personal sense of irritation at her self-assurance and boldness, which he may have considered an insult to the court. Perhaps it reflected deep-rooted sexual prejudice and rank misogyny on his part. More likely, his fictitious account sprang, above all, from a feeling that the Countess had by her actions betrayed both her religion and her class (she had been presented at court to Queen Victoria in

SCHEDULE.

Date   May 4th   19 16 .   No.

Name of Alleged Offender (a)	Offence charged	Plea	Finding, and if Convicted, Sentence (b)	How dealt with by Confirming Officer
Constance Georgina Markievicz	1. Did an act to wit did take part in an armed rebellion and in the waging of war against His Majesty the King, such act being of such a nature as to be calculated to be prejudicial to the Defence of the Realm and being done with the intention and for the purpose of assisting the enemy.	Not Guilty	Guilty. Death by being shot The Court recommend the prisoner to mercy solely & only on account of her sex.	Confirmed. But I commute the sentence to one of Penal Servitude for life.
Alternative 2.	Did attempt to cause disaffection among the civilian population of His Majesty.	Guilty.		

(a) If the name of the person charged is unknown, he may be described as unknown, with such addition as will identify him.

(b) Recommendation to mercy to be inserted in this column.

J.G.MAXWELL.   C.G.Blackader,
                                                    Brig. Genl.

_____   _____
          Convening Officer.   *President.*

Promulgated this sixth day of May 1916.
                                    H. Anderson, Capt.
Kilmainham Goal, Dublin.   3/ The Royal Irish Regt.

her jubilee year, 1887). Such considerations certainly influenced Miss Mahaffy's assessment of her; she writes of Markievicz that she was 'the one woman amongst them of high birth and therefore the most depraved ... She took to politics and left our class.'[132]

The verdict reached in Markievicz's court martial was unique: 'Guilty. Death by being shot. The Court recommend the prisoner to mercy solely and only on account of her sex.' Next day, 5 May, Maxwell informed the Cabinet that he would commute the death sentence in her case. He did so officially on the 6, recording that the

The 'Schedule' taken from the proceedings of the court martial of Countess Markievicz. It contains the charge, the defendant's plea, the unique verdict reached by the court in her case, and the text of Maxwell's decision to commute the sentence.

PRO LONDON

verdict was 'Confirmed. But I commute the sentence to one of Penal Servitude for life.'[133] His decision was conveyed to her soon afterwards at Kilmainham. She later complained in characteristically melodramatic fashion that whilst there she had lain 'awake night after night, until dawn, when each morning some of her friends were shot under her window, [with] two volleys ... often necessary to kill them'.[134] She was then held at Mountjoy until July, when Maxwell had her transferred to England; she was at the time 'the only prisoner convicted for rebellion ... [then] ... in Ireland' and was becoming the focus of extremist attention.[135] There were fears that her continued presence might precipitate an attempted breakout. She was moved to HMP Aylesbury, joining at least one other Irish rebel there. They were held alongside two dozen other women, of all classes and nationalities, including some German aliens. They complained less about conditions than about the other inmates – their 'frequent brawling, filthy language,' emotional instability and immorality. The Countess later told her sister that her 'company ... [had] ... been the dregs of the population ... no one to speak to except prostitutes who have been convicted for murder or violence. The atmosphere is the conversation of the brothel.'[136] The Home Office denied her claims. Later she stated that during her thirteen month imprisonment, Thomas Clarke had been her 'inspiration'.

Overall, in seventy-five of the ninety cases (84 per cent), in which the courts martial had imposed the death sentence, Maxwell commuted the verdict to varying terms of penal servitude, ranging from life in ten cases to six months with hard labour in four.[137] One can only speculate on how many more he would have executed without Asquith's government applying pressure to desist. But the evidence suggests, as Maxwell stated privately to his wife, that he had never intended to 'overdo' them; he had clearly implied the same in his conversation with Wimborne. When the trials began on 2 May, he privately predicted that 'there would be as many as 70', his assumed upper limit (in fact they totalled over one hundred and ninety who were either identified by the detectives at Richmond Barracks as meriting courts martial, or picked up during the security forces' sweep of the countryside).[138] He found their on-going nature 'very tiresome' and, from the outset, overturned most of the death penalties imposed by the courts – by 3 May, he had confirmed seven (24 per cent) out of twenty-seven and, by 5 May, thirteen out of sixty-eight (19 per cent).[139] The proportion consistently fell, but this was not mainly due to any external criticism. Rather it was because the Dublin rebels were tried first, and amongst them were the assumed ringleaders. On 9 May, Maxwell had written to Asquith: 'The courts under Defence of the Realm Act in regard to rebellion in the city of DUBLIN are practically finished. Those on rebellion in the Provinces are still to be done ... Today still remain to be tried Connolly and MacEgmot [sic].' He believed that they were likely to be 'the last to suffer Capital punishment, as far as I can now state'. Next day, he repeated: 'I sincerely trust that no such case will now arise.'[40]

The pressure actually applied by Asquith appears to have been very limited in nature and to have had little measureable effect. Certainly, some was applied. A number of government ministers had been uneasy over the introduction of martial law and from the out- set had sought to circumscribe its impact by constraining Maxwell's powers. Later, after the first executions, the Cabinet had summoned the GOC to explain and defend his actions. On Sunday, 7 May, when there were rumours that more executions were pending, Redmond sent an urgent message to Asquith; the nationalist leader threatened to resign if the death sentences continued. In response, the Prime Minister sent what he termed a 'strong telegram' to Maxwell saying that he hoped the shootings would stop, except in some quite exceptional cases.[141] In fact, at dawn the following day, Colbert, Mallin, Heuston and Ceannt faced the firing squad, and the GOC showed no inclination to slacken the pace of the courts martial. Wylie records: 'I got to know Maxwell pretty well and this particu- lar day I could see he was in a bit of a splutter. "Read that," he said, handing me a telegram. It was from Asquith, then Prime Minister ... "Who is next on your list," barked Maxwell. "Connolly, Sir." "Well I insist on him being tried."'[142]

At the outset, 27 April, Asquith had informed the commons that the 'paramount duty of the Government is to restore order, and to stamp out rebellion with all possible vigour and promptitude'. Apparently convinced by Maxwell's defence of the death penalty, he strongly defended his later application of its use against those who argued that 'you have done enough already'. On 11 May, Asquith said of Thomas Kent that he was 'executed – most properly execut- ed as everybody will admit – for murder at Fermoy'. He continued:

There are still two other persons who are under sentence of

death [MacDermott and Connolly] – a sentence which has
been confirmed by the General – both of whom signed the
Proclamation and took an active part, one of them the most
active part of all, in the actual rebellion in Dublin. I do not
see my way, and the Government do not see their way, to
interfere with the decision of Sir John Maxwell that in
these two cases the extreme penalty must be paid. If it was
justifiable, as we think it was, in the case of the five other
persons who signed the Proclamation, it would be
extremely difficult, on any ground of justice ... to
discriminate between them and these two others simply for
the reason that they happen to have been tried a little later
... I cannot – I tell the House fairly and frankly – reconcile
it with my conscience or my judgement, believing as I do
that the five other sentences [on those who signed the
proclamation] were properly given ... simply because we
have reached this stage in point of time and numbers, that a
differential or preferential treatment should be accorded to
men equally or even more guilty.

He added: 'That, I am glad to think and believe, completes the tale.
So far as I know, so far as the General ... knows, there will be no
reason to resort to this extreme penalty to any other case.' He also
strongly defended Maxwell stating: 'We believe that under very
trying conditions, in the exercise of a very delicate and difficult
jurisdiction, he has shown, as far as we can judge, discretion, depth
of mind and humanity, and so far as I am concerned I am perfectly
satisfied with the manner in which he has discharged and is
discharging the exceptionally difficult duty which was confided to
him'.[143]

When Asquith came to Ireland on 12 May, in his most decisive
intervention, it was largely to evaluate the impact of the executions
and imprisonments. He stated then with evident relief, 'on the
whole ... there have been fewer bad blunders than might have been
expected with the soldiery for a whole week in exclusive charge'.[144]
In a letter to Maxwell, written on the day of his arrival, Asquith
appeared even to envisage the possibility of further executions and
to be most concerned about introducing procedural changes into
the courts martial – such as to the wording of the indictment. He
gave Maxwell instructions that 'in all further cases of murder (like

[Thomas] Kent's) if there are any, the charge should be framed in the terms suggested by the Attorney-General "'for an act,'" citing the language of Regulation 50, and going on "'to wit that he did feloniously and of malice aforethought kill and murder AB etc.'"[145] When they met, Maxwell reassured him that there 'need be no further executions.'[146] The GOC's overall impression was that the Prime Minister 'appeared to approve all that he had done hitherto and reposed entire confidence in him for future dealings'.[147] In his private correspondence, Maxwell commented: '[Asquith] has not interfered with me but ... has helped me very much' (18 May), and described him as 'a remarkable man ... clear headed' (30 May). In Maxwell's opinion, Asquith's defect was that he was 'not very strong,' too responsive to the Irish Parliamentary Party and too willing to pander to public criticism.[148] That Maxwell's relationship with the government remained more or less satisfactory throughout is suggested by the fact that he remained at his position in Ireland so long. When it was decided to replace him as GOC, on 26 October 1916, ministers recorded their anxiety to offer him an appointment 'of such a kind as to show that ... [they] ... fully appreciated his services'.[149]

Those whose death sentences had been commuted were in due course transferred to England to serve their time. Jack Plunkett recalls how, after the details of Maxwell's decision to revoke the sentences had been brought to Kilmainham, 'a lot of us sentenced men were brought out and driven to Mountjoy.' There, they were held for approximately one week, given prison clothes and kept in their separate cells throughout each day. Then, he continues, 'one night we were given back our ... uniforms, after all badges had been removed, and we were rushed out in military lorries in a mystifying manner' to the North Wall. Under heavy guard, they were ordered onto a cattle boat which was then getting up steam. 'There were twenty-one of us together at this time,' he recalls 'and we were located in the steerage, separated by a timber fence from the cattle.' As they crossed the Irish Sea, they inevitably reflected on the insurrection. Plunkett remembers W.T. Cosgrave, who had fought bravely at the South Dublin Union stating emphatically that 'he had come out against his conscience and he would never do it again'.[150] They next boarded the train at Holyhead en route to Portland Prison; according to one of them, Maurice Brennan, 'at all the stations we passed we were booed by the people'.[151]

In contrast, within Ireland the extent of public sympathy for the Rising was already increasing measureably. On 29 May, Percy Bick, a British officer noted with evident disillusion: 'People are already sympathising with the rebels and have forgotten the poor soldiers who have lost their lives through the wicked folly of the people. I am sorry the authorities put a stop to the shooting of prisoners found guilty.'[152] During May, the Inspector General of the RIC had likewise detected a growing 'wave of resentment'; the courts martial and executions, mass arrests and deportations had, he thought, caused many nationalists who had at first condemned the Rising to consider that unnecessary severity had been deployed in suppressing it.[153] Ominously, he observed that the extreme nationalists were 'by no means cowed'. 'In some quarters,' he noted, 'it is sought to brand the Sinn Fein rebellion as a Roman Catholic ... Rising'; as evidence, in August, he quoted a Belfast priest referring to those 'Holy martyrs who went to heaven last Easter'.[154]

It was of course natural to depict the insurrection in such terms. It was justified in part by the religious identity and devout nature of many of the Volunteers. Large numbers of them had crowded into Dublin churches on Easter Sunday, regarding this as an essential part of their preparation. Thomas Ashe observed: 'Let me carry your cross for Ireland, Lord ... We have to rely on prayer. The rosary in particular'.[155] Throughout Easter week the garrisons had routinely assembled to recite the Rosary, even in the midst of heavy fighting. Though there were a number of angry confrontations with hostile priests during the insurrection, others had made regular and treasured visits to the rebels' posts to hear confession. At the surrender the Capuchin Fathers had played an especially prominent role arranging localised truces, delivering Pearse's order and later attending to the spiritual needs of the

---

CHIEF SECRETARY.

Regarding this question of the publication of photographs of rebel leaders, I would refer to a minute of my predecessor, No. 71297 (A.-2.) dated November 4th (Government file 12638/B) in which you concurred.

In that minute, it was pointed out that the sale of these photographs had been allowed since the rebellion, and that the test of any act which is considered likely to cause disaffection must be that it promotes incitement to break the law - otherwise it seems impossible to draw the line.

In applying that test to the present case of the calendar with the O'Rahilly's photograph on it, there does not appear to be sufficient grounds for inferring that it would promote incitement to others to break the law - The inscription "Killed in Action" is no worse than "Executed" which appears on photographs of other rebel leaders which are now exposed for sale in shops in all parts of the country.

I think that the Executive should decide whether the policy of taking no action in regard to these photographs is to be altogether changed, and that they are to be seized.

(sd) B. Mahon, Lieut.-General,
COMMANDING-In-CHIEF THE FORCES IN IRELAND.

Memorandum indicating that the production of photographs of the executed rebels in 1916 was a cause of concern to the British authorities

PRO LONDON

condemned men at Kilmainham before and after their execution. The religious charactar of the insurrection was reinforced by the devotional nature of the writings, especially of some of its leaders, many published posthumously. These features contributed to the readiness of the public to identify with their actions.

The monthly Crime Special Branch reports by the RIC county inspectors recorded symptoms of a palpable change in public attitudes to the Rising: – the increasing frequency of memorial masses for the executed rebels; the growing sales of photographs of them and distribution of leaflets about them; the setting up of aid funds for their families; the appearance of songs and ballads celebrating their actions; the ubiquity of republican flags and badges; the numerous accounts of young men marching, military-style, at GAA football matches; the enthusiastic reaction of cinema audiances to newsreels of the Rising; the shouting of pro-rebel slogans anywhere people gathered together anonymously. Moreover, there were ominous signs that militant nationalists were re-organising, reflected in the rise in arms thefts and in the noticeable hardening of attitudes towards the police.[156] Rumours of a further rising persisted until the end of the First World War (on 14 December 1917, with surprising prescience, de Valera stated that: 'the Germans were about to throw $6^{1}/2$ million men against the Western Front and that Ireland's opportunity would come sooner than expected').[157] After Easter week, recruitment levels fell sharply; even amongst the Irish in Australia it had 'come almost to a standstill'. At a Cabinet meeting, the Chief Secretary, on 19 September 1916, 'drew a very gloomy picture of the present state of feeling'; he estimated that 'three-quarters of the population are more or less sore and embittered'.[158]

Maxwell was fully aware of the transformation in public mood. He observed that 'the first results of the punishments inflicted were good ... The majority of people recognised that they were not excessive'; but since then 'a revulsion of feeling had set in'.[159] He predicted, as early as mid-June, that 'if there was a general election ... there is a danger Mr Redmond's party would be replaced by others perhaps less amenable to reason'.[160] Maxwell was then monitoring the changing content of the censored correspondence written by rebel prisoners; he regarded it as a depressing barometer of the shifting balance of opinion in Ireland. He informed Asquith that, 'it had shown a decided turn for the worse, for whereas in the first flush of captivity their letters were more or less apologetic and humble, now the tone is defiant and shows that they are not in the least repentant. In fact, they think they are very gallant fellows.'[161] He was also aware of, and indeed had foreseen, his own growing unpopularity – a more personal measure of public attitudes. He observed in early July: 'Some of the Irish call me very nasty names "Bloody Butcher" and such like'. Elsewhere he commented: 'I will be the best hated man wherever there are Irish,' adding 'I am getting sick of the job.'[162]

Maxwell accepted that the courts martial, the executions, the mass arrests and the deportations had helped cause the change, but, in his view, a number of 'misrepresentations' of the truth lay at the root of the growing popular sympathy for the Rising and its leaders. Amongst these, he claimed, were suggestions that: 'the leaders were executed or murdered in cold blood without trial; that people were deported who took no part ... without trials or charges ... That the Military have been harsh, unjust and oppressive, etc, trials in camera.'[163] He noted with disapproval: 'the Irish are beginning to think that all ... should be let off ... The tendency, of course, is to make martyrs of all those who have been executed.' When he considered the sources and purveyors of these 'misrepresentations', his list was a lengthy one and, by implication, an indictment of much of Irish society and culture. He thought some of the catholic clergy were 'really intensely disloyal and keep any sores there are open', and castigated especially the 'infernal requiem masses for the repose of the souls of those who died and have been executed'. The Pope, he suggested to Asquith, might be 'induced to prevent priests messing themselves up in matters political'. He also ridiculed the Irish nationalist MPs whom he described as, 'hard at it throwing mud' and 'making political capital out of events'. John Dillon he thought the worst offender, in particular his widely reported speech to the Commons, on 11 May, when he had stated: 'It would be a damned good thing for you if your soldiers were able to put up as good a fight as those in Dublin.' The GOC regarded this statement as 'rotten and untrue', considered that it had done 'enormous harm' and felt angered that it had been in his view so inadequately refuted by Asquith and his ministers. In addition, Maxwell censured the public bodies in Ireland who he alleged failed to provide balanced leadership. The press, he said, 'magnify every incident which could reflect on military or government'. He also wrote scathingly of a 'conspiracy to get at the boys in schools and inculcate revolutionary ideas'.

The consequence of such a shift in public opinion was that, as he observed forlornly, that: 'I am looked on as the embodyment of military excess' and 'the rising generations ... is [sic] more bitter than their predecessor'.[164]

Maxwell's comments in relation to education in this period were perhaps the most apposite. All statistics point to the unusually high numbers of Christian Brothers' past pupils involved in both the rank and file and the administration of the physical force republican movement. A survey of four Christian Brothers' Schools in Dublin reveals that in 1916, of those who took part in the Rising, twenty-four were from Marino, thirty were past pupils of Synge Street and thirty from Westland Row. Remarkably, one hundred and twenty-five of those involved in the Rising were from the O'Connell Schools, North Richmond Street (including Sean Heuston, Con Colbert and Eamonn Ceannt), yet there were just five from Belvedere College, located a short distance away. One study concludes that the Christian Brothers' Schools turned out young men 'with a passion for the Irish identity, who lent themselves readily to organisations like the Irish Volunteer Force and the Irish Republican Brotherhood'.[165] An essential characteristic of the Brothers' curricular and extra-curricular activities (especially in the teaching of the Irish language, history and Gaelic sports) was that they instilled in those who attended an intense sense of pride in their Irishness. It was this feature, combined with the creation of a well-educated lower middle class, which helped create what Barry Coldrey describes as 'the ideal revolutionary group'.[166]

Quite possibly, even without the perceived cruelty and brutality of Britain's response to the Rising, public attitudes would in any case have changed. Even during Easter week, the public had shown growing sympathy towards the rebels. The Irish MP, Tim Healy, considered that a turning point was the treatment of the Volunteers from the GPO and Four Courts after their surrender; on Saturday night, between 29 and 30 April, they had been made to stand or sit under armed guard in the open at the Rotunda Garden before being escorted to Richmond Barracks next morning. He wrote: 'since it was not possible to make immediate arrangements for the decent custody ... [of them] ... this led to conditions which left a memory as bitter as that enkindled by the executions'.[167] During the spring and summer of 1916, the police reports suggest other factors also contributed to shifting attitudes. They stress the importance of the persistent and widespread fear of conscription especially amongst the young, their numbers swollen by the large number of labourers who, unable to find employment in Britain, were forced to return home, 'owing to the reaction against them' there.[168] With justification, opinion in Ireland generally attributed Westminster's decision not to impose conscription to the impact of militant nationalists.[169]

The Crime Special Branch reports claimed that the prisoner releases, far from earning Irish gratitude, fuelled resentment by providing evidence that the arrests had been made 'without just cause'; indeed the return of the rebels was widely interpreted by the public as a 'triumph over the government'. Special Branch also agreed strongly with the GOC's view on Dillon's speech after the Rising, suggesting that it had had a 'deplorable' and 'mischevious effect' and had 'changed the whole feeling' – influencing especially those of moderate opinion who had previously been hostile to the rebels. Moreover, they criticised Asquith's role. They considered that his visit to Ireland, during which he had met some of the prisoners at Richmond Barracks, had merely served to raise their profile and enhance their credibility; one report stated tersely: 'it did an infinity of harm'. Likewise, they asserted that his subsequent attempt to achieve a settlement through negotiation based on Home Rule, was regarded by the rebels as a vindication of their actions; leading them to 'feel that they have taken the right steps'.[170] Far from killing Ireland's hopes of self-government, as the GOC himself phrased it, 'out of rebellion more had been got than by constitutional methods'.[171]

The palpable ineffectiveness and repeated failure of constitutional nationalism over the past fifty years had thus been highlighted. For British ministers the Irish question remained an apparently intractable problem. The velvet glove approach, combined with a commitment to Home Rule associated with Birrell and Nathan, was perceived to have been a failure; they were amongst the first casualties of the Rising. In its aftermath, the measures identified in Ireland with Maxwell had helped cause bitterness which, when eventually translated into politcal terms, sounded the death knell for the Parliamentary Party, and its replacement by Sinn Féin.

The Leaders

The spelling and setting of the transcripts of the official record of the fifteen court martial proceedings which follow are identical to the original documents. The sequence adopted for the fifteen sections has been determined by the official prisoner numbers given to each man on surrender. In keeping with the period the portraits of the executed men are original memorial postcards circulated shortly after their executions.

IRISH REBELLION, MAY 1916.

P. H. PEARSE.
Commandant-General of the Army of the Irish Republic).
Executed May 3rd, 1916.
One of the signatories of the "Irish Republic Proclamation."

Patrick Pearse

REBELLION IN IRELAND, 1916.

Short History of rebels on whom it has been necessary to
inflict the supreme penalty.

PATRICK H. PEARSE.

  This man was a member of the Irish Bar and was
Principal of a college for boys at Rathfarnham,Co Dublin. He
was 36 years of age.

  He had taken an active part in the volunteer movement from its inception,and joined the Sinn Fein or Irish
Volunteers when that body became a separate organization.

  He was a member of the Central Council of the Irish
Volunteers and a regular attendant at the meetings of that
body.

  He was one of the signatories to the Declaration of

Extract from a
memorandum entitled
'Short History of
rebels on whom it has
been necessary to
inflict the supreme
penalty' sent by
General Sir John
Maxwell to Herbert
Asquith, on 11 May
1916.

Irish Independence which document contains, inter alia, the following passage- "She (viz-Ireland) now seizes that moment "and supported by her exiled children in America and by gallant "allies in Europe ⁂ she strikes in the full confidence "of victory."

He was "Commandant General of the Army of the Irish Republic" and "President of the Provisional Government", and, as such, issued a Proclamation to the people of Ireland which was printed and distributed in Dublin and elsewhere.

At his trial a letter written by him on May 1st was produced and proved containing the following passage- "I "understand that the German expedition on which I was counting "actually set sail but was defeated by the British." He stated at his trial that he was in communication with Germany and that his object was to defeat England.

PATRICK PEARSE WAS BORN IN DUBLIN on 10 September 1879, the first son of a self-educated, free-thinking English monumental sculptor, who had come to Ireland in the 1850s, and his second wife, Mary Brady from County Meath. Patrick probably inherited some of his aloofness from his father, together with his taste for literature and his striving for respectability. His piety, strong national identity and love for the Irish language he derived from his mother and her family, as well as from attendance at the Christian Brothers' School, Westland Row. He had a happy, comfortable, somewhat isolated, middle-class upbringing. Through his strong personality, he dominated his two sisters and younger brother, Willliam. Even as a child, he had a vivid, morbid imagination, with unusual fantasies of self-sacrifice for his country derived from his knowledge of celtic myths and religious literature. He was intelligent and industrious, ascetic by nature, and won a scholarship to the Royal University where he studied law; he was afterwards called to the Irish Bar though he may only have practised on one occasion.

Pearse had joined the Gaelic League on leaving school and

became immersed in the Irish cultural revival. He developed an abnormally single-minded commitment to the revival of the Irish language, valuing it particularly as the repository of Irish culture and a vital component of Ireland's contribution to world civilisation. His involvement in the movement was ultimately to prove disillusioning. He gained rapid promotion, finally becoming editor of its newspaper in 1903. He became first a cultural nationalist, pillorying the educational system which in his view intimidated Irish people, did not cater for the national ideal and was the prime source of Ireland's anglicisation. Initially he regarded educational reform as more important than political independence. In September 1908 he founded an independent, Irish-speaking school for boys, St Enda's (St Enda had abondoned the heroic life of a warrior to teach a devoted band of scholars on Aran Island). In it, the direct method of language teaching was adopted, and the atmosphere was unusually liberal – in Pearse's phrase, a 'child republic'; it was as exciting for the pupils as it was initially fulfilling for their headmaster. But there was always a tension between the desire to provide those attending with freedom to develop and the intention also to groom them for a heroic sacrificial gesture. Its prospectus stated that the object was to inculcate in those attending, 'the desire to spend their lives working hard and zealously for their fatherland and if it should ever be necessary, to die for it.'[1] Celtic myth and legend were a central part of its curriculum. Revolutionary politics became second nature to those educated there; fifteen of its former pupils and four of the teachers who had taught them participated in the Rising.

Until 1912, Pearse appeared on Home Rule platforms, regarding Irish devolution as the best available stepping stone to independence – though he issued a warning: 'If we are cheated now there will be red war in Ireland.'[2] His conversion to physical force republicanism was gradual, and had complex roots. One milestone was his decision to transfer his school to the Hermitage, Rathfarnham; this imposing house was built in the 1780s in a beautiful and isolated location, and had associations with Robert Emmet, whose presence Pearse claimed to feel. There he became more politically minded, immersing himself in the thoughts and actions of the Irish revolutionaries and interjecting his undiluted admiration for them into the curriculum and mores of the school. He was also influenced by contemporary events. He said of the deprivation which he observed during the Dublin lockout, that 'the root of the matter lies in foreign domination'.[3] The delay over the passing of the third Home Rule bill and the considerable political impact of militant unionist resistance to it, eroded further his faith in the efficacy of constitutional methods. He joined the Irish Volunteers at their foundation in November 1913. His involvement confirmed his shift towards physical force nationalism, provided an increasingly obsessive outlet for his energies and gave him an escape from worry over the possible bankruptcy of his school and the associated prospect of public humiliation and ridicule. He had in any case come to believe that true educational freedom was conditional on the attainment of full political independence.

In October 1913, his financial concerns prompted Pearse to approach Bulmer Hobson, a leading figure in the IRB. Through his revolutionary contacts, Hobson organised a three-month lecturing tour for Pearse in the United States and, before his departure, swore him into the Brotherhood, partly to help ensure the success of the venture (December 1913). Whilst in the US, Pearse made repeated and successful appearances before militant Irish–American audiences. By the time of his return in May 1914, he felt himself to be morally committed to organising a rising in Ireland – a heroic role commensurate with his own perceived abilities and growing sense of destiny.

Like the other rebel leaders, Pearse came to believe that through his death and martyrdom in an insurrection, militant Irish nationalism would be revived and Ireland's right to freedom 'proven'. But for him, the idea of the blood sacrifice had additional appeal. He gradually fused together his nationalism and his catholic faith. His Christian devotion had always centred on Christ's passion and crucifixion, and he developed a consuming yearning for self-sacrifice, in conscious emulation of Christ's sacrifice on the cross. He wrote: 'One man can free a people, as one man redeemed the world.'[4] He was also influenced by a mystical belief, then widespread, in the assumed benefit to mankind of blood split in violent conflict. He wrote in 1913: 'Bloodshed is a cleansing and sanctifying thing', and in 1915: 'The old heart of the earth needed to be warmed by the red wine of the battlefield.'[5]

The outbreak of the First World War, with soldiers sacrificing themselves in unprecedented numbers for political goals, kindled his enthusiasm still further and also instilled a conviction that the time was opportune. On 12 August 1914, he wrote to John Devoy, an ardent supporter of physical force nationalism: 'A supreme moment for Ireland may be at hand. We shall go down to our graves beaten and disgraced men if we are not ready for it.'[6] A craving for action had progressively come to dominate his thinking. This, combined with his literacy and oratorical gifts, made him an object of interest to revolutionary groups in Ireland and he was himself keen to impress them. The dominant IRB figure, Thomas Clarke, was initially suspicious of Pearse due to his earlier record of political moderation. But he was persuaded by Sean MacDermott to invite him to give the oration in 1913 commemorating Wolfe Tone's death. Clarke afterwards observed: 'I never thought there was such stuff in Pearse.'[7] The view that Pearse was one of themselves was confirmed by his panegyric at the graveside of the Fenian and physical force campaigner O'Donovan Rossa in 1915. Afterwards Pearse commented effusively: 'The Rossa funeral was wonderful.'[8] Republicans were impressed by his extraordinary magnetism as a public speaker and came to appreciate how he might, by articulating their deepest convictions, act as a figurehead in a future insurrection, explaining and justifying it. So thoroughly did he in the end accomplish this, that after Easter week it became 'almost impossible to see the man'.[9] In May 1915, Pearse was made a member of the IRB Military Council which planned the Rising. He had meanwhile been appointed to the Volunteer headquarters staff as Director of Organisation, whilst still remaining as headmaster of his school. The hectic pattern of his life deflected him from the introspection to which he was prone; in an unpublished autobiography he referred to himself as 'the strange thing that I am'.[10]

Already, in the spring of 1915, Pearse had put his financial affairs in order, 'in view of the probability of my being arrested or losing my life ... [in] ... the call to action for my country'.[11] Throughout the months which followed, the dominant members of the IRB revolutionary cell planning the insurrection remained Clarke and MacDermott, and they successfully focussed the energies of their romantic nationalist colleagues on the immediate preparations. Pearse's role included involvement, from September 1915, in making arrangements for the landing and distribution of German arms on the Kerry coast; when asked just after the outbreak of war what he thought would be a sufficient German force, he had replied 'about 5,000 men'.[12] (This was a not a realistic figure, the actual number asked for from Germany was much higher.) In January

1916, he played a central part in the secret negotiations with Connolly to ensure Irish Citizen Army collaboration in a future rising. Meanwhile, from January to April 1916, he wrote a series of pamphlets (*Ghosts*, *The Separatist Ideal*, *The Sovereign People*, *The Spiritual Nation*) to help explain and justify the Military Council's future actions. He also sought, in a series of delicately phrased and ambiguous speeches, to psychologically prepare the Irish Volunteers for action. He subtly strove to instill an offensive cast of mind whilst trying to avoid alerting the British government or those members of the organisation who were opposed to the idea of a rising.

The authorities tended to regard Pearse as a literary visionary and discount his remarks, unaware of the extent and nature of his republican contacts. He sought further to reassure them by deliberately toning down public displays of extremism by the Volunteers. Thus he proscribed their use of the tricolour, substituting instead a flag associated with conservative nationalism. The plan to present the rebels when they assembled at the outbreak of the Rising as being on a routine Easter training exercise had a similar purpose. Their manoeuvres were to be publicised by Pearse in advance; he even requested that officers report back, by 1 May, on how the day had passed off. He was likewise deeply implicated in the Military Council's efforts to conceal the plans for the Rising from Eoin MacNeill. As soon as the latter became aware of its true intentions, he called at St Enda's early on Friday morning (21 April). There Pearse, who had earlier described MacNeill as 'weak, hopelessly weak',[13] disclosed the truth with brutal frankness and radiated an air of indifference, even condescension, 'as if what he [Pearse] had done was of no importance'.[14]

Following news of MacNeill's countermand order, Pearse assembled with the other Military Council members in emergency session at Liberty Hall, on Sunday morning, 23 April. There, he agreed with the majority view that the Rising be postponed until noon next day. At this session he was appointed Commandant General of the Army of the Irish Republic and President of the Provisional Government of the Republic that was soon to be declared. As President he would read the Proclamation: this was appropriate, as he had drafted most, if not all of it. He was thought to have the requisite presence and oratorical ability, he was a respected headmaster, and his demeanour and appearance suited him to the task. That afternoon he wrote to MacNeill confirming that the Sunday manoeuvres had been cancelled: this had in fact been done to lessen the likelihood of a premature strike by country commandants. But that evening, Pearse sent out couriers with despatches nationwide, which stated: 'We start at noon today, Monday. Carry out your instructions.'[15]

Some days earlier, Pearse had gathered the boys together at St Enda's, bidden them farewell and commented, referring to the school, that: 'Its work is done.'[16] Those ex-pupils who had joined the Volunteers and were involved the Rising, considered themselves to be 'entirely at the disposal of' their former headmaster.[17] To reduce the risk of arrest, Patrick (with William Pearse) stayed in a house in Rutland Street, central Dublin, for several nights before the Rising, protected by an armed bodyguard with instructions to protect him to the death. On Easter Monday morning, Father Aloysius, a Capuchin priest going to celebrate mass, saw the two brothers cycling past, Patrick wearing 'a loose overcoat or mackintosh, which covered some luggage'. The cleric added: 'I at once concluded that something was in the air.'[18]

Before he left Liberty Hall with the headquarters battalion, Pearse's sister, Mary Brigid, implored him: 'Come home, Pat, and leave all the foolishness', while The O'Rahilly's sister berated him saying: 'This is all your fault.'[19] Pearse marched at or near the head of the column to the GPO. His most decisive action of the week occurred soon after the building had been occupied. At 12:45 p.m., Clarke handed Pearse the Proclamation and accompanied by an armed bodyguard, the doors locked behind him, Pearse stood on the step outside the building and read it. One rebel who was present records that Pearse was observed by 'an indifferent looking crowd [of perhaps three or four hundred] ... For once the magnetism left him. The response was chilling. A few perfunctory cheers. No enthusiasm whatsoever.'[20] Copies of the document were then posted around neighbouring streets and distributed to the other rebel garrisons. When Dick Humphries, The O'Rahilly's nephew, arrived at the GPO, Pearse immediately asked him, 'if I had seen ... [them] ... His eyes light up with intense joy when I say that these posters are attracting great attraction and excitement.'[21]

At the GPO, Pearse held titular command only; Connolly provided the military leadership. Though Pearse looked the part, he was neither a soldier nor a tactician. W.J. Brennan Whitmore, who was in command of a unit inside the GPO at the time, was singularly unimpressed by Pearse's inspection of their defences; such was his sense of gratitude at any effort in the cause that it inhibited his critical faculties. There is no reason to believe that Pearse fired a single shot at the enemy during the entire week. He may also have considered that building barricades or tunnelling through walls sat uneasily with the dignity of his offices. Rather, he exuded a calm confidence, offered appreciation and encouragement, and sought to inspire the men: he caused some wonderment with his constant assurances that German U-boats would soon be appearing in Dublin Bay. One rebel recalls that throughout the proceedings: 'he was very approachable. The Volunteer privates took every opportunity to have a word with him, like schoolchildren with a favourite teacher.'[22] He tried to ensure a high moral tone. When he sent Desmond Fitzgerald out to acquire supplies, he insisted that payment be made in cash, to show that they were men of honour. He was appalled by the looting, having hoped that Dublin slum-dwellers would join rather than exploit the Rising. Like Connolly, he suggested without conviction that those culpable should be shot, but shrank back from implementing this punishment. Earlier, in 1914, he had described some of the ammunition landed at Howth as, 'useless ... explosive bullets [dum-dum bullets] which are against the rules of civilised warfare and which therefore we are not giving out to the men'.[23]

Despite his surface optimism, Pearse privately supported the view that there was 'no hope of victory'. Fitzgerald records that in his conversations with him, Pearse always 'came back to the moral rectitude of what we had undertaken ... Every theological argument and quotation was noted to justify it ... By Tuesday he was already depressed as prolonged resistance would mean all the rebels being killed in action or shot by the British ... [His face conveyed] a sense of great tragedy.' Pearse felt a heavy personal responsibility for the death and injury he had brought both to his men and to the citizens of Dublin, and he lamented the crippling impact of MacNeill's countermand order on the scale of their action. On Easter Monday, one of his first acts was to send for a priest from the pro-cathedral to hear the confession of garrison members. Nonetheless, he derived consolation from the fact that 'Ireland had risen in arms and that his life would be given in service of his people', and that the insurrection 'would revivify the spirit of the Irish nation'.[24]

Pearse spent much of his time preparing morale boosting

statements for the men and addressing the public. On Tuesday morning, he informed the Volunteers that there had been heavy gun-battles, but that British troops had been 'everywhere repulsed', republican forces were 'fighting with splendid gallantry' and controlled the city, and that 'the populace of Dublin are plainly with the republic ... and the country is rising.' That day, he also appealed directly to the citizens of the capital. He distributed *Irish War News*. Only one issue was ever produced – it was priced one penny and carried details of the declaration of a republic and establishment of a provisional government. During the afternoon, standing on a table in Sackville Street, he read out a manifesto on behalf of the insurgents. He described as 'momentous ... the proclamation of a sovereign, independent Irish State', and stated that 'the final achievement of Ireland's freedom is now with God's help only a matter of days' away. He made various claims – that Ireland's honour had 'already been redeemed', that the Irish Regiments had mutinied, that the looting was by 'hangers-on of the British Army', and that the 'vast bulk' of Dubliners were behind the republicans. He also appealed for support, stating: 'There is work for everyone.'[25] In a draft of one of his statements Pearse had included, but then excised, a claim that the looting was being done by supporters of the British government. In the later Commons debates on the Rising on 11 May, John Dillon asserted that: 'nine out of ten of the Irish people were on the side of the law. This is the first time such a statement could be made of any serious rising in Irish history.' He also added: 'one of the most horrible tragedies of this fighting was that brother met brother in the streets of Dublin. I asked Sir John Maxwell himself, "Have you any cause of complaint of the Dublins [the Royal Dublin Fusiliers] who had to go down and fight their own people in the streets of Dublin? Did a single man turn back and betray the uniform he wears?" He told me, "Not a man"'.[26]

As time went on, Pearse believed that the rebels would hold out for longer than he had initially anticipated; he thus ordered that food supplies be rationed in expectation of a three-week siege. By Tuesday, he genuinely felt gratified that already they had performed better than Emmet in 1803. But he was also fully aware that the initiative was passing to crown forces, that despite his appeals and dispatches, the country had failed to rise and that troop reinforcements were flooding into the city. Connolly therefore made preparations for a furious mass infantry attack on the GPO: Desmond Ryan records that, 'all seemed to take it for granted that we would be finally crushed. By common consent it would be a fight to the finish.' Pearse said to him: 'When we are all wiped out, people will blame us for everything. Condemn us ... In a few years, they will see the meaning of what we tried to do.'[27] When addressing a group of Volunteers newly arrived at the GPO late on Tuesday evening, his comments echoed these themes. He stated: 'If [they] did nothing else [they] at least had redeemed the fair name of Dublin city, which was dishonoured when Emmet was allowed to die before a large crowd of its people ... Be assured that here will find victory, even though that victory may be found in death'. One of the rebels present describes it as 'a terribly thrilling moment'.[28]

On Wednesday, Pearse wrote to his mother, reassuring her that 'all [were] safe', the St Enda's boys were 'in excellent spirits', the food was 'as good as if served in a hotel' and they slept on mattresses. He concluded: 'The men have fought with wonderful courage and gaiety, and whatever happens to us, the name of Dublin will be splendid in history for ever.'[29] In fact Gerald Keogh, one of his ex-pupils, had been killed in action on Easter Tuesday: he had been sent by Pearse on an errand on Easter Monday and gunned down while returning next day. Also, the rebels had been surprised at the lack of facilities in the GPO; most bedded down under a table or desk. Pearse himself slept badly all week; he was sustained mainly by nervous energy. His exhaustion is evident from a war bulletin he composed on Wednesday evening: it was inaccurately dated and though it repeated his now-familiar sentiments, his prose lacked its usual fluency and power.

Nonetheless, Pearse persisted with his efforts to sustain Volunteer morale – producing statements, reading out dispatches from the commandants of other garrisons, and making regular inspection tours of the building. Though Michael Collins (who was Plunkett's aide-de-camp in the GPO during Easter week) later commented that he did not consider the Rising an 'appropriate time for the issue of memoranda couched in poetic phrases', a prepared speech Pearse delivered on Thursday afternoon appears to have been particularly effective.[30] In it he claimed that a large body of Volunteers was marching on Dublin, and that as they had already held out as a republic for three days, under international law they would be entitled to send a delegation to the peace conference at the end of the war in Europe. After he had concluded, one rebel present recalls that there was 'a deafening outburst ... [which] ... spread throughout the whole building. The account put new vitality into the men which three days of uncertainty and suspense had rather depressed ... The everlasting wait for the unexpected is truly nerve wrecking [sic].'[31] Certainly, the speech was timely. Earlier that day Connolly's ankle had been shattered by gunfire, and during the afternoon, shells began pounding Sackville Street, so that by evening fires were engulfing its lower east side. 'While night darkens,' one rebel wrote 'the interior of our room is as bright as day.'[32] Twenty-four hours earlier, the insurgents had shot out the lights in neighbouring streets. Tim Healy, a nationalist MP, later claimed in the Commons that 'for forty-eight hours you [British troops] rained shells upon the poor old city, sometimes of the rate of fifteen to twenty shells a minute, sounding like the thuds of the clods on a father's coffin to those who love that city'.[33]

Almost certainly, the rebel leadership at the GPO met early on Friday morning, 28 April, and agreed that if the attempt was made to annihilate the garrison with shells or incinerate the building, they would evacuate it. At 9:30 a.m., Pearse issued what he clearly recognised would be his last memorandum. In it, he claimed with justification that the insurgents were still holding their main positions in the city, while 'we are busy completing arrangements for the final defence of headquarters, and are determined to hold it while the buildings last'. He took the opportunity to pay tribute to the 'gallantry' of the Volunteers. He described their actions as 'the most glorious in the later history of Ireland' and added: 'If they do not win this fight, they will ... have deserved to win it ... They may win it in death ... [They had] redeemed Dublin ... [and] ... saved Ireland's honour.' He concluded: 'We should have accomplished more ... enthroning ... the Irish Republic as a Sovereign State, had our arrangements ... been allowed to go through on Easter Sunday.' But, he added magnanimously: 'Both Eoin MacNeill and we have acted in the best interests of Ireland.' He paid special tribute to Connolly, describing him as 'still the guiding brain of our resistance', and declared on his own behalf: 'I am not afraid to face either the judgement of God or the judgement of posterity.'[34] Volunteer Joe Good recalls that despite its doleful references to 'winning in death' and 'final defence', the speech was greeted by 'an amazing and spontaneous cheer, as the men marched back to their positions'.[35]

Around noon, the evacuation process began. Pearse assembled

about thirty of the women (they were mostly members of Cumann na mBan) in the main hall. He expressed his appreciation of their bravery and devotion and indicated to them that for their own safety they must leave. Amidst tearful and angry protests, they were then ushered out of the building into Henry Street during a lull in the fighting. Soon afterwards, the wounded were likewise led out, escorted by a priest. Pearse himself was by then almost helpless with exhaustion. Jim Ryan, a medical student, recalls how he came to him that Friday afternoon and said that he 'had not slept for the week and asked if I could help'. Ryan 'gave him a draft ... [but] ... it had no effect ... as the fire alarm sounded almost immediately'.[36]

As the British bombardment intensified, Pearse ordered the snipers down from the roof of the GPO, and they assisted in fighting the blaze. Sean MacEntee recalls how he 'walked up and down behind me. He seldom spoke except when a spark fell or burning matter from the roof set some of our defences ablaze. Then he would direct his men to extinguishing the fire ... He appeared cool and unmoved.'[37] Others remember him having a brief verbal confrontation with Joseph Plunkett in a doorway; for the first and last time in Easter week he lost his composure. Prior to the evacuation of the full garrison, Pearse selected a group of twenty-five men, under The O'Rahilly, and instructed them to secure possession of a new headquarters, at Williams and Woods factory in Parnell Street. Shortly after they had gone he ordered the main party to assemble and before leaving told them to 'go out and face the machine-guns as if you are on parade'.[38] He stood in the doorway as they scattered in batches into Henry Street. When the last contingent had passed, he conducted a final tour of the building to search for any left behind; he returned begrimed with soot and dirt, his face swollen with the heat. A fusillade of shots rang out as he and several others, including his brother, then fled, eventually reaching the sanctuary of a grocer's shop in Moore Street. Once there, Oscar Traynor recalls being ordered by Connolly to begin tunnelling to the end of the terrace, but then being summoned back by Pearse. Together, they scrutinised a map of Dublin, Traynor indicating where they were, the shortest route to William and Wood's, and the acute difficulties of reaching there, given the disposition of British troops.[39]

Next morning, 29 April, the rebel leaders met and conferred in a shop at 16 Moore Street. Though they were isolated, surrounded by troops firing artillery shells, and seventeen of their men had been injured during the evacuation, initially no agreement appears to have been reached. Some, including Pearse, favoured making a dash for the Four Courts. Joe Good describes the event which was probably vital in enabling them to achieve consensus. Before noon a party of civilians was attempting to vacate some houses across the street and, he writes, 'some men among ... [them] ... had been warned not to go but they persisted. I heard this order shouted by the enemy: "Females advance and males stand." There was a burst of fire ... One man at least was riddled with bullets. . . . It was that incident ... which determined Pearse and his staff to treat for terms.'[40]

At 12:45 p.m. the leaders met again. Pearse recorded their decision to 'open negotiations with the British commander ... believing that the glorious stand ... during the last five days ... has been sufficient to gain recognition of Ireland's national claim at an international peace conference.' They wished also to prevent 'further slaughter of the civilian population and to save the lives of as many as possible of our followers'.[41] When afterwards describing these events to his mother, he said that he had himself favoured 'one more desperate sally ... but I yielded to the majority'. He added: 'I think now the majority was right as the sally would have resulted only in losing the lives of perhaps 50 or 100 of our men and we should have had to surrender in the long run.'[42] Acting as go-between, Elizabeth O'Farrell (she had previously brought by hand Pearse's instructions to the west of Ireland that the Rising would begin on Easter Monday) relayed verbally the provisional government's decision to Brigadier-General William Lowe. He demanded unconditional surrender, indicating that if Pearse failed to appear inside half an hour, followed by Connolly, hostilities would be resumed. The insurgents considered that they had no option but to comply.

Pearse left the garrison, walked up Moore Street and, at exactly 2:30 p.m., surrendered to General Lowe at the junction of Moore Street and Parnell Street. He handed over his sword, automatic pistol in its holster, a pouch for ammunition and a canteen. Lowe proposed that O'Farrell convey the surrender order to the other rebel garrisons. She recalls: 'Pearse turned to me and said: "Will you agree to this?" I said: "Yes, if you wish it." He said: "I do wish it." [He] then shook hands with me and spoke no word.' A number of armed troops stood by and two army motor vehicles were waiting. Pearse and Lowe's ADC, along with another officer, were then driven off in the GOC's car, down Sackville Street to Irish Command headquarters, the Royal Hospital. It was preceded by the other vehicle, containing Lowe and Captain de Courcy Wheeler. According to O'Farrell, as the rebel leader was driven off, one of several officers standing near her commented: 'It would be interesting to know how many [German] marks that fellow has in his pocket.'[43] The staff car was driven by Lowe's ADC (who was also the British Brigadier-General's son). He later recalled that 'a priest came with us', and that when they had reached their destination Pearse 'had not finished giving his last messages to his family, so I told the driver to keep on driving. When Pearse had finished he turned to me and said, "That was indeed kind of you and I would like to give you a small token of my gratitude." He took off his … hat and removed the … cap badge and gave it to me.'[44]

After seeing Maxwell, Pearse wrote and, when it had been typed, signed the order instructing 'Commandants of the various districts in the city and country to lay down arms.' It stated that the decision to accept 'unconditional surrender' had been taken by the members of the provisional government at Moore Street, in order 'to prevent further slaughter of Dublin's citizens and in the hope of saving the lives of our followers now surrounded and hopelessly outnumbered.'[45] Afterwards, Pearse was escorted to a sitting room. The door was locked and Wheeler kept his revolver aimed at Pearse the entire time. Wheeler was under orders 'to shoot if he tried to escape.' Wheeler recalls: 'Pearse smiled at me across the table and did not seem in the least perturbed.'[46] Some personal effects and a little over seven pounds were taken from the prisoner before he was transferred to a cell at Arbour Hill Detention Barracks that evening.

During Sunday, several visits were made to Pearse in his cell by those seeking verification of his order. Two priests from Church Street (Father Aloysius and Father Augustine) were officially permitted to see him. He gave them written surrender instructions for a rebel unit in the Four Courts area which had been unwilling to accept verbal assurances that the Rising was over. From north of Dublin, Thomas Ashe sent Richard Mulachy to authenticate that unconditional terms had been agreed; Pearse assured him that this was so and confirmed that they applied to 'the whole of Ireland'. With the same purpose, two rebel officers from Wexford were given safe conduct by their local British OC and brought by military vehicle to Arbour Hill. Pearse gave them a somewhat modified order – to 'lay down arms or disband' – whispering, when opportunity arose, that they should hide their weapons as 'they will be needed later'. Afterwards, they described him as 'physically exhausted but spiritually exultant, his uniform ... complete except for the Sam Browne belt' which had been taken from him.[47] His watch and whistle were also gone.

On 1 May, removed from comrades and free from interruption, Pearse threw himself into a 'frenzy of creation'.[48] He wrote three poems – 'To my Brother', 'To my Mother' and 'A Mother Speaks'. His mother had asked him to write 'a little poem which would seem to be said by you about me'. These he handed over to one of the soldiers on duty and he wrote to Maxwell the next day asking that they be forwarded to Mrs Pearse. The GOC, however, thought them 'seditious' and sent them instead to Asquith, amongst whose papers two of them first came to light some fifty years later; when at Kilmainham, Pearse gave a copy of the third, 'A Mother Speaks', to a priest who handed it to Mrs Pearse on 3 May. Pearse also wrote three statements on his financial affairs, again requesting that Maxwell forward these to his mother; this request was respected. In these he referred to his 'one source of personal regret in embarking in this enterprise ... Its failure will involve loss, more or less considerable, to various persons.'[49]

In addition, on 1 May, Pearse wrote a letter to his mother, his first since leaving the GPO. In it he briefly summarised events since the previous Friday. No doubt due to exhaustion, his account contains factual errors. Moreover, he mistakenly assumed that the men from Moore Street, including his brother and the St Enda's boys, had been brought to Arbour Hill; in fact they had been escorted to Richmond Barracks early the previous day (Sean Heuston was the only other rebel leader then being held at the Detention Barracks). He repeated the 'hope also expressed by provisional government members', immediately after their decision to surrender, that the British authorities would 'spare the lives of our followers ... We do not expect that they will spare the lives of the leaders.' He continued: 'Personally I do not hope or even desire to live but I do hope ... that the lives of all our followers will be saved including the lives dear to you and me (my own accepted) and this will be a great consolation to me when dying.' He added: 'We have preserved Ireland's honour and our own. Our deeds of last week are the most splendid in Ireland's history. People will say hard things of us now but we will be remembered by posterity and blessed by unborn generations.'

Finally, he suggested to his mother that she would be allowed to see him and added in a postscript: 'I understand that the German expedition which I was counting on actually set sail but was defeated by the British' (possibly implying that he believed the *Aud* had been carrying troops as well as arms).[50] Pearse also handed this letter to a soldier on duty – Sergeant G. Goshman. It was shown to Maxwell, who decided not to deliver it to the prisoner's mother; as with the other material written by the rebel leader that day, he found 'some of it objectionable', and instead forwarded it with the rest to Asquith (it also first came to light amongst Asquith's papers in 1965).[51] It was, however, typed up and used as evidence at Pearse's court martial.

On 2 May, Pearse was transferred from Arbour Hall to Richmond Barracks, where he stood trial that afternoon (prisoner number one), Brigadier-General Blackader presiding. The prosecution called three witnesses, each of whom spoke briefly. The first was Lieutenant S.O. King, Royal Enniskillen Fusiliers, who had been held captive by the rebels at the GPO from Monday to Friday of Easter week along with fifteen other prisoners. He indicated that he had been on duty at the Rotunda, Dublin on Saturday, 29 April. He continued: 'The Sinn Fein was firing at the soldiers. The accused came from the neighbourhood from which the shots were being fired. The accused was in the same uniform in which he is now with belt, sword, revolver ... The accused surrendered to General Lowe.' The defendant cross-examined him asking: 'Were you a prisoner in our hands and how were you treated?', to which King replied: 'I was, and was very well treated.'[52]

A DMP detective, Constable Daniel Coffey, was next to testify. He stated: 'I was present when the accused, Pearse, was in custody at Irish Command Headquarters at about 5 P.M. on Saturday, 29 April. I identify him as a member of the Irish Volunteers. I have seen him several times going through the city with bodies of men and acting as an officer.' The defendant did not question either Coffey or the third witness Sergeant G. Goshman, who said simply: 'I was on duty at Arbour Hill Detention Barracks on 1 May. I saw the accused writing the letter now produced to the court. He handed it to me.'[53]

Recalling the trial many years later, William Wylie the prosecution counsel, wrote: 'I had never seen him [Pearse] before, a schoolmaster, and looked a decent chap. Lots of evidence against him, apart from the fact that he had been OC at the GPO. He had been in close touch with Casement and letters were found on him showing this [this statement was wholly inaccurate on both counts]. When I had finished with the evidence against him, I asked him should he wish to make a statement. He said he did.'[54] The official court record states tersely: 'Prosecution closed. The accused calls no witness in his defence,' and adds that when asked by the president of the court, Pearse made the following statement:

> My sole object in surrendering unconditionally was to save the slaughter of the civil population and to save the lives of our followers, who had been led into this thing [illegible word] by us. It is my hope that the British government who has shown its strength will also be magnanimous and spare the lives and give an amnesty to my followers, as I am one of the persons chiefly responsible, have acted as C-in-C and President of the provisional government. I am prepared to take the consequences of my act, but I should like my followers to receive an amnesty. I went down on my knees as a child and told God that I would work all my life to gain the freedom of Ireland. I have deemed it my duty as an Irishman to fight for the freedom of my country. I admit I have organised men to fight against Britain. I admit having opened negotiations with Germany. We have kept our word with her and as far as I can see she did her best to help us. She sent a ship with arms. Germany has not sent us gold.[55]

Wylie described the speech as 'very eloquent ... what I always call a Robert Emmet type'.[56] While Emmet may have influenced the framing of the Proclamation, it was Tone's statement from the dock which was Pearse's inspiration. Like his mentor, Pearse fully accepted his responsibility for the insurrection, acknowledged and implicitly justified the call for foreign aid, and employed some poetic license when depicting his own 'developing militance for Irish freedom.'[57] In fact, he consciously overstated his role in the Rising, reflecting the strength of his yearning for self-sacrifice. By comparison, his letter to his mother (1 May) was noticeably more circumspect. His fearless performance in court impressed Blackader. The Countess of Fingall famously recalled how the officer: 'came to dinner one night greatly depressed. I asked him: "What is the matter?" He answered: "I have just done one of the hardest things I have ever had to do. I have had to condemn to death one of the finest characters I have ever come across. There must be something very wrong in the state of things that makes a man like that a rebel. I don't wonder his pupils adored him.'"[58]

The court found Pearse guilty and sentenced him to 'Death by being shot'. Soon afterwards, Maxwell confirmed this verdict. When justifying this decision later, Maxwell first noted the prisoner's impeccable background: 'This man was a member of the Irish Bar and was principal of a college.' But, the GOC stated: 'He had taken an active part in the Volunteer movement from its inception ... joined the Sinn Fein or Irish Volunteers when that body became a separate organisation ... was a member of [its] Central Council ... was "Commandant-General of the Army of the Irish Republic" and "President of the provisional government" and as such issued a Proclamation to the people of Ireland.' Maxwell highlighted Pearse's contacts with Germany, observing: 'He was one of the signatories to the Declaration of Irish Independence, which document contains, *inter alia*, the following passage: "She (viz. Ireland) now seizes that moment and supported by her exiled children in America and by gallant allies in Europe ... she strikes in the full confidence of victory."' He also noted that 'at his trial a letter written by him on May 1 was produced and proved containing the following passage: "I understand that the German expedition on which I was counting actually set sail but was defeated by the British"' [this section of the text the GOC had underlined]. Maxwell concluded: 'He [Pearse] stated at his trial that he was in communication with Germany and that his object was to defeat England.'[59]

Pearse was transferred the short distance to Kilmainham during the evening of 2 May. There, like Clarke and MacDonagh, he heard that he was to be executed at dawn the next morning. Pearse was kept in a separate cell under observation throughout the night – Father Aloysius was his only visitor. The priest recalls that he had just retired for the night, (at Church Street Friary), when he 'was called to learn that a military car was at the gate and a letter was handed to me to say that prisoner Pearse desired to see me and that I had permission to see him ... I accompanied the military and we drove in the direction of Charlemont Bridge. The sniping was so fierce that we did not continue ... and turning back, we went direct to Kilmainham.'[60] He heard later that the driver had intended to collect Mrs Pearse at St Enda's and also MacDonagh's wife.

At the prison, Father Aloysius was informed that Thomas

MacDonagh had also 'asked for my ministrations'. He continues: 'I spent some hours between the two cells ... [which was] ... inspiring and edifying. When I met Pearse, I said: "I am sure you will be glad to know that I gave Holy Communion to James Connolly this morning." I cannot forget the fervour with which, looking to heaven, he said: "Thank God. It was the one thing I was anxious about."' Father Aloysius writes of Pearse's 'intense devotion'; he heard his confession, gave him Holy Communion and the rest of the time was spent in prayer. The prisoner 'assured' him that he was 'not in the least worried or afraid' and spoke of the 'privilege of dying for his country'.[61] Along with all the other visitors to the prison, Father Aloysius was ordered to leave despite his protests, at between 2 and 3 a.m. Before doing so, Pearse gave him a poem for his mother and told him to ask the officer in charge to forward his other correspondence to her; it was arranged that the priest would call with her at the earliest possible moment to inform her of her son's death.

During his short time at Kilmainham, Pearse wrote an expanded and more polished version of the speech he had given at his court martial. In it he amplified Germany's role in the Rising and pleaded that his own admissions in court 'must not be used against anyone who acted with me.' He concluded: 'You cannot extinguish the Irish passion for freedom. If our deed has not been sufficient to win freedom, then our children will win it by a better deed.'[62] He also wrote one further poem ('The Wayfarer'), lighter in spirit than the others, evoking memories possibly of his last holiday in Connemara the previous summer, and two letters – one to his brother William, and a final one to his mother. It is probable that whilst writing the latter Father Aloysius called and that he completed it therefore within an hour of his execution. In it he expressed regret that it did 'not seem possible' that she would be able to visit him and his belief that 'Willie and the St Enda's boys will be safe'. He told her that he had just received Holy Communion and repeated some of the sentiments he had expressed earlier, both to the priest and to the men in his garrison during the Rising. He stated: 'I am happy apart from the great grief of parting from you. This is the death I should have asked for if God had given me the choice of all deaths – to die as a soldier for Ireland's freedom. We have done right. People will say hard things of us now, but later they will praise us.' He then bade a last farewell to his family by name and concluded: 'I have not words to tell my love of you and how my heart yearns to you all. I will call

P.S. — I understand that the German expedition on which ~~[crossed out]~~ coming
~~[crossed out]~~ sail - but was defeated by
the British.

4

Arbour Hill Barracks,
Dublin, 1st May 1916.

Dearest Mother,
You will, I know, have been longing to hear from me. I don't
know how much you have heard
since the last note I sent
you from the G. P. O.
On Friday evg. the Post Office
was set on fire, and we had to
abandon it. We dashed into
Moore Street, and remained
in the houses in Moore Street until
Saturday afternoon. We then
found that we were surrounded
by troops, and that we had
practically no food. We decided,

The first page of the original letter written at Arbour Hill Barracks on 1 May 1916, by Patrick Pearse to his mother was found among his court martial papers. He had given it to one of his guards, Sergeant G. Goodman, to arrange for its delivery, but it was instead passed on to General Maxwell and used by the prosecution as evidence during Pearse's court martial.

PRO LONDON

to you in my heart at the last moment.'[63]

In this final correspondence, Pearse completed a body of literature aimed at explaining and justifying the insurrection, and at preserving and imprinting the memory both of it and of himself in the national memory. Had the insurrection gone as originally planned, his own role would have inevitably been diminished. Given its rapid and heroic collapse, he fulfilled in these last days the then vital function of promoting and legitimising the Rising. Though his role in planning it had been secondary, he become through his writings and the offices he held in Easter week, its incarnation and icon. His in order to prevent further slaughter of the civil population and in the hope of saving the lives of our followers, to ask the General commanding the British forces to discuss the terms. He replied that he would receive me only if I surrendered unconditionally, and this I did. I was taken to the Headquarters of the British command in Ireland, and there I ~~~~ wrote and signed an order to our men to lay down their arms. This I did in accordance with the decision of the members of our Provisional Govt. who were with us in Moore Street. My own ~~~~ was in favour of our more desperate sally before

public image was that of a pious, selfless patriot, unconcerned with the practicalities of this world. He was the perfect role model for the sort of Ireland that emerged in the years following the Rising. His executioners contributed vitally to this metamorphosis, enabling him to fulfil his martyr fantasy – that of the prisoner, who died alone, in public for the people, like Christ or Cu Chulainn. At his court martial, he had begged that others be saved and he alone face the firing squad. Desmond Ryan states: 'Pearse's ideal insurrection would have had one signature to the Proclamation and one casualty.'[64]

Pearse was executed between 3:30 and 4 a.m. on 3 May. The

Page two of Pearse's letter to his mother.

opening ~~negotiations~~, but I yielded to
the majority, and I think now
& ~~...~~ the majority were
right, as the sally would have
resulted only in losing the lives of
perhaps 50 or 100 of our men,
and we should have had to
surrender in the long run, as
we were without food.
I was brought here on Saturday
evg. and later on all the men
with us in Moore Street were
brought here. Those in the other
parts of the city have, I understand,
been taken to other barracks and
prisons.
All here are safe and well.
Willie and all the St. Enda's boys
are here. I have not seen them
since Saturday, but I believe that
they are all well, and that they
are not now in any danger. Our
hope and belief is that the Govt.
will spare the lives of all our followers,

Page three of Pearse's
letter to his mother.
PRO LONDON

proceedings were delayed briefly as the initial orders to authorise
the death sentence had not been signed to the satisfaction of
Brigadier Maconchy, the OC of 59th Division which supplied the
firing squad. The unit's official history states that Pearse, like Clarke
and MacDonagh, met his fate bravely. Captain H.V. Stanley, certified that the 'prisoners were dead, before the commandant disposed
of the bodies', though for some reason no labels were attached to
them as the procedures, hurriedly devised beforehand, had stipulat-
ed.[65] They were then buried in quicklime adjacent to an east facing

but we do not expect that they will **6**
spare the lives of the leaders. We
are ready to die and we shall
die cheerfully and proudly. P really
die ... I do not hope or even, desire to ...
But I do hope and desire and believe that the lives of all our
followers will be saved, including
the lives dear to you and me (my
own excepted) and this will be
a great consolation. You must not
grieve for all this. We have preserved Ireland's honour and
our own. Our deeds of last week
are the most splendid in Ireland's history. People will say hard
things of us now, but we shall be
remembered by posterity and blessed
by unborn generations. You too will
be blessed because you were my
mother.
"If you would like to see
me, I think you will be allowed to
visit me by applying to ... the Park.
Irish Command, near ...
I ... have another opportunity of
... Love W.W., M.B., ...
until ... and to your own dear self

wall at nearby Arbour Hill Detention Barracks. Pearse was interred
first, then MacDonagh beside him, followed by Clarke. Some hours
later, Mrs Pearse was informed of her son's execution. Her daughter, Margaret, recalls that 'on the morning of Low Sunday we heard
of the surrender and then no news whatever until the following
Wednesday, 3 May, when at about 10 a.m. the Reverend Father
Aloysius arrived to break the terrible news that Pat had made the
supreme sacrifice – that he had died that morning at a quarter to
four.'[66]

Page four of Pearse's
letter to his mother.
PRO LONDON

Trial of P.H. Pearse

prisoner number one

REFERENCE: PRO WO71/345

DATE: 2 May 1916

LOCATION: Richmond Barracks

JUDGES: Brigadier-General C.G. Blackader (President), Lieutenant
Colonel G. German, Lieutenant Colonel W.J. Kent

CHARGE

'Did an act to wit did take part in an armed rebellion and in the
waging of war against His Majesty the King, such act being o such
a nature as to be calculated to be prejudicial to the Defence to the
Realm and being done with the intention and for the purpose of
assisting the enemy'

PLEA: Not guilty

(The members of the court and witnesses were duly sworn in)

VERDICT: Guilty. Death by being shot

Text of Trial

2nd Lt. S.O. King 12th Royal Inniskillen Fusiliers (12th Batt)
being duly sworn states –

> I was on duty at the Rotunda Dublin on Saturday the 29th
> April. The Sinn Fein was firing at the soldiers. The accused
> came from the neighbourhood from which the shots were
> being fired. The accused was in the same uniform in which
> he is now with belt, sword and revolver on and 3 with
> ammunition. The accused surrendered to General Lowe.

The accused crossexamines the witness.–

Q. Were you a prisoner in our hands and how were you treated.

A. I was and was very well treated.

The witness withdraws.

Constable Daniel Coffey Detective Department Dublin
Metropolitan Police being duly sworn states.–

> I was present when the accused Pearse was in custody at
> Irish Command HQ at about 5pm on Saturday the 29th
> April. I identify him as a member of the Irish Volunteers. I
> have seen him several times going through the city with
> bodies of men and acting as an officer.

The Accused does not cross examine this witness.

Sgt G. Goodman Military Press at Staff Corps being duly sworn
states –I was on duty at Arbour Hill Detention Barracks on the 1st
May.
I saw the accused writing the letter now produced to the Court.
He handed it to me. The letter is marked X and attached signed
by the President.

> The Accused does not cross-examine this witness –

> Prosecution closed.

> The accused calls no witnesses in his defence.

The accused makes the following statement.–

> My sole object in surrendering unconditionally was to save
> the slaughter of the civil population and to save the lives of
> our followers who had been led into this thing by us. It is
> my hope that the British Government who has shown its
> strength will also be magnanimous and spare the lives and
> give an amnesty to my followers, as I am one of the persons
> chiefly responsible, have acted as C-in-C and president of
> the provisional Government. I am prepared to take the
> consequences of my act, but I should like my followers to
> receive an amnesty. I went down on my knees as a child and
> told God that I would work all my life to gain the freedom
> of Ireland. I have deemed it my duty as an Irishman to fight
> for the freedom of my country. I admit I have organised
> men to fight against Britain. I admit having opened
> negotiations with Germany. We have kept our word with
> her and as far as I can see she did her best to help us. She
> sent a ship with men. Germany has not sent us gold.

Thomas MacDonagh

IRISH REBELLION, MAY 1916.

THOMAS MacDONAGH
(Commandant of Bishop Street Area),
Executed May 3rd, 1916.
One of the signatories of the "Irish Republic Proclamation."

THOMAS MACDONAGH.

This man was an M.A. of the National University in Ireland and a tutor in English Literature in the University College,Dublin. He took an active part in the Sinn Fein movement since its inauguration and was a prominent officer and Director of Training. He was also a signatory to the Declaration of Irish Independence previously mentioned in connection with P.H.Pearse's case. He signed a document headed "Army of the Irish Republic" which set out the various "Commands" and described himself there as "Commandant General and member of the Provisional Government of the Irish Republic."

He was in command of the party of the rebels who occupied and held Jacob's Biscuit factory from the neighbourhood of which the British troops were fired on and numerous casualties occurred.

THOMAS MacDONAGH WAS BORN ON 1 FEBRUARY 1878 at Cloughjordan, County Tipperary, the fourth of nine children, three of whom died in infancy. Neither of his parents, both teachers, held strong political opinions. It was probably from his father, who was imbued with a deep distrust of patriotism and patriots, that he derived his gregarious nature. His mother had been Unitarian, but converted to Catholicism; it may have been from her that he inherited his early religious fervour and his more enduring literary interests. Both of her parents had been English, and she 'had early decided that her sons would receive the nearest equivalent to an English upbringing which she could give them ... at an early age two of them joined the British Army. [In 1892] Tom was sent to the Holy Ghost Fathers at Rockwell College'. MacDonagh at first had the intention of becoming a priest, a course which he abandoned in 1901 for want of a vocation.[27]

Following family tradition, he entered teaching – at schools in Kilkenny and Fermoy, from 1901 to 1908 and then at St Enda's, Pearse's school in Dublin, 1908-10. In 1911, following completion of an MA at University College Dublin, he became an English lecturer there, so transferring to an atmosphere markedly more secular than had been familiar to him. In 1902, he joined the Gaelic League and from being non-political hitherto, he became an ardent cultural nationalist, single-mindedly committed to the revival of the Irish language. Until 1914, his creative output was prodigious; writing prose, scholarly analyses, poetry and drama, with W.B. Yeats in large part his mentor and inspiration. The main basis for his reputation rests on the publication, *Literature in Ireland*, which traced and championed the distinctive mode of thought and use of language by those in Ireland who wrote in English. He was also a theatre director and closely associated with the *Irish Review*, a literary/political weekly publication. Overall, Johann Norstedt, his biographer, regards MacDonagh as a 'minor' literary figure and derivative thinker, whose poems never developed beyond promise and whose plays were largely ignored – 'a man of too many parts'.[2]

James Stephens recalls that from 1910, MacDonagh 'lived a kind of semi-detached life at the gate-lodge ... [at Grange House, Rathfarnham, near St Enda's] ... in the Dublin hills. To this house all literary Dublin used to repair and MacDonagh was constantly to be seen. He was a quaint recluse who delighted in company and fled into and out of solitude with equal precipitancy. He had a longing for the hermit's existence and a gift for gregarious life.'[3] In January 1912, he married Muriel Gifford; she was one of the three daughters of a conservative unionist Dublin solicitor. MacDonagh's son writes of his father: 'His was a peaceful and regular life at the beginning of the First World War. Happily married, surrounded by his friends, and his books, a friend to artist and scholar, he was as Yeats said, "coming into his force".'[4]

Bulmer Hobson found MacDonagh's political development at that time 'a complete puzzle'.[5] MacDonagh had been unconnected with militant nationalism until he joined the Volunteers on 3 December 1913. Through membership, he undoubtedly found a new direction and purpose. In due course, he was appointed Commandant, Second Battalion, and then Commandant of the entire Dublin Brigade and Director-General of Training. He took part in the Howth gun-running (later exaggerating his own role), and he was 'acting Commandant General' at the funeral of O'Donovan Rossa in 1915. As the force came increasingly to absorb his energies, his literary output dwindled. More crucially, and partly due to this involvement, he had become by 1916, a convert to and enthusiastic advocate of physical force as the only means whereby Ireland could 'win freedom'. His close personal friendship with the more radical Volunteers, including Pearse and Plunkett, helped to facilitate this conversion. Moreover, though his participation in the Rising was 'something ... of a last minute decision', he had over previous years been fusing together the Irish literary revival and the reassertion of Ireland's national spirit.[6] Many of his poems spoke of death and dying for Ireland. In essence, he fought in 1916 for the spiritual liberation of his country from its progressive anglicisation and cultural assimilation.

It may be, as MacNeill suggests, that MacDonagh 'believed firmly in the blood sacrifice theory according to which nothing less than a symbolic spilling of blood by Irishmen would re-awaken the national consciousness'.[7] This is suggested by the recollections of one Volunteer, Oscar Traynor. He vividly remembered during the weeks preceding the Rising MacDonagh hinting that: 'on Easter Sunday there was going to be something more than manoeuvers ... written up in the newspapers'. Traynor continues: 'I remember distinctly one of his lectures [at Volunteer headquarters] ... when he made an extraordinary forecast of the future. He said that the

Volunteers would eventually go into action, that they would appear to be defeated, and that they would rally again, and have another fight in which they would appear to be successful. He said that in the course of this fight they would have their Army recognized, and that in a third great effort the Irish would be freed ... his forecast now appears to be fully justified.'[8]

MacDonagh did not become a member of the IRB Military Council until early April 1916, by which time its preparations for insurrection were almost complete. The reason for his inclusion was to improve the channel of communication with Eoin MacNeill, his colleague at UCD and the Volunteer Chief of Staff. It was hoped that MacNeill might yet be persuaded that a rising was justified. It is unclear when MacDonagh himself first became aware that one was being planned. A police spy informed the Castle that in a speech he made to Volunteers on 22 March 1916, MacDonagh stated: 'we have to make sacrifices ... When we go out, some of us may never come back.'[9] According to the same source, he repeated these sentiments on 19 April. Such indiscretion would have appalled Clarke or MacDermott but it reflects MacDonagh's heightened emotional state as the appointed day drew near. One of MacDonagh's university students, Austin Clarke, noted how during the spring of 1916, his behaviour became noticeably more erratic and he seemed distracted and tense. He writes: 'I began to realise, with a feeling of foreboding, that something was about to happen for I noticed at times, though only for a few seconds, how abstracted and worried Thomas MacDonagh looked. Suddenly, one day, during a lecture on the Young Ireland poets, he took a large revolver from his pocket and laid it on the desk. "Ireland can only win freedom by force," he remarked, as if to himself.'[10] Though on the surface, MacDonagh always appeared to be a light-hearted, humorous and expansive young man, he always had a gloomy despairing, self-doubting side and a persistent fondness for solitude. He lacked the steely resolve, which is a trademark of the natural revolutionary.

Neither the Military Council's arguments nor its deceits proved effective with MacNeill. MacDonagh called to see him on at least three occasions between Good Friday morning and Easter Sunday evening and on Easter Saturday night his discussion with MacNeill became heated and 'some of MacDonagh's remarks were overheard'. He stated: 'You realise your [countermand] order may not be obeyed...I must act under the authority of my [Military] Council'.[11]

Nonetheless, at 8 p.m. on Easter Sunday, after returning home from his final unsuccessful visit, MacDonagh wrote out a statement in which he generously described MacNeill as an 'honest and sincere' patriot, though in his view 'wrong'.[12] Sean Fitzgibbon described this as 'a complete exculpation of MacNeill'; the romantic nationalists, Pearse included, were much more sympathetic in their response to MacNeill's countermand order than their republican colleagues, Clarke and MacDermott.[13] In his statement, MacDonagh also declared: 'I have only one motive ... the good of my country.'[14] It was he who issued the mobilisation orders for Easter Monday to the entire Dublin Brigade and so set the insurrection in motion. That morning, 24 April, he donned the uniform, cloak, cap and accoutrements of a Volunteer commandant and joined members of his Second Battalion at St Stephen's Green West, their pre-arranged assembly point. From there, at around noon he led the main body to Jacob's Biscuit Factory. The building occupied a dominant position on the route north from Portobello Barracks to Dublin Castle, and its two huge towers provided ideal vantage points for snipers. But it proved to be the least eventful post in the Rising: the military assault anticipated by the rebels never materialised. The British OC, General Lowe, did not regard it as of sufficient political or strategic significance. Moreover, because of its fortress-like impregnability and its location amidst densely populated streets, a direct attack would have required substantial numbers of troops, resulted in heavy casualties and devastated much adjacent civilian property. Hence, the tactics preferred by the military were to contain the position and wear down the garrison by means of low intensity pressure.[15]

In the course of the week, it was John MacBride who emerged as the most effective leader at the factory. Though MacDonagh looked the part and exuded optimism and cheerfulness, he lacked the necessary drive, ruthlessness and decisiveness. His tendency to issue orders, then amend or retract them, caused confusion, exasperation and resentment within the Battalion. On one occasion he awakened a group of the Volunteers who had just bedded down and ordered them to take food supplies to the College of Surgeons and return with rifles. When they had completed their mission they were complimented by MacDonagh but he then asked the officer in charge what had happened to the bayonets? Peadar Kearney, the composer of 'A Soldier's Song' recalls: 'The officer replied that he had heard nothing about them. MacDonagh then said that there were bayonets in the College of Surgeons to fit the rifles and that they would have to be brought over. He then told the officer that as the men present knew the way he had better take them back and get them!' Kearney adds: 'That was nearly the last straw.'[16] On another occasion, when Mallin requested the transfer of Citizen Army members from Jacob's to the College of Surgeons, MacDonagh told one of the members, William Oman, '"I'm not letting you go. I am keeping you beside myself." Then he asked me what I thought of that arrangement. "Well," I said, "you are in command, sir." However, just as the party was about to depart, he changed his mind and released me to go with them.'[17]

The regime he permitted at his post was lax and casual. Douglas Hyde records in his diary his amazement when he heard from a visitor that: 'Volunteers were passing in and out of it [Jacob's] freely. He says they were dancing inside and taking it by turns to fight. As one goes out in order to go home and sleep, he takes off his bandolier and hands it along with his rifle to another man coming in.'[18] Those Volunteers who were transferred to Mallin's garrison at the College of Surgeons were at once struck by the harsher, military-like discipline there, the more purposeful, structured daily routine and generally quieter atmosphere. False rumours proliferated at Jacob's partly because MacDonagh failed to communicate information received from other posts. Instead, he offered bland assurances that 'the fighting was going well ... We might be at Jacob's for months ... that the position was so well in hand nothing could stop republican victory.'[19] Tragically, as his post became more isolated from outside, MacDonagh seems to have begun to believe these sentiments himself.

The shock to the garrison at Jacob's was therefore all the greater when, on Sunday morning, 30 April, Elizabeth O'Farrell delivered Pearse's surrender order. She recalls: 'I was blindfolded and was walked about for a few minutes. I then heard Commandant MacDonagh's voice and the bandage was taken off my eyes. I gave him the order from Commandant Pearse and told him of our position in the GPO and Moore Street.'[20] MacDonagh later professed himself to have been 'astonished' and initially rejected it, stating that it was invalid because its author when writing, was a British prisoner.[21] He was also convinced both that 'the country was up and the British wanted to quell us before attacking them', and that the strategic balance in the First World War was shifting rapidly to the insurgent's advantage ('England is down and out,' he asserted).[22] He expressed confidence that the Jacob's garrison could hold out for months and if successful could secure a seat for Ireland at the future peace conference. As Pearse and Connolly had been arrested, he claimed that the 'chief command devolved to him' and he insisted on negotiating directly with the British GOC.[23] When eventually he met General Lowe, the utter hopelessness of his military position was made clear to him and he recognised the need to surrender, hoping, he said later, that 'It would save ... good lives for Ireland.'[24] A two-hour truce was arranged to enable him to consult with his battalion and with Eamonn Ceannt at the South Dublin Union.

The pace and drama of these events placed enormous additional physical and emotional strains on MacDonagh. After the accumulating pressures of the week, he had been forced to accept the sudden, irretrievable collapse of all his hopes. That British retribution would follow was certain: he wrote later 'I knew it would involve my death.'[25] Both his decision to accept surrender and its inept delivery caused uproar within his garrison. On his return to Jacob's, he consulted his officers but could not bring himself personally to face the rank and file. When compelled to confront them, a woman present observed 'one could never imagine him looking so sad'.[26] Tearful, unshaven and covered with the debris of the week, he stressed that he was acting under instruction from Pearse, claimed that under international law they had succeeded in establishing a republic and indicated that those in civilian clothes might simply go home (he might easily have escaped himself). According to Kearney, he added, hardly reassuringly: 'They might shoot some of us. They can't shoot us all.'[27] Another Volunteer, Michael Walker, also present, records him as having said 'Although I have assurance from his reverence here that nobody will be shot, I know I will be shot, but you men (or comrades – I am not sure of exact words here) will be treated as prisoners.' Walker continues: 'uproar broke out on this declaration and numbers of the garrison shouted: "We will not trust their word".'[28] At this point, the timely intervention of John MacBride and of Father Augustine (one of two priests who had acted as intermediaries) helped silence the incipient revolt. Kearney recalls, 'Father Augustine held up his hand, his impressive appearance commanding immediate attention. "Not one amongst you will be shot," he said. "The stand you have made this week has gone round the world and the enemy dare not shoot you. But let me impress on you all. The man who fires another shot in this building will incur a terrible responsibility."'[29] Lowe had earlier told the priests that if the men did not surrender, 'he would be obliged to attack and demolish the factory with great loss of life'.[30] Meanwhile, MacDonagh had 'appeared to be overcome with emotion and retired from the room, [and] several of the garrison commenced to destroy their arms'.[31]

At 3:15 p.m., MacDonagh issued an order, stating: 'On consultation with Commandant Ceannt and other officers, I have decided to agree to unconditional surrender also.'[32] He had already met Lowe fifteen minutes earlier, to inform him of the decision (handing over his gun and belt as token), and to finalise the formal arrangements and procedures. Before their departure the Volunteers destroyed any papers thought to be incriminating. Just as they were leaving the building, looters smashed their way into some of its offices at Bishop Street. An enraged MacDonagh could not be dissuaded from the erroneous opinion that the noise had been caused by rampaging British soldiers throwing bombs, and shooting and bayoneting his men.

At 4:30 p.m. MacDonagh led his men on the half-mile march from the factory to St Patrick's Park, the agreed surrender point. For some time, British troops had been assembling there in preparation for their arrival. Earlier in the day they had been forced to scatter after firing in their direction by Volunteers in the Jacob's command area. At least one sniper, who was either unaware of or indifferent to the surrender of his garrison, had persisted shooting, causing casualties amongst the waiting soldiers.[33] When the rebels reached the park at 5 p.m., Major J.E. Armstrong, (First Royal Enniskillen Fusiliers and Provost Marshal, 76th Brigade) the British Officer Commanding, was waiting to question them. He had some days earlier complained to Wylie that he had been 'home on leave, and [was] dropped into this bloody mess [the Rising]'. Wylie recalls that: 'At about 12 o'clock [on 30 April, Armstrong] had come to me and told me that he heard they had sent for a railway boiler on a lorry, that it was to be filled with troops, driven up to the door of Jacob's factory, which was full of rebels, and then unloaded and the factory rushed. I feel sure he said, in his dry way, that they will want one or two officers of local experience to lead the troops. "In my opinion," Armstrong added, "it is a death trap, as each man jumps out at the open end he will be shot, so in view of these facts I think it is lunch.'" Later that afternoon, Wylie witnessed the surrender of the Jacob's garrison – two long lines of men, with MacDonagh, in full uniform and brown field boots, and MacBride, still in an ordinary lounge suit, at the front. On arrival, the leaders stood, talked and laughed, whilst Wylie himself was detailed to note down the names and ranks of the insurgents; MacDonagh, he later described as 'a poet, a dreamer and an idealist'. In addition, a list was made of those who were unarmed, and all weapons were handed over to the troops. After about an hour, the men from the South Dublin Union had also made their way to the park to surrender. Both rebel garrisons were then escorted by two companies of the Second and Sixth Staffordshires to Richmond Barracks. Wylie recalls that the military guard was 'expecting an attempted rescue', but that the 'prisoners needed more protection from the crowd than the soldiers did'.[34]

MacDonagh (prisoner number thirty) was tried after Pearse, on the afternoon of 2 May, Brigadier-General Blackader presiding. The prosecution called just one witness, Major J.E. Armstrong, who gave essentially the same largely circumstantial evidence in each of the cases involving rebels who had surrendered at St Patrick's Park on 30 April. As on each subsequent occasion, he began by stating that at the time of the surrender there had been firing from the neighbourhood of Jacob's which had caused several casualties amongst the troops in the park (this gave a rather inaccurate impression of the extent of the fighting in the area during the week). He said that he had been aware of MacDonagh making 'several journeys through our lines': Major Armstrong was initially unaware that this had been 'at the invitation of General Lowe'. He claimed that at about 5 p.m., he had witnessed the defendant arrive 'with over 100 others' and that he had then 'made a statement to me that he was a Commandant ... [and] ... it was no use my searching for papers as they had all been destroyed'. Armstrong also implied that the prisoner had been armed, as his name did not appear on 'a list [made] of the unarmed men.'[35] In fact, it is certain that MacDonagh was bearing no arms at that time. Father Augustine, who was present throughout the surrender process, later recorded unambiguously: 'Having regained the car we were soon at Jacob's, and at 3 pm arrived again at St Patrick's Park, where MacDonagh informed General Lowe of the decision to surrender and handed his revolver and belt to an officer'.[36]

William Wylie, the prosecution counsel, who asserted that he had arrested MacDonagh at St Patrick's Park on 30 April (acting as a member of Trinity College Officer Training Corps), later recalled his court martial. He states: 'The evidence was very black against him ... I asked him if he wished to make a statement. He merely shook his head. He never spoke during the trial.'[37] The official proceedings, however, indicate that MacDonagh did respond briefly when invited to speak in his own defence. Having cross-examined Armstrong, he stated: 'I did everything I could to assist the officers in the matter of the Surrender, telling them where the arms and ammunition were after the surrender was decided upon.'[38]

Afterwards, on reflection, MacDonagh clearly felt concerned that his comments in court might be misinterpreted by others as a plea for clemency or taken to imply a rejection on his part of his republican principles. At around midnight, 2 May, a few hours before his execution, he wrote to his wife, Muriel, a letter which is more in the nature of a will than a political testament or item of personal correspondence. Nonetheless, the letter states: 'At my court martial in rebutting some trifling evidence I made a statement ... On hearing it read after, it struck me that it might sound like an appeal. It was not such. I made no appeal, no recantation, no apology for my acts. In what I said I merely claimed that I acted honourably and thoroughly in all that I set myself to do.' In the document, he expressed no regrets about his role in the Rising or his impending death. Rather, returning to some of the themes contained in a note he had written on Easter Sunday, he declared: 'In all my acts ... I have been actuated by one motive only, the love of my country, the desire to make her a sovereign independent state ... I am ready to die and I thank God that I die in such a holy cause.'[39] The letter contains a subtle act of defiance to British authority; MacDermott inverted the official stationery so that the embossed crown appears at the bottom of each page.

In June 1916, a document first appeared in Dublin purporting to be MacDonagh's address to the court. Its circulation led to the prosecution of four businessmen – J.M. Butler, a newsagent and three printers, P.P. Curtis, W.H. West and R. Latchford. Roughly twelve thousand copies appear to have been published at the time, at least 3,500 being promptly seized by the authorities. It is an impassioned and articulate vindication of physical force, of the Rising and of the republican tradition. Its authenticity has been the subject of much controversy. Certainly, its sentiments, style and phrasing contain echoes of its claimed author. The official proceedings prove, however, that Mr Robertson of the Chief Crown Solicitor's office was entirely justified in describing it at Butler's trial as, 'pure fiction ... absolutely bogus'.[40]

Wylie records that 'the next accused [Thomas Clarke] was waiting outside when the court closed to consider their verdict on the one just tried'; after deliberating, it found MacDonagh guilty and sentenced him to death.[41] That same day, 2 May, Maxwell confirmed its judgement. He later justified this decision on the grounds that the defendant had played 'an active part in the Sinn Fein movement since its inauguration ... was a prominent officer ... Director of Training ... [and] ... in command' at Jacob's, 'from the neighbourhood of which ... British troops were fired on', causing casualties. He also referred to a typed document, found during a search on John MacBride. It was headed 'Army of the Irish Republic' and in it MacDonagh had described himself as 'Commandant General' of the force and 'Member of the Provisional Government of the Irish Republic'.[42] Along with the five other prisoners who had been court-martialled that day, after his trial MacDonagh was brought briefly back to the gymnasium at Richmond Barracks and there was able to converse freely with his comrades. He reiterated some of the comments that he had made to his garrison at the time of the surrender. One of those present, Piaras Beaslai, recalls that he 'chatted gaily and told them all that the Germans had landed in England and that very soon the British Empire would be finished'. Beaslai's explanation for MacDonagh's remarks was that he might have 'heard some rumour of the German bombardment of Yarmouth and Lowestoft on Easter Tuesday'. In contrast, Patrick Pearse 'sat on the floor, deep in his own thoughts, so full of them that he noticed nothing around him'.[43]

After the trial, MacDonagh was transferred to Kilmainham and like Patrick Pearse and Thomas Clarke, was kept in a separate cell under observation. That evening, 2 May, he was officially informed that the court's verdict had been confirmed and that he would be shot at dawn the next morning. It was the sentence he had fully anticipated since the surrender; after the Rising he had written to his wife indicating that it would result in 'the deaths of other leaders,' including himself.[44] Years later, Wylie wrote: 'I was always sorry

MacDonagh was executed. It was particularly unnecessary in his case.'[45] However, if the supreme penalty was to be imposed on any of the rebels after the Rising, there can never have been any doubt that it would be applied to the signatories of the Proclamation and those who had served as commandants of the four Dublin battalions. Amongst the fourteen rebels executed in the city after the Rising, MacDonagh was one of the few who 'qualified' on both counts.

Father Aloysius, of Church Street, attended MacDonagh before his execution. The drivers of the vehicle dispatched to escort him to Kilmainham had intended to collect the prisoner's wife as well, but the 'sniping from the roofs was so fierce' that they were forced to turn back without her. They did, however, call for Sister Francesa, his sister, at Basin Lane Convent; on leaving him, she is reported to have 'flung her rosary around his neck'.[46] Father Aloysius prayed with him, heard his confession, gave him Holy Communion and administered the last rites. He described him afterwards as 'happy', and unlike earlier, as having 'no trace of fear or anxiety'. When writing to his wife, after being told that she could not be reached, he had said: 'Perhaps it is better so.'[47]

Between 2 and 3 a.m., all visitors to Kilmainham without exception were ordered to leave. At between 3:30 and 4 a.m., 3 May, Thomas MacDonagh was executed. He was interred at Arbour Hill Detention Barracks; two signatories of the Proclamation, Patrick Pearse and Thomas Clarke, were buried on either side of him. Later that morning, Father Aloysius returned to the prison to lodge a complaint at not being permitted to 'remain with the prisoner to be present at his execution ... and administer extreme unction'.[48] His protests were successful; at each of the subsequent executions, priests were permitted to remain with the condemned men in their cells and then to accompany them when they faced the firing squad. This was significant not just for the present but also for the future. The clergy not only provided the rebels with the consolations of religion but also ultimately helped influence popular perceptions of the Rising itself, by later providing some of the most graphic accounts of the final hours of the condemned men.

Donagh MacDonagh, a future judge and poet, was an infant when his father was executed. He writes: 'This man was my father, but he was a stranger to me in all but blood. I have a dim, child's memory of a uniformed figure on a motor-bicycle, of a person who gave me a red wagon. One of my earliest and most vivid memories is of Father Aloysius coming to our house in Oakley Road with the news of the executions. I was playing in a rockery and fled in terror from the bogeyman who came riding on a breadvan with news which terrified.'[49]

Trial of Thomas MacDonagh

prisoner number thirty

REFERENCE: PRO WO71/346

DATE: 2 May 1916

LOCATION: Richmond Barracks

JUDGES: Brigadier-General C.G. Blackader (President), Lieutenant
        Colonel G. German, Lieutenant Colonel W.J. Kent

CHARGE:

'Did an act to wit did take part in an armed rebellion and in the
waging of war against His Majesty the King, such act being o such
a nature as to be calculated to be prejudical to the Defence to the
Realm and being done with the intention and for the purpose of
assisting the enemy'

PLEA: Not guilty

(The members of the court and witnesses were duly sworn in)

VERDICT: Guilty. Death by being shot

Text of Trial

PROSECUTION

1st witness
Major J. A. Armstrong. 1st Royal Inniskillen Fusiliers–
Provost Marshall 176th Brigade states

> I was present at St. Patricks Park Dublin on 30th April
> 1916.
>
> There were British Troops there and I saw them fired on. I
> was under fire myself. The shots came from the direction of
> Jacobs Factory. There were several casualties among the
> British Troops. At a later hour I saw the accused coming
> from the direction of Jacobs Factory under a white flag. He
> made several journeys through our lines – about 5 p.m he
> surrendered with over 100 others to General Carleton. He
> was acting as an officer when he surrendered.

> I made a list of the unarmed men and the accused was not on that list.
>
> He made a statement to me that he was a Commandant. He was subsequently sent under escort to Richmond Barracks.

Cross examined by the accused.

> I did not know that the accused came out at the invitation of General Lowe. The accused made the statement to me that it was no use my searching for papers as they had all been destroyed.

The witness withdraws

Prosecution closed.

The accused calls no witness in his defence.

The accused in his defence states.

> I did everything I could to assist the officers in the matter of the Surrender telling them where the arms and ammunition were after the surrender was decided upon.

IRISH REBELLION, MAY 1916.

THOMAS J. CLARKE,
Executed May 3rd, 1916.
One of the signatories of the "Irish Republic Proclamation."

Thomas Clarke

<u>THOMAS J.CLARKE.</u>

This man was a signatory to the Declaration of Irish Independence already adverted to. He was one of the most prominent leaders in the Sinn Fein movement in Dublin. He was present with the rebels in the G.Post Office,Sackville Street, where some of the heaviest fighting took place and was proved to have been in a position of authority there.

On the 28th May 1883,under the name of Henry H.Wilson, he was sentenced in London to Penal Servitude for life for treason felony,and was released on licence on the 20th September 1898.

He exercised a great influence over the younger members of the organization with which he was connected.

Extract from a memorandum entitled 'Short History of rebels on whom it has been necessary to inflict the supreme penalty' sent by General Sir John Maxwell to Herbert Asquith, on 11 May 1916.

THOMAS CLARKE WAS BORN on the Isle of Wight in 1858, the son of a British army sergeant, who while posted previously in Ireland, had married Mary Palmer of Cloghern, County Tipperary. Clarke thought of himself as a native of Dungannon, County Tyrone, where his family subsequently settled and where he first acquired his belief in Ireland's right to full independence. His father warned him that in seeking to overthrow British rule he was 'knocking against a stone wall'. Anticipating his future lifelong struggle, his son replied that he 'would knock away in the hope that one day the wall would give'.[1]

Clarke was admitted into the IRB in Dublin, before emigrating to the United States in 1881; there he joined Clan na Gael which dispatched him (under the name Henry Hammond Wilson) on a bombing mission to England, targeting public buildings. It was Clarke's misfortune that the entire operation had been infiltrated by British agents from its inception. Little attempt was made at secrecy. On Wednesday 4 April 1883, Clarke was seen with two other men, 'placing a black bag which seemed very heavy on the top of a cab' at Euston Station, in London. The following afternoon, the cab driver led police to a private boarding house, 17 Nelson Square, near Waterloo Station, to which he had previously conveyed a 'suspicious man and a box'. Head Constable Shea describes how he, with colleagues, watched as later two men entered the dwelling. He writes: 'We followed immediately. They [the two men] went to a bedroom and locked the door from the inside. Inspector Littlechild got the landlady to request that the door should be opened and immediately that was done we rushed in. Inspector Littlechild seized Wilson. I did the same with the other man who gave his name as Doctor Thomas Gallagher of Brooklyn, New York. On the floor between the two men was a black leather portmanteau, which contained two ... bags full of ... explosive substances ... After searching the prisoners, we conveyed them to Bow Street.'[2]

He was arrested, charged with treason felony and sentenced in London on 28 May 1883 to penal servitude for life – in effect twenty years in custody. In prison, he endured brutal conditions characterised by prolonged confinement, intellectual starvation, constantly disrupted sleep, inadequate nutrition and little exercise. He witnessed these remorseless conditions impel close comrades towards insanity. This fate he avoided by practising mental calculations and also by frequent reflection on the lessons to be drawn from his ill-judged enterprise. He served part of his term in Millbank Prison, where his hair was cropped and he was dressed in the prison uniform which bore his identity – J464. He later recalled: 'I remembered with what relentless savagery the English Government had always dealt with the Irishman it gets into its clutches, and the future appeared as black and appalling as imagination could picture it. But the worst my imagination could then picture was outdone by the horrors of Chatham Prison that I was afterwards to experience.' He recalled one of his colleagues 'going mad ... there in the stillness, between two of the hourly inspections, I heard the poor fellow fighting against insanity, cursing England and English brutality from the bottom of his heart, and beseeching God to strike him dead sooner than allow him to lose his reason. Such episodes are ineffaceable in the memory; they burn their impress into a man's soul.'[3]

On 20 September 1898, after serving fifteen years, Clarke was released early on licence as part of a government amnesty. When he re-entered civil society he was socially inept, introverted, suspicious of others, his faith in the catholic church had been weakened if not shattered, and he had a harsh unforgiving attitude towards anyone he believed had betrayed the republican cause. His prison experience 'left on his features a mark that death alone could remove but had been powerless to subdue the fire that glowed within and animated every thought and action of his life'. His revolutionary commitment remained intact and undiminished. Desmond Ryan wrote of him: 'What had burned into his soul was something akin to the Miltonic hate, unconquerable will ... [a] ... study of revenge, and most certainly a courage never to submit or yield until the flame of insurrection and a flood of rifles rounded off the tragic glory and integrity of his life'.[4]

After his release he lived for seven years in the United States where, as during his first visit there, he worked at variety of ill-paid jobs. On this occasion, he was employed for a time sweeping the streets in New York, before being engaged as John Devoy's secretary at Clan na Gael. In 1903, he helped Devoy found and edit a new newspaper, *The Gaelic American,* but he felt constantly frustrated by the extent of Irish-American absorption in American politics. Nonetheless, during this period he found deep personal fulfilment through his marriage to Kathleen Daly, a niece of John Daly and a member of a staunch republican family from Limerick. When he returned to Ireland in 1907, he found his life transformed; his earlier sacrifices now earned him status, power and admiration. He was soon co-opted onto the Supreme Council (in 1909) and was made Secretary of the IRB, and thus held influence at the heart of Irish republicanism. Its younger, more vigorous members were humbled and awed by his sacrifices, captivated by his force and vigour which belied his age and appearance and looked to him for advice and instruction. He became in effect a full-time subversive; the shop he opened in Parnell Street served as the public front for his clandestine activities. The business was of course closely monitored by the British authorities, who came to regard its owner, with his ex-Fenian associates, as being at the hub of revolutionary activity in Ireland, consequently neglecting the potential threat from others. DMP detectives rented a front room in the street opposite and kept him under constant surveillance, none of which deterred Clarke.[5]

Soon after his return to Ireland Clarke formed with Sean MacDermott the political friendship of his life. From 1908, initially with Bulmer Hobson's help, they rejuvenated the IRB – they determined its strategies, promoted those who shared their objectives, expelled or demoted those thought less zealous or committed, and fashioned it into an instrument capable of fomenting insurrection. Apart from their obvious differences in age and temperament, MacDermott and Clarke had shared goals. Both were impatient for revolution, fearing that Home Rule would result in Ireland's permanent absorption within the United Kingdom. Clarke discovered a talent for political manipulation which more than compensated for his distaste for public oratory and preference for spurning the limelight: MacDermott, likewise, possessed this skill. Both were elitist, part of a despotic republican tradition which was characterised by indifference to the will of the majority. More than any others, they drove forward the entire revolutionary enterprise and generated the dynamism which resulted in the Rising.

Opportunities for insurrection soon arose. A leading member of the IRB recalled how Clarke rubbed his hands with glee whenever he spoke of the UVF. Its formation helped radicalise nationalist opinion in Ireland during 1913, leading to the setting up of the IVF, which he joined but in which he took up no position of leadership. On 9 September 1914, when he presided over a meeting of extreme nationalists in Dublin called to discuss insurrection, he declared that 'Ireland had now a wonderful chance to rid herself of English rule'.[6]

The control which he and MacDermott exercised over the IRB became virtually absolute from June 1914; at that time Bulmer Hobson (one of the major figures in nationalist Ireland) resigned from his official positions in the IRB after an irreparable rift with Clarke over Redmond's proposal to enlarge the Provisional Committee of the Irish Volunteers. Hobson recalls, with bitterness, how afterwards Clarke 'asked me how much Redmond had paid me for letting his nominees in', and how he subsequently set out 'to undermine my influence in the movement'.[7]

MacDermott and Clarke were overjoyed by the split in the IVF three months later, precipitated this time by Redmond's Woodenbridge speech, in which he had called for its members to enlist in the British army. As a result the force was reduced to a small militant rump which they might more easily infiltrate and fashion for use in a future insurrection. Also, the danger of its emasculation by Parliamentary Party moderates had vanished. In May 1915, the IRB Military Council was established on Clarke's initiative. It was initially composed of just three like-minded and trusted members and was thus a body which was both conducive to secrecy and amenable to Clarke's control (both Clarke and MacDermott joined in September 1915). This was the dynamic force which over the next twelve months, conceived, meticulously orchestrated and ultimately brought to bear, the Easter Rising. One Volunteer, Joe Good, wrote of Clarke that he was, 'a quiet, gentle little man ... very frail ... But,' he added with ample justification, 'he was the revolution.'[8]

At around midnight, on 22 April 1916, Military Council members first began to hear the shattering news that Eoin MacNeill was despatching orders cancelling the Volunteer manoeuvres arranged for the following day. Initially, Clarke could not be contacted; like the other Military Council members, he was staying at a safe house (a hotel in Gardiner Place), with an armed guard, having told his wife to open their shop as usual on Easter Sunday. At the emergency Military Council session held that morning (23 April), he argued passionately that they proceed with the Rising as arranged. This, he suggested, would cause less confusion to the men in the field, who once it had begun would assume that MacNeill's order had been a hoax. In essence, he was terrified that his life's work would now fizzle out, with no result. To his chagrin, his views were rejected by each of the other members (including MacDermott), the men he himself had groomed and promoted. Despite his best efforts, the majority agreed that the Rising should be postponed until noon next day, Easter Monday.[9]

The Military Council next discussed who should hold the position of President of the Irish Republic, about to be proclaimed. The post was offered to Clarke, who, true to his nature, declined; possibly he also thought it inappropriate given his previous record as a felon. His pre-eminence was, however, recognised by the placing of his name first below the Proclamation. This he accepted only after persuasion. After the business had been completed, he returned home once more. Reflecting on MacNeill's actions, Clarke fulminated to his wife: 'We've been betrayed,' and told guests that 'it was a piece of the blackest treachery'.[10]

The next morning, Clarke proceeded to Liberty Hall on foot with two bodyguards, arriving by 9:45 a.m. At just before noon he travelled by car with MacDermott, stopping at the side of the GPO at much the same time as the headquarters battalion approached. His first action once they had entered the building was to help smash down the glass partition and door which separated the public section on the ground floor from the large sorting office which extended to Henry Street. At 12:45 p.m. he locked the main doors and handed the Proclamation to Pearse, who, standing on the step outside, read it to a muted and bewildered crowd. His comrades noted that Clarke, like MacDermott, was clearly in his element, physically and emotionally revived. Desmond Fitzgerald recalls: 'He was clearly elated that Ireland had indeed risen in arms though so few were our numbers. He did not hide the fact that he had been and still was bitterly angry that the countermanding order had been sent out.'[11] Similarly, Volunteer Pat Rankin states simply: 'He looked about thirty years younger and seemed so happy.'[12] It was after all the culmination of all Clarke's endeavours since returning from America almost ten years before. He had last taken up arms against English rule in Ireland in one April, thirty-three years earlier in London – in a plot riddled by informers, which had ended in fiasco, and for which he had paid a heavy personal price. But now, he was taking action in the heart of Dublin, Ireland's capital city, with trusted comrades, in a rebellion largely orchestrated and brought to fruition by himself.

During the early afternoon, he derived particular pleasure from reading through reports found in the pigeon-holes of the RIC relating to the strength and activities of the Irish Volunteers. Diarmuid

Lynch recalled: 'We chuckled in the fact that all their spying was in vain and that neither they nor their superiors realised the imminence of the climax.'[13] That evening Clarke wrote the first of at least two letters he sent from the GPO to his wife.[14]

Morale amongst the Volunteers was high as they busied themselves fortifying their position, occupying outposts and erecting barricades. But it was soon evident to their leaders that the initiative was already passing to British forces. There had been no hoped for nationwide revolt, troop reinforcements were pouring into Ireland virtually unopposed and by mid-week a military cordon was already tightening around the GPO. The leaders expected a massed infantry assault with furious hand-to-hand fighting. On Tuesday, Clarke said to Sean Reynolds, a Volunteer at the GPO: 'I suppose, Sean, you know the game is up. We have lost.'[15] From his comments to Jim Ryan the next day, it is evident that Clarke did not expect to survive the conflict. Ryan recalls that Clarke came to see him and 'for no apparent reason launched into a full history of the IRB ... Then he gave me a detailed account of the events leading up to the Rising ... for two hours and at the end I was aware of the reason for it. I was now Red Cross and so he said I might be spared by the enemy in the final bayonet charge. If therefore I should survive he hoped I now understood and would make known the motives of those who signed the Proclamation.'[16] Also on Wednesday, Clarke pointed out to another Volunteer a concrete shelter in a yard: it was where he suggested all the women should be placed when the final moments came. When Desmond Fitzgerald asked him the following day how did he think they would be executed – '"hanging or shooting", Clarke responded "I should think it would be shooting after a Rising like this and in the middle of a war".'[17]

It was evident to the British officers held captive in the building that Clarke, though not in uniform, held a position of authority. He was recognised as a leader by the garrison on account of his past record of sacrifice and commitment, his membership of the provisional government (he was seen presiding at its meetings) and his dominant position within the IRB. After Connolly's injury on Thursday, his prominent role was further enhanced. By then, due to the military's use of incendiaries, a conflagration was engulfing the east side of Sackville Street, and with no sign of infantry massing, it became increasingly apparent that the same strategy would be deployed against the GPO itself. The leaders agreed on Friday morning that in these circumstances they would evacuate; later that day their fears were realised.

At 5 p.m., Clarke transferred the prisoners to the cellar, informing them: 'It is the only place of safety ... We are making our last stand. If we leave the building, you will leave along with us.'[18] By then, the week was clearly taking its emotional toll on him. When it was decided, one hour later, to move the rebel wounded to a nearby hospital, he approached one of those accompanying them and said: 'If you see my wife, tell her the men fought ... ' He was unable to finish and turned away.[19] It was while the whole garrison was evacuating at 8 p.m. that he was observed with a revolver in his hand, having just fired what was probably his only shot of the entire Rising. He had attempted unsuccessfully to blow the lock off a gate to gain access to a building and so enable his men to evade British fire.

That night in Moore Street, Clarke ordered a party of Volunteers to tunnel through to the end of the terrace (their work was not completed until daybreak). Clearly, he assumed that a long gun-battle lay ahead. However, at noon next day, 29 April, the rebel leaders conferred and decided by majority vote to seek surrender terms in order to prevent 'further slaughter'. Almost certainly Clarke's was the only dissenting voice. After the meeting, Joe Good describes seeing the others, 'talking quietly ... like men who had made a decision and were passing time'. He and others noticed that Clarke 'stood near a window, silent and alone'. According to Louis Le Roux, on Tuesday, 'he [had] exhorted his colleagues "to die fighting as they would in any case be executed if they surrendered"' (his view on this apparently changed later in the week), and again on Saturday, 'he alone asked till the very end that they should fight on till death'.[20] The revolutionary enterprise to which he had dedicated his life had collapsed, and he knew full well that he would take no part in any future action; at the time, Clarke told Jim Ryan that the signatories of the Proclamation would be shot and the rest set free.[21] When Elizabeth O'Farrell was leaving, white flag in hand, to establish contact with British forces, 'Clarke turned his face to the wall and broke down, sobbing.'[22]

At 4:30 p.m., O'Farrell returned to Moore Street with Pearse's surrender order in hand and General Lowe's instructions summarising the arrangements that had been agreed. These were very specific, and read: 'Carrying a white flag, proceed down Moore Street, turn into Moore Lane and Henry Place out into Henry Street, and around the Pillar to the right hand side of O'Connell Street, march up to within a hundred yards of the military drawn up at the Parnell Statue, halt, advance five paces and lay down arms.'[23] Clarke, showing solidarity with the other leaders, addressed the Volunteers in an attempt to quell those who objected. Joe Good writes: 'He did his best to persuade us and I was impressed by his eloquence. He insisted that only himself and the other leaders would be shot ... he mentioned his fifteen years in English jails ... he told us that there was no need for us to fight to the death, that we had done well already. He said he was confident as a result of our action the Irish people would now assert themselves ... He spoke at length and with great force and sincerity but,' he adds, 'he failed to convince me.'[24] MacDermott, speaking perhaps with more genuine conviction, appears to have been the more effective.

Shortly afterwards the Volunteers lined up in the street outside and marched to the surrender point. Clarke and MacDermott stood near to each other in line, whilst Lieutenant S.A.L. Downing, Irish Regiment, took a list of names and addresses. One of the women present describes how 'Two officers came down and one said to the other "Thomas Clarke". One of them called Mr Clarke out of line and several other officers came over to look at him.'[25] In due course, the Volunteers were escorted to a grassed area beside the Rotunda Hospital and there they spent the night in the open, under armed guard.

Jim Ryan 'awoke towards morning and found [his] head resting on Tom Clarke's shoulder. "Are you awake?" he whispered, "I was waiting for opportunity to turn."'[26] According to Julia Grenan, a Cumann na mBan member who remained with the garrison until surrender early that morning (30 April), 'detectives came up with a military officer and brought away Mr Clarke under armed guard. He returned after some time and told us they had searched and taken away all he had and that the record of his whole life was read out to him. His life in prison, his conduct there, his life in the United States, even to the cut of the clothes he wore there, his life from his return to Ireland up to the present day. "Everything, they have everything," he said'.[27]

On arrival at Richmond Barracks, Clarke wrote in pencil his last letter to his wife (MacDermott also scribbled a note on the back) and gave it to a British soldier for delivery; Kathleen Clarke later explained that both men had 'thought they would be shot at once, without trial'.[28] In the letter, her husband expressed something of his feelings of pride and contentment. He stated: 'I am in better health and more satisfied than for many a day – all will be well eventually – but this is my goodbye and now you are ever before me to cheer me – God bless you and the boys. Let them be proud to follow the same path – Sean is with me and McG. [probably Sean McGarry, who was with him in the GPO] – They are all heroes.'[29]

Liam O'Briain saw Clarke at the barracks, 'sitting there just as we had seen him twenty times in his shop in Parnell Street, with the same clothes, the same look, quiet, silent, with the suspicion of a smile. Tom was very satisfied with himself and the situation.' He continues: 'After a while Sean fell asleep with his head on Tom's chest ... I don't think Tom slept at all. Sean would start a little and we would hear a mutter from him saying "The fire! The fire! Get the men out!" Then you would hear Tom's quiet voice saying gently: "Quiet Sean, we're in the Barracks now. We're prisoners now, Sean."'[30]

Clarke was court-martialled during the afternoon of 2 May (prisoner number thirty-one), Brigadier-General Blackader presiding. It is unlikely that the trial lasted more than fifteen minutes. The prosecution called just one witness, Lieutenant S.L. King, Enniskillen Fusiliers. He recalled that between 10 and 11 a.m., Tuesday, 25 April, 1916, while in Sackville Street, 'two men rushed across from the direction of the Post Office and took me prisoner, taking me into the main entrance.' Whilst held captive, he claimed that he 'often saw the prisoner [Clarke]. He appeared to be a person in authority although he was not in uniform. Some of the men obtained a key from him at different times and some wore uniform [this may be related to the fact that bank notes, postal orders and other securities of value were handed over to the defendant in the GPO dining room on Easter Monday]'. He concluded less than convincingly: 'I have no doubt that he was one of the Rebels.'[31] None of the DMP detectives who had been monitoring Clarke's activities so closely over the years was called upon to testify.

Under cross-examination by Clarke, King conceded that: 'whilst in the Post Office I was very well treated'; it contrasted with the prisoner's own experience of captivity. The record of the court proceedings then ends abruptly, noting only: 'The prosecution closed. The accused does not call any witnesses and makes no statement.'

Many years later William Wylie, the prosecution counsel, could 'remember distinctly ... Thomas J. Clarke. He was the oldest of them and had been a Fenian and a member of the IRB all his life.' He continues: 'He did not defend himself either and was perfectly calm and brave throughout the proceedings. He struck me as a particularly kindly man, who could not injure anyone.'[32]

Immediately after his trial, Clarke informed Piaras Beaslai that 'he was convinced that the Rising would have a very good effect on the morale of the country'.[33] Like Pearse and MacDonagh, Clarke was taken to Kilmainham that evening, and was told there that Maxwell had confirmed the verdict of the court, 'Death, by being shot'. His execution was to take place the next morning. One week later, when justifying this decision, the GOC stated: 'This man was a signatory of the Declaration of Independence ... [and] ... one of the most prominent leaders of the Sinn Fein movement in Dublin. He was present with the rebels in the G. Post office, Sackville Street, where some of the heaviest fighting took place and was proved to have been in a position of authority there.' Drawing on his intelligence sources, he concluded by noting that Clarke had 'exercised a great influence over the younger members of the organisation with which he was connected'.[34] He also included details of his earlier period of imprisonment: like John McBride, Clarke's past record counted against him in Maxwell's eyes. The GOC's observations regarding his influence had justification. One historian wrote of Clarke that though he was 'known to scarcely more than a couple of thousand people in all Ireland ... [and] ... even in the national movements which he helped to control he was almost unknown ... he was more than an "inspiration" to the young men, he was in fact their assurance of the apostolic succession of their movement, and the fact that he shared their ideas and drove them forward towards an ultimate sacrifice increased their confidence in themselves and their aim.'[35]

Kathleen Clarke was a prisoner in Dublin Castle (from 1 to 3 May 1916) at the time of her husband's execution. In the early hours of 3 May she was brought under military escort to Kilmainham to pay a farewell visit to her husband. She spent an hour with him in a cell illuminated only by the shadowy light of a candle held by a soldier. Clarke once more forthrightly condemned MacNeill's action, 'a continuation of what he had said to her about ... [him] ... in his return from the meeting in Liberty Hall on Easter Sunday'.[36] The

Volunteer Chief of Staff had clearly displaced Hobson as his *bête noire*, and had by now become his wife's as well. Clarke also described, with some justification, his court martial as a 'farce' and indicated that 'he had made no speech from the dock or anything like that'. He stated that he was 'relieved' that he was to be executed; his one dread had been that he would be sent back to prison again.[37]

Overall, Mrs Clarke said of her husband: 'he was in a most exalted frame of mind'. She claims he entrusted her with a message to the Irish people which read: 'I and my fellow-signatories believe that we have struck the first blow for Freedom. The next blow, which we have no doubt will strike, will win through. In this belief, we die happy.'[38] Before facing the firing squad, Clarke was attended by Father Columbus and Father Tom Ryan of Inchicore. The official records indicate that he was executed, with Patrick Pearse and Thomas MacDonagh 'by 4:15 a.m.' on 3 May 1916. Evidence of his meticulous forward planning and calculation, stretching it seems even beyond the grave, is provided by the intimation made in the first list of subscriptions to the Irish Volunteer Dependants' Fund (set up to aid the families of the rebels). It reads: 'Left by the late Thomas J. Clarke, c/o Mrs Clarke, for the relief of distress, £3,100'.[39]

Trial of Thomas Clarke

prisoner number thirty-one

REFERENCE: PRO WO71/347

DATE: 2 May 1916

LOCATION: Richmond Barracks

JUDGES: Brigadier-General C.G. Blackader (President), Lieutenant
Colonel G. German, Lieutenant Colonel W.J. Kent

CHARGE:

'Did an act to wit did take part in an armed rebellion and in the
waging of war against His Majesty the King, such act being o such
a nature as to be calculated to be prejudical to the Defence to the
Realm and being done with the intention and for the purpose of
assisting the enemy'

PLEA: Not guilty

(The members of the court and witnesses were duly sworn in)

VERDICT: Guilty. Death by being shot

Text of Trial

PROSECUTION

1st witness

Second Lieut S.L. King 12th Enniskillen Fusiliers being duly
sworn states.

> Between 10 and 11 am. Tuesday 25 April 1916 I was in
> Sackville St. 2 men rushed across from the direction of the
> Post office, and took me prisoner taking me into the main
> entrance of the Post office. While I was detained there I
> often saw the prisoner. He appeared to be a person in
> authority although he was not in uniform.
> Some of the men obtained a key from him at different
> times and some wore uniform. I have no doubt that he was
> one of the rebels.

XX'd [cross-examined] by the accused.

Whilst I was in the Post Office I was very well treated.

The prosecution closed.

The accused does not call any witnesses and makes no statement.

IRISH REBELLION, MAY 1916.

E. DALY
(Commandant of the North-West Dublin Area).
Executed May 4th, 1916.

Edward Daly

__EDWARD DALY.__

This man was one of the most prominent extremists in the Sinn Fein organization.

He held the rank of Commandant and was in command of the body of rebels who held the Four Courts where heavy fighting took place and casualties occurred. He admitted being at the meeting of officers which decided to carry out the orders of the executive council and commence the armed rebellion.

Extract from a memorandum entitled a 'Short History of rebels on whom it has been necessary to inflict the supreme penalty' sent by General Sir John Maxwell to Herbet Asquith, on 11 May 1916.

EDWARD DALY, POPULARLY KNOWN AS NED, was born in 1891 and brought up in Limerick, an only son with nine sisters, in a family steeped in republican politics. His father had taken part in the 1867 Fenian Rising, his uncle, John Daly, was given life imprisonment in 1884 for alleged physical force involvement, serving twelve years, and Tom Clarke was his brother-in-law. He attended the local Christian Brothers' School, Roxborough Road, where he was considered 'not by any means a brilliant pupil'.[1] After working as a baker's apprentice in Glasgow and a clerk at a timber yard in Limerick, he moved to Dublin in 1912. There he lived with the Clarkes, initially helping to run their shop, before finding employment with a firm of wholesale chemists in Westmoreland Street. He was amongst the first to join the Irish Volunteers in 1913, and soon became absorbed in their training and organisation. He rose to the rank of Captain, before being elected Commandant, in January 1915, of First Battalion, Dublin Brigade. This particular division drew its recruits from a large area north of the Liffey, which included some of the most deprived neighbourhoods in the city. It was by means of Daly and the three other commandants that the IRB Military Council tightened its control over the Irish Volunteers in the capital.

Daly led his unit, B Company, at the Howth gun-running in July 1914, and the following year he helped organise the funeral of the veteran Fenian, O'Donovon Rossa. At Sean MacDermott's request, he worked full-time with the Volunteers during the weeks immediately preceding the insurrection (though he probably did not know its precise date until 19 April). In retrospect, at least some of the members recognised that they were 'consciously preparing for the day' by the spring of 1916; ex-soldiers were then honing their street-fighting skills and they were identifying within their garrison area strategic buildings that might be occupied, potential snipers' vantage-points and commercial properties with food and other essential supplies.[2] At 8 p.m. on Easter Sunday evening, Daly attended a War Council with the other officers in his battalion at their training centre, Colmcille Hall, 5 Blackhall Street. They met to finalise arrangements in the aftermath of MacNeill's countermand order and the Military Council's decision to postpone the Rising until the next day.

On Easter Monday morning, as had been hastily arranged, First

Battalion assembled in Blackhall Street at 11 A.M.; Daly, smartly
turned-out as usual in his Volunteer uniform, was there to greet
them. He was a frail, sparce figure, quiet by temperament (a colleague described him as 'very withdrawn') but he was to provide
highly competent, humane and dignified leadership throughout
Easter week. He disclosed to those present – about one-third of the
number anticipated – the true purpose of their mobilisation, and
that an Irish Republic would be declared at noon; he stressed that
forthwith they should regard themselves as members of the Irish
Republican Army. He added that whilst 'he expected them to take
part in the coming fight with the only enemy Ireland ever had with
courage and conviction', those who did not wish to do so were at
liberty to leave.[3] Two did so, as they could see no prospect of success; the remainder cheered his remarks, a number requesting to see
a priest.

The area assigned to Daly's command was extensive and strategically vital. The battalion's successful occupation by noon of the Four
Courts, an imposing, fortress-like building of classical design, was
intended to prevent troops being deployed eastwards from the
Royal Barracks. Likewise, through the seizure of adjacent properties
in North King Street, the battalion hoped to contain crown forces
based at Marlborough Cavalry Barracks on the north-west fringe of
the city. The Volunteers were in action almost immediately, firing on
a party of hapless Lancers transporting munitions from the docks at
North Wall to the Magazine Fort in Phoenix Park. Meanwhile, they
worked feverishly, building up the defences of their vulnerable
posts. The Four Courts itself was heavily fortified; it was the
Volunteers' most secure position throughout the fighting, a base
from which units could be dispatched, a haven into which rebels
deployed elsewhere could retreat with relative safety and from
Friday it served as battalion headquarters.[4]

Meanwhile, the whole area around the Four Courts was honey-
combed with barricades. A British military source observed that in
the surrounding 'mean and compact streets', these were indeed 'formidable obstacles'. The source added that their supreme effective-
ness lay in the fact that the insurgents simultaneously occupied a
considerable number of strategically placed outposts, so 'situated as
to be able to inflict maximum casualties on English troops with
minimum loss to themselves'.[5] Meanwhile, food and other supplies
were commandeered and the manpower shortage was eased, as

modest reinforcements reported to battalion headquarters. The garrison's strength, however, peaked at two hundred and sixty men; numerical weakness imposed a constant constraint on Daly's strategy and tactics throughout the week.

Until Thursday, the battalion had little direct contact with crown forces, apart from minor, sporadic and inconclusive engagements. Nonetheless, some of its most vulnerable outputs on the periphery of the occupied area were quickly cleared by troops, as they established a military cordon along the north side of the city. Daly's greatest initial triumph was a successful assault on the Linenhall Barracks, which was subsequently burnt out to prevent re-occupation in a substantial, morale-raising conflagration. Thirty-two unarmed army pay clerks were taken captive, swelling the number of prisoners held by the rebels. These included two civilians suspected of being spies and twenty-five DMP members discovered hiding in the basement of Bridewell Police Station near the rear of the Four Courts.[6] Daly personally sought to ensure that they were humanely treated, moving them to safe, less exposed locations when the fighting became intense, consciously observing, as he remarked later, 'the rules of civilised warfare'.[7] One of the prisoners, a British officer, afterwards stated that the rebels 'fought like gentlemen ... they treated ... [him] ... with the utmost courtesy and consideration'; he added that they were 'incapable of acts of brutality'.[8] They won admiration also for their attempts to regulate the distribution of bread to the public within the garrison-held area and they appear to have contained local looting with comparative success. Though there was extensive damage to property throughout the district, the Four Courts itself, both the building and its records, survived largely intact.

By Wednesday, one Volunteer records, Daly was 'beginning to look very tired and haggard. His tunic was torn at the sleeve. I believe that he had not closed his eyes since the outbreak on Monday. He cared nothing for himself or any hardship he endured ... [and was] ... at all times solicitous for each and every one of his men.'[9] On Thursday it was evident that the British military net was closing in; the intensity of the encircling sniper barrage had increased, and soldiers had taken up positions in Capel Street and Great Britain Street, so severing the close contact which Daly had hitherto maintained with headquarters at the GPO. With an all-out assault thought imminent, the rebels made their final defensive preparations. On

Friday, at 6:45 p.m., the onslaught began; Maxwell observed later that the arrival of the South Staffordshires at TCD that afternoon, 'allowed me to begin the task of placing a cordon around the Four Courts'. He also stated that the 'very desperate fighting' which followed, was 'by far the worst ... that occurred in Dublin' apart from at Mount Street Bridge.[10]

The gun-battles at North King Street in particular have been described in later years as being like a 'miniature Stalingrad'.[11] There, the troops adopted a pincer strategy, separate units attempting to advance from east and west and deploying armoured cars to approach and gain a foothold amongst rebel strongholds, the precise location of which they had no accurate knowledge. They regarded it as 'one of the most disaffected streets in Dublin ... Practically all the inhabitants were connected with the [Sinn Féin] movement.' Along stretches of the street, rebel snipers had taken up positions in 'practically every house'.[12] The most desperate encounter occurred at the first barricade (adjacent to number twenty-seven), as the military pushed east from Bolton Street. At a later military enquiry into the civilian deaths which occurred during the fighting there, the British officer commanding gave a vivid impression of the nature of the battle. He stated:

> This whole neighbourhood was strongly held by the rebels, who had elaborately prepared and fortified it against the military with barricades across the street, and by taking out house windows and sandbagging them, etc ... The moment they [the troops] showed themselves in the street, they were subjected to heavy fire, and were carrying their lives in their hands; their first object was to force their way into the first house they came to ... they were held up by heavy fire from a strong barricade across the street exactly where no 27 is situated ... I do not think ... it ... was taken much – if anything – before 8 o' clock in the morning. The barricade was from 8–10 feet high, and was constructed of vehicles, carts, boarding, bedding and all sorts of things ... The men who made the first rush were practically all killed or wounded. I lost 13 men out of my company in front of that barricade.[13]

Only after fourteen hours of sustained fighting did the soldiers succeed in advancing the 150 yards into Church Street; in the process they sustained heavy losses – sixteen dead and thirty-one wounded. For much of the time, both defending and attacking forces were engaged on opposite sides of the street, firing at point-blank range across the narrow roadway.

By 8:30 a.m. on Saturday, 29 April, the military cordon around the Four Courts had been completed. Most of the rebels had by then retreated to the Four Courts building itself. But about sixty still occupied heavily fortified outposts, north of the streets taken by the troops at such cost, and lying outside the cordoned area. The court martial records provide a vivid insight into Daly's own assessment of how 'hopeless' the garrison's strategic position had by then become. He discussed with his officers the possibility of launching a desperate counter-attack to regain lost positions, re-establish contact with rebel headquarters (still believed to be at the GPO), and also to 'save the lives of as many people as possible in the building [the Four Courts]'; it was at the time under a sustained shell barrage from artillery located in Wood Quay.[14]

Consideration of these desperate measures ended abruptly with the delivery of Pearse's surrender order late on Saturday afternoon. The British authorities had arranged for Elizabeth O'Farrell to convey it to the Four Courts. She recalls: 'Daly was very cut up about it, but accepted it as a soldier should.'[15] A Cumann na mBan member who was present described the garrison's reaction to the news. She writes: 'it was a terrible, shattering moment. They cried and they wept and they protested and they did their best to destroy their guns. I could see them hacking away at them. But there was no escape for them then.'[16] Daly's response to those who had been anxious to 'fight it out' was to 'appeal to discipline. They must obey the order of the Commander-in-Chief.'[17] Acutely aware of how precarious their military position had become, he must surely have felt relieved that the end had come without further loss of life. Characteristically, his first concern was to make arrangements for the safe transit home of the Cumann na mBan members.

News of what had happened soon filtered through the immediate neighbourhood. John Clarke, a shopkeeper who lived close by, recorded his impression of events: 'About 5 pm, we heard noises in the street. Gaining courage the ladies opened the hall door. At once we could see something had occurred. People were about and speaking. Soldiers on roof ... looked on alert with rifles pointed. I ventured out with my arms raised high and, not being ordered in, I remained out ... we learned that the volunteers in the Four Courts had surrendered.' Soon afterwards, Clarke watched as the insurgents 'handed up their arms through the railings' of the building. He concluded his account sorrowfully: 'Thus ends the last attempt for poor Ireland. What noble fellows! The cream of the land! None of your corner boy class!'[18]

After the surrender Daly led his men under heavy military guard along the largely deserted quays, reaching Sackville Street at 9:15 p.m. Volunteer Piaras Beaslai claims that 'when the English general asked one of his own officers "Who is in charge of these men?" Daly personally responded: "I am. At all events I was," a remark which he must have known signed his death warrant.'[19] In an expert analysis of Daly's command, Major General Pat Hally has written that it was 'an excellent area, well held, well defended and well led'.[20] He considered that the commandant showed fine military judgement, concentrating his forces on account of their unexpectedly small number, establishing strong, well-selected outposts, organising local attacks to retake lost ground, impeding the deployment of troops from the Royal Barracks and finally marching his forces into Sackville Street in a disciplined, orderly manner.

Along with the Volunteers from the GPO, Daly and his garrison were held under armed guard overnight on the grass plot beside the Rotunda Hospital, before being escorted next morning to Richmond Barracks. There, having been identified for court martial by DMP detectives, Daly was tried two days later, on 3 May (prisoner number twenty-one), Brigadier-General Blackader presiding. The prosecution called two witnesses, Lieutenant Halpin and Lieutenant A.P. Lindsay, both of whom were cross-examined by the defendant. They were military officers who had been captured by First Battalion early in Easter week and detained at the Four Courts until the surrender. From their testimony, it was evident that both had been treated well. Lindsay confirmed that Daly had been commandant. He also disclosed that he had been taken into his confidence on 29 April; the rebel leader consulted him over plans then being considered to mount an insurgent counter-attack. Lindsay had advised that surrender was the wisest option.[21]

In a short statement in his defence, Daly made a determined effort to evade the death sentence. He justified his plea of not guilty on the grounds that he had had 'no dealings with any outside forces' (the enemy). He also claimed that he had not been aware of the plans for an insurrection until Easter Monday morning. He concluded: 'The officers including myself when we heard the news held a meeting and decided that the whole thing was foolish but that being under orders we had no option but to obey.'[22]

On 3 May, within hours of the trial, Maxwell confirmed the verdict of the court – 'death, by being shot'; at the same time, he confirmed three other death sentences – on William Pearse, Plunkett and O'Hanrahan. Later that same day, Daly was informed that he would face the firing squad early next morning. The GOC later justified his decision on the grounds that the defendant had been commandant at the Four Courts 'where heavy fighting took place and casualties occurred', and was also, he alleged, 'one of the most prominent extremists in the Sinn Fein organisation'.[23] His family's long republican associations and having Thomas Clarke as his brother-in-law are unlikely to have passed unnoticed.

After the trial, Daly was transferred to Kilmainham. Late that evening, 3 May, his sister, Catherine, received a message at her home in Dublin from the military officer in charge there, stating that her brother was 'a prisoner in the above prison and would like to see you tonight. I am sending a car with an attendant to bring you here.'[24] The night before she had visited her husband, Thomas Clarke, at the gaol before his execution and he had told her then that 'he felt sure Ned [Daly] would be shot as well as Willie Pearse'.[25] Two of her sisters had arrived to offer her consolation and were with her when the letter arrived. In the early hours of 4 May, the three women arrived at Daly's cell, number sixty-six, and found him lying on a blanket on the floor, clearly exhausted, in Volunteer uniform but without cap, belt, bandolier and sword. During their short time together, he paid glowing tribute to his men: 'Such heroes never lived,' he said. Having fought hard, though unsuccessfully, for his life at his trial, he now seemed as 'cool as ever', and faced the final hours with courage and dignity, entirely reconciled to his fate. He stated emphatically that he felt 'glad and proud to die for his country and that he knew the week's work would bring new life to Ireland', He reiterated points he had made at his court martial, insisting that, 'All he did ... was for Ireland, his own land' and that he had 'acted as he was bound to as a soldier of Ireland in all matters under the orders of his superior officers'.[26] Before they left, he gave them momentoes – buttons, coins, a purse and a pencil. On their way out, they spoke to some British officers and officially laid claim to his body. They had told him of the deaths of Patrick Pearse, MacDonagh and Clarke, and themselves drew consolation from knowing that he would not have to serve long, hard years in prison as his brother-in-law had done.

A priest who heard Daly's confession and gave him Holy Communion in his cell likewise described him before he faced the firing squad as 'calm and brave'.[27] At between 4 and 4:30 a.m. on 4 May, the four condemned rebels – Daly, William Pearse, O'Hanrahan and Plunkett – were executed. Their bodies were then brought to Arbour Hill Detention Barracks for burial alongside those shot and interred the previous morning. Appropriately, though entirely accidentally, Daly was placed beside Thomas Clarke.[28]

Request, dated 20 September 1917, made by Catherine Daly, mother of Edward Daly, for a 'report' of the court-martial records of her son; her appeal was unsuccessful.

PRO LONDON

Trial of Edward Daly

prisoner number twenty-one

REFERENCE: PRO WO71/344

DATE: 3 May 1916

LOCATION: Richmond Barracks

JUDGES: Brigadier-General C.G. Blackader (President), Lieutenant
Colonel G. German, Lieutenant Colonel W.J. Kent

CHARGE:

'Did an act to wit did take part in an armed rebellion and in the
waging of war against His Majesty the King, such act being o such
a nature as to be calculated to be prejudical to the Defence to the
Realm and being done with the intention and for the purpose of
assisting the enemy'

PLEA: Not guilty

(The members of the court and witnesses were duly sworn in)

VERDICT: Guilty. Death by being shot

Text of Trial

PROSECUTION

1st witness

Lieu. Halpin 3rd Sherwood Forresters being duly sworn states.

> I was arrested opposite the Four Courts on Monday April
> 24 and I was taken into the Four Courts and detained in
> Custody until the Saturday following. I first saw the accused
> on Thursday April 27, he was armed, and in uniform. I
> don't know if he was in authority. There was firing from the
> Four Courts while I was there.

Cross examined by the accused.

> I first saw the accused in the room in which I was detained
> and he asked if I was properly treated and on the second
> occasion he told me there was a danger of the wing in

which I was being shelled and he had me removed. On the third occasion he asked me if I had my meals and bedding all right.

The witness withdraws

2nd witness

Lieut A.P. Lindsay 5th Bn Inniskillen Fusiliers being duly sworn states.

I was arrested on Tuesday April 25 by the rebels at the Four Courts and was fired on prior to arrest. Another officer with me was wounded (Lord Dunsany).

We were both taken into the Four Courts and confined there.

I saw the accused during my confinement. I did not see the accused giving any orders. I saw him on Thursday, Friday and Saturday and had conversation with him. On Saturday I was informed that Commandant Duly wanted to see me and I went down to see him. Commandant Duly is the accused. He said he intended to make a counter attack as the position was hopeless. I told him it was useless and that he had better surrender. He said that he could not surrender without orders from his superior.

Cross examined by the accused.

He told me he had had a conference with the officers and that a counter attack had been decided upon. He also said that he did not expect anyone who took part in this counter attack would come back alive. He said the object of making this counter attack was to save the lives of as many people as possible in the building.

The witness withdraws

Prosecution closed.

The accused calls no witnesses and makes the following statement.

The reason I pleaded "Not guilty" was because I had no dealings with any outside forces. I had no knowledge of the insurrection until Monday morning April 24. The officers including myself when we heard the news held a meeting and decided that the whole thing was foolish but that being under orders we had no option but to obey.

Statement ends.

IRISH REBELLION, MAY, 1916.

WILLIAM PEARSE
(Younger Brother of P. H. Pearse, also Executed),
Executed at Kilmainham Prison, 4th May, 1916.

William Pearse

Extract from a memorandum entitled 'Short History of rebels on whom it has been necessary to inflict the supreme penalty' sent by General Sir John Maxwell to Herbert Asquith, on 11 May 1916.

BODLEIAN LIBRARY, UNIVERSITY OF OXFORD

<u>WILLIAM PEARSE.</u>

     This man was a brother of P.H.Pearse, the President of the Irish Republic. He was associated with the Sinn Fein movement from its inception.

     He held the rank of Commandant in the rebel army. He was present in the G.P.O. during the fighting and was acting as an officer and surrendered with the rebels in Sackville Street.

WILLIAM PEARSE WAS BORN IN DUBLIN on 15 November 1881, the third child of his father's second marriage. Like his more famous brother, he was educated at the Christian Brothers' School, Westland Row. He left, aged sixteen, after an unimpressive performance in his Junior Certificate, and transferred to the Metropolitan School of Art, attending it at first full-time, then part-time, from 1898 to 1910. While a student there, Patrick provided him with the funds to enable him also to study in Paris and at the Kensington School of Art in London. He had, in consequence, a keener awareness of movements in modern art than most of his contemporaries. He was more gifted artistically than his brother, showing genuine, if slight, talent especially up to his late twenties, in both drawing and sculpture. In essence, he did 'the best he could with the gifts he had', driven initially by strong creative ambitions to earn a living as a sculptor.[1] He exhibited his work and bought and sold pieces of Irish art through his involvment in the Irish Art Company. Despite his father's more high-flown artistic ambitions, the family trade lay mostly in producing stock carvings of established popularity and traditional design for Irish churches. Given William's interests, he was from an early age marked out as the natural inheritor of the family business. However, the company was dissolved in 1910, partly because of William's lack of commercial acumen as well as a depression in the building trade.

William also had a passion for drama: according to Ruth Dudley Edwards, 'apart from his work and his preoccupation with his family, this appeared to be his great interest in life. He gazed at the stage and at actors with a sort of awe.'[2] With his younger sister Mary Brigid, he formed a small troupe, the Leinster Stage Society, which was moderately successful, putting on plays at the Abbey Theatre, between 1910 and 1912, and elsewhere. Maire Nic Shiubhlaigh reluctantly withheld praise for Pearse's acting abilities, writing: 'It seems a hard thing to say that he was never terribly successful as an actor. He never lost his self-consciousness on a stage. He was acutely aware of the unsuitability of his speech ... [he spoke slowly, with a lisp] ... His voice never completely became his servant. But what he lacked in ability he made up in enthusiasm.'[3]

Nonetheless, William's artistic and theatrical interests gave him in many ways a more liberal view of the world than his older brother, and he certainly looked the part. He had pleasing features, was stockily built, with sad, sensitive eyes, a receding chin and a mass of black hair brushed well back from the forehead and worn rather long. His hair was a vital element in the artistic appearance which he carefully cultivated. He moved as he spoke – slowly; one observer wrote of him that 'his legs resembled the progress of a compass as he seemed to move ... [them] ... from the hips without bending his knees'.[4] He had an unassuming, gentle manner; to T. K. Moylan, 'he was such a quiet, unassertive, inoffensive individual, one could not associate him with bloodshed. I doubt if he ever fired a gun, even in Easter Week. I could not think of anyone less likely to take the life of a fellow man.'[5]

His involvement in the Rising stemmed directly from the all-pervading influence of Patrick, who was two years his senior. William felt an unswerving loyalty towards him and a constant unquestioning determination to assist him; he emulated him in word and deed, though lacking either the intelligence or aptitude to do so academically They were as inseparable as their busy lives permitted, addressed each other often, to the consternation of friends, in a sort of baby-talk, and spent leisure-time together, sharing holidays in the west of Ireland. Instead of developing as a sculptor, William abandoned all his creative ambitions to further his brother's interest. He sold the family business and formed the theatre company with his sister, partly to raise money for St Enda's, and he taught art at the school though possessing few natural gifts as a teacher. Overall, he had a greater influence on Patrick than anyone else and helped moderate his priggishness. His criticisms were the more acceptable because they came from a securely held position of affection and trust. Just before his execution, Patrick wrote to him to express his appreciation, saying: 'No-one can ever have had so faithful a brother as you.' He paid tribute to him also in one of his last poems, stating: 'Of all the men I have known on earth, you only have been my familiar friend, nor needed I another.'[6] It was a reflection of his dedication to Patrick's enthusiasms that William too joined both the IRB and the Irish Volunteers. In due course, he was promoted to Captain of E Company, Fourth Battalion, Dublin Brigade (which included a number of senior students at St Enda's). Later, he was appointed to his brother's headquarters staff to serve as Staff Captain. In the flurry of activity immediately prior to the Rising he was even permitted to issue mobilisation orders, signing them as 'Acting Chief of Staff'.[7] Nonetheless, he remained, according to

Bulmer Hobson, 'just a shadow ... a wee fellow'. Hobson continues: 'he used to come in with messages ... [I] ... never got a word out of him', and concludes that 'he had taken no part in the movement' beyond joining a Volunteer unit, and ultimately was executed solely because he was Patrick Pearse's brother. Oscar Traynor recalls the tense atmosphere at Volunteer headquarters when Patrick delivered his final lecture before the Rising. Characteristically, William entered the room with his brother, and 'helped him take off' his greatcoat and slouch hat.[8]

On Friday 21 April, as a precautionary measure, IRB Military Council members left their homes and stayed, protected by bodyguards, at various safe houses which were unknown to the police and therefore unlikely to be raided before the appointed day. Both Pearse brothers slept at 27 Rutland Street. On Easter Sunday morning, William was at Liberty Hall when the leaders held their crisis meeting following news of MacNeill's countermand order, and in the afternoon he went with Patrick to St Enda's, to bid their mother farewell. After 8:30 a.m. on Easter Monday morning, Father Aloysius was on his way 'from Church Street to say mass at Gloucester Street' when he met the two of them on bicycles. Patrick was wearing a loose overcoat or mackintosh and it confirmed the priest's suspicion that 'something was in the air'.[9] They were making their way back to Liberty Hall. Ruth Dudley Edwards writes: 'There is bathos in the image of Mrs Pearse's two sons going out to fight: the heavy balding schoolmaster with a sword he could not use and the inarticulate, long-haired, slight young man, whose talents had been dissipated in the service of causes he could barely understand.'[10]

During the two weeks prior to the Rising, it was said that William 'was never out of ... [Patrick's] ... sight'.[11] From the brief glimpses of his activities documented by those who saw him there, this seems to have been the case at the GPO as well. Eamonn Dore states that 'he was at his brother's side all week', serving him as ADC.[12] The two of them made frequent visits to the roof and parapet where, until Wednesday, many of the defenders were members of E Company, Forth Battalion and from St Enda's. They were also seen together making tours of inspection of the building's defences. Likewise, Sean MacEntee recalls that: 'In the space almost immediately opposite ... [its] ... main entrance hall ... a small office had been contrived.' He describes seeing Patrick in it 'writing busily. Except for ... Willie ... who stood a little way from him, he was quite alone.'[13] When on

Wednesday, the former wrote a letter to his mother, William was there to append a footnote, stating merely: 'Have really nothing to say. We are still here. Don't worry. I saw a priest again (confession) and was talking to Fr. Bowden also.'[14]

William Pearse played a minor and exclusively supportive role throughout, and appears to have been somewhat detached from the momentous events going on around him. Desmond Ryan recalls him inspecting, with Patrick, the former St Enda's boys who were posted as snipers on the roof of the GPO. He records him saying in his 'slow, lisping voice as he looks in passing at the fires and the chaos in view ... "A curious business this. I wonder how it will all end? I know a lot of good work has been done, but there is a great deal more to do."'[15] This rather limp and self-conscious attempt to raise morale illustrates the fact that by temperament he was wholly unsuited to the atmosphere of war; nonetheless, his convictions, however vicariously acquired, did not betray him.[16]

On Friday morning, 28 April, it is likely that William attended a crisis meeting of the leadership at which evacuation was agreed if the GPO was shelled or set ablaze by British incendiaries. At 1 p.m., as the inferno spread and the ceilings began collapsing, Patrick ordered the snipers on the roof to abandon their posts; when some delayed, it was his brother who went up on his behalf to chase them down. Both brothers left the post office as part of the last group to evacuate and were greeted by a 'fusillade of shots' as they stepped into Henry Street; Frank Henderson recalls: 'we succeeded in getting across one by one'.[17] Next day, William was present when at noon the members of the provisional government held a council of war at 16 Moore Street and agreed to seek surrender terms. Desmond Ryan recalls that after it, William emerged and told him of the proposal to 'save the men from slaughter, for slaughter it is'. Ryan continues: 'He shook his head sadly and then sighed with relief at the thought that the men might be saved.'[18] He returned moments later and asked for a razor for his brother. Julia Grenan records that 'all in number 16 ... were in tears' as Patrick then left to meet General Lowe, 'except MacDiarmada and Willie Pearse'.[19]

Soon afterwards, when the surrender terms had been accepted by the GPO garrison, William helped round-up its members. Sean MacEntee, who had slept in a stable off Moore Street on Friday night, writes: 'It was about 3:00 in the afternoon when we heard voices from the street crying: "Any Volunteers here?" Wondering who could be calling out as boldly in that area I opened the stable door and saw two Volunteers standing at the top of the street. One of them ... was Captain Breen ... the other was Willie Pearse. Leaving the gate I ran up to the two men. "What," I cried, speaking to Pearse and breaking down with emotion, "has it come to this?" "It has," Pearse replied sorrowfully, "but we have got terms, the best terms. We are all to march out with arms in our hands and no-one will be detained but the leaders."[20] As the battalion marched down Henry Street, towards Sackville Street and the Parnell Monument, William was at their head, carrying a white flag. Soon, when the rebels were standing adjacent to the Gresham Hotel under military guard, Captain Henry de Courcy Wheeler took a note of his name and address, along with the others positioned close by; these included Michael Collins, Sean MacEntee and Jack Plunkett.[21]

Next morning, Sunday 30 April, the rebels were escorted from the Rotunda Hospital to Richmond Barracks. That night Liam O'Briain records seeing William in the crowded billits there. He states: 'There was a dreamy-eyed, young man with rather long hair who looked like an artist and was wearing Volunteer uniform ... Young Pearse was turning from side to side on my left, very disturbed, though he was fast asleep.'[22] On Monday, when the Volunteers were assembled in the gymnasium, Sean MacEntee was sitting beside William Pearse. He describes the arrival of the DMP detectives, stating: 'They went among us scrutinising our faces closely and intently, here and there tapping a man on the shoulder and telling him to gather at the side of the room. In this way William Pearse was taken ... [he] ... had had a premonition of his fate. Naturally, we began to discuss what the outcome of our situation could be. He did not feel that the rank and file Volunteers would be treated badly but he was certain that the officers would be harshly dealt with. He was taken to the far side of the room with some others ... Sean MacDermott ... Joe Plunkett ... and that was the last I saw of him.'[23]

During the following night, 2 May, Patrick Pearse who was then at Kilmainham awaiting execution, almost certainly asked to see his brother. This would have become all the more urgent in view of the fact that the authorities had been unsuccessful in their efforts to contact his mother. Lily O'Brennan stated that 'when the military escort reached Oakley Road they found that Mrs Pearse was out in Rathfarnham which is about three miles away. The driver of the car said it was too dangerous to go there as sniping by the rebels was still going on.'[24] This account is broadly corroborated by Father Aloysius who was in the vehicle at the time. He recalled that 'sniping from the roofs of the houses was so bad that when we got as far as Charlemont Bridge the soldiers thought it advisable to abandon their plan and return'.[25]

Possibly, after this failed attempt had been reported, the military authorities decided to have William escorted to Kilmainham from Richmond Barracks. On 3 May, he told Margaret, his sister: 'Last night ... I had a terrible experience. I was in prison over there (indicating across the road) when a group of soldiers brought me here [he was then in Kilmainham himself]. About half-way over we heard shots. The men looked at each other and one said "Too late".' He added: 'I think they were bringing me to see Pat but we heard only the volley that took him.' According to Mrs Pearse's account, William said to her: 'I was brought across a yard. When we got to a gate, the man with me knocked and the answer we got was: "You are too late." On the minute, the spirit in me grew strong.' He continued: 'I never shed a tear, there were seven men there and one officer. They had candles in their hands.'[26]

Later on 3 May, after his horrifying ordeal of the night before, William Pearse was court-martialled (prisoner number twenty-seven), Brigadier Maconchy presiding. He was tried along with three other Volunteers from the headquarters garrison – John Dougherty, John McGarry and J.J. Walsh. The prosecution called just one witness for all four accused, Lieutenant S.L. King, Royal Enniskillen Fusiliers; he had also testified at the trials of Patrick Pearse and Thomas Clarke held on the previous day. Lieutent King had been held as a prisoner at the GPO from Tuesday to Friday of Easter week. He said that he recognised Dougherty as one of the two rebels who had taken him captive at gunpoint in Sackville Street (he 'threatened to blow my brains out') and claimed also to have seen the others whilst confined there. There could never have been any real evidence against Pearse, whose role throughout the Rising had been wholly passive. King merely said: 'I know that ... [he] ... was an officer but do not know his rank.' He shed even less light on the respective actions of the others. He stated that Walsh was in uniform but 'did not appear to be in any authoritative position.' He also alleged that Pearse, McGarry and Walsh were 'wearing equipment,' and 'Dougherty had a revolver but no equipment'.[27]

None of the accused cross-examined the witness. When speaking in his own defence, Dougherty denied making the statement attributed to him by King; Walsh and McGarry claimed that they had not known the 'intention of the mobilisation' on Easter Monday.[28] It is often suggested that Pearse 'practically condemned himself to death by the exultant attitude he adopted' in court and that he 'insisted that he had been immersed in the plans for the Rising from the beginning'.[29] From the official record of proceedings it is clear that the only justification for such an interpretation is that he alone of the fifteen rebels executed and of the four court-martialled at his trial, pleaded guilty to the charge (that he 'did take part in armed rebellion ... with the intention and for the purpose of assisting the enemy'). McGarry stated in his response: 'I had no intention of assisting the enemy'. It is impossible to know now whether Pearse was at the time 'exultant', nervous or merely mentally confused, but the statement he made subsequently was clear, concise, restrained and accurate. He said simply: 'I had no authority or say in the arrangements for the starting of the rebellion. I was throughout only a personal attaché to my brother, P.H. Pearse. I had no direct command.'[30]

The court found all four Volunteers guilty and sentenced them to death, but beside the verdict on McGarry the record states 'recommend to mercy on the grounds that he was misled by the leaders'.[31] Maxwell commuted the sentences on Dougherty and Walsh to ten years penal servitude and in McGarry's case to eight years. He confirmed the death penalty on Pearse. Maxwell seems to have had some reservations about doing so – perhaps having heard of his ponderous, lisping delivery during his trial and his rakish youthful appearance, or perhaps as a result of reading his statement in court. This seems to be the only explanation for the dispatching of a messenger from his military headquarters on 3 May, just after the case had been heard, to the commandant at Kilmainham with an urgent request: 'Please inform me by bearer of the age of William Pearse who was tried by FGCM [Field General Court Martial] today' (signed Brigadier-General Byrne). On the reverse side Major W.J. Lennon responded: 'I beg to inform you that the age of William Pearse is 33 last November' (it was actually 34).[32]

Later, Maxwell summarised his reasons for confirming the sentence of death, stating that Pearse 'was a brother of P.H. Pearse, the President of the Irish Republic. He was associated with the Sinn

Féin movement from its inception. He held the rank of Commandant in the rebel army. He was present in the GPO during the fighting and was acting as an officer and surrendered with the rebels in Sackville Street.'[33] The assertion that he was a commandant was wholly inaccurate, but may have been inferred from the fact that he had led the GPO garrison on its march from Moore Street after the surrender. That he was executed was certainly in part because he was Patrick's brother and also because he was tried at an early stage when clemency was smothered by the overweening desire to make examples of the leaders. The authorities already knew how little reliance could be placed on personal appearance: Patrick Pearse was headmaster of a school and MacDonagh a university lecturer. Also, Maxwell was relying on police intelligence reports. As has been stated: 'In the welter of contradictory orders preceding the Rising, William had set his hand to papers as "Acting Chief of Staff". He was as likely a service officer as some of the others on brief acquaintance ... Patrick Pearse was too embroiled in the complexities of those days to consider the position he was putting ... [his brother] ... in.'[34] Despite a poem to his mother about the prospective sacrifice of her two sons, Pearse's 'hope and belief' when in less romantic mode, was that William would survive him and be released from prison soon.[35]

The record of court proceedings suggests that William Pearse's trial was a travesty of justice, with no genuine attempt made to establish the truth regarding his role in the Rising or the extent of his involvement in revolutionary politics prior to it. As F.S.L. Lyons writes, his 'only crime was to have loved his famous brother enough to be at his side wherever he went and whatever he did'.[36] On 3 May, William Pearse was officially informed that Maxwell had confirmed his death sentence and that he would be executed next morning. He had been transferred to Kilmainham and whilst there requested that his mother and sister visit him. Margaret writes: 'Towards midnight we were aroused from an attempt to get a few hours sleep [at 10 a.m. that morning they had first heard of Patrick's execution] by the arrival of a military lorry. I went to the hall door and was given a note saying that the prisoner, William Pearse, desired to see us. I returned to the bedroom and said to mother: "More bad news. Willie wants to see us as he is going too."' After arriving at the prison, she continues: 'We talked quietly, calmly [to him] and chiefly about personal matters ... We told him how proud we were of him and Pat and that we were satisfied they had done right ... [Then] ... we bade [him] ... a last goodbye and left him gazing after us, one longing, sad look till the cell door closed.' She concluded: 'Though our sorrow and loss are very great indeed, we were resigned. Pat and Willie, so wonderfully united in life, were also united in death.'[37]

There was a 'slight postponement of the fixed time' for the executions of Pearse, O'Hanrahan, Plunkett and Daly, in order to give the priests from Church Street 'an opportunity of attending to the men'. When Father Augustine arrived at William Pearse's cell his 'hands were already tied behind his back ... [But] ... he was beautifully calm, made his confession, as if he were doing it on an ordinary occasion, and received Holy Communion with great devotion. A few minutes later he stood before the firing squad.'[38] William Pearse was executed at between 4 and 4:30 a.m., 4 May, and subsequently interred at Arbour Hill between the bodies of Michael O'Hanrahan and Joseph Plunkett.

Trial of William Pearse

prisoner number twenty-seven

REFERENCE: PRO WO71/358

William Pearse was tried along with John Dougherty (prisoner number twenty-six), John McGarry (prisoner number twenty-eight), and J.J. Walsh (prisoner number twenty-nine

DATE: 3 May 1916
LOCATION: Richmond Barracks
JUDGES: Colonel E.W.S.K. Maconchy (President), Lieutenant Colonel
      A.M. Bent, Major F.W. Woodward

CHARGE:

'Did an act to wit did take part in an armed rebellion and in the waging of war against His Majesty the King, such act being o such a nature as to be calculated to be prejudical to the Defence to the Realm and being done with the intention and for the purpose of assisting the enemy

PLEA: William Pearse was the only one of the four here accused to plead guilty. The others pleaded not guilty.

(The members of the court and witnesses were duly sworn in)

VERDICT: All were found Guilty. Death
('John McGarry is recommended to mercy on the grounds that he was misled by the leaders')

Text of Trial

1st witness

Lieu. S.L. King 12th Batn. R. Inniskilling Fusiliers states:-

> On Tuesday the 25th April at 11 a.m. I was seized by two armed men outside Clery's shop opposite the General Post Office. John Dougherty was one of the two. He held a revolver at me and told me if I did not put my hands up he would blow my brains out.
>
> He took me to the General Post office where I was held as

a prisoner till Friday night.

I was in uniform.

I saw each of the other prisoners in the G.P.O. while I was there and during that time the Post Office was held against His Majesty's troops by men firing against the troops.

There was another officer there Lieut Chalmers who was wounded, also in uniform.

I know that William Pearce was an officer but do not know his rank.

I do not know what McGarry's position was. He was not in uniform.

J. Walsh did not appear to be in any authoritative position but was dressed in uniform.

I saw Pearse, McGarry and Walsh wearing equipment, belts and pouches. Dougherty had a revolver but no equipment.

It was Dougherty who threatened to blow my brains out, not the man with him.

I am quite certain that I saw McGarry with equipment on.

DEFENCE

John Dougherty states:–

I did not say that I would blow Lieut King's brains out.

William Pearse states:–

I had no authority or say in the arrangements for the starting of the rebellion. I was throughout – only a personal attache to my brother P.H. Pearse. I had no direct command.

John McGarry states:–

I had no intention of assisting the enemy. I had no position or rank of any sort. I was employed as a messenger. I did not know of the rebellion until the Post Office was taken. I had no rifle.

J.J. Walsh states:

During the past eighteen months I have held no official position either big or little in the Irish Volunteers or any other national movement and my whole attention was confined to business.

I gave it up at the time of the split between the Redmondites and the Irish Volunteers. I mean my official position. I remained in the Volunteers as a private and on being mobilised on Monday I knew nothing whatever of the intention of the mobilisation.

I fired on nobody during the time in the Post Office. I had no arms whatever. I was told off to attend to the water and sand arrangements in case of fire.

E.W.

KEOGH BROS. LTD.   MICHEAL O' HANNRACHAIN   DUBLIN

Michael O'Hanrahan

MICHAEL O'HANRAHAN.

This man was employed at the office of the Headquarters of the Irish Volunteers.

He was one of the most active members of that body, took part in all their parades and was a constant associate with the leaders of the rebellion. He was arrested in uniform and armed, and there had been heavy firing and casualties amongst the British troops in the neighbourhood of the place where this man with others surrendered. He was an officer in the rebel army.

Extract from a memorandum entitled 'Short History of rebels on whom it has been necessary to inflict the supreme penalty' sent by General Sir John Maxwell to Herbert Asquith, on 11 May 1916.

BODLEIAN LIBRARY, UNIVERSITY OF OXFORD

MICHAEL O'HANRAHAN WAS BORN in New Ross, County Wexford, in 1877, and spent his early years in Carlow before moving to Dublin. His republicanism may in part have been inherited from his family, some of whom were involved in 1798; his father took part in the 1867 Fenian Rising, and subsequently went on the run to evade arrest. A priest said of O'Hanrahan that he 'always showed that the national spirit of his forebears was strongly implanted in him'.[1] He was educated at the local Christian Brothers' school and the College Academy. In his adolescence, he became an Irish language enthusiast, acquiring his knowledge through attending classes and private study. He founded the first branch of the Gaelic League in Carlow and was its delegate at the organisation's second national representative congress, held in 1900. He remained active as an official in the movement after going to Dublin. He was also a keen member of the Sinn Féin movement, joining it soon after its foundation, sitting on its National Council, and addressing often hostile audiences, particularly in the north.

He had considerable literary ability. His style and outlook were thought to be reminiscent of the Young Irelander, Finton Lalor. He made regular and respected contributions to the nationalist press. His first book, *A Swordsman of the Brigade*, was described as a 'simple romantic tale' and related the actions of a soldier in the Irish Brigade fighting in eighteenth century Ireland and France.[2] In a review, Thomas MacDonagh wrote of it; 'The author knows his history and has caught the atmosphere of the life of the time. The book is full of military adventure; a manly, healthy story of the Gael by a Gael.'[3] O'Hanrahan dedicated it 'To the memory of a father to whom I owe so much and whose life's quest is over, and to ... my mother who whispered hope when days were black'.[4] A second volume, *Irish Heroines*, was published posthumously by his family, and was comprised of a series of lectures which he had given just weeks before the Rising. His support for physical force to achieve independence is implicit in the contents of the lectures. When addressing some members of Cumann na mBan, he had advised: 'Strive to be heroines in your daily lives, to be mothers, sisters, lovers of heroes ... Work, train yourselves for the days to come ... when we ... shall gaze on a free flag and a free people ... [in] ... peace and freedom.'[5] A further volume, *When the Norman Came*, was published in 1918; characteristically it was a work of romantic and heroic historical fiction, and became an Irish schools textbook.

In 1916, O'Hanrahan was employed, along with his brother, Henry, as a clerk at the headquarters of the Irish Volunteer Force, in Dawson Street, Dublin. It was said of him at the time that he was 'among the most trusted men in the Volunteer organisation'[6] and that 'his integrity and sincerity inspired confidence'.[7] In a Foreword to *Irish Heroines*, Father M. O'Flanaghan described O'Hanrahan as 'one of those modest, silent, earnest workers who do not seek applause, who are only revealed to the public in the flair of a great crisis'.[8] On first meeting him, Pat Rankin, an Ulsterman who fought at the GPO, was struck by his 'kind features'.[9] He was living then in Connaught Street, Phibsborough, with his mother, eight sisters and brother. It is unlikely that he had any knowledge of the actual plans for a Rising until Wednesday, 19 April. Nonetheless, during the months preceding it, developments at his family home had been drawn to the attention of Dublin Castle. Whilst describing 'renewed activity by the Volunteer movement', an informer code-named Granite, indicated to the authorities in two separate reports, that O'Hanrahan's residence was one of those being used to store rifles and ammunition.[10]

On Easter Monday morning, O'Hanrahan accompanied by his brother, marched in Volunteer uniform with Second Battalion, Dublin Brigade to Jacob's Biscuit Factory. As the garrison entered the building one of the women present stated: 'Down the street, swaying from side to side, came an open two-seater car. As it drew abreast of Jacob's a figure in Citizen Army uniform stood up in the front seat and waved its hat above its head. It was Madame Markievicz ... "Ho at it, boys!" she yelled. "The Citizen Army are taking the Green! Dublin Castle in falling!" There was a pause amongst the figures on the street. Everyone looked after the noisy vehicle. In the hush that followed, the shouts of its [Jacob's] occupants could be heard distinctly. Then there was a cheer.'[11]

O'Hanrahan's sister described him as an 'intimate friend' of Thomas MacDonagh, and he served throughout Easter week on his personal staff as quartermaster, with responsibilities for the layout and administration of the post and for supplies. These were daunting tasks at the factory. Set in a warren of narrow streets, it was a huge, impregnable building, with high towers which gave spectacular views of much of the city south of the river. The occupying garrison numbered about one hundred and eighty men, with Fianna and Cumann na mBan units giving support. One of the women observed that the 'little force seemed to have been swallowed up in the vastness of the place. There was an eeriness about ... [it] ... a feeling of having been cut off from the outside world'.[12] Its pervasive gloom and creaking floorboards added to the oppressive, surreal atmosphere, whilst the rebels' sense of isolation was progressively heightened by their diminishing knowledge of developments elsewhere. Surprisingly, food was scarce. Maire Nic Shiubhlaigh states that 'despite constant foraging ... on the first day, no food suitable for hungry men could be found'.[13] According to Peadar Kearney, 'hearty meals' of the available biscuits – cream crackers, rich fruitcake and shortbread – rapidly induced even among the most 'sweet toothed members ... a feeling of nausea. Bread became the whole desire.'[14]

There is no record of O'Hanrahan being directly involved in the conflict. The British army leadership did not regard the biscuit factory as a significant military or political objective and opted for a strategy of containment and psychological attrition. This involved 'sleep deprivation and unnerving the insurgents by sniping and having armoured cars speed noisily past the factory at night-time, a shrewd and effective tactic which had a cumulative effect on the defenders'.[15] One Volunteer recalls: 'the ear-splitting crash of all sorts of arms gave the impression that the building was being attacked front and rear. All this meant that nerves were as taut as a violin at pitch.'[16] The garrison sustained just one fatality during the week – Joe O'Grady, shot by troops near St Stephen's Green whilst returning from an unsuccessful attempt to deliver relief supplies to de Valera's Third Battalion at Boland's Bakery on Easter Thursday. Most of the actual fighting at Jacob's took place around its more vulnerable outposts: in the opinion of one Volunteer, 'the strain ... was probably more intense for some of us because of the comparative inactivity'.[17]

Given these circumstances, the shock to the battalion must have been all the greater when, on Sunday morning, 30 April, Elizabeth O'Farrell called at Jacobs' to deliver Pearse's surrender order. Anticipating the inevitable outcome, she records that during her visit, 'Michael O'Hanrahan and his brother ... asked me if I would take charge of some silver (about £3 in all) they had in their pockets and convey it to their mother. This I consented to do.'[18] When finally MacDonagh had accepted the unconditional terms on offer,

O'Hanrahan marched with the rest of the garrison the half mile from the factory to the surrender point, St Patrick's Park (it had been arranged that the Volunteers from the South Dublin Union would follow them there). One Volunteer recalls that 'before we reached the British ... some of the boys just walked out into the crowd which lined most of the way ... and escaped'. He adds that the leaders, including O'Hanrahan 'could have easily escaped. However, they presumably thought that they were honour-bound by their agreement to surrender.'[19]

Throughout the day's proceedings the sound of gunfire persisted. Earlier on the Sunday morning, Sean O'Caileagh states: 'our men fired on scattered groups of soldiers in St Patrick's Park' who were preparing for the arrival of the Volunteers. He also noted that 'all the time' whilst they were marching there, a 'sniper continued firing. We afterwards learned it was one of our own men, located in some high position in Jacob's factory who had not heard of the surrender.'[20] On their arrival, Major J.A. Armstrong, Enniskillen Fusiliers, the British officer commanding at the park, 'personally questioned' the rebels and demanded that the arms be handed over. They were then conducted under escort to Richmond Barracks. John MacDonald, a member of the Jacob's garrison, recalled seeing the O'Hanrahan brothers, after they had reached the military base, 'crying together, locked in each others' arms'.[21] Michael was not downcast, however; he is reported at some point to have said to Henry: 'We may go under and have to suffer the penalty but in my opinion Ireland is saved.'[22]

O'Hanrahan was court-martialled on 3 May (prisoner number thirty-six), Brigadier-General Blackader presiding. The prosecution called just one witness, Major J.A. Armstrong: he gave essentially the same circumstantial evidence in all five cases involving the rebels who had surrendered at St Patrick's Park. At O'Hanrahan's trial he began as usual by referring to the shots fired at the troops in the park on 30 April, from 'the neighbourhood of Jacob's', causing 'several casualties'. He said that he had seen the Volunteers arrive from the factory and also 'another large body ... from the same direction'. With regard to the defendant specifically, he could affirm only that he had been in 'one of the parties', was in uniform, and had stated at the time of the surrender that he was an officer. He also alleged that he had been armed. When cross-examined by the accused he justified this claim on the rather unconvincing grounds that his name did not appear on a list compiled of those men who were unarmed, and that all insurgent officers appeared to have 'pistols or revolvers'. But he was forced to concede: 'I cannot say whether [the prisoner] was armed or not.' In his defence, O'Hanrahan made a concise, lucid and defiant statement, in which he affirmed his recognition of the Republic proclaimed on Easter Monday and hence his obligation to carry out the instructions of its officers. He stated: 'As a soldier of the Republican army acting under the orders of the Provisional Government of that Republic duly constituted I acted under the orders of my superiors.'[23]

On 3 May, a total of fifteen rebels were sentenced to death by the courts martial. O'Hanrahan's case was one of four in which Maxwell confirmed this verdict. In justifying this decision, the GOC claimed that he had been 'one of the most active members' of the Volunteers, a 'constant associate' of the leaders of the Rising and an officer in the rebel army. While clearly there was truth in these assertions, they could hardly be said to have been sufficient to merit the imposition of the death penalty in this particular case, any more than in those of the many other rebels who were similarly involved but who received lesser sentences. Maxwell also reiterated Armstrong's unsubstantiated allegations that O'Hanrahan had been armed and he too made vague reference to the 'casualties amongst British troops' in the area of St Patrick's park.[24] The accused had served at Jacob's which had been uniquely inactive throughout, and may well never personally have been engaged in the fighting at any time during the week.

Towards evening on 3 May, O'Hanrahan was informed that he was to be executed at dawn next morning and was transferred to Kilmainham. During the early hours of 4 May, a police officer delivered an official letter from the prison authorities to his family's home. For some inexplicable reason, it stated: 'Michael O'Hanrahan, a prisoner in Kilmainham, wished to see his mother and sisters before his deportation to England.'[25] It was their first indication of his whereabouts since the surrender, and reassured by the content of the message just two of his sisters left to visit him in the waiting car. They were brought on arrival to a room off the front hall. While waiting, one of them, Eily, describes how they noted 'three young women on their way out, Mrs Tom Clarke and her sisters, who had been to see their brother, Ned Daly. They told us Ned was to be shot at dawn. We were horror struck,' she adds, 'as we realised that the same fate awaited our own brother.' Mrs Clarke later recalled how she tried to prepare them for 'something worse than deportation'.[26] Their worst fears were confirmed by one of the group of soldiers who led them up to O'Hanrahan's cell, number sixty-seven, on the second floor.

On entering, Michael immediately enquired 'if they knew why they had been brought'. He appeared to them to be 'his usual calm and gentle self' and to 'have no fear of death'; his main concern was for his mother and for his brother, Harry, with whom he had lost all contact. Though warned by the soldiers present that they 'must only speak of personal matters', Eily told him, 'Ned Daly is going with you, Michael' and that Pearse, Clarke and MacDonagh 'had gone on the morning of the 3rd'.[27] Before leaving, his sisters confirmed that arrangements had been made for him to see a priest and he made his will, witnessed by two of his gaolers (bequeathing his rights in *A Swordsman of the Brigade*). Soon afterwards, Father Augustine arrived and accompanied him to the execution yard; on his return journey the priest glimpsed Joseph Plunkett who was also being led before the firing squad. He is later reported to have said of O'Hanrahan, 'He was one of the truest and noblest characters that it has ever been my privilege to meet.'[28]

O'Hanrahan was executed on 4 May between 4 and 4:30 a.m. He was interred at Arbour Hill Detention Barracks between the bodies of Ned Daly and William Pearse. In his last hours, he said to Father Augustine, 'Father, I would like you saw my mother and sisters to console them.'[29] Honouring the promise he had then given, the priest set out later that morning to break the news to his mother: on his way he met Eily and one of her sisters going to the Church Street Priory to contact him as they 'could not bring [themselves] to tell her the real truth'. Afterwards, Father Augustine returned to Kilmainham to inform Henry of the execution of his brother; he had been 'put in the same cell from which Michael had been shot'.[30] He had been court-martialled earlier that day, 4 May, and was sentenced to penal servitude for life.[31]

Commenting on the courts martial and the death sentences, an eminent study of the Rising concludes: 'the justification for O'Hanrahan's execution, for one, is unknown to this day'.[32] The release of the official records of the proceedings has shed little further light on this issue. They cast much more perhaps on the comment made in January 1917 by Sir Reginald Brade, when he was arguing strongly against the records being made open to the public. In justification of this, he stated: 'There are one or two cases in which the evidence is very thin.'[33] The trial of Michael O'Hanrahan must surely have been one of those he had in mind. O'Hanrahan was unfortunate to have been tried so soon after the Rising – 3 May. Also, the fact that he was employed full-time by the Irish Volunteers probably led the authorities to assume that he had played a more prominent role in the outbreak than was actually the case. But if, like him, leading Volunteers were going to be executed on such grounds alone, the inevitable result would have been an excessive number of executions. Peadar Kearney, who had served with him during Easter week, commented later: 'Jacob's garrison gave three brave men to freedom's altar, when British vengence glutted itself with Irish blood in Kilmainham, Thomas MacDonagh, Michael O'Hanrahan and Major John MacBride.'[34] Certainly, O'Hanrahan's case was one of those which was likely to raise the suspicion in Irish minds that from the outset 'the authorities intended to execute certain of the Sinn Féiners whether there was evidence against them or not', and that this was the reason why the trials had been held in secret.[35]

Trial of Michael O'Haurehan

prisoner number thirty-six

REFERENCE: PRO WO71/357

DATE: 3 May 1916

LOCATION: Richmond Barracks

JUDGES: Brigadier-General C.G. Blackader (President), Lieutenant
Colonel G. German, Lieutenant Colonel W.J. Kent

CHARGE:

'Did an act to wit did take part in an armed rebellion and in the
waging of war against His Majesty the King, such act being o such
a nature as to be calculated to be prejudical to the Defence to the
Realm and being done with the intention and for the purpose of
assisting the enemy'

PLEA: Not guilty

(The members of the court and witnesses were duly sworn in)

VERDICT: Guilty. Death by being shot

Text of Trial

PROSECUTION

1st witness
Major J. A. Armstrong being duly sworn states

> I was present at St. Patricks Park on April 30. The British
> Troops were fired upon and there were several casualties –
> the fire came from the neighbourhood of Jacobs factory.
> The same day a surrender was arranged. I saw the surrender
> being arranged by Mr MacDonagh. Over 100 men arrived
> from Jacobs factory as a result of the surrender and another
> large body arrived from the same direction as a result of the
> surrender. The accused belonged to one of the parties. He
> was in uniform and armed. After the surrender he was
> removed in custody to Richmond Barracks. He said he was
> an officer.

Cross examined by the accused

All the officers appeared to be armed with pistols or revolvers.

I cannot say whether he was armed or not but all unarmed were placed on a separate list and the accused is not on that list. – the shots which caused the casualties came from the immediate neighbourhood of Jacobs Factory.

The witness withdraws

Persecution closed.

The Accused in his defence makes the following statement

As a soldier of the Republican army acting under the orders of the Provisional Government of that Republic duly constituted I acted under the orders of my superiors.

Statement ends.

IRISH REBELLION, MAY 1916.

EAMONN CEANNT
(Commandant of the South Dublin Area),
Executed May 8th, 1916.
One of the signatories of the "Irish Republic Proclamation."

Eamonn Ceannt

EDMUND KENT.

This man was one of the signatories to the Declaration
of Irish Independence previously adverted to.

He was on the Executive Committee and Central Council
of the Irish Volunteers and attended all their meetings. He was
an extremist in his views and identified himself with all
pro-German movements. He held the rank of Commandant in the rebel
army and was in command at the South Dublin Union in the capture
of which the British troops suffered heavily, losing both officers
and men. He was armed at the time of his surrender.

Extract from a
memorandum entitled
'Short History of
rebels on whom it has
been necessary to
inflict the supreme
penalty' sent by
General Sir John
Maxwell to Herbert
Asquith, on 11 May
1916.

EAMONN CEANNT WAS BORN in Galway in 1881, but brought up and educated in Dublin, where, like Colbert and Heuston, he attended the Christian Brothers' School, North Richmond Street. After leaving there, he found employment as a clerk in the city's Corporation Treasury Department. He was not an especially sociable man. Shortly before his execution he wrote that his 'cold exterior was but a mask': certainly he was regarded as dour and taciturn by contemporaries, some of whom thought him 'hard to get on with' and 'grave and rather expressionless'.[1] In 1900, Ceannt joined the Gaelic League. He was eventually elected to its governing body and he became a teacher of the Irish language. His wedding ceremony in 1905, was conducted in Irish. He became an ardent Irish-Irelander, with a particular passion for music. He mastered the Irish war pipes, playing them before Pope Pius X in October 1911, during the pontiff's jubilee celebrations. In his journey to Rome, he had accompanied a band of Irish athletes who, when his weird shrill tones were completed, burst into wild cheering. Throughout the entire trip, Ceannt insisted on conversing only in Irish.[2]

Sean Fitzgibbon wrote of Ceannt that he 'believed in the logic of the pike' and was 'more naturally a physical force man that any of the other leaders'.[3] Aged sixteen, he enthusiastically participated in Dublin's celebrations commemorating the 1798 rebellion. His republicanism was rooted initially in his cultural nationalism, and confirmed later by contemporary events and by his reading. In 1912, at the beginning of the Third Home Rule crisis, he declared: 'Once the weapon of peace breaks in the hands of the parliamentary leaders there should be no further recourse to it in our time. Force is winning in Ulster, winning a political battle. It is up to the nationalists of Ireland to adopt similar means. It is the duty of all men to be skilled in the use of arms' – he became so himself.[4] He wrote a well-received appreciation of a new edition of John Mitchel's *Jail Journal* – Mitchel had come to advocate an armed insurrection to achieve an Irish republic. In his review, Ceannt stated that the publication would encourage Irish readers to 'drink at the undiluted font of eternal national principles ... it proved [England's] law was a formula for converting Irish patriots into English felons'.[5] Bulmer Hobson, who disagreed profoundly with Ceannt's views, described him as 'a good fellow, very sincere, a very good son of man, but not much grasp of the political situation'.[6]

Ceannt first met Sean MacDermott at an anti-imperialist demonstration in Dublin, and it was the latter who, recognising him as a kindred spirit, swore him into the Irish Republican Brotherhood in 1911. MacDermott also encouraged Ceannt to join the Irish Volunteers from its inception in order to advance the IRB's infiltration of the force. Ceannt found in the IVF his natural milieu and rose rapidly from Captain of A Company, Fourth Battalion to Commandant and then to Director of Communications on its headquarters staff. Predictably, he voted against Redmond's attempt to assert control over its executive in June 1914 and during the following month, he took a prominent part in the Howth gunrunning.

From the outset, Ceannt was personally involved in the planning and preparation for the Rising. On 9 September 1914 he organised a conference, held in the library of the Gaelic League in Dublin and attended by leading republicans, at which it was agreed to prepare for an insurrection and to seek German support. In the period which followed, Ceannt was trusted by the principal architects of the Rising, Clarke and MacDermott; they recognised his zealous commitment to the whole revolutionary enterprise and sensed his absolute loyalty to themselves. Thus, he was part of the small secretive IRB group which began formulating plans in 1914. When this body was formalised (on Clarke's initiative) into a Military Council, in May 1915, Ceannt was one of its three original members. Even he, however, may not have been apprised of all the actions of the revolutionary cell preparing for the Rising. His wife later recalled him telling her, in mid-January 1916, that 'Connolly had disappeared and he [Connolly] had arranged with the Citizen Army that should he ever be missing, the men after three days were to attack Dublin Castle'. Ceannt stated that: 'we [the IVF] must come out with them. I am going to see if Mallin will hold his hand for a few days. I have called the officers of [Fourth] Battalion.' Mrs Ceannt adds: 'It seems extraordinary to me that Eamonn, a member of the IRB and of the Military Council should have been unaware that the IRB were detaining Connolly.'[7]

At its meeting on 17 April 1916, the Military Council approved the draft Proclamation, and Ceannt was one of its signatories. He was outraged when informed early on Easter Sunday, 23 April, that MacNeill had sent out a countermand order. Sean T. O'Kelly, who was present at the time, recalls that he said, 'very fiercely, "some people deserve to be shot and it's possible they might be".'[8] Ceannt hastily arranged for the officers in his battalion to assemble that morning at his home in the Dublin suburb of Dolphin's Barn; they arrived with such frequency that the door had to be left ajar. The same day, he attended a crisis session of the Military Council at Liberty Hall. At the meeting, he supported the majority view that the insurrection should be postponed for twenty-four hours. He then returned home and instructed his officers to await further instructions at their own homes. Later that day, a guest noted that he looked 'tired and strained', was more than usually 'preoccupied' and 'withdrawn', and spent most of the time 'writing industriously'.[9] He was actually composing, and arranging for the dispatch of, mobilisation orders for the Rising next day.

Early on Easter Monday morning, his sister describes seeing him, in uniform, sitting at a table, 'nearby his gun, a splendid Mauser, adding up the units of Volunteers who were answering the call'.[10] Afterwards, he joined the members of his battalion, who were assembling as had been arranged at Emerald Square, Dolphin's Barn. Their primary military objective was the occupation of a poor-house, the South Dublin Union, and close by it, several strategically positioned supporting outposts (Watkins Brewery, Jameson's Distillery and Roe's Distillery). The Union sprawled like a small town over fifty acres and comprised the largest complex of build-ings on the western fringes of the city, south of the river. On a low rise east of it stood the Royal Hospital, residence of the British GOC. Adjacent to the Union was Kingsbridge Railway Station, ter-minus of the Cork line, and to the north, just across the Liffey, lay the Royal Barracks. Given its military and strategic significance, its seizure was certain to provoke a determined military response. In anticipation of this, Ceannt refused to permit Cumann na mBan members to accompany his unit.[11]

As elsewhere, the turnout of Volunteers was disappointing: by 11:30 a.m., a little over one hundred members of the Fourth Battalion had assembled. Nonetheless, they proceeded to occupy their allotted targets virtually unhindered. Ceannt's unit, with the redoubtable Cathal Brugha as second-in-command, entered the Union, front and rear, at approximately twelve noon. Almost imme-diately, they proclaimed their presence by firing on a party of sol-diers marching along James Street and by provocatively unfurling a republican flag from a high window in its west wing; their emblem would have been clearly visible from the GOC's quarters. Their immediate priority was to prepare the Union's defences, which included selecting a headquarters, evacuating buildings, and erecting barricades at gates and doors and along passageways. However, given their small number, it proved impossible to make the complex of buildings secure. It was so stretched and scattered that even internal communication within it could not be satisfactorily maintained: units lost all contact with each other for much of the week. From the outset, the rebels were exposed to sniper fire on virtually every side. Their position was made more vulnerable by virtue of the fact that only one of the three support outposts taken by the rebels (Jameson's Distillery) was held for long.

Already, during Easter Monday, British troops entered the Union's grounds, some simply by scaling the half-mile long wall which identified its perimeter, where it bordered the Grand Canal. At an early stage, Ceannt's unit was surrounded and he was nearly captured. Almost immediately, the uncompromising character of the fighting at the outpost was established: nervous and frightened combatants confronted each other in an unfamiliar labyrinthine battleground with innumerable hiding places and long intersecting corridors. Both sides proceeded with extreme caution, often separated only by a thin stone wall from where the slightest sound was likely to be greeted by a fusillade. Night fighting held especial terrors. Though precautions were taken, casualties among inmates and nursing staff were inevitable. When on Monday evening, Ceannt offered the troops a one-hour truce, so that the dead could be buried and wounded treated, he received the uncompromising response: 'We shall give you no terms. You have killed our major.'[12]

Despite their vulnerability and low turnout, Volunteer morale remained high, sustained by the evident sympathy of local civilians and, above all, by the heroic and inspirational leadership provided by Ceannt and Brugha. Unlike other Military Council members such as Pearse and MacDonagh, Ceannt was by instinct a soldier, a man of action. In the Union he revealed the necessary qualities of energy, resourcefulness, resilience and physical courage to inspire the confidence and win the admiration of his unit. Leading by example, Mauser in hand, he ensured that when the main assault by British troops came, they had to struggle for every yard gained.

Having built-up their reserves, the military launched a co-ordinated attack on Ceannt's base, the Night Nurses' Home, at 3 p.m.

on Thursday, 27 April, with (one rebel estimated) six hundred troops. They moved methodically by sections, attacking first with machine-guns and hand grenades. Later, in the face of fanatical resistance and after Ceannt had dismissed appeals for surrender, they varied their tactics, boring through walls or blowing them up using high explosives. The battle lasted five hours. Its emotional climax came when Brugha, gravely injured and cut off from comrades, could be heard shouting: 'Come on you curs to I get one shot before I die. I am a wounded man. Eamonn Ceannt come here and sing '"God Save Ireland" before I die.' Eventually, Ceannt broke through to save him and found him sitting, propped up against a wall, a revolver to his shoulder, waiting for the enemy to appear. Joseph Doolin described the moment when the two leaders met: 'Both men dropped their revolvers, Ceannt went down on one knee and put his arm around Brugha. The conversation in Irish ... After about a minute, Ceannt rose and a tear fell.'[13] After further desperate rebel resistance, the troops finally withdrew at 8 p.m. They attacked once more briefly on Friday morning, but thereafter, did not return. In total, the garrison at the Union lost six men killed in action during Easter week.

Despite the Union's growing isolation, on Friday Ceannt had been informed that the Rising was not going well elsewhere – 'in the provinces, all was quiet' and the military seemed 'determined to level the city'.[14] When asked if he thought that the British would use artillery, he had replied 'exultantly, slapping his thigh, "the moment they fire the first shell, we win"'.[15] This sketchy knowledge of events outside his garrison area must have cushioned the impact when MacDonagh arrived on Sunday afternoon to tell him of Pearse's surrender order. The leaders conferred briefly, agreed that acceptance was their only option, and Ceannt informed his garrison of the decision. Peadar Doyle, Ceannt's staff orderly, recalls: 'Suggestions were made that all should escape, as there was no military guard. I was one of those to make the case for a complete surrender on the grounds that we had stood together all through the fight and ought to stand together to the end. This was agreed to but, nevertheless, several broke away.'[16] Ceannt was clearly proud of the achievements of his unit. He was overheard observing to a British officer, that 'it would surprise him to see the small number who held the place',[17] and he wrote afterwards of the 'magnificent gallantry and fearless, calm determination of the men'.[18] One of the rebels spoke to one of the soldiers, and he 'admitted that the authorities were of the opinion that there were at least 500 men defending the Union and had they known there were only 50 he said: "none of us would ever have left alive".'[19] When the garrison was led into the street, it was met with 'marked enthusiasm' by local civilians, and along the route was 'greeted with great jubilation particularly in the poorer areas'.[20] Ceannt acidly enquired of some of them, 'Where were you when you were wanted?'; his words were echoed by de Valera in identical circumstances at Boland's Bakery at about the same time.[21]

In fulfilment of arrangements agreed beforehand with General Lowe, the garrison proceeded to Jameson's Distillery. After some initial resistance, the Volunteers at the distillery fell in behind and both units, (numbering about two hundred in all), marched to the agreed surrender point, St Patrick's Park; approximately one hundred and eighty men who had served with MacDonagh at Jacob's Biscuit Factory were already at the park. In preparation for their arrival, a substantial British force had assembled, under the command of Major J.A. Armstrong. A list was then made of those who were unarmed, the names and addresses of all the rebels were taken and their weapons collected. William Wylie later claimed: 'It was I who ... [took Ceannt's] ... name, rank, etc., when he surrendered.'[22] The insurgents were then conducted under escort to Richmond Barracks. Next morning, when they assembled in the gymnasium, Ceannt was one of those identified by DMP detectives as warranting a court martial and asked to stand aside.

Ceannt was tried on 3 and 4 May, (prisoner number thirty-two), Brigadier-General Blackader presiding. Major Armstrong was the only prosecution witness called and mantra-like he proceeded to deliver his litany of mainly circumstantial evidence. As usual, he stated first that he had been present at St Patrick's Park, on 30 April, that the troops had been fired on from the direction of Jacob's, causing casualties, and that he had seen the Jacob's party surrender at around 5 p.m. With regard to Ceannt, Armstrong said vacuously that he had 'surrendered as one of the party [implying, from Jacob's] and was at the head of it', that his name was on a list of armed men and that 'from information he gave he is described as Commandant'. He added, in substantiation, 'I asked him to give orders and he did so, they were obeyed.'[23]

Ceannt was well prepared for his trial. Whilst waiting for it at

Richmond Barracks, he may have been made aware of the weak nature of prosecution evidence in some cases at least, and its heavy reliance on Armstrong's testimony. One Volunteer, P.S. Doyle, recalls that Ceannt 'came to see us early one morning and gave instructions that each of us was to make the best defence possible'.[24] Ceannt's notes relating to his own court martial were later found written on the back of his charge sheet (and were probably made at the end of its first session, on 3 May). They included: '(1) My position – shall not deny anything proven or admit what is not proven. Legal advise necessary. Deny portion of the charge [presumably regarding 'assisting the enemy']. (2) Is Crown case closed? (3) Rebut Major's evidence [Armstrong's] (4) 1. Republic duly established. English were the aggressors. [This last point he did not make in court].'[25] A barrister was in fact 'allowed to advise' him, according to an entry in his brother's diary.[26]

In court, on 3 May, Ceannt cross-examined Armstrong aggressively, attempting to cast doubts on the reliability of the list of armed men made at St Patrick's Park on 30 April, to which Armstrong had referred in his evidence. The major conceded that it had been drawn up after the Volunteers had been disarmed 'by a process of elimination ... and ... recollection' (by which he meant, a list of the rebels who had no arms was made before the battalion had been disarmed and compared with a list of all those known to have surrendered at the park). Armstrong continued to insist, however, that the accused had 'a revolver or automatic pistol which he took out of his pocket and laid on the ground'.[27] It was not possible for the defendant either to know or to expose the real background to the list to which the witness kept referring. Many years later, Wylie recalled: 'As a matter of fact it was ... my notebook, which Jimmy Armstrong produced when he gave evidence of this.' He continues: 'I remember General Blackader asked Armstrong did he take the particulars himself and Armstrong said: "No, but they were taken by a responsible officer."' Wylie concludes: 'I was the officer but, as there was nothing irregular in the proceedings, I said nothing.'[28]

The crown prosecutor also records that Ceannt, 'asked to have witnesses produced and his case was adjourned to see if we could get them. The police, however, failed to find them as ... [he] ... was very vague about their addresses.' He added, 'I do not blame them.'[29] On 3 May, the defendant did, however, call John MacBride (he was at Richmond Barracks waiting to be tried next day) who testified that Ceannt had not been a member of the Jacob's garrison. He attempted also to summon Thomas MacDonagh, who had been Commandant at the factory, but was told he was 'not available' (MacDonagh had been executed at dawn that morning). The court then adjourned to enable Ceannt to contact others. It reconvened at 12:48 p.m. next day, 4 May, and Ceannt then produced two further defence witnesses – Richard Davies and Patrick Emmet Sweeny (both, like MacBride, were being held at the barracks, awaiting court martial). They also confirmed that he had not been at Jacob's and, though pressed by the prosecution, provided no incriminating evidence about Ceannt's role in the Rising.[30]

In his own closely reasoned statement, Ceannt insisted that his witnesses had successfully established that he had not been at Jacob's, that MacDonagh 'would have been able to corroborate' this and therefore that he could not be held responsible for any firing from the area of the factory. He asserted that the evidence suggesting he been armed was 'not conclusive'. He stated: 'I claim at least that there is reasonable doubt and the benefit of the doubt should be given to the accused.' He declared: 'I gave away my automatic pistol.' (This was somewhat disingenuous; Father Augustine, who witnessed the surrender at St Patrick's Park, records that Ceannt, 'gave up his gun and then his belt to an English officer').[31] Ceannt also pointed out that 'the Volunteer uniform, more often than not, does not indicate the rank of the wearer'. Finally, prompted perhaps by his preparatory notes, he denied 'assisting the enemy' and stated that no attempt had been made by the prosecution in court to substantiate this portion of the charge. He did admit, rather ambiguously, that he had surrendered at St Patrick's Park and had come 'at the head of 2 bodies of men, but was only connected with one'.[32]

Twenty years later, Wylie described Ceannt as a 'brave man [who] showed no sign whatever of nervousness before the court. I would say, in fact, that he was the most dignified of any of the accused.' However, he indicated that the manner in which the defendant had conducted his defence may actually have been counter-productive; he states that 'the court got it into their heads that the accused was only playing for time'. Expanding on this, he added – quite erroneously – that Ceannt 'would make no statement himself, they refused to adjourn again and he was executed'.[33] It seems evident now that the three judges were more concerned to expedite their progress through the long list of those to be court-martialled than to reach an accurate verdict as to the guilt or innocence of the accused on the basis of the best evidence available. It is not surprising then that in 1917, Sir Reginald Brade advised the government against making public the court proceedings in Ceannt's case specifically. He stated: '[I do not] think it would be wise if we were to publish the evidence ... and we had to publish the fact that he [the defendant] summoned as one of his witnesses Thomas MacDonagh and we had to state that [quoting from the court record] "Thomas MacDonagh was not available as a witness as he was shot this morning."'[34] In April 1917, solicitors acting for Ceannt's widow (and also the executor of his will), sought the text of the proceedings. They were needed, they claimed, in connection with two life insurance policies. The request was rejected. The grounds given by Army Council were that the application was 'not made on behalf of the person tried,' that the trial had taken place 'in camera,' and that it was claiming privilege from the production of the records 'for reasons of public policy'.[35]

On 6 May, Maxwell confirmed the court's verdict of guilty. In doing so, he relied on information provided by his intelligence sources, rather than any evidence produced by the prosecution during the trial. When justifying his decision, he stated that Ceannt was 'extremist in his views,' identified 'with all pro-German movements,' had signed the Proclamation, had held high office in the Volunteers, was Commandant at the South Dublin Union where British troops suffered heavily and, he alleged, was 'armed at the time of his surrender.'[36] On 7 May, Ceannt was officially informed that he would be shot at dawn next morning: it was as he had anticipated. On 5 May, he had written to his wife: 'Trial closed. I expect the death sentence ... I shall die like a man for Ireland's sake.'[37] He had always considered the fact that 'his name was to the proclamation' would be decisive, though one contemporary newspaper report claimed that he had been sentenced to three years penal servitude.[38] That evening he was transferred to Kilmainham. One of the women held there records being roused 'some time in the night [5 May] by singing outside gate, the strains of "A Nation Once Again" and cheering and great commotion inside. We heard afterwards it was Eamonn Ceannt coming in'; a report which was confirmed when she saw him attending the prison chapel next morning.[39] Ceannt was initially placed in cell eighty-eight, on the top landing of the central compound (where Joseph Plunkett had been held). He was transferred on Sunday, 7 May, to number twenty on the ground floor, nearer the execution yard; the other rebels condemned to death next morning were in adjacent cells.

Ceannt faced his execution with courage and dignity. In his last letter to his wife, he wrote: 'Not wife but widow before these lines reach you. I am here without hope of this world and without fear, calmly awaiting the end ... I die a noble death, for Ireland's freedom ... you will be – you are, the wife of one of the Leaders of the Revolution.'[40] He believed that through the Rising, 'Ireland has shown she is a nation', and in time, would 'honour those who risked all'.[41] In his final hours, he was visited briefly by his family, including his brother, Michael. He did not share Eamonn's political opinions; from the moment the Rising had begun he had regarded it as 'utter madness' and had the feeling that the rebels were 'mere boys ... playing at soldiers'. But he did state emphatically: 'Lord, if we thought they had the least chance, wouldn't we all be in it.' During the week, he had had premonitions of Eamonn's death, given the strength of British forces and their willingness to deploy incendiary bombs – in his words, 'burning out brave fellows when they could not defeat them'. He writes: 'We were all in a terrible state of anxiety', until on Wednesday morning they had read a newspaper report stating that Eamonn had been sentenced to three years penal servitude; as a result their 'hearts bounded with joy'.

When the official summons from Kilmainham was delivered to the family home, Michael knew then that there was no hope. He writes:

> Arrived at the gaol ... admitted, handed up our letter, names registered, lanterns procured and then down the dark corridors into the bowels of his hellish abode ... The keys rattled, the door is opened to find poor Eamonn after rising from a little table lit by one candle, where his correspondence is arranged. Several envelopes are addressed in his fine, clear style. He received us and shook hands quite calmly ... we were allowed 20 minutes. A few minutes before time was up, Ned called us over and we knelt around him for our last chat. He said Father McCarthy [sic] who was with him, hinted that there was hope of a reprieve ... there was something strained in his manner and it was evident from his letter afterwards that he had absolutely no

> hope ... I never saw him look so well. When the sentry said
> kindly that the time was up, we stood up and had a few
> words more ... after we left the cell and before the sentry
> shut the door, I looked back at poor Ned and that picture I
> shall bear with me to the end. He stood sideways, right side
> towards me, the candle showing him up clearly from the
> external darkness, looking down at the little table were he
> had been writing, wrapped in thought, silent ... my heart
> welled up with infinite pity for him. Before the door
> closed, I cried out "God's Blessing with you," to which he
> replied: "May God favour you".[42]

Father Augustine records saying to him, just before he faced the firing squad, 'When you fall, I will run out and anoint you' and his reply: 'Oh, that will be a grand consolation, Father.'[43]

According to Father Augustine's account, Ceannt 'died with forgiveness of his enemies on his lips'.[44] But he did not die without the most profound regrets. In a statement composed on 7 May, he wrote: 'I leave for the guidance of other revolutionaries who may tread the path that I have trod, this advice. Never to treat with the enemy, never to surrender at his mercy, but to fight to a finish. I see nothing gained but grave disaster caused by the surrender, which has marked the end of the Irish insurrection of 1916 ... the enemy has not cherished one generous thought for those who withstood his forces for one glorious week.'[45]

After seeing his brother for the last time, Michael returned home. He writes that it was a

> drab weary drive ... twice as long, as the car broke down ...
> I arrived at 1 a.m. ... I prayed on as I never prayed before,
> bringing down my Sacred Heart statue and altar lamp to
> the dining room. I said five rosaries, as many or more
> litanies and numerous other prayers, keeping a glass of water
> near me to moisten my lips, sometimes kneeling,
> occasionally sitting ... coming on to 4 o'clock, I redoubled
> my prayers and made special appeals to the great object of
> my particular devotion, the Sacred Heart of Jesus. When
> 3:45 passed, I said to myself "Well, I suppose it's all over
> now, and I won't know a thing about it" ... soon afterwards
> I heard clearly the faint click of a rifle. It was faint, but in
> that solemn stillness, perfectly distinct ... I pulled out my

watch ... 7 minutes to 4. I felt I knew then definitely that all
was over with poor Eamonn. I put out the light and as I
went upstairs and into bed I cried bitterly from the depths
of my heart.[46]

However fanciful this account may appear, the official records show
that Eamonn Ceannt was executed between 3:45 and 4:05 a.m. on
8 May 1916.[47]

Trial of E. Ceannt (E. Kent)
prisoner number thirty-two

REFERENCE: PRO WO71/348

DATE: 3–4 May 1916

LOCATION: Richmond Barracks

JUDGES: Brigadier-General C.G. Blackader (President), Lieutenant
Colonel G. German, Lieutenant Colonel W.J. Kent

CHARGE:

'Did an act to wit did take part in an armed rebellion and in the
waging of war against His Majesty the King, such act being o such
a nature as to be calculated to be prejudical to the Defence to the
Realm and being done with the intention and for the purpose of
assisting the enemy'

PLEA: Not guilty

(The members of the court and witnesses were duly sworn in)

VERDICT: Guilty. Death by being shot

Text of Trial

PROSECUTION

1st witness
Major J.A. Armstrong. Enniskillen Fusiliers states:–

> I was at Patricks Park on the 30th April 1916. The British
> troops were fired on, the fire came from the neighbourhood
> of Jacobs Factory. Several casualties occurred. I was under
> fire. I was present about 5 pm when the party from Jacobs
> Factory surrendered.

> I directed an officer to make a list of the unarmed men. The
> accused surrendered as one of the party and was at the head
> of it, his name was not on the unarmed list. There was an
> armed list made and his name appears at the head and from
> information he gave he is described as commandant. I asked
> him to give orders and he did so, they were obeyed.

Cross-examined by the accused.

> A list of all the man on parade was made and that is the list
> of armed men, it does not follow that all men on parade
> were armed men. I have a perfect recollection of the time
> the list was commenced, it was commenced after the men
> were disarmed. I succeeded in making a list of all armed
> men after they had been disarmed because I had had a
> separate list of the unarmed men made before the disarming
> look place. I arrived at list of armed men by a process of
> elimination only, and a recollection of men seen with arms,
> the accused was one of them. He had no rifle; either a
> revolver or automatic pistol, which he took out of his
> pocket, and laid on the ground.

Prosecution closed.

DEFENCE

The accused calls witnesses.

1st witness
John McBride sworn, states.

> I know the accused intimately, I should be in no doubt as
> to his identity, I remember Sunday the 30th April 1916 and
> preceding days, I was in Jacob's factory, I left it on Sunday
> afternoon between 4 and 5 pm. The accused was not in my
> company before I left. It was impossible for the accused to
> be in Jacob's Factory without my knowledge, he had no
> connection with the party that occupied Jacob's Factory.

Cross-examined by the Prosecution

> I saw the accused in the neighbourhood of St Patricks Park
> when my party surrendered. I did not see the accused at
> any time between Easter Monday and Sunday the 30th
> April 1916. I have not the slightest knowledge that he is
> Commandant of the 4th Battalion. I saw him in uniform at
> the time the surrender took place drawn up in line.

The Prisoner calls on Thomas McDonagh who was not available
as he was shot this morning.

The Court adjourns this case for further evidence.

At 12.45 pm on the 4th May 1916 the Court re-opens.

2nd witness

Richard Davys being duly sworn states.

> I was in Jacobs Factory from Monday the 24th April till
> Sunday the 30th The accused was not in Jacobs during any
> part of that time. He was not of the party which
> surrendered from Jacob's Factory. I know the accused
> perfectly well. I don't think accused could have been in
> Jacobs factory or been one of the party surrendering from
> Jacobs Factory without my knowledge. I did not hear
> accused's name mentioned at any time in connection with
> Jacob's Factory.

Cross-examined by Prosecution.

> The Party at Jacobs Factory surrendered about 5pm on
> Sunday the 30th. The surrender took place near Patricks
> Park. When I surrendered accused was at the far corner of
> the same square. I could not say if he was of the same party
> with me that came to Richmond Barracks. I heard shots
> fired from near Jacobs Bakery but could not say who fired.

> I saw a proclamation declaring Ireland a Republic on
> Wednesday 26th April, I did not take any notice of the
> names appended.

3rd Witness

> Patrick [Emmet?] Sweeney being duly worn states.
> I was in Jacobs Factory from Easter Monday to Sunday 30th
> April 1916. I never saw accused in Jacobs factory the whole
> time I was there.

The accused in his defence states.

> Three witnesses who were in Jacob's factory from Monday
> the 24th April 1916 to about 5 pm on Sunday the 30th
> have sworn that I was not in Jacobs Factory during any of
> that period and was not one of a party which surrendered
> from Jacobs Factory on Sunday 30th April. Another witness
> who was not available would have been able to corroborate
> these 3. The evidence makes it quite clear that I cannot
> have had anything to do with the firing from the
> neighbourhood of Jacobs which resulted in casualties to
> British troops at St Patricks Park as referred to. I do not
> accuse Major Armstrong of endeavouring to mislead the
> Court, but it is clear that he was deceived in thinking that I

was attached in any way to the Jacobs party which as deposed fired on British troops in the neighbourhood of Patricks park. He has admitted that his plan of making a list of armed men was by a process of elimination of the unarmed men from the whole list on parade and from recollection. He has admitted that the list of armed men was compiled after all men had been disarmed. I submit that this evidence is not conclusive except insofar as it concerned the unarmed men and is not evidence as to the men who were armed. I claim at least that there is reasonable double and the benefit of the doubt should be given to the accused. In regard to my carrying arms there is no positive or direct evidence except that Major Armstrong believes I carried a revolver or automatic pistol which he says I took from my pocket and laid upon the ground. As to my having surrendered to the military authorities this is sufficiently proved by my presence at Richmond Barracks and is hereby freely admitted. As to the accusation that I did an act "with the intention and for the purpose of assisting the enemy" I content myself with a simple denial. The Crown did not even tender evidence in this regard.

I gave away my automatic pistol. The Volunteer uniform more often than not does not indicate the rank of the wearer.

The witness I intended to call and could not be found from the description I gave to the Police would have proven that I did not come from the neighbourhood of Jacobs factory.

I came at the head of 2 bodies of men but was only connected with one body.

IRISH REBELLION, MAY 1916.

JOSEPH PLUNKETT (son of Count Plunkett),
Commandant-General Irish Republican Army,
Executed May 4th, 1916.
Who was married a few hours before his execution.

Joseph Plunkett

JOSEPH PLUNKETT.

     This man was also a signatory to the Declaration of Irish Independence. He was a member of the Central Council of the Sinn Fein Volunteers and took part in their meetings and parades. His residence was a training ground and arsenal for the rebels.

     This man, being of good education, exercised great influence for evil over the other members.

     He took an active part in the fighting in and around the G.P.O. where the British troops suffered severely. He held the rank of Captain.

JOSEPH PLUNKETT WAS BORN IN DUBLIN in November 1887, the eldest son of seven children. All his life he was plagued by health problems; by the age of thirteen, he had had pleurisy and pneumonia; later, repeated surgery on his neck to remove tubercular glands left him with appalling scars. He looked thin and pale, was short-sighted, and although above average height, he seemed smaller because of a stoop. He was educated by tutors at home, by Jesuits at Belvedere College and Stoneyhurst in England, and at the National University of Ireland. He was precociously intelligent, well-read, with eclectic interests – in philosophy, languages, literature, the sciences, poetry and later military strategy. He was also an accomplished skater and dancer, enjoyed food and wine, and was witty and convivial company. Partly because of ill-health, he had travelled extensively since his youth, living abroad for long periods. He inherited some of these traits from his father. George Plunkett was a Papal Count (from 1884) who was descended from the seventeenth century martyr, Oliver Plunkett. He had been called to the Irish Bar, became Director of the National Museum and lived 'like an 18th century gentleman of means' at Larkfield House, an estate in the Dublin suburb of Kimmage.[1]

Plunkett was devoutly catholic and a romantic nationalist becoming, like Pearse and MacDonagh, publicly committed to an insurrection to achieve independence. The influence of his family background was 'for revolution' (two of his brothers were also involved in the Rising).[2] The family was intensely catholic, keenly interested in Ireland's culture and language, and ardently nationalist. Though his father had supported the moderate Home Rule movement, he was later involved in Sinn Féin and in 1916, took an active part in the preparations for insurrection. The development of Joseph's own political ideas may well be related to his decision to learn Irish for matriculation – as a result he became a Gaelic enthusiast. Thomas MacDonagh was chosen as his teacher, became his inseparable friend and may have influenced the development of his political views; it was he who arranged for the publication of Plunkett's first volume of poetry, *The Circle and the Sword,* in 1911.

Plunkett had greater natural literary talent than either MacDonagh or Pearse, and drew much of his inspiration from the mystics, especially St John of the Cross, rather than from Irish sources. However, he blended mysticism and nationalism. His poems were obsessed with sacrifice, but whilst Pearse emphasised the solitary sacrificial gesture – the individual dying publicly for his people – Plunkett's vision was dramatic and epic, setting the sacrificial figure against a cosmic background. His romantic morality sanctioned not only the sacrifice of himself but also of others in pursuit of self-realisation; he has been described as being 'as hard as nails ... prepared to die for his beliefs and see others die for them'.[3] Plunkett was dying of consumption in any case, and he sought a more heroic end. He had ambitions to be cast in a significant and historic role as a consequence of which Irish nationalism would be revived. The development of his ideas is reflected in the content of the *Irish Review*, a weekly literary journal he edited from mid-1913. It became increasingly militant and was thus suppressed in November 1914.

Plunkett joined the Irish Volunteer Force at its foundation, and was elected to its Provisional Committee. Though he voted for Redmond being permitted to appoint half the members of the committee in June 1914, he strongly opposed his appeal in September that IVF members join crown forces. The *Irish Review* carried a manifesto which argued that the purpose of the force was to secure Ireland's rights and liberties, not to serve England and her empire. He welcomed the resulting Volunteer split, remained in the IVF and became its Director of Military Operations. Despite his lifetime obsession with secrecy, his involvement with the force in time attracted the attention of DMP detectives. He had earlier (mid-1914) joined the IRB, rising to membership of the Supreme Council.

From the outset of the First World War, Plunkett favoured and was involved in preparations for a rising. He was appointed a member of the IRB Military Council at its formation in May 1915, and there collaborated closely with Pearse and Ceannt in developing plans. He was its most effective, valued and dominant figure, as he was a formidable and knowledgeable military strategist and tactician. His fascination with such matters had grown as his political opinions had become more extreme. Thus, in April 1915, he was sent to Germany by the IRB revolutionary cell in order to convince the authorities there of the IRB's commitment to revolution, and to establish what support Germany was prepared to provide. His constant need to convalesce provided an ideal cover for European travel. The trip also enabled him to indulge his theatrical nature; he assumed various aliases, grew a moustache and beard, destroyed all previous photographs of himself and travelled by a circuitous route. Perversely, he kept a diary which in the wrong hands, 'would have been a virtual death warrant'.[4]

In Berlin, Plunkett collaborated with Casement (who referred to him as an 'invalid') in submitting to the General Staff a thirty-one-page memorandum, the *Ireland Report*, in June 1915.[5] The report gives a clear indication of the scale of the military operations Plunkett and his comrades were envisaging and went far beyond the levels associated with notions of a blood sacrifice. The report contained a request for a twelve-thousand-strong German expeditionary force to land at Limerick, with forty thousand rifles. This, it was hoped, would incite a popular rising in the west to coincide with the insurrection in Dublin. The objective was the destruction of Britain's military and political power in Ireland; in the process, it was suggested that Britain's resources would be so stretched as to transform the European war to Germany's advantage. It was a comprehensive and daring plan, complemented by incisive military argument and analysis aimed at convincing sceptics of its overall feasibility. It helps explain why Plunkett's expertise was held in such high esteem by his colleagues. Though the German response was cautious, Plunkett was rightly convinced that support would be forthcoming if the Military Council could prove that its military undertaking was a serious enterprise, to which it was genuinely committed. His subsequent report – he returned in June – provided its members with every incentive to pursue their preparations with renewed vigour. Shortly afterwards he travelled to the United States to consult with and update the Clan na Gael leadership.[6]

Plunkett and his family were actively involved in the final preparations before Easter week. In March, his sister Philomena was sent to New York by the Military Council to inform Clan leaders that the date of the Rising had been deferred until 23 April, from the 21, and consequently that the German arms shipment should not arrive before the amended date. In early April, Count Plunkett, whilst in Berne en route for an audience with the Pope, made contact with the German authorities on behalf of the insurgents to press on them the necessity of sending officers and a submarine as well as arms to Ireland. By then Larkfield House was itself more akin to a fort. Arms production – hand grenades, cartridges, and so on – was in full progress. Also, from February, a derelict flour mill on the estate, hitherto used for training by Dublin Volunteers, was being utilised as a camp by the 'Kimmage garrison'. This had between sixty and seventy members and was composed mainly of Irishmen, either fleeing from conscription in Britain or on the run in Ireland itself. Plunkett asked one of them, Michael Collins, to act as his aide-de-camp in Easter week.[7]

Despite his failing health, Plunkett remained actively involved in the preparations for the Rising. He participated in the Military Council's discussions with Connolly, which took place between 19 and 22 January, 1916, commenting afterwards that he had 'never talked so much in his life'.[8] Consumed by the need for secrecy, he disclosed little to rank and file Volunteers. He assured them: 'We have done nothing and intend to do nothing without the approval of Eoin MacNeill'.[9] He downplayed the significance of his visit to Germany, depicting it as a chastening experience, owing to the General Staff's entrenched indifference to events in Ireland. He therefore felt acutely uneasy about the speeches made by Pearse in which he sought psychologically to prepare the Volunteers for action, fearing that his comments might arouse the suspicions of the British authorities.

Plunkett's most decisive intervention lay in his authorship and circulation, with Military Council approval (17 April), of the 'Castle Document' (it was read out at a meeting of Dublin Corporation two days later so guaranteeing extensive press coverage). It purported to be a secret Dublin Castle memorandum, written in code, containing details of imminent British repressive measures directed against the Irish and National Volunteers amongst others, including mass arrests and the occupation of strategic locations. Though the government immediately condemned it as a forgery, its effect, as intended, was to electrify the political atmosphere in Dublin. It was calculated to induce all Volunteers, both National and Irish, to join in the Rising. It was also a convenient smokescreen behind which the Military Council's final preparations could be completed. Moreover, had the authorities been considering action they would have had good reason to pause, as the element of surprise would have been entirely lost. Initially, MacNeill himself was completely hoodwinked; the forgery was a key factor in causing him briefly to support an insurrection; Plunkett even suggested to him that he sign the Proclamation. The suspicions of Colm O'Lochlainn, who printed the document, were raised at the outset when Plunkett 'told [him] things to leave out'.[10]

Plunkett received word of MacNeill's countermand order early on Easter Sunday morning, 23 April. At 9 a.m. that day, he assembled with the other Military Council members for a four-hour emergency session, and concurred with the majority view that the Rising be postponed until Easter Monday. It was probably just afterwards that he made out his will – in anticipation of his death as a signatory of the Proclamation. It read: 'I give and bequeath everything of which I am possessed to Grace Evelyn (Mary Vandeleur) Gifford.'[11] It may well be that he ought to have been marrying Grace that Sunday. They had become engaged in December 1915 after he had written to her: 'Will you marry me and nobody else? I have been a d....d fool and blind imbecile, but that thank God I see I love you'; they were engaged that same day, 2 December.[12] Though she had been a protestant – the daughter of a well-known Dublin unionist, a solicitor – they both shared an intense interest in catholicism, which had resulted in a breach with her parents. Reflecting back on this period, Grace writes: 'We practically talked of nothing else ... [It was] ... how we got to know each other.' She recalled that Thomas MacDonagh was 'rather irreligious', and how she frequently 'stood listening to their [MacDonagh and Plunkett's] arguments'.[13] On 7 April 1916, she was baptised into the catholic faith in a ceremony held at University Church, St Stephen's Green.[14] When she suggested an Easter wedding, Plunkett had warned: 'We may be running a revolution then'.[15] But later he had himself suggested Easter Sunday so that they could go into the Rising together, and possibly also because one of Grace's sisters was marrying that day. Grace claimed later that the wedding did not take place because a friend bungled the arrangements and the priest did not read out the banns. But according to another of her sisters: 'MacNeill's orders countermanded not only the Rising but also the wedding, for Joe was so involved in Military Council affairs that morning that he had time for nothing else.' She adds: 'Grace and he agreed that if he were arrested she would marry him in prison.' This account is confirmed by a letter written by Plunkett to Grace at the time of the surrender (noon, 29 April), which stated: 'I did everything I could to arrange for us to meet and get married but ... it was impossible.'[16] His enthusiasm for marriage partly stemmed from his anxiety to ensure that Grace should inherit his property after his death; he was aware that she had been forced to leave her parents' home.

On the eve of the Rising Plunkett was acutely unwell. Weeks

earlier, probably in early April, he had had an operation to remove
tubercular glands in his throat; he left a nursing home in Mountjoy
Square on Good Friday or Holy Saturday. He told one of the rebels
during Easter week: 'The doctor gave me six months to live.'[17] For
one or two nights just before the insurrection, he stayed in an apart-
ment in the Metropole Hotel, close by the GPO. Grace called to see
him there early on Saturday evening. She describes his mood as
relaxed and carefree, though in appearance, he looked acutely ill; she
notes that he was always 'reckless'[18] with his health. On Easter
Monday morning, Michael Collins helped him to get dressed in his
Volunteer uniform, with its captain's badges on its sleeve and high
stiff tunic collar; it did not conceal his neck which was swathed in
bandages. He was then driven the short distance to Liberty Hall.
When Joe Good arrived there he immediately (and rather dramatically) noticed Plunkett 'beautifully dressed with riding boots and
spurs, standing in the roadway going over a plan with a number of
our officers around him. Tall, aristocratic, with pince-nez glasses and
clever-looking face, he was the picture of a traditional staff officer ...
Some wit beside me said "Ludendorff", and I replied: "Dressed to
death".'[19] As Plunkett joined the headquarters garrison behind
Connolly to march to the GPO, he extracted his sword and, in a dramatic gesture, threw away the sheath.

Accounts which depict him lying helpless and ineffectual
throughout the week which followed, do less than justice to his role.
There are enough sightings of him at the GPO, animated and in
good spirits, to confirm that he enjoyed periods of remission. He
had full possession of his faculties, certainly at times he continued to
display qualities of leadership and decisiveness, and he undoubtedly
acted throughout as an inspiration to his colleagues. On Easter
Monday, he was clearly unwell but in excellent heart. Desmond
Fitzgerald, who felt 'great pity' for him, writes that shortly after they
had occupied the post office 'Plunkett looked appallingly ill, but at
the same time very cheerful ... Though he looked like a dying man,
he seemed to be supremely happy.'[20] Good noticed that he was still
'examining maps and dispatches ... smiling a lot, with occasional
laughter'.[21] Likewise, Dick Humphries recalls seeing him and The
O'Rahilly, 'come in from his tour of the defences. The former as
usual relating some joke at which both laughed heartily.'[22]

It is also evident that Plunkett was capable of following orders and
giving his own. When on Tuesday, Lawrence's toy shop, (Sackville

Street) with its stock of fireworks was set ablaze by looters, Connolly ordered him and Diarmuid Lynch to take over a squad of Volunteers and extinguish the flames. Lynch recalls: 'We had to resort to pistol fire over the heads of the crowd to force them back and enable the firemen to work'; ultimately their best efforts proved futile.[23] Plunkett also had some responsibility for the various outposts seized by the rebels in the post office area. Volunteer Cormac Turner, whose unit occupied the jewellers Hopkins and Hopkins at O'Connell Bridge on Easter Monday, relates how Plunkett was the officer he routinely dealt with at headquarters. It was he who arranged for Turner's men to be provided with food, tunnelling equipment and bombs, and who on Wednesday, after British shelling had begun, gave him orders regarding the disposition of his men.[24]

Like Pearse, Plunkett spent part of the week writing; he had an office close to Pearse's in the wing of the post office which fronted Sackville Street. As on his trip to Germany in 1915, he kept a diary throughout the week in a Field Message Book; some of its pages bear the circle and sword symbol, similar to a Celtic cross, which he used in his literary work. Though little of it survives and it is far from being entirely accurate – especially regarding events outside his garrison's command – it gives some impression of the Rising. It begins, 'Easter Monday, 1916. The GPO occupied in the Name of the Republic shortly after noon (about 12:15). Republic declared.' It then provides a brief chronological summary of the fighting in Sackville Street (detailing Connolly's injuries, etc) and elsewhere in the city and the provinces. An entry for Wednesday, 26 April, day three of the Republic, reads: 'News from Navan says 200 IRA moving on Dublin'.[25] It concludes with extracts from documents relating to the garrison's surrender.

The diary offers no insights into Plunkett's own innermost thoughts, but he disclosed some of these to Desmond Fitzgerald who spoke to him frequently in Easter week. Fitzgerald records that, unlike Pearse whose conversation constantly returned to consideration of the moral rectitude of their actions, Plunkett was happy to expound on other matters, particularly his views on literature and on various authors. It is clear that when they discussed the Rising, Plunkett was far from optimistic regarding the outcome. According to Fitzgerald, he stated on Easter Monday that it was, 'only a matter of hours until we should be dead, and I am sure,' Fitzgerald adds, 'they both [Pearse as well] shared this conviction.'[26] In the event of their being captured, both leaders considered that hanging was a possible means of execution. From their comments at the GPO it is also clear that they were prepared to compromise on the republican ideal. They were willing to accept the possibility that a German prince could be installed as the king of an independent Ireland if Germany won the war, even nominating Prince Joachim as a potential candidate. Their view was that the German leadership would support policies of de-Angicization, promote nationalist elements in Ireland and favour its independence as a means of making Britain strategically more vulnerable. Ernest Blythe states that Plunkett and MacDonagh had put forward a similar proposal at Volunteer headquarters in January 1915.

By Tuesday, 25 April, the balance of military advantage was already shifting decisively in favour of crown forces as, despite rumours to the contrary, the country failed to rise and military reinforcements began streaming into Dublin. As the week progressed, however, Plunkett appears if anything to have become more animated. Though he was reputedly seen reading Erasmus' *In Praise of Folly* as shells began exploding around the GPO, he certainly seems to have been exhilarated by the sight of the raging conflagration which steadily engulfed the eastern side of Lower Sackville Street on Thursday evening.[27] He exuberantly observed to a fellow officer: 'It is the first time that this has happened since Moscow. The first time a capital city has burned since 1812.'[28] Desmond Ryan recalls that 'during the worst stages of the shelling, no one was more assiduous in keeping up the spirit of the defenders [than Plunkett]. He walked past a long line of men in the front windows smiling carelessly, his sabre and pistol dancing merrily.'[29]

Joe Good broadly confirms Ryan's account. Reflecting on the period before the rebel evacuation of the GPO, he writes:

> As time dragged on, our morale would have begun to weaken, I'm sure, if it hadn't been for Joseph Plunkett. Pearse seemed to have shot his bolt. Connolly was gravely wounded, out of action and out of sight ... but Joe moved amongst us all the time, his eloquent comforting words at odds with his bizarre, eccentric appearance, his dangling sabre and jewelled fingers. We all somehow, and in many different ways responded to his gentle sayings and praise. He was greatly loved. Most of us knew that he had risen from his deathbed

to lead us ... [His] high collar didn't any longer hide that bandaged throat.[30]

Plunkett's elation suggests that the final Wagnerian scenes at the post office resonated with his own private, apocalyptic vision of sacrifice and martyrdom.

Almost certainly, early on Friday morning, 28 April, the five members of the provisional government at the GPO met and agreed to evacuate the building, should British troops begin shelling it with explosives or bombarding it with incendiaries. That evening, Plunkett helped in rallying the men as they dashed from their headquarters amidst a hail of machine-gun, rifle and artillery fire. One rebel recalls him 'ordering a van to be dragged across one of the lanes down which the machine-guns rattled, a feeble enough screen but it served its turn'.[31] That night he, along with most of the other leaders, slept in a single room in a house in Moore Street. At around midday on Saturday 29 April, all of them assembled for a council of war at number 16. From Good's testimony, Plunkett appears to have been content with the majority vote that they negotiate terms. This is suggested also by the tone of a letter he wrote, probably just afterwards, to his fiancée, Grace Gifford. It is headed '6th day of the Irish Republic, 29 April 1916. About noon. Somewhere in Moore Street', and appears to have been his first attempt to establish contact with her since the outbreak of the Rising. He began by expressing his devotion to her, and then stated that apart from his failure to 'meet [her] and get married', he had 'no regrets ... My other actions have been as right as I could see and make them.' The letter's closing sentiments suggest that at the time Plunkett felt little or no hope that he would survive for long after the surrender. He wrote: 'Love me always as I love you. For the rest all you do will please me. I told a few people that I wish you to have everything that belongs to me. That is my last wish so please see to it.'[32] He entrusted delivery of the letter to Winifred Carney, Connolly's loyal secretary and colleague in the ITGWU, in the erroneous expectation that she would not be imprisoned; she gave it to Grace after her release from prison in December 1916. A further insight into Plunkett's views is provided by a conversation he had with Jim Ryan, after Pearse had left the garrison at Moore Street to meet Brigadier-General Lowe. Ryan recalls probing him as to what surrender terms he was expecting to be agreed. His reply – similar to that given by other rebel leaders in answer to the same question – was that the signatories of the Proclamation would be executed, and the rest set free.[33]

When news reached the garrison in Moore Street that Pearse and Connolly had agreed to unconditional surrender, Plunkett was one of four leaders who attempted to persuade those who were opposed, to accept the decision. He met with little success. Good recalls: 'Even poor Joe ... already at the point of death, dragging himself to us and pleading with that austere, stoic passion could not move us.' It was Sean MacDermott's intervention which proved to be decisive. Following the instructions received from Lowe regarding surrender procedure, the men filtered out of the houses they had been taking shelter in. One of them recalls how Plunkett at that moment, 'stood in the middle of Moore Street holding a white flag, his back turned to the enemy ... his attitude looked scornful. For him, the enemy did not appear to exist.'[34] As they marched to Sackville Street, Plunkett caught the attention of military observers. His prominent position in the column suggested that he was one of the leaders. His appearance must have seemed striking and eccentric – the gaunt sickly features, the swathe of bandages around his throat, the sword and pistol by his side; the spurs he had worn on Easter Monday had disappeared – lost in the course of the week's fighting.

Julia Grenan later recalled the garrison spending that Saturday under armed guard on the grass forecourt at the Rotunda Hospital. She described how Plunkett 'suffered intensely from the cold ... [and] ... Miss Carney spread over her own coat and Commandant Connolly's coat ... on the ground and insisted on Sean MacDermott and Joe Plunkett having a little warmth and rest.' She adds that, next morning, by the time the rebels had completed the march to Richmond Barracks, he was at the point of exhaustion. 'We saw him carried in through the prison gates' she claims.[35] Other accounts give different versions of the incident, but confirm that he looked extremely ill; so much so that, under instruction from MacDermott, Liam O'Briain gave him a quilt he had carried with him since his garrison had surrendered at the College of Surgeons.

Plunkett was held at Richmond Barracks until 3 May. Shortly after his arrival, he was one of those identified by DMP detectives in the gymnasium and asked to stand aside, with the other suspected leaders, for court martial later; so too were both of his brothers, George and Jack. At 6:25 p.m. on Sunday evening, he wrote a short note to his family, confirming that all three of them were 'well and happy, but detained'.[36] Two days later, he wrote again to Grace, his letter written on the back of the page on which he had recorded his will on Easter Sunday and which he had clearly kept with him all week. It was surprisingly optimistic in tone. He stated: 'I have no notion what they intend to do with me, but I have heard a rumour that I am to be sent to England. The only thing I care about is that I am not with you, everything else is cheerful.' He concluded, 'We have not had one word of news from outside since Monday 24 April, except wild rumour. Listen, if I live, it might be possible to get the church to marry us by proxy – there is such a thing but it is very difficult. Father Sherwin might be able to do it ... I am very happy.'[37] He gave the letter to a British soldier who had it delivered to Grace's home in Rathmines.

On 2 May Father Augustine, who was visiting the barracks, noticed Plunkett. He was sitting in the sun on a grassy plot with several other Volunteers, opposite a large building, 'awaiting his turn for court martial'. He commented: 'My heart went out to him, but I did not then know I was to see him so soon again.'[38] The next day, 3 May, was the most traumatic in Plunkett's short life; in the course of it, he was tried (prisoner number thirty-three), sentenced to death, the verdict confirmed, and that evening he was married.

Brigadier Maconchy presided at Plunkett's court martial (he also heard William Pearse's case that same day). The prosecution called three witnesses. The evidence they provided was thin, largely circumstantial, and in one instance, factually inaccurate. Two of the witnesses were soldiers who said that they had noticed Plunkett when the GPO garrison had surrendered in Sackville Street on 29 April. Major Holmes, Royal Irish Regiment, identified him as 'one of the leaders' and stated that 'he was dressed in the green uniform he is now wearing, with a Captain's badges of rank on his sleeves'. He also noted that 'the party at the head of which he surrendered was armed', and that 'the Sin Feiners in the Post Office had been firing on the troops for several days and had killed and wounded a number of soldiers'. In his very brief statement Lieutenant Colonel Hodgkin, Sherwood Foresters, merely added that Plunkett, 'when he surrendered ... [was] ... wearing a sword and pistol'.[39]

The other prosecution witness was a DMP sergeant, John Bruton, who was called to provide evidence relating to Plunkett's previous revolutionary activities. He claimed to 'know the prisoner'. He testified that he had 'seen him on two occasions entering and leaving no. 2 Dawson Street [Irish Volunteer headquarters], dressed as well as I could see in the uniform of the Irish Volunteers on at least one occasion.' He concluded by observing that 'his name appears on the Proclamation issued by the Irish Volunteers and I believe him to be a member of the Executive Council of that body.' When he had finished, Plunkett cross-examined him; he had not challenged the evidence given by either of the soldiers. He asked Bruton: 'How do you know the Proclamation was issued by the Irish Volunteers?' The sergeant replied: 'I know that the names of the men which appear at the foot of ... [it] ... are connected with the Irish Volunteers. They include P.H. Pearse, Edmund Kent, Thomas Macdonagh, John McDermot, who are members of the Council of the Irish Volunteers and who constantly attended meetings at No. 2 Dawson Street.'[40]

When the prosecution case had been completed and Plunkett was asked to address the court, he confined himself to addressing the obvious factual errors contained in the police officer's statement. He observed: 'I have nothing to say in my defence but desire to state that the Proclamation referred to in Sergt. Brutons evidence is signed by persons who are not connected with the Irish Volunteers and the proclamation was not issued by the Irish Volunteers.'[41] During a trial held on the previous day, 2 May, William Wylie, the prosecution counsel, had advised the presiding judge that the Proclamation could not be adduced as evidence 'unless I could get the original and prove the accused's signature to it'.[42] Plunkett's was the only case in which the document was given such prominence by the Crown, but he did not challenge the legitimacy of using it, or claim either that he had not signed it.

Twenty-two rebels were tried by court martial on 3 May, and of these, twenty were given death sentences by the court. In four cases, Maxwell confirmed this verdict, and Plunkett was one of them (the others were William Pearse, O'Hanrahan and Daly). The GOC later summarised the reasons for his decision; in doing so, as in the other instances, he relied much more heavily on his intelligence sources at Dublin Castle than on the sparse evidence that had been actually produced by the prosecution. He stated that Plunkett had been a 'signatory to the Declaration of Irish Independence ... [an active] ... member of the Central Council of the Sinn Fein Volunteers,' had 'held the rank of Captain' and had taken 'an active part in the fighting in and around the GPO where British troops suffered severely.'

He also added that 'this man, being of good education, exercised great influence for evil over the other members,' and that 'his residence was a training ground and arsenal for the rebels'.[43] His comments were broadly accurate; only his assessment of Plunkett's role in the fighting is really open to challenge. Later on 3 May, the prisoner was informed of the court's verdict, of Maxwell's confirmation of his sentence, and that he was to be executed at dawn next morning. The outcome can have come as no great surprise to him. Early that evening he was escorted to Kilmainham.

When Grace Gifford had heard of the first three rebel executions (they had taken place at dawn on 3 May and included her brother-in-law Thomas MacDonagh), she had a premonition that Joseph would share a similar fate. She hurriedly acquired the requisite marriage papers from a priest, bought a wedding ring at a jeweller's in Grafton Street at 5 p.m. just before closing, and proceeded quickly to Kilmainham. There, she was eventually taken to the prison chapel and placed in front of the altar. At 8 p.m. Plunkett arrived, escorted by armed troops; he seemed to Grace to be calm and composed. When his handcuffs had been removed, the prison chaplain Father Eugene McCarthy conducted the ceremony by candlelight, the city's gas supplies having been disrupted by the Rising. Two of the soldiers present acted as witnesses. After the service had ended, the bride and groom were not permitted any private conversation; Plunkett's handcuffs were replaced and he was ushered back to his cell. Two days later, the *Irish Times* carried a marriage notice 'Plunkett and Gifford – May 3 1916, at Dublin, Joseph Plunkett to Grace Gifford'.[44]

After the ceremony, Father McCarthy found Grace lodgings for the night a short distance from the gaol. She had been there roughly four hours when an official letter was delivered to her from Major W.S. Lennon, Commandant at Kilmainham. It stated: 'I beg to inform you that your husband is a prisoner in the above prison and wishes to see you tonight. I am sending a car to bring you here.'[45] She saw her husband in his cell – number eighty-eight, on the top landing of the central compound – briefly and for the last time that evening. Even before the armed guard, who was standing by with a watch, told them 'ten minutes', her conversation had dried up. She later drew an artistic impression of their final meeting together. Several of the Capuchin priests from Church Street also saw Plunkett during his final hours. Father Augustine confirmed the account given by the prisoner's wife that he seemed cool, calm and self-possessed; he caught a last glimpse of him while he was escorting Michael O'Hanrahan to the execution yard. Father Sebastian later recorded that while he was waiting to face the firing squad, Plunkett had said, 'Father I am very happy. I am dying for the glory of God and the honour of Ireland.'[46] He is also reported as having spoken in similar terms to Father Albert.

Joseph Plunkett was shot between 4 and 4:30 a.m. on Thursday, 4 May, and was afterwards buried at Arbour Hill Detention Barracks; he was the youngest of the rebels to be executed. Diarmuid Lynch, who was being held at Kilmainham prior to deportation, heard the volleys. He recalls that he at once 'felt certain' that it was Plunkett, because on Wednesday he had spoken to him briefly when they were allowed some brief exercise – 'He had been court-martialled earlier in the day but received no verdict.'[47] Plunkett's cell was later occupied for a time by Eamon Ceannt; a partially indecipherable inscription written in pencil on a wooden panel on the wall of number eighty-eight read, 'This is Joseph Plunkett's cell ... [signed] Grace Plunkett.'[48] Both of Plunkett's brothers, George and Jack were court-martialled on 4 May; they also received death sentences, but these were commuted by Maxwell to ten years penal servitude.[49]

Trial of Joseph Plunkett

prisoner number thirty-three

REFERENCE: PRO WO71/349

DATE: 3 May 1916

LOCATION: Richmond Barracks

JUDGES: Colonel E.W.S.K. Maconchy (President), Lieutenant
      Colonel A.M. Bent, Major F.W. Woodward

CHARGE:

'Did an act to wit did take part in an armed rebellion and in the
waging of war against His Majesty the King, such act being o such
a nature as to be calculated to be prejudical to the Defence to the
Realm and being done with the intention and for the purpose of
assisting the enemy'

PLEA: Not guilty

(The members of the court and witnesses were duly sworn in)

VERDICT: Guilty. Death.

Text of Trial

PROSECUTION

1st witness
Major Philip Holmes 5th Batn (attached 3rd Batn) R. Irish Regt.
states after being duly sworn:–

> I identify the prisoner as a man who was one of the leaders
> of a large company of Sin feiners who surrendered on the
> evening of the 29th April. They surrendered at the northern
> end of Sackville Street in the area to which the Sin Feiners
> who had been in the Post Office for several days had retired
> when the Post office was burnt. The Sin Feiners in the Post
> Office had been firing on the troops for several days and had
> killed and wounded a number of soldiers. He was dressed in
> the green uniform he is now wearing with a Captain's
> badges of rank on his sleeves when he surrendered.

The party at the head of which he surrendered was armed.

2nd witness

Sergeant John Bruton, Dublin Metropolitan Police states

I know the prisoner Joseph Plunkett. The Head Quarters of the Irish Volunteer movement – are at No. 2 Dawson Street.

I have seen him on two occasions entering and leaving No. 2 Dawson Street dressed, as well as I could see, in the uniform of the Irish Volunteers on at least one occasion.

His name appears on the Proclamation issued by the Irish Volunteers and I believe him to be a member of the Executive Council of that body.

Cross examined by the Prisoner.

How do you know the proclamation was issued by the Irish Volunteers.

Answer.

I know that the names of the men which appear at the foot of the Proclamation are connected with the Irish Volunteers.
They include P.H. Pearse, Edmund Kent, Thomas Macdonagh, John McDermot, who are members of the Council of the Irish Volunteers and who constantly attended meetings at No. 2 Dawson St.

3rd Witness

Lt. Colonel H.S. Hodgkin D.S.O. 6th Batn Sherwood Foresters states:–

I saw the prisoner when he surrendered on the 29th April. He was wearing a sword and pistol.

DEFENCE:

The prisoner in this Defence states.

I have nothing to say in my defence but desire to state that the proclamation referred to in Sergt. Brutons evidence is signed by persons who are not connected with the Irish Volunteers and the Proclamation was not issued by the Irish Volunteers.

IRISH REBELLION, MAY 1916.

MAJOR JOHN McBRIDE
(Born in Westport, May 7th, 1868).
Executed in Kilmainham Prison, May 5th, 1916.

John MacBride

JOHN McBRIDE.

This man fought on the side of the Boers in the South African war of 1899 and held the rank of Major in that Army, being in command of a body known as the Irish Brigade. He was always one of the most active advocates of the anti-enlistment propoganda and the Irish Volunteer movement. He was appointed to the rank of Commandant in the rebel army, and papers were found in his possession showing that he was in close touch with the other rebel leaders and was issuing and receiving despatches from rebels in various parts of the city.

He voluntarily stated at his trial that he had been appointed second in command of portion of the rebel forces and considered it his duty to accept that position. He was accompanied by over 100 men at the time no surrendered.

He had great influence over the younger men in the associations with which he was connected.

Extract from a memorandum entitled 'Short History of rebels on whom it has been necessary to inflict the supreme penalty' sent by General Sir John Maxwell to Herbert Asquith, on 11 May 1916.

BODLEIAN LIBRARY, UNIVERSITY OF OXFORD

John MacBride was born in Westport, County Mayo, on 8 May 1865, into a middle-class merchant family and was the youngest of five sons. In unpublished memoirs, he described being educated at the local Christian Brothers' School and at St Malachy's College, Belfast. MacBride claimed to have inherited his physical force republicanism: his father and uncles had been active in the IRB and involved in the 1867 Fenian Rising and he had a great grand-parent who was in the 1798 rebellion. A militant speech delivered by Parnell at the height of the Land League agitation in Mayo may also have inspired him. Certainly in autobiographical notes, MacBride recalls as a young man taking a private oath, 'to establish a free and independent Irish nation'. It was while working briefly as a draper's apprentice in County Roscommon, and then at a whole-sale druggist's in Dublin, that he first became active in the IRB; he attended the movement's convention in 1895 as a district repre-sentative.[1]

In the late 1890s, he left Ireland for South Africa, hoping to make his fortune in the gold mines there. It was to prove a fateful step which propelled him ultimately to a pinnacle of popularity in Ireland. While employed as an assayer, he was drawn into the region's politics. Some Irish workers had fought on the British side during the Jameson Raid; though devoid of military experience and training, he decided to form an Irish Brigade – a title justified nei-ther by its numbers nor its composition. His intention was to ensure that, should the occasion arise again, there would be some Irishmen ready to fight 'the hereditary enemy, the oppressor of our race', at a time when 'they could not unfortunately do so at home'.[2] He was elected a Major, receiving his commission from Paul Kruger, in October 1899. From all accounts, he led his unit well and he fought bravely against British forces in the second Boer War, employing aggressive guerrilla tactics and earning a reputation for recklessness and daring. His actions won him the gratitude of the Boer leader-ship and a national reputation in Ireland, where MacBride Clubs were formed. Arguably, he helped inspire 'the modern physical force movement'.[3]

Unable to return home for fear of arrest, MacBride sought employment in Paris and there first met Maud Gonne. Initially, their relationship and subsequent marriage further enhanced his celebrity status; she was a renowned beauty, wealthy and moved in fashionable circles. Though he was an unemployed, penniless, polit-ical exile, they shared a common hatred of England. Gonne believed his brigade had 'saved Ireland's honour' and that his popularity with his countrymen would enhance her own political influence with them: it seemed in her own words that she was 'marrying Ireland'.[4] Within months of the ceremony it was evident that their tempera-ments and lifestyles were wholly incompatible. Amidst much pub-licity, recrimination and bitterness (particularly over access to their son), they separated in September 1905. As friends had foreseen, the scandal damaged both their reputations and possibly, as both had feared, Ireland's as well. Maud Gonne never fully recovered her pop-ularity with the Irish people and though they still regarded him as a hero, much obloquy was heaped on MacBride as well. Most famously, W.B. Yeats described him as 'a drunken, vain-glorious lout'. One historian has described him as 'not a polished man'. At the height of his marital quarrels, in 1904, MacBride advised his wife in characteristically melodramatic fashion and with unintended pre-science, to remarry 'in case he was hung or died in prison'.[5]

Meanwhile, MacBride left Paris and returned to Dublin, where he lodged with the city's Mayor, Fred Allen. He became a 'somewhat pathetic figure' – unemployed and in financial hardship, until in 1910, he secured a position as water bailiff for the corporation, with offices on the quays.[6] He remained politically active: in 1911 he was elected onto the Supreme Council of the IRB, as representative for Connaught. But, shortly afterwards, he was displaced by Sean MacDermott. His demotion was symptomatic of the emergence of a younger, more ruthless element within the movement, for whom Thomas Clarke was mentor: it counted for nothing that MacBride had acted as best man at Clarke's wedding in New York. He was thought to be of an older generation, his excessive drinking raised doubts as to his reliability and discretion, and his personal life was regarded as a source of embarrassment. Nonetheless, he had remained politically active. In 1911, he had been instrumental in ensuring that no loyal address was presented by Dublin Corporation during a royal visit to the city; he had canvassed its members. On 9 September 1914, he attended a meeting of militant nationalists, which was convened to discuss the prospects for a rising in wartime. Subsequently, he was active in the Irish Neutrality League, which focused its attention on an anti-recruiting campaign. Consistently, he allied himself with the new, more militant IRB leadership. It was mindful that one day MacBride's military experience and reputation for daring might be of value, though he played no part in the formation or development of the Irish Volunteer Force.[7]

On Easter Monday morning, 1916, MacBride occupied Jacob's Biscuit Factory as a member of MacDonagh's Second Battalion, Irish Volunteers, and served as his second-in-command throughout the week. There has been much speculation as to how these circumstances arose – had he heard of the Rising and did he thus proceed deliberately to this location? In which case had it perhaps been previously arranged that he would assume such a position of responsibility? Alternatively, did he happen to be passing Jacob's whilst it was being seized by the Volunteers and decide there and then to join in? Or did he fortuitously encounter MacDonagh and his garrison as they assembled near St Stephen's Green and on impulse offer his services? It is certainly possible that he was aware an insurrection was being planned, given his membership of the IRB and the fact that he was seen both at Clarke's shop and at First Battalion Headquarters on Easter Sunday morning. But the talk then was exclusively of MacNeill's countermand order. That he had not been informed of the Military Council's subsequent decision merely to postpone their action is suggested by the fact that MacDermott attempted unsuccessfully to send him an 'urgent message' at 11:15 a.m. the next morning, via his office on the quays.[8] It was known that MacBride frequented there even on public holidays to inspect ships which had docked at the port overnight, as part of his duties for the corporation.

The court martial proceedings help clarify how MacBride came to be involved in the Rising. According to his own evidence, he left his lodgings on Easter Monday morning intending to meet his brother Anthony, a doctor from Castleton, whom he had arranged to have lunch with at the Wicklow Hotel; MacBride was shortly to act as best man at his wedding. He stated: 'In waiting round town I went up as far as Stephen's Green and there I saw a band of Irish Volunteers. I knew some of the members personally and the Commander told me that an Irish Republic was virtually proclaimed ... Although I had no previous connection with the Irish Volunteers I considered it my duty to join them.' Having marched with them to Jacob's, he told the court that 'after being a few hours there' it was arranged that he should serve as second-in-command; once again he had accepted from a sense of 'duty'.[9] This account was corroborated during the trial by his landlady. During Easter week, MacDonagh had told his brother, Michael, with obvious delight, that MacBride had 'walked up to me and said, "Here I am if I am any use to you":[10] the two men (MacBride and MacDonagh) were seen on Easter Monday talking together at the corner of York Street and St Stephen's Green. Furthermore, amongst the papers found on MacBride after the surrender, and cited at his court martial, was an undated instruction, issued by MacDonagh, typed on the back of a Jacob's invoice, stating that he was 'to be commandant'.[11] (In fact, MacDonagh was himself Volunteer Commandant of Second Battalion, one of four such officers in the city, and in command at Jacob's.) This suggests that MacBride's appointment was not pre-planned, but improvised after he had unexpectedly turned up, and that he acted on impulse. In 1908 he had written a scrawled note on an envelope: 'To fight in Ireland for Ireland is the greatest ambition of my life.'[12] Having suddenly been presented with an opportunity, perhaps his last, to fight the English at home, to live up to his own rhetoric and to compensate for years of drift, failure and dissipation, he had seized the moment. He must have looked incongruous as he marched with MacDonagh at the head of the column of Volunteers from St Stephen's Green, dressed in a navy blue suit, grey hat and with a malacca cane on his arm – his 'uniform' throughout the Rising.[13]

On reaching Jacob's, the rebels quickly gained entry by smashing open one of the main gates with a sledgehammer. They immediately set about fortifying the factory, establishing outposts in nearby strategically placed properties, and erecting barricades in anticipation of a British assault. Meanwhile, MacDonagh not only designated his officers but indicated their responsibilities – MacBride was allocated the defence of the Bishop Street section of the building. To the immense frustration of the garrison, the only real action of the week came in the first hour when the rebels opened fire on a party of thirty soldiers which had been hastily despatched from Portobello Barracks to reinforce Dublin Castle. Though they were driven out of their various outposts, the expected, full-scale military attack on Jacob's never came. Thus they had to endure long periods of inactivity and boredom, relieved only by the despatching of small groups to carry out reconnaissance or to attempt small-scale ambushes of troops. In the course of the week effective leadership gradually gravitated from MacDonagh towards the more experienced, dynamic and decisive MacBride. He personally led some of the expeditions: characteristically he was observed after dawn one morning leaving by a ground-floor factory window to direct Volunteers nearby to take up new positions. One of them described him during the Rising as, 'a soldier of courage and resource, a gentleman, quiet, witty, always unruffled ... Without exception ... [they] ... admired and respected him.'[14]

Volunteer Peadar Kearney describes how during Saturday, 29 April, the Volunteers at Jacob's, unaware of the dramatic events elsewhere in the city, were still 'toiling away ... strengthening defences',[15] preparing for a last stand, hoping at least to inflict substantial casualties on crown forces. Next morning, Elizabeth O'Farrell arrived bearing Pearse's surrender order and informed MacDonagh of the evacuation of the GPO and events in Moore Street. Stunned and bewildered, he initially dismissed the terms and insisted on face-to-face negotiations with the British Commander-in-Chief. Eventually, intermediaries – two Capuchin priests – arranged for him to meet General Lowe at around noon in St Patrick's Park. MacBride, likewise, at first rejected any capitulation, stating he would 'oppose it with all the strength he could command'.[16] He offered to accompany his commandant, but was dissuaded after being reminded by Father Augustine 'of the fine part he had played in the Boer War', and the likelihood that the British military leaders remembering it too, would be 'ill-disposed towards him'.[17]

Lowe persuaded MacDonagh of the need to accept surrender and a truce was agreed to allow him to consult his comrades at the factory and deliberate with Ceannt's garrison at the South Dublin Union. The shock of his decision and his inept delivery of it on his return to Jacob's caused uproar amongst the Volunteers there, who strongly suspected that 'a deal had been done behind their backs'.[18] Some were implacably opposed; others who favoured a mass breakout to freedom were denounced as deserters. MacBride, still immaculately dressed, with 'all the appearance of having just walked out of a dining room' interjected at the opportune moment.[19] His commanding presence and his serenity, based on his acceptance of capture and certain death, contrasted sharply with MacDonagh's dishevelled look and virtual emotional collapse. He spoke simply and with clarity, stating: 'Liberty is a precious thing and anyone of you who sees a chance, take it. I'd do the same myself but my

liberty days are over. Good luck, Boys.' Reflecting on the lessons to
be learnt from the week, he concluded: 'Many of you may live to
fight some other day. Take my advice – never allow yourselves to
be cooped up inside a building again.'[20] His courage was recognised
by those present; one of the Cumann na mBan women noted later
that, as 'a marked man by Dublin Castle detectives, his execution was
inevitable if he was taken prisoner'.[21] Nonetheless, he spurned the
ample opportunities to make good his escape. Some of the men
acted on his instructions. After he had spoken, Kearney writes: 'That
settled it, and a half dozen of us faced the streets of a hostile and
fear-stricken city.'[22] Others waited until the garrison had marched
out of the factory led by MacDonagh and MacBride; they then simply melted into the surrounding crowds, unimpeded and unnoticed
by the authorities during the half-mile march to the surrender
point, St Patrick's Park. The remainder arrived there at about 5 p.m.
William Wylie recognised MacBride there: he was to be the prosecution counsel at his trial. The Volunteers then proceeded under
escort to Richmond Barracks.

There, the rebels were searched and their names, addresses and
occupations noted. On Monday morning, Robert Holland recalls
that they were ushered into the gymnasium, followed by DMP
detectives who at first scrutinised them through a glass screen. Then,
he writes, 'after about twenty minutes they came in, in groups of
two's ... Now and again ... [one of them] ... said: "You, and you and
you, get up and over to the other side of the hall" ... These called
themselves Irishmen, the very scum that kept us in British bondage.'
He concludes: "that identity parade will never leave my memory, as
I saw Con Colbert, Eamonn Ceannt ... Major McBride ... and
scores of others in derision being pointed out and shouted at "Get
up and over here". This went on for the best part of two hours, and
when they had completed their job to their satisfaction they then
marched them out of the hall.'[23] Volunteer Padraig O Ceallaigh
recalls seeing MacBride for the last time, jingling some coins as he
sat in one of the rooms, smiling when O Ceallaigh observed: 'I suppose that's some of the German gold.'[24]

MacBride was court-martialled on 4 May, (prisoner number thir-
ty-four). Brigadier-General Blackader presided: MacBride had
stood before him in court the previous day, appearing for the
defence in the trial of Eammon Ceannt. The prosecution called
three witnesses, two of them army officers who in their testimony

described seeing MacBride surrender at St Patrick's Park and hearing him give his name, 'Major John MacBride'. Though lacking convincing evidence, they also alleged that he had been armed. Papers found when he was searched were also placed before the bench – MacDonagh's note appointing him Commandant, and a dispatch, which it was claimed was proof that he had had contact with other rebel leaders during the Rising. (Another document also found on him on 1 May was used in the trial of James Connolly.) The evidence of a third witness, a police inspector who had searched MacBride's lodgings on 2 May, was disallowed.[25]

MacBride cross-examined one of the witnesses. In an ante-room before his trial, he had informed Wylie that he, 'had no defence but wished to make a statement ... if permitted.' The counsel offered to make it on his behalf, but the defendant insisted 'he would do so himself'.[26] In the course of the statement MacBride outlined the chance turn of events which had preceded his involvement in the Rising (this was confirmed by Mrs Allen, his landlady and the only witness he called). He also stressed that he had not 'influenced any other person to join' and pointed out with justification, that he 'could have escaped' from Jacob's before the surrender, but had 'considered it a dishonourable thing to do.' According to Wylie, when finished he thanked the officers of the court for their 'attention and courtesy' and Wylie for 'his fairness and offer of assistance'.[27]

Throughout, MacBride appears to have accepted that his fate was sealed. S.T. O'Kelly had seen him from the window of his cell at Richmond barracks being escorted across the barrack square to his court martial, along with several other prisoners, and had himself at that time felt there was little hope. After the trial he saw him again, and MacBride shouted up to him: 'Nothing will save me, Sean. This is the end. Remember this is the second time I have sinned against them.'[28] Nonetheless, he had impressed Blackader who is said to have described MacBride as the 'most soldierly' of the rebels he tried.[29] At the time, Wylie recalls the British officer declaring that 'when in South Africa, he thought of MacBride as about the lowest thing that crawled' but as a result of the Rising, however, Blackader confessed, 'I will never think of him now without taking my hat off to a brave man.'[30]

Maxwell had taken part in the Jameson Raid and was at the time fortunate to have escaped execution by the Boers. He can only therefore have harboured the most negative of memories of

MacBride. On 4 May, he expeditiously confirmed the sentence of the court – 'Death by being shot': MacBride's was one of just three trial cases he processed, out of over thirty waiting to be dealt with, before hurriedly leaving Dublin to attend a Cabinet meeting in London held next day. When justifying his decision later, the first point he noted was that the defendant had 'fought on the side of the Boers in the South African War': clearly MacBride's past helped damn him in the eyes of the British officer class. The GOC also claimed that he was 'one of the most active advocates of the anti-enlistment propaganda and the Irish Volunteer movement' as well as a 'commandant' during the Rising.[31] Most of these statements were incorrect. MacBride had never joined the Irish Volunteers and was not a Volunteer commandant. MacDonagh had erroneously referred to him as such in his typed instruction, which in effect made him second-in-command at Jacob's. Nonetheless, this almost certainly helped to confirm the presumption that he was and had been a leading figure in the movement. Moreover, at the surrender, the accused had openly and defiantly declared himself to be: 'Major John MacBride'. Historian Robert Kee concludes: 'It is difficult not to think that he was shot partly as a simple act of revenge by the military for an offence for which the common law had long for-given him.'[32] All in all, this assessment seems somewhat overstated.

On the evening of 4 May, MacBride was officially informed that his sentence had been confirmed and that accordingly he would be executed at dawn next morning. During his final hours Father Augustine visited him in his cell: the priest later said of him that he 'knew no fear', was 'quiet and natural' and that he had in his 'first words expressed sorrow for the surrender'. He heard MacBride's confession, gave him Holy Communion and they prayed together. When the soldiers came to lead him to the execution yard, the pris-oner requested not to be blindfolded or have his hands bound, but on both counts received the same reply: 'Sorry Sir, but these are the orders.'[33] Tom Kettle, a Volunteer who had joined British forces after the outbreak of war to uphold the rights of small nations, overheard him say to the firing squad: 'Fire away. I have been looking down the barrels of rifles all my life.'[34] 'This was a lie,' Kettle continues, 'but a magnificent lie. He had been looking down porter bottles all his life.'

MacBride's certificate of execution states that he was shot at 3:47 a.m., 5 May 1916. According to British Special Branch reports,

Maud Gonne only heard the news later, while reading the *Daily Mail* in Paris. Both she and her son then immediately donned mourning clothes. She had long since lost touch with the progress of Irish nationalism, but no doubt she still understood MacBride. She wrote to W.B. Yeats soon afterwards, saying: 'He made a fine heroic end which has atoned for all. It was a death he had always desired.'[35]

Trial of John MacBride
prisoner number thirty-four

REFERENCE: PRO WO71/350

DATE: 4 May 1916

LOCATION: Richmond Barracks

JUDGES: Brigadier-General C.G. Blackader (President), Lieutenant
Colonel G. German, Lieutenant Colonel W.J. Kent

CHARGE:

'Did an act to wit did take part in an armed rebellion and in the
waging of war against His Majesty the King, such act being o such
a nature as to be calculated to be prejudical to the Defence to the
Realm and being done with the intention and for the purpose of
assisting the enemy'

PLEA: Not guilty

(The members of the court and witnesses were duly sworn in)

VERDICT: Guilty. Death by being shot

Text of Trial

PROSECUTION

1st witness
Major J.E. Armstrong Inniskillen Fusiliers duly sworn states

> I was present at Patricks Park Dublin on April 30. The
> British troops were fired on on that occasion and there
> were casualties. The fire came from the neighbourhood of
> Jacobs Factory. I was present when the prisoners from
> Jacobs Factory surrendered at 5 pm.

> I recognise the accused as one of them. He gave his rank as
> an officer. I had a list of the unarmed men made before the
> party was disarmed and the accused does not appear on that
> list. I was present when a Summary of Evidence was taken
> and I gave the same evidence as I have given now to the
> best of my relief. The accused did not cross examine me –

he was not in uniform.

Cross examined by the accused.

> I identify the accused as one of the party that surrendered. I do not produce a list with the accused's name on it.

The witness withdraws.

2nd witness

2/Lieut. S.H. Jackson 3rd Royal Irish Regt. duly sworn states.

> I recognise the accused as John McBride. He gave his name as Major John McBride.
>
> I was in charge of the searching party in the gymnasium. The accused handed his note book to me there, the date being 1.5.16. Papers attached marked X were found in the note book.

The accused declines to cross examine the witness.

The witness withdraws.

3rd Witness

Inspector Richard H. Boyne Dublin Metropolitan Police duly sworn states.

> I am an Inspector of the Dublin Metropolitan Police.
>
> On May 2 about 11 a. m I visited the lodgings of the accused and I found

(evidence of this witness disallowed)
Prosecution closed.

DEFENCE

1st Witness

Mrs. Allan 8 Spencer Villas Glenaquary duly sworn states.

> I have known the accused 25 years. I remember you leaving my house last Easter Monday morning dressed in civilian clothes. I remember receiving a letter from the accused's brother Dr. McBride saying that he was coming up from Castle Bar and asking the accused to meet him at the Wicklow Hotel Dublin. I remember the accused saying that he was going to lunch with his brother and would be back about 5 o/c.

I remember that Dr McBride was to be married the following Wednesday and that the accused was to be best man.

I have never seen him in uniform nor has he got such a thing so far as I know.

The Prosecution asked no question.

The accused in his defence states

On the morning of Easter Monday I left my home at Glengeary with the intention of going to meet my brother who was coming to Dublin to get married. In waiting round town I went up as far as Stephens Green and there I saw a band of Irish Volunteers. I knew some of the members personally and the Commander told me that an Irish Republic was virtually proclaimed. As he knew my rather advanced opinions and although I had no previous connection with the Irish Volunteers I considered it my duty to join them. I knew there was no chance of success, and I never advised nor influenced any other person to join. I did not even know the positions they were about to take up. I marched with them to Jacobs Factory. After being a few hours there I was appointed second in command and I felt it my duty to occupy that position. I could have escaped from Jacobs Factory before the surrender had I so desired but I considered it a dishonourable thing to do. I do not say this with the idea of mitigating any penalty they may impose but in order [to] make clear my position in the matter.

Statement ends.

IRISH REBELLION. MAY 1916.

J. J. HEUSTON,
One of the leaders of the Rebellion.
Executed May 8th, 1916.

Sean Heuston

Deputy Adjutant General
11 MAY. 1918
NO.
Richmond Barracks

Extract from a
memorandum entitled
'Short History of
rebels on whom it has
been necessary to
inflict the supreme
penalty' sent by
General Sir John
Maxwell to Herbert
Asquith, on 11 May
1916.

BODLEIAN LIBRARY,
UNIVERSITY OF
OXFORD

This man was in command of the Mendicity Institute, Usher's Island. One British Officer and 9 men were killed by the fire from the building which had to be carried by assault. Twenty-three rebels were captured in it amongst them this man, and large stores of revolver and rifle ammunition and bombs were found. Orders and despatches were also discovered showing that this man was in constant communication with the leaders. In all of these despatches he described himself and was described as Captain.

SEAN HEUSTON WAS A THICKSET, somewhat taciturn Dubliner, born on 21 February 1891, the son of a clerk. Like Con Colbert, and many others involved in the Rising, a formative influence on him was his attendance at the Christian Brothers' School, North Richmond Street, Dublin. In 1907, aged sixteen, he joined the Great Southern and Western Railway Company as a clerk; its report on his suitability for permanent employment after his probation year described him as 'particularly satisfactory' and proficient, especially at bookkeeping.[1] Until 1913 he worked at Limerick Goods Depot, and at the same time was also active locally, organising and instructing the members of Fianna. After six years, he transferred to the Traffic Manager's Office in Dublin's Kingsbridge (now Heuston) Station, where his main duties were abstracting and furnishing traders' accounts. He was unmarried and lived in Broadstone with his mother, sister and aunt. His was the main source of income for the family; his parents were estranged and his father was then living and working in London.

Heuston joined the Irish Volunteers in the spring of 1914, becoming Captain of D company, First Battalion, Dublin Brigade, a reflection of his commitment, reliability and competence. The battalion drew its recruits from the area north of the river between Phoenix Park and Sackville Street. Heuston was also a keen member of the Gaelic League and joined the IRB. He rose to become Lieutenant and Director of Training in the Fianna and Pearse employed him as a drill instructor for the boys at St Enda's; Pearse favoured using members of the Fianna organisation for this purpose.[2]

It is probable that Heuston first heard of the Rising on Wednesday, 19 April 1916, though there is an account of him delivering a pair of 'two feet high lamps' to insurgents from Tralee on 17 April, who had come up to Dublin partly to collect them.[3] These were to be used to signal to the *Aud* whose arrival off the coast of Kerry was imminent. During the days leading up to the Rising, Heuston involved himself in making the necessary preparations within his battalion area. He is reported to have been dumbfounded on Easter Sunday, when, after attending mass, he heard the 'terrible' news of MacNeill's countermand order. He spent most of the day at D company headquarters, Colmcille Hall, Blackhall Street, where he had advised Volunteers to wait until further notice. At 3:05 p.m. he issued a written instruction to them stating: 'There is no parade today. Take this as definite and ignore all orders.' But twenty-five minutes later, having meanwhile perhaps heard that the Military Council had postponed the Rising until Easter Monday, he wrote a second, urging members to 'remain in the city.'[4]

At 8 p.m. that evening he attended an hour long war council at Colmcille Hall, along with other First Battalion officers, including its Commandant, Ned Daly, to finalise arrangements for the following day. At midnight he asked several Volunteers to check if any DMP detectives were watching the building; box-loads of arms, ammunition and high explosives were being stored there. He then dismissed all but one, and together they remained on guard-duty at company headquarters overnight.[5] On Easter Monday morning, he returned home for breakfast at 10 a.m. and left half an hour later with his haversack and a day's rations, informing his mother that he was leaving to take part in a route march. She wrote later: 'He never told us about the rising. I did not hear anything about him until Low Monday [1 May].'[6]

Heuston went straight to St George's Street Church, Temple Street North, where he had arranged for the members of D company to assemble; owing to the confusion, however, fewer than a dozen turned out. He led them first to Liberty Hall, where he was provided with some modest reinforcements and was also almost certainly handed a typed order from Connolly. It stated simply: 'Seize the Mendicity [Institution] at all costs.' This 250-year-old building had been used since 1907 to 'house the very poorest of [Dublin's] poor'; it occupied a commanding position south of the quays and was therefore regarded as having a vital role in at least delaying any military advance from the Royal (now Collins) Barracks towards the rebel-held GPO and Four Courts.[7] The small garrison, thirteen in number, occupied it without resistance, as the midday angelus sounded.[8]

The unit had scarcely taken up defensive positions when a substantial force of unsuspecting British troops (Royal Dublin Fusiliers) approached from the direction of the Royal Barracks; they were marching along the north side of the river having been hastily summoned to reinforce Dublin Castle. On receiving the order, the rebels fired several volleys; in panic the soldiers scattered for cover and in the ensuing gun-battle, one officer was killed and up to nine other ranks injured. At 2:45 p.m., Heuston was able to inform headquarters at the GPO: 'We hold position firmly. No casualties.'[9] He also requested additional supplies of ammunition.

Though under increasing sniper attack, Tuesday was a relatively quiet day for the small and exposed unit. At 9:10 a.m. Heuston reported to Connolly: 'Still here with 13 men. A little enemy activity in vicinity at present ... Have you any special instructions or news?' In response, headquarters dispatched further reinforcements – a dozen Volunteers, members of the Fingal Brigade. Overnight the rebels remained on high alert. Heuston devised a detailed, handwritten rota under which never fewer than half the company were on duty at any one time, whilst the remainder were instructed to sleep 'with full equipment'.[10]

As at other isolated, but strategically significant rebel-held positions in the city (the City Hall, Liberty Hall), on Wednesday, the military net rapidly closed in around the Mendicity Institution. A force of Royal Dublin Fusiliers, its estimated strength three to four hundred, surrounded the outpost during the morning, some of the soldiers occupying adjacent houses, and deluged the building with machine-gun and rifle fire. Meanwhile others, crouching under its low front wall for cover, hurled grenades through the windows. Two Volunteers received serious injuries in their despairing efforts to pick up the grenades and propel them back at their assailants. A member of the company later recalled that after a short time 'the small garrison had reached the end of its endurance ... Hopelessly outnumbered and trapped, our commandant after a consultation with us decided that the only hope for the safety of us all was to surrender.'[11] One of the rebels walked out into the yard at the rear of the building, bearing a white flag; the rest followed, most of them having cast aside their arms. However, as they approached the rear gate of the Mendicity Institution, a distant British sniper, unaware of their capitulation, fired, fatally wounding one of them. By this time a number of the rebels, including Heuston, had discarded their Volunteer uniforms. In explanation, one of them stated later at his trial: 'I took it off when we were about to surrender', presumably so as not to besmirch the honour of the force. The troops then meticulously searched the building, finding amongst other things, 'several rifles and several thousand rounds of ammunition for revolvers and rifles (.303) ... 6–7 bombs charged and with fuses ... [and] ... an order signed by James Connolly'.[12]

The two dozen Volunteers who had survived unscathed, were escorted past troops lying prone in the street outside the Institution, with rifles cocked. One of the rebels afterwards stated that they 'were forced to march to the Royal Barracks with our hands up, held behind our heads ... [we were] ... lined up in the parade ground ... attacked by British solders ... then ... marched under heavy guard by an underground passage to Arbour Hill Detention Barracks where we were searched'. In due course, all the rebels were court-martialled and sentenced: they believed this was because they had given their opponents such a 'hard time'.[13]

Heuston was transferred to Richmond Barracks on 4 May and tried (prisoner number forty-six) later that day, together with three other members of his garrison (W. O'Dea, P. Kelly and J. Crenegan): he appears only to have received a copy of the charge that morning. Brigadier Maconchy presided over the court. Two officers from the Royal Dublin Fusiliers were called to testify for the prosecution. Both had been present when their unit had been fired on from the Mendicity Institution on 24 April and both had participated in the successful assault two days later. One of them claimed to recognise Heuston as having been in command of the rebels at the time of the surrender. Some of the documents uncovered by the military during their subsequent search of the building were also produced as evidence. These included Connolly's typed instruction to 'Seize the Mendicity at all costs' and hand-written papers detailing men for defence duties after it had been seized.[14] Two small Field Report Pads they had found were also shown to the court; they had cost 4d and the London printers had included on the cover 'hints in writing reports, etc., useful to scouts and others for writing orders and reports in the field'. They contained the carbon copies of several messages clearly sent by the Volunteers, dated between 22 and 26 April; it was strongly implied in court that these had been written by Heuston. They included one which was unsigned, dated Easter Sunday, 23 April, and stated cryptically: 'I hope we will be able to do better next time.'[15]

When speaking in his own defence, Heuston focussed on challenging the validity of some of the documentary evidence. He stated categorically that the note which referred to doing 'better next time' was 'not mine'. It is evident even from a cursory glance that it is not in his handwriting; he methodically signed those he actually wrote 'Captain Heuston'. The notepads were clearly for general use; two of the entries bear the signatures of other Volunteers – (one of them, Sean MacDermott). On shakier ground, the defendant also claimed that since Connolly's order was addressed to 'Captain Houston', it was 'not addressed to me as my name is "Heuston"'.[16] It seems obvious that the ICA leader had used the Scottish spelling, more familiar to himself, rather than the Irish equivalent. In short statements, the three garrison members who were tried at the same time as Heuston, each claimed in effect that they had been duped by their leaders: they alleged that they had gone out on Easter Monday, believing themselves merely to be taking part in manoeuvres, unaware until too late that they were in fact participating in a rising.

On 6 May, Maxwell confirmed the death sentence which the court had imposed on Heuston (the others received terms of imprisonment of up to three years). The GOC later justified the punishment on the grounds that though Heuston's unit had been small and had surrendered on the third day of the Rising, 'substantial military casualties had been sustained in the fighting' at the Mendicity Institution.[17] Meanwhile, the prisoners had been transferred to Kilmainham, either on the day of Heuston's court martial or during the following evening. Heuston appears fully to have anticipated his fate: when asked by a comrade whether he had heard his sentence yet, he replied: 'There is no hope for me. I expect to be shot.'[18] He went to confession and received Holy Communion on Sunday morning, 7 May; later that day he was officially informed of Maxwell's decision, and that he was to be executed at dawn the next morning.

On the previous Monday, Heuston's aunt, Miss Theresa McDonald, 'met someone who said he [Sean] had been taken prisoner at the Mendicity'; it was the family's first news of his 'activities' since he had left home exactly one week earlier.[19] At 10 p.m. on the eve of his execution, a policeman arrived at his home and delivered an official letter, stating: 'John Heuston desires to see you and also his sister, Theresa, and his aunt, Theresa. I am sending a motor car to convey you and his aunt here.'[20] It was signed by the Commandant of Kilmainham, Major W.S. Lennon, and the car awaited them, driven by an officer. Heuston was also permitted to summon his brother, Michael, a novice priest at a priory in Dublin. He wrote to him: 'I suppose you have been wondering why I did not communicate with you since Easter, but the explanation is simple. I have been locked up by His Britannic Majesty's Government. They have just instructed me that I am to be executed in the morning. If the rules of the order allow it I want you to get permission at once and come in here and see me for the last time in this world. I feel quite prepared to go, thank God.' The envelope containing the note was marked 'Urgent, Await Reply'.[21]

Whilst he waited for the arrival of his family, Heuston wrote several other letters, one to his sister, Mary, a Dominican nun living in Galway. It is somewhat defensive in tone; it suggests resignation as to his own fate and hope, rather than certainty, as to the likely impact of the insurrection. He stated:

> Do not blame me for the part I have taken. As a soldier, I
> merely carried out the orders of my superiors who should
> have been in a position to know what was in Ireland's best
> interest. Let there be no talk of foolish enterprises. I have no
> vain regrets … If you really love me teach the children in
> your class the history of their own land, and teach them that
> the cause of Caitlin Ni Uallachain never dies. Ireland shall
> be free … as soon as the people of Ireland believe in the
> necessity for Ireland's Freedom and are prepared to make
> the necessary sacrifices to obtain it … Let us pray that
> Ireland will benefit from it ultimately. Let you do your share
> by teaching Ireland's history as it should be taught.[22]

Heuston expressed similar sentiments when writing to a work colleague on the railways, saying: 'I ask all to pray fervently for the repose of my soul. Whatever I have done I have done as a soldier of Ireland in what I believed to be my country's best interests. I have, thank God, no vain regrets. After all, it is better to be a corpse than a coward.' He concluded: 'won't you as a last favour see that my mother gets whatever assistance you can give obtaining whatever salary is due to me, and whatever refund is due from the Superannuation Fund? She will stand badly in need of it all.'[23] His mother's future financial position was clearly a cause of deep concern to Heuston and it prompted him to write one further letter – perhaps the most difficult of all. He wrote to his father: 'I have been sentenced to death for taking part in the recent rising. I have for years past been my mother's main support and I now make this appeal to you from the jaws of death to assist my mother as far as lies within your powers.'[24]

After being stopped several times at military roadblocks on the way, the family eventually arrived at Kilmainham. They were led to Heuston's sparcely furnished, ground floor cell (number nineteen) in the central compound, beside those of the three other rebels who were also to face the firing squad (Ceannt, Colbert and Mallin), and adjacent to the execution yard. His sister recalls that 'one soldier holding a lighted candle was in ... with them. He was young and deeply effected. He was crying.' Theresa overheard an officer comment: 'These men must be got away by three.' Father Browne, who had accompanied Michael Heuston, describes how at the end the family 'bade him [Sean] a long and fond farewell, and so we left him, serene as he had been during the whole of our visit'.[25]

Father Albert, a Capuchin priest from Church Street, visited Heuston at 3:20 a.m. on Monday morning, and found him 'kneeling beside a table, his rosary beads in his hand'. He recalls that 'during the last quarter of an hour, we knelt in the cell in complete darkness' and confirms that the condemned man 'awaited the end' with 'calmness and fortitude'. At 3:45 a.m., a sentry knocked at the door, and the priest then accompanied the prisoner to the execution yard, repeating with him some of the prayers they had said together earlier, and glimpsing briefly Michael Mallin as he was being led away from his cell. Before confronting the firing squad, Heuston kissed a crucifix in the priest's hand and whispered: 'Father, sure you won't forget to anoint me.'[26] He was executed at between 3:45 and 4:05 a.m. on Monday, 8 May. One of the rebels who knew him well observed later:

> There are some people you'd never think they'd execute, like Sean Heuston. He was just an ordinary person, a young lad, who was working in Kingsbridge Railway Station and wasn't of any importance. He did command the men in the Mendicity Institution, and it's said he did play certain havoc with the soldiers coming out of the Barracks and around the quays, but other than that I wouldn't say he was the sort of person who should have been executed. An ordinary army would never have shot the likes of Sean Heuston.[27]

It was, of course, precisely these actions at the Mendicity which had convinced Maxwell that the death penalty was appropriate in Heuston's case – however unjustified this decision soon came to appear to nationalist opinion in Ireland. Shortly after his execution, newspapers reported:

> A remarkable scene occurred outside the Dominican
> Church, Dominick Street ... After requiem mass for S. S.
> Heuston, on his relatives making their appearance on the
> street, they were loudly cheered by a large crowd who had
> assembled outside the church. Members of the throng
> afterwards sang verses of 'A Nation Once Again', 'Who
> Fears to Speak of '98' and 'God Save Ireland'. Members of
> the crowd were observed to be wearing republican badges
> with mourning tokens.[28]

Trial of J.J. Heuston

prisoner number forty-six

REFERENCE: PRO WO71/351

J.J. Heuston was tried along with W. O'Dea (prisoner number forty-seven), P. Kelly (prisoner number forty-eight), and J. Crenigan (prisoner number forty-nine).

DATE: 4 May 1916

LOCATION: Richmond Barracks

JUDGES: Colonel E.W.S.K. Maconchy (President), Lieutenant Colonel Bent, Major F.W. Woodward

CHARGE:

'Did an act to wit did take part in an armed rebellion and in the waging of war against His Majesty the King, such act being o such a nature as to be calculated to be prejudical to the Defence to the Realm and being done with the intention and for the purpose of assisting the enemy'

PLEA: All defendants pleaded not guilty

(The members of the court and witnesses were duly sworn in)

VERDICT: Heuston, O'Dea and Kelly were found 'Guilty. Death.' J. Crenigan was found 'Guilty. Two years imprisonment; recommended to mercy on account of his youth'

Text of Trial

PROSECUTION

1st witness

Capt. A.W. MacDermot 7th Btn R. Dublin Fusiliers states:–

> On the 26th April I was present when the Mendicity Institution was taken by assault by a party of the 10th Batn. R. Dublin Fusiliers.

> 23 men surrendered on that occasion. I identify the four prisoners J.J. Heuston, W. O'Dea, P. Kelly and J.Crenigan as

having been in the body of men who surrendered.

They left their arms except their revolvers in the Mendicity Institute when they surrendered. Some of them still wore revolvers.

One officer of the 70th [sic] R. Dublin Fusiliers was killed and 9 men wounded by fire from this Institute on the 24th April.

I searched the building when they surrendered. I found several rifles several thousand rounds of ammunition for both revolvers and rifles (.303).

I found 6 or 7 bombs charged and with fuses in them ready for use.

I found the following papers.

An order signed by James Connolly, one of the signatories to the Irish Republic Proclamation, directing "Capt. Houston" (Sic) to "Seize the Mendicity at all costs." It was dated the 24th April 1916.

James Connolly signed as

> "Commandant General
> Dublin Division".

Also papers detailing men for various duties in the Mendicity Institute. All these papers are headed

> "Army of the Irish Republic."

Also two message books signed by Heuston "Capt."

One contains copies of messages sent to "Comdt. General Connolly" giving particulars of the situation in the Institute.

The other message book contains copies of messages commencing on the 22nd April two days before the outbreak. One message contains a reference to Macdonagh who is stated to have just left Heuston

Another is a message to "all members of D Coy. 1st Batn." stating that the parade for the 23rd is cancelled and all rumours are to be ignored.

Another message dated the 23rd states "I hope we will be able to do better next time."

These documents are attached to the proceedings by the court.

Examined by the Court Capt. MacDermot states:–

Heuston commanded the party of men who surrendered.

2nd Witness

Lieut W.P. Connolly 10th R. Dublin Fusiliers states:–

I was present when 23 men surrendered on the 26th April at the Mendicity Institute.

I identify the four prisoners before the court as being amongst them.
The leader was J.J. Heuston.

I was present when the troops were fired on from the Mendicity Institute on the 24th April, when Lieut G.A. Neilan was killed and 6 men wounded to my knowledge.

Heuston was without a coat when he surrendered and also had no hat on. He was not in the uniform of the Irish Volunteers.
I was present when the building was searched and found arms and ammunition in it and also the documents now before the court.

Cross-examined by J.J. Heuston

I cannot say exactly where I found the message books but they were in the building.

Examined by the Court.

Among the arms there were some old German Mausers. Among the ammunition there were two cardboard boxes of "Spange" German ammunition.

DEFENCE

W. O'Dea states.

I was perfectly ignorant of what was going to occur. I understood it was an ordinary route march when I was called out as we had been told for some time previously that the best equipped Company was to get a prize at the Easter Manoeuvres. It was to have taken place on Easter Sunday but was postponed.

I do not know why it was postponed. I turned out in full uniform but I took it off when we were about to surrender.

J.J. Heuston states.

The message in the notebook produced saying "I hope we will be able to do better next time" is not mine.

The order from Connolly addressed to "Captain Houston" is not addressed to me as my name is "Heuston".

I had no intimation of the nature of the charge against me until this morning.

P. Kelly states.

I did not know anything about the rebellion beforehand or what I was coming out for. I came out because I was asked to. I thought it was for manoeuvres. I did not fire any shots.

J. Crenigan states.

I did not know what I was called out for. I thought it was for manoeuvres. I am 16 years old.

Con Colbert

CORNELIUS COLBERT.

This men was one of the most active members of the Sinn Fein organisation. He was a close associate with all the leaders, and took a prominent part in the organization of the rebel army in which he held the rank of Captain. He was armed at the time of his surrender and came from the neighbourhood of houses from which heavy firing had taken place earlier in the day.

Extract from a memorandum entitled 'Short History of rebels on whom it has been necessary to inflict the supreme penalty' sent by General Sir John Maxwell to Herbert Asquith, on 11 May 1916.

Con colbert was born in 1888 and brought up in Athea, County Limerick. He may have derived his republicanism from his father who was active in the Fenian movement. Like many others involved in the Rising, republican tendencies either confirmed or instilled by attendance at the Christian Brothers' School, North Richmond Street, Dublin. There the syllabus included hour–long, inspirational, lunchtime lectures delivered each Friday 'about the mass rock, and the Famine, of Blessed Oliver Plunkett, and of Emmet and Tone, McCracken'.[1] After leaving, Colbert became a junior clerk at a bakery in the city, and more crucially, he was amongst the first to join the Fianna movement. He was given command of the Inchicore branch and eventually made Chief Scout of Ireland. He enlisted in the Irish Volunteer Force from its inception, assisting with training. He was made Captain of F Company (Fourth Battalion), based in Inchicore. This was a poor recruitment area, as it was very much a British garrison district; this was evident from the hostile reaction of local people to the rebels when, after their surrender, they were being escorted through these streets to Richmond Barracks. Most members of his unit were aged between eighteen and twenty, and like himself had graduated through the Fianna. Like Heuston, Colbert also taught at Pearse's school, St Enda's, instructing the boys in physical exercises and in drilling.[2]

Colbert was small, no more than 5 feet 4 inches in height, of stocky build and fastidious about his dress and appearance – a characteristic he tried to instil in Fianna members; he was a fluent Irish speaker and a devout catholic. His ascetic lifestyle (he was a total abstainer and non-smoker), derived in part from his study of Irish history. Robert Holland, who was second-in-command of his company, recalls that 'he had one ambition only – to free Ireland. In fact he never spoke of anything else unless it was connected with Irish history ... All his lectures centred around the subject of why we failed. His answer was always: "Drink and want of discipline and loose talk".' One of Colbert's favourite sayings was: 'First serve God and then your country'. He was deeply respected in the organisations he joined; he was both generous and totally trustworthy. Holland states: 'All his pocket money went for equipment ... for the Fianna ...You could never doubt anything he would tell you. He was never abusive.'[3] He was also fearless in his commitment to Irish independence and to an insurrection to achieve it. In mid-1915, during Volunteer manoeuvres in County Tipperary, he told Sean Fitzgibbon enthusiastically that: 'He [Colbert] was to guard the line of the Shannon in the event of a rising.'[4] P.S. Doyle, a member of Fourth Battalion, writes: 'He had remarkable courage and daring throughout the period. He warned us one night in a lecture "if there was anyone in the company who was afraid to die, they should make up their minds in the coming week of their future intentions".'[5] These same values and attitudes he sought to inculate into the members of both Fianna and the IVF. Yet despite his own single-mindedness, he was sensitive to the likely sacrifices of the Volunteers when action came. At a meeting held shortly before the insurrection, he asked Pearse about the position of those men who might come out, and who were concerned about the prospect of losing their jobs. Pearse replied, somewhat scornfully, that if anyone was worried by such concerns, then he would advise that they should not come out.

In June 1914, Colbert voted against John Redmond's attempt to gain Parliamentary Party control of the Executive Council of the Irish Volunteers. By late 1915, he was convinced that soon 'an opportunity might arise' for a rising. He probably first heard of the IRB Military Council's plans on Wednesday, 19 April 1916. He informed a close colleague then that 'the time is near ripe' and on Good Friday, that 'the next mobilisation would probably be the last … [There] … would be street fighting … the men [should] bring the principle tools of their particular trades, such as hammers, saws, picks, crowbars and such like'; he urged them 'to go to confession and make sure that the others went also'.[6] Immediately before the Rising, he served as bodyguard for Patrick Pearse. Meanwhile, Colbert was also arranging for the delivery of arms, preparing for the seizure of properties identified within the allotted Fourth Battalion area and seeking to ensure the fullest possible turnout of Volunteers for the mobilisation on Easter Sunday. But he declared with characteristic zeal that if he did not get the men to turn out, he would fight on his own. However, following MacNeill's countermanding order and the subsequent Military Council decision to postpone the insurrection, he issued an order to his men at 6 a.m. that morning instructing them to 'stay in their own homes' and await further instructions.

Under revised orders, Fourth Battalion members assembled at 11 a.m. on Easter Monday in Emerald Square, some with 'pikes of the crudest kind'. Their main objective under Eamonn Ceannt as Commandant, was the occupation of the South Dublin Union, a poorhouse which sprawled over fifty acres on the western fringe of the city, just south of the river. Three supporting outposts were also to be taken – Roe's Distillery, Mount Brown, Walker's Brewery, Ardee Street and Jameson's Distillery, Marrowbone Lane. Watkin's Brewery was allocated to F Company. After first dispatching scouts to check that no soldiers lay in ambush and that there was no unusual activity at Wellington Barracks nearby, Colbert and his unit effortlessly occupied their target. But on Tuesday evening, he decided on evacuation. By then, it had become evident to him that Watkin's Brewery 'covered nothing of strategic importance', was too remote from the South Dublin Union to contribute to its defence and was too large for his small garrison to hold securely. From the outset, Colbert had been bitterly disappointed at the poor turnout of Volunteers. He had fewer than twenty in his unit: 'If they had turned out, we would need no outside assistance,'[9] he complained. He estimated that fewer than one in ten had mobilised, when compared with the numbers who had attended for training on Holy Thursday. Nonetheless, in anticipation of bitter fighting ahead, he, like Ceannt, had not permitted any members of Cumann na mBan to accompany his group.

Unlike the unit at Roe's Distillery who simply abandoned its position on Tuesday and dispersed, Colbert transferred his unit to Jameson's Distillery. There, though limping badly and clearly tired, he assumed de facto command. The post was vital to the defence of the South Dublin Union, commanding approaches from the south and east. Here too the garrison was small and also vulnerable: the fighting around it had already become intense. Typically, Colbert and most of his men took up exposed positions on the 'most open side to the enemy'. Between Wednesday and Friday, both Volunteers and troops were locked, in Holland's phrase, in a 'battle royal'.[10] British snipers sustained an intense and accurate barrage, taking cover behind tree trunks, the distillery's walls, and rapidly dug trenches along both sides of the Grand Canal and in adjacent fields. The rebels responded with rifle fire and, after receiving instruction from Colbert, with grenades of dubious reliability.

Throughout the week, Volunteer morale remained high despite their disappointingly small number, their growing isolation and, from Thursday, the ominous glow of fires spreading in the city centre. Their position was well fortified and they had ample supplies of food – milk-churns, bakery carts, chickens and even live cattle had been successfully commandeered. On Wednesday, one Volunteer proudly declared that they had already lasted 'longer than the four previous rebellions put together'. The rebels had sustained no fatalities, whilst it was evident that 'the British were suffering heavy losses'. The casualties among the troops and the fact that they appeared to belong to different regiments encouraged the hope that 'there could not be many left'.[11] Rumours proliferated of rebel victories elsewhere in Ireland, of country units and German forces marching on Dublin and of English defeats in France. It appeared to Holland that 'we were winning. Failure was the last thing ... [we] ... thought of ... There was no mention of any of us surrendering.' He says of Colbert that, 'all the time he seemed to think that we must win and said to me that we must come in at the peace negotiations when the war had finished'.[12]

On Saturday morning, to the surprise of the rebels, the British troops moved out of range; they had disappeared from view entirely by Sunday morning. Nonetheless, that morning when Colbert addressed the Volunteers, he again confirmed that there was 'good news' from all fronts and, still anticipating a military assault, they responded with cries of 'Yes!' when he asked if they were ready to fight to the last man.[13] One of the women present recalls 'there was a feeling that we were going to be there for a long spell'.[14] The mood altered dramatically however, when at 4 p.m. on Sunday afternoon, Thomas MacDonagh arrived at the distillery to deliver Pearse's surrender order. His visit was a protracted one as the leaders there protested vigorously, but in the end impotently. Colbert was seen 'crying very bitterly', he was inconsolable, disoriented by the sudden and unexpected turn of events.[15] He told Holland forlornly, 'I do not know what to say or think, but if what I think comes true, our cause is postponed to a future generation ... we must have been let down very badly as we have not had the support of our people that we had expected.'[16]

An hour or so later, Ceannt arrived at Jameson's with a British officer, and conferred briefly with the leaders while the Volunteers from the South Dublin Union stood outside waiting to march to St Patrick's Park, the agreed surrender point. Colbert confirmed to Holland that: 'All was over ... [He] ... could hardly speak ... He was completely stunned. The tears rolled down his cheeks.' However, he had sufficient resolve to summon his bewildered garrison to the distillery yard, where he announced that 'we were surrendering unconditionally' and that 'anyone wishing to go or escape could do so'.[17] Soon afterwards, looking 'quite right by this time', he led his men through the main gate, where they fell in behind Ceannt's Volunteers and marched to Bride Street, adjacent to the park.[18] There, British troops had formed-up two deep on each side of the road, with bayonets fixed and machine-guns strategically located. A rebel recalls: 'Major Armstrong who was in charge of the military personally questioned all ... as to their names and addresses, made a demand for the surrender of all arms', and once these had been collected 'a group of officers and NCOs gave every one of us a minute search'.[19] Holland also recorded his impression of these events, stating that:

> people were ordered to get away from the windows of the
> buildings on each side and to close them ... A military
> officer from the path in front of us gave the command for
> us to lay down all our arms on the road in front of us. He
> then ordered us to march forward towards him, and when
> we got to the kerb brought us to a halt. A military lorry was
> then passed down behind us, and soldiers started to throw
> our rifles and revolvers into the lorry. A few shots went off
> as a few of the late owners had forgotten to extract the
> cartridges.

They were then conducted under escort to Richmond Barracks. Nearing their own company recruitment area, Holland recalls that jeering and abusive crowds had gathered who insulted them by name. He adds that the rebels 'appreciated the British troops [who] saved us from manhandling.'[20]

That evening, crammed tightly into billets, the prisoners contemplated their future. Holland records that after a pause Colbert spoke, stating that 'from his point of view he would prefer to be executed'. He continued: 'We are all ready to meet our God ... Now that we are defeated, outside that barrack wall the people whom we have tried to emancipate have demonstrated nothing but hatred and contempt for us. We would be better off dead as life would be a torture. We thank the Mother of God for her kindness in her intercession for us that we have had the time to prepare ourselves to meet our

Redeemer.'[21] Colbert then called on everyone to recite the rosary for the spiritual and temporal welfare of those who fought in the cause of Irish freedom, past, present and future generations. His comments reveal the devastating psychological impact of the day's events; they were dramatic, sudden, and beyond his capacity to control or even to influence. The morning's euphoria and high expectations based on his own company's successes had been shattered by defeat – a defeat apparently celebrated most by those he knew best, the inhabitants of Inchicore. The experience left him traumatised and deeply disillusioned – his religious faith providing his only consolation.

Next day, 1 May, when the rebels were ushered into the gymnasium at Richmond Barracks, Colbert was one of those whom DMP detectives thought merited a court martial and ordered to one side. He was tried on 4 May, (prisoner number seventy), under an inaccurately spelt Irish version of his name. Colonel D. Sapte presided, as he was to do at the trials of MacDermott and Connolly. The proceedings can only have lasted a matter of minutes. Major J.A. Armstrong was the only prosecution witness; he was called in the cases of all five rebels who surrendered at St Patrick's Park and were later executed. On each occasion, he gave essentially the same vacuous and circumstantial evidence. He began by stating that he had been present at 'Bride Street and Patrick's Park,' on 30 April, 'where the British Troops were fired on'. He claimed that the accused was 'one of a party which surrendered about 5 p.m.,' that he was dressed in a Volunteer captain's uniform and was armed. This last assertion he justified on the grounds that the officers generally 'were armed with pistols or revolvers'. He concluded by stating that 'these men who surrendered came from the direction in which firing had taken place'.[22]

Little of Armstrong's testimony bore any direct relation to Colbert's case and was therefore of little relevance in establishing the extent of his guilt or innocence. Most, if not all the firing which Armstrong referred to, had come from snipers (possibly just one) based in Jacob's Biscuit Factory or surrounding buildings who were probably unaware of Pearse's surrender order. The defendant had come from Jameson's Distillery, Marrowbone Lane, which had been militarily inactive since Friday. Moreover, Holland states that the Volunteers did not leave there until 6:30 p.m.; those based at Jacob's had arrived earlier, at 5 P.M. It is thus evident that Armstrong knew with certainty little or nothing about Colbert – neither which rebel garrison he had belonged to nor which outpost he had served in, let alone what his specific role in the Rising had been. The insurgents had taken prisoners at Marrowbone Lane – a gatekeeper and British army sergeant – and had they been called by the prosecution they might have been able to provide relevant testimony. Colbert did not cross-examine the witness; he was the only one of the rebels not to challenge Armstrong's evidence. When asked for a statement 'in his defence', he merely replied: 'I have nothing to say.'[23]

The court found the defendant guilty and, on 6 May, Maxwell confirmed its sentence of death. He later justified his decision on the highly dubious grounds that the accused was 'one of the most active members of the Sinn Féin organisation,' (as in other cases this was only valid if it was taken to include Fianna and the Irish Volunteers) and a 'close associate of the leaders'. The GOC accepted without question, Armstrong's claims that Colbert had been armed at the time of surrender and had come from the 'neighbourhood of houses from which heavy firing had taken place earlier in the day'. More accurately, Maxwell noted that he was 'prominent in the rebel army' and had held the rank of captain.[24]

Colbert was transferred to Kilmainham prison, probably on 4 May. Unlike the other rebels executed, he did not request either his family or friends to visit him there. In a letter to his sister, Lila, he explained: 'I did not call you to this jail ... I felt it would grieve us both too much.' During his final hours, he wrote ten letters in all, to relatives and friends, bidding them farewell and asking for their prayers. In one he expressed the hope that he would 'die well', and in others stated: 'Don't blame me, perhaps it is God's way of saving my soul', and 'May God grant you freedom soon in the fullest possible sense'.[25]

In the evening before his execution, 7 May, he requested that a fellow prisoner, Mrs Seamus Murphy, be brought to his cell (both she and her husband had served at Jameson's and were being held in Kilmainham). Mrs Murphy's meeting with Colbert reveals something of his mental state before his execution.

When I entered the cell Con was lying on the floor with a blanket over him. There was no plank bed or mattress of any kind in the cell and the night was bitterly cold. There was a little table and stool in the cell, and a candle lighting

on the table as Con was expecting the priest. He jumped
up when he saw me and said: 'How are you? I am one of
the lucky ones.' Of course I knew what was going to
happen to him when he said that. 'I am proud,' he said, 'to
die for such a cause, I will be passing away at the dawning
of the day'. I said: 'What about Eamonn Ceannt?' He was
the only other one of the men I knew. He replied: 'He has
drawn the lucky lot as well' ... He said he never felt happier
... the soldier who was present was crying.[26]

He asked her to give his prayer book to one of his sisters and to say,
along with the other Cumann na mBan members, a Hail Mary
when they heard the volleys next mornings. Father Augustine had
accompanied Colbert to the execution yard, and noted as they
walked, 'his lips moving in prayer'.[27] He was executed at between
3:45 and 4:05 a.m. on the morning of 8 May. Robert Holland who
knew him so well writes: 'I am of the opinion that he got the death
he prayed and wished for ... [It was] ... a happy release ... He had as
much as told me so.'[28] Colbert was the second of the executed leaders to be a leading figure in Fianna, the other being Sean Heuston
(in addition, two youths in the organisation were killed in action
while delivering dispatches).[29] Colbert's case was raised in the
House of Commons at Westminster. Mr P.J. O'Shaughnessy asked:
'what grounds there were for the execution of Con Colbert, a
native of Athea, whether his youthful age was taken into account
before sentence, whether he was a signatory of the republican
Proclamation and whether he had the ministration of a priest before
death?' Mr H.J. Tennant, the Under Secretary of State for War,
replied that: 'Con Colbert was a captain in the rebel army. Every cir-
cumstance connected with the case including that mentioned by
the honourable member was given due consideration before the
sentence of death was confirmed.' He added that: 'Colbert was not
a signatory of the republican Proclamation, [and that] the ministration of a priest was given in his case, as in others, before the
sentence was carried out'.[30]

Trial of Cornelius Colbert
(Concobar O' Colbaird)
prisoner number seventy

REFERENCE: PRO WO71/352

DATE: 4 May 1916

LOCATION: Richmond Barracks

JUDGES: Colonel D. Sapte (President), Major W.R. James,
Major D.B. Frew

CHARGE:

'Did an act to wit did take part in an armed rebellion and in the
waging of war against His Majesty the King, such act being o such
a nature as to be calculated to be prejudical to the Defence to the
Realm and being done with the intention and for the purpose of
assisting the enemy'

PLEA: Not guilty

(The members of the court and witnesses were duly sworn in)

VERDICT: Guilty. Death

Text of Trial

Summary of Evidence

Accused – Concobar O'Colbaird

PROSECUTION

Major J.A. Armstrong Royal Inniskilling Fusiliers states –

On 30th April 1916 I was present at Bride Street and
Patrick's Park where the British Troops were fired upon.
The accused was one of a party which surrendered about 5
pm. He was dressed in a Volunteer Captain's uniform and
was armed. These officers were armed with pistols or
revolvers.

These men who surrendered came from the direction in
which firing had taken place.

DEFENCE

The accused in his defence states:

I have nothing to say.

THOMAS R. KENT

(Courtmartialled May 4th and Shot at Cork Barracks, 4th May, 1916).

Thomas Kent

__THOMAS KENT__. (Executed 9th May at Cork)

This man's crime was in effect the murder of Head Constable Rowe near Fermoy on 2nd May. Some Police Officers were sent to arrest him and his brother, and shots were fired from the house in a most deliberate manner, killing the Chief Constable.

Extract from a memorandum entitled 'Short History of rebels on whom it has been necessary to inflict the supreme penalty' sent by General Sir John Maxwell to Herbert Asquith, on 11 May 1916.

THOMAS KENT WAS BORN IN 1865, the fourth in a family of nine children. In 1916, he was the oldest of the four sons still living at home with their mother, then in her eighties, at Bawnard House, four miles from Fermoy, County Cork; the house was located on a prosperous two hundred-acre, owner-occupied farm. He was a total abstainer, an earnest Irish language student and an enthusiastic exponent of Irish music and dancing. Aged nineteen, and after the death of his father, he had emigrated briefly to the United States, and there worked for a catholic church furniture-maker in Boston, before being forced by ill-health to return to Ireland. He and some of his brothers acquired a local reputation for their active involve-ment in the Land League agitation during the late 1880s when they were arrested. Following the Parnellite split in the Home Rule party Kent appears to have held aloof from political activity for some years.[1]

After the Irish Volunteer Force was launched, Kent helped Terence MacSwiney organise companies in North-East Cork; his own unit claimed to be the first teetotal corps in Ireland. His brother, William, said of him in 1916, that he had by then become 'very active' in the movement, 'devoted all his time to it ... that was his whole study'.[2] Local police frequently observed him attending, in uniform, Volunteer recruitment meetings, parades and demonstrations, in Cork, Limerick and Dublin, where he represented his district at an IVF convention in October 1915. They regarded him as a 'local leader' both in the force and in Sinn Féin, an active anti-enlistment campaigner (regarding crown forces) and 'dangerous'.[3] During and after 1914, he was again arrested several times for the collection and possession of arms and for making seditious speeches. The last occa-sion before the Rising was for remarks he was alleged to have made at Ballymac, near Fermoy, on 13 January 1916. Though he was tried and subsequently acquited, a substantial arms cache was discovered by police in the course of a search at Bawnard House.

Of the other brothers then living at home, local police considered David to be 'as strongly associated with the volunteer movement as Thomas'. Richard had been regarded as 'decent' and 'inoffensive', but more recently was thought to be imitating their example. He had been a fine athlete, holding all-Ireland medals under the GAA for hurdling and hammer throwing, but a serious sporting accident had caused irreparable brain damage and had noticeably changed his personality. As a consequence, he was placed in Cork Lunatic Asylum for four years. The fourth brother, William, appears to have held consistently moderate political opinions: the RIC described him as being 'always opposed to his brothers' actions'.[4]

According to one newspaper account 'Cork's reputation was worthily redeemed' during the Rising by the actions of Thomas Kent.[5] The county was virtually inactive during Easter week, even though the IRB Military Council had successfully infiltrated its Volunteer leadership with pro-insurrection officers, and elaborate plans for the area had been devised. The revolt in Dublin and arrival of the *Aud* on the west coast were to have been the trigger for a sudden, dramatic eruption of activity throughout Munster in which crown forces were to have been overwhelmed. Once the *Aud* had landed, Tralee was to have been cut off, isolated and taken over by Volunteers and a goods train despatched to Fenit pier to receive and then help distribute the weapons throughout much of the west of Ireland. Initially the role of the force in Cork was to assist the branches in Kerry, under the cover of a three-day Volunteer mobilisation to begin on Easter Sunday. It was to prevent police and troops moving by road or rail and interfering with activities so strategically vital to the insurrection.[6]

Police in the county had from the outset been highly suspicious as to the true purpose of these publicised IVF mobilisation plans. They had been forewarned in March by headquarters in Dublin to be 'especially vigilant in watching Irish Volunteer movements in view of the probability of a hostile landing of arms and men'. They monitored with growing concern the increased pace of the local force's activities as the appointed day, Sunday 23 April, approached. To their immense relief when the day came, though a number of Volunteer branches assembled 'to their entire strength' (especially those in areas adjoining Kerry), and marched or held manoeuvres, they then quietly returned to their homes 'in scattered groups'.[7]

After all the preceding 'feverish activity', the rank and file Volunteers felt 'confused, fatigued and harassed'.[8] Local police dismissed the force's publicised explanation for abandoning its manoeuvres – 'the very bad weather'. They instead attributed it to Casement's arrest and the 'failure of his expedition'. The RIC County Inspector for Cork reported: 'Only that the plans misfired for the landing of arms on the Kerry coast the whole country would have been ablaze.'[9] A further factor of which he was unaware was the impact on the local leadership of MacNeill's countermand order, stating that the Easter Sunday manoeuvres had been cancelled. It had been delivered by hand on Good Friday morning by J.J. O'Connell. It was in fact to be the first of many such instructions: between 21 and 24 April, 'nine separate dispatches arrived in Cork, some contradictory or countermanding, others confirming, previous orders'.[10] A later Volunteer headquarters inquiry into the inactivity of the county's units during Easter week, concluded that 'there was nothing but confusion as to what Dublin wanted them to do'. Cathal Brugha likewise concluded that 'owing to the sinking of the arms ship and subsequent conflicting orders, Cork could not have acted other than they did'.[11]

The County Inspector recorded that after Easter Sunday, the Volunteers remained 'very excited and aggressive' for much of the following week: there was a 'state of tension ... We were nightly expecting attacks on RIC barracks and Post Offices and banks.' In fact the only incidents which he reported were that a police sergeant was held-up, searched and threatened on the public road by an IVF unit and that a single telegraph pole was cut down (both incidents occurring on Sunday, 30 April). On Friday, 28 April, he was instructed by the RIC Inspector General in Dublin that it was time to 'proceed vigorously against the Rebels'. However, next day, the military Officer Commanding, Cork district, advised the County Inspector to 'avoid friction' until he received further orders. At 1 a.m., 2 May, they were issued: the police were informed that the temporary armistice had expired and that they could proceed with the arrest of local extremists and the seizure of arms. By then, normality was returning to Dublin, and Enniscorthy had surrendered on 1 May, the final episode of the Rising in the provinces. Mobile platoons of troops were being despatched to Cork and elsewhere to complete the pacification of the country and to crush 'disloyalty.'[12]

At 2:30 a.m. on 2 May, seven RIC members under the command of Head Constable Rowe, left Fermoy by motor ambulance. They had already made two arrests in the Castlelyons area, before proceeding to Bawnard House nearby to take Thomas and David Kent into custody. Both were described as 'prominent Sinn Féiners'; prior to the night of 1 May, Thomas had been 'on the run' for some weeks. The policemen arrived after daybreak, at between 3:45 and 4 a.m. and stood 'with swords fixed and magazines loaded' as the Head

Constable knocked the back door and ordered the occupants to come out. The police reports are inconsistent: certainly a verbal exchange followed during which a voice from inside (possibly Thomas's) retorted either: 'We will not surrender. We will leave some of you dead,' or 'We will die before we surrender.' An RIC officer, Sergeant S. Coldbeck, then advised Rowe to take cover. Rowe stepped back and was standing in a gateway looking towards the house when, minutes later, the Kents opened fire. Three shots rang out – one from a bedroom window and two from a shotgun positioned at a lobby window, overlooking the back door. The second of these struck the Head Constable just above the ear, killing him instantly. A medical officer from Fermoy Hospital who later attended the scene reported that his 'brain matter was lying around him'.[13]

An hour-long gun-battle ensued, during which police reinforcements were requested from Fermoy, and David Kent was gravely wounded. At about 4:50 a.m., someone from inside the building called out that 'one of the occupants was dying' and requested that a priest be sent for. Sergeant Coldbeck replied that this would be done, but only after the family had thrown out its weapons and ammunition. After a 5 to 10 minute delay, two shotguns and an ancient, ex-British army service, Lee Enfield rifle were despatched from one of the windows; inspection later showed that all had been recently fired. The occupants themselves did not come out. Once more the police accounts are conflicting. It appears that the family did offer to surrender, but was instructed by Coldbeck to 'hold back'. He had summoned military assistance from Fermoy, requesting that troops come and help the police to 'prevent anyone escaping from the house'. He wished therefore to delay until the soldiers had arrived. During the intervening period (lasting at least an hour) the RIC officers continued to shoot in the direction of the house. This they justified later in court by saying that they suspected the Kents had retained some of their arms. Though the Kents did not return fire, in a later search of the property one firearm and some ammunition were removed.[14]

It was after 6 a.m. when the troops at last arrived. When requested by the police sergeant, the occupants of the house surrendered, having first received assurances that a military officer was present. They emerged 'one by one through a window in the ground floor', which itself suggests that the doors of the building had been barricaded. William came first, then Thomas. Richard followed: he was later described in court as being 'semi-demented' at the time. Once outside, he instantly made a dash for freedom, despite calls from his brothers as well as from the soldiers to stop. He was shot and severely wounded having gone barely twenty-five yards; though taken to Fermoy Hospital he died of his injuries on 4 May. David who was also brought there, recovered and stood trial at Richmond Barracks on 15 and 16 June 1916. On 3 May, Thomas and William were escorted to Cork Detention Barracks, where both were court-martialled next day (military officers commanding in the provinces had been empowered by Maxwell to try within their own district any rebels who resisted arrest). William was acquitted. At the time of the family's surrender, he had said: 'Do not blame me I had nothing to do with this business,' and police were satisfied that he had taken no active part in the resistance.[15] Meanwhile, Mrs Kent had been released from custody at noon on 2 May. Seamus Fitzgerald, who occupied the cell next to Thomas Kent in the Detention Barracks, states that, prior to his appearance in court, he was very strictly isolated from the other prisoners and that none of them had any contact with him.[16]

Thomas Kent after his arrest on 2 May 1916, with his brother, William

ALLEN LIBRARY

Surprisingly, the charge brought against Thomas Kent was identical to that used in the trial of each of the rebels court-martialled in Dublin after the Rising and subsequently executed ('that he did take

Irish Rebellion, May, 1916.
Arrest of Edmund Kent. at 4 a.m.
THOMAS
He was subsequently shot.

part in an armed rebellion ... for the purpose of assisting the enemy'). Maxwell's legal advisor, A.T. Bucknill, was to comment at a later date in reference to the trial of David Kent: 'The difficulty ... in ... [this] ... case is that no rebellion took place in Cork and the case appears to be more one of ordinary murder'.[17] The prosecution called five witnesses – three RIC members who were involved in the gun-battle at Bawnard House and two of the military officers summoned by the police to provide assistance when the family was surrendering. Each gave a graphic description of the episode but said nothing directly implicating Thomas Kent in Rowe's death. It is, however, difficult to disagree with the judge's summing up in the case of David Kent, which was held by General Court-Martial with the same five prosecution witnesses. He stated that the Kent family had been 'determined to resist the police in the execution of their duty ... not stopping short of using deadly force against them'.[18]

Thomas Kent entered a plea of not guilty. He cross-examined three of those giving evidence. In so doing, he established that he had not on the most recent previous occasion (January 1916) resisted being arrested, that the police had continued firing after the Kents had discarded their weapons (though RIC accounts suggest that they had not handed over all of them) and that Richard had been in an asylum. He also made a brief statement emphatically denying the charge. He stated: 'On 2 May 1916 during the night I was awakened by the sound of firearms and I immediately went into my mother's room, where my brother William was. They were standing on the bed in the corner of the room. I immediately went into the corner where they were, where the three of us remained till the military officers arrived when we immediately surrendered. I never fired or had arms in my hand.'[19] At David's trial in June, William, who was called as a defence witness, conceded that Thomas had taken an active part in the gun-battle, because he was 'so enthusiastic in the Sinn Féin movement'. The Defence Counsel went further, stating that Thomas 'was engaged in the shooting of the Head Constable', adding 'I am satisfied that he was convicted by satisfactory evidence'.[20] At the time, the barrister was, of course, more concerned to exculpate David Kent from blame than to assess objectively the strength of the prosecution's case in Thomas's trial.

The court found Thomas Kent guilty, and on 6 May Maxwell confirmed its sentence of death. The GOC rejected a plea for clemency from the Mayor of Cork, writing in reply: 'I think it unwise to comply with the request. Thomas Kent murdered a policeman.'[21] He justified his decision to Asquith on identical grounds, stating: 'shots were fired from the house [Bawnard House] in the most deliberate manner'.[22] The Prime Minister's only reservation appears to have been the wording of the charge used in the trial. He stated: 'It should have been made clear that ... [Thomas Kent] ... was executed for murder' (in David Kent's case the indictment included the phrase – '[he] did kill and murder' Head Constable Rowe).[23] No doubt the severity of Thomas Kent's punishment for involvement in a relatively minor skirmish reflected the government's concern to demonstrate to the Irish people that now the rebellion had been crushed, it would not tolerate any further violent opposition to its authority. In this it may have been effective as shortly after the shoot-out at Bawnard House, the Cork Volunteers began handing over some of their weapons to crown forces. Nonetheless, the case does highlight the inconsistency of the courts; on 8 May 1916, Thomas Ashe was sentenced to death for his part in the Battle of Ashbourne in which a dozen or more RIC men were killed, yet the court's verdict was commuted by the GOC to penal servitude for life. Arguably, David Kent's injury had the effect of saving his life. By June, when he was fit to stand trial, Maxwell was more conscious of the disastrous impact that the executions were having on public opinion, and he commuted his death sentence to five years penal servitude. David was in fact released in June 1917; his mother died during the period of his captivity.

The execution of Thomas Kent, and the critical fact that it had occurred outside the capital, served further to enrage John Dillon, the moderate Irish Parliamentary Party MP. Speaking in the Commons on 11 May, he highlighted its likely impact on Irish opinion. He stated: 'I have received word that a man named Kent had been executed in Fermoy, which is the first execution that has taken place outside Dublin. The fact is one which will create a very grave shock in Ireland. Because it looks like a roving commission to carry these horrible executions all over the country. This, I say, was the first execution outside the city of Dublin. In a district where there have been no serious disturbances.' He continued, referring to Maxwell: 'Would not any sensible statesman think he had enough to do in Dublin and the other centres where disturbance broke out without doing everything possible to raise disturbance and spread disaffection over the whole country?' It was in the context of these observations that he proceeded to warn the Prime Minister: 'You are letting loose a river of blood and, make no mistake about it, between two races who, after three hundred years of hatred and of strife, we had nearly succeeded in bringing together.' Asquith appeared to be unimpressed by Dillon's comments on the Kent case. During the debate, he responded by commenting: 'There is ... a man called Thomas Kent who has been executed – most properly executed as everybody will admit – for murder at Fermoy.' In actual fact Asquith may have been more impressed by Dillon's remarks than was immediately apparent. As a consequence of Asquith's pressure on Maxwell, when David Kent was tried in mid-June, his case was heard by the highest form of military court, a General Court Martial (his brother had been tried by Field General Court Martial). He was thus able to call on legal representation when presenting his defence. Also, unlike Thomas, he was charged with murder and his trial was held in open court. Again, this was partly on the Prime Minister's insistence; he had informed the commons on 11 May 1916, that if there were any future cases 'in which a charge of murder is preferred, instructions will be given that the court-martial shall be held in public with open doors'.[24]

Thomas Kent was informed of Maxwell's decision in his case on 8 May. Before his execution his spiritual needs were attended to by Father John Sexton, the priest at a church nearby and chaplain to the military hospital. Kent was shot at Cork Detention Barracks in the early hours of 9 May. Some years later, Volunteer Liam O'Briain described meeting a serviceman in 1925 who had been posted to Cobh by the Royal Navy during the First World War, and who claimed to have been in charge of Kent's firing squad. He stated that the prisoner died 'very bravely. Not a feather out of him.'[25] He was buried in the grounds of the barracks (requests for his body to be transferred to the family vault at Castlelyons were dismissed). David Kent, who was briefly detained at the same military post before being transferred to stand trial in Dublin, recalled afterwards how 'three mornings in succession he passed over a newly made grave there and realised only on the fourth from a rough cross painted upon it that there lay the ashes of his brother'.[26]

Overleaf:
The complete text of the official proceedings of the court martial of Thomas Kent. The trial took place at Cork Detention Barracks, on 4 May 1916.

Trial of Thomas Kent

Statement against Thomas Kent.

1st Witness.

Sgt S. Caldbeck R.I.C. being duly sworn is examined by the prosecutor & states: —

On 2nd May 1916 between 3.45: a.m. & 4. a.m. I proceeded with Hd Con: Rowe to the house of Mrs Kent, with instructions to arrest Thomas Kent & his brother David Kent. Four other police accompanied us. The Head Constable knocked at the door, and when challenged said he was a policeman, & ordered the occupants to come down & open the door. A reply from the lobby window to the effect that "we will never surrender, we will leave some of you dead." The shot was fired from the lobby window on North side, a second shot was fired from a bed room window facing East: a third shot was again fired from the lobby window, which blew the face off Hd Con: Rowe. This happened about five minutes after they were told to come down. About 4.50 a.m. someone from within called out that one of the occupants was dying, & asked for the priest. I answered "If you throw out all your arms I may send for the priest." At about ten minutes after this three fire arms were thrown out, but the occupants did not come out themselves. All these arms, on examining them, had recently been fired on the arrival of the military. Four men, including the prisoner, who came out second

and his mother came out
+ surrendered to the officer in
charge. Constable Dolan brought me
another fire arm which he found
in a bed room in searching the
house. I examined it, It had
quite recently been fired

Cross-examined

Did not Constable Dolan let this   Q. 1
fire arm off by mistake?

Yes.
                                     A 1

after the fire arms had been thrown   Q. 2
out of the house, did not the police
continue to fire into the house?

Yes, occasionally
                                     A. 2

Was there any firing from
the house after the three   Q. 3
arms had been thrown out?

No
                                     A. 3

Why did you continue to fire   Q. 4
after we threw out our arms?

Having reason to believe that all   A. 4
the arms were not surrendered

Constable F. Kuc R.I.C. being duly   2nd Witness
sworn is examined by the prosecutor
+ states :-
On 2nd May 1916, I accompanied
Hd Con: Rowe + other R.I.C. to Mrs Kent's
house to carry out an arrest. I
was posted on the west side of the

house almost immediately I
heard some shots fired. on the third
shot being fired, I saw it hit H.
Con: Rowe & he dropped dead. The
shot came from the house.

9

3rd Witness.

Constable J. Norris R.I.C. being duly sworn
is examined by the prosecutor states:—
on 2nd May 1916 at about 4. am.
I arrived at Mrs Kent's House, in company
with H. Con: Rowe & other R.I.C. I accompanied
H. Con: Rowe to the back door. The Head
Constable Knocked at the door. a voice
from the window asked who was
there & H. Con: Rowe answered "police"
& to come down & let him in. Shortly
after a shot was fired from the
lobby window, where the voice came
from. Shortly after two more shots
were fired in succession. Previous
to this when the occupants were told
to come down & open the door, a voice
from inside called out "we will
die before we surrender". Later, after
the firing had taken place, & the Hd
Constable had been Killed, a man
inside the house called out, that
one of them had been wounded, &
asked for a priest, About 4. 55 am.
three fire arms were thrown out of
the windows, and they offered to
surrender, but they were told by
Sgt Caldbeck to hold back, until
military assistance arrived. On
the military arriving the occupants
came out & surrendered. On entering
the house later I saw six cartridges
£ 12. Bore, No 6 shot. lying on the floor
The accused was the second man
to come out of the house. We which

10/

to Mrs Kents' house originally to
arrest Thomas (the prisoner) & David
his brother as being prominent
Sinn Feiners.

10

Cross-examined.

Had you previously come to my house
with the intention of arresting me?

Q. 5

Yes, for an offence against the
Defence of the Realm act.

A. 5

Did I resist?

Q. 6

No.

A 6

Was I not acquitted for this offence
at Cork?

Q. 7

Yes.

A. 7

Was not my brother Richard in an
asylum?

Q. 8

Yes, but is now released.

A. 8

2nd Lieut. P. J. McChesney, 15th Rl. Fusiliers
being duly sworn is examined by
the prosecutor & states:—

4th Witness.

On 2nd May 1916 at some time between
6. am & 8. am. I proceeded with
some of other officers to the house of
the Kents, with orders to prevent any
one escaping from the house. On my
arrival I found a police sergt.
& a Constable, also the body of
the dead Head Constable. I heard
the Sergt. R.I.C ask the occupants
to "surrender" onwards & that

11

4th Witness
(Continued)

effect. Someone inside asked if
there was an officer present. I said
that I was one, & called upon them
to surrender. They did so, coming down
one by one through a window on the
ground floor. The prisoner now before
the Court was the second to come out.
Four men & one woman came out **11**
altogether. One of the men tried to escape
& was severely wounded, when he had
gone about 25 yards. An old service
rifle was lying outside the house, also
another fire arm. I handed these over to
the Sergt R.I.C. I then searched the house.
There were two shot guns also leaning
against the wall of the house outside,
one had an empty cartridge case
in it. There was also a bandolier
with ammunition with these guns. The
McCristelle revolver was also with
these arms.

Cross - examined.

Did I attempt to escape?

9   Q.

9   A.   No.

5th Witness   2nd Lieut. R.S. Page   14th Royal Fusiliers
being duly
Sworn is examined by the Prosecutor
states:-
On 2d May 1916 about 6. a.m. I proceed
with four other officers to the house
occupied by the Kents, close to Fermoy,
with instructions to prevent anyone
from escaping from the house. The
occupants of the house were called

12

upon to surrender by the police
Sergt. and they said they would
surrender to an officer. On being
informed that an officer was
present, they came out & surrendered.
There were four men & one woman
came out of the house.

13
13

The Prisoner Thomas Keith states:-
On 2nd May 1916, during the night I
was awakened by the sound of
fire arms, & I immediately went into
my mother's room where my brother
William was. They were standing in
the bed in the corner of the room, I immediately went into the corner where they were.
When the three of us remained till the
military officers arrived. When we
immediately surrendered. I never fired
or had arms in my hand.

R.G.B. Jeffreys Major

Padt.

Field Gen. C.M.

4th May 1916

Michael Mallin

MICHAEL MALLIN.

This man was second in command of the Larkinite or Citizen Army with which organisation he had been connected since its inception. He was in command of the rebels who occupied Stephens Green and the College of Surgeons. At those places serious encounters took place and there were many casualties both amongst the military and civilians. He surrendered on the 30th April and was accompanied by a body of 109 rebels all of whom were armed.

Extract from a memorandum entitled 'Short History of rebels on whom it has been necessary to inflict the supreme penalty' sent by General Sir John Maxwell to Herbert Asquith, on 11 May 1916.

BODLEIAN LIBRARY, UNIVERSITY OF OXFORD

MICHAEL MALLIN WAS FORTY-TWO YEARS OF AGE in 1916. He was a small, slight, dapper looking Dubliner, with thick dark hair and a long moustache. He was a silk weaver by trade, a labour organiser (Secretary of the Silk Weavers' Union from 1909) and for a time a shop owner; his premises had been forced to close owing to the poverty in the city in 1913. He was an accomplished flautist, a band instructor with the Transport Union, a devout catholic and member of a Working Men's Temperance Committee. His grandfather had taken part in the Fenian Rising of 1867. The most formative phase in his own political development appears to have come after he enlisted in the British army, the Royal Fusiliers, in 1888, aged fourteen. Over the next twelve years he saw service in India and then in South Africa and it was there he acquired strong pro-Boer and anti-imperialist sympathies.

Before the First World War, Mallin's home in Inchicore (Emmet Hall, the premises of the Irish Transport Union), was used by local Volunteers for indoor training; it was in a strategically sensitive location, adjacent to Richmond Barracks. He joined the Irish Citizen Army at its inception in 1913, becoming its Chief of Staff when Connolly became its Commandant in 1914 and was second in authority only to him. As part of his duties, he organised manoeuvres and indoor exercises, taught scouting and signalling; he was 'very keen on drilling' and an enthusiastic student of military strategy. He was particularly active in acquiring arms for the force; he was said to have a 'genius' for coaxing weapons from soldiers. Training sessions always ended with an address, often delivered by Mallin in his 'quiet, pleasing, well-modulated voice'. In these, he always made it clear that he 'regarded the Citizen Army as as a practical military force for use in the near future'. Though he was initially distrusted by its members because of his British army service, R.M. Fox, who wrote the Irish Citizen Army's history, states that Mallin became with Connolly 'the mainstream of the CA' and was a 'good soldier and vivid personality'. He won respect and admiration as he was likeable, tireless, resourceful and selfless. Fox continues: 'He distinguished himself by those qualities of personal leadership and military discipline which the situation demanded ... He endeared himself ... by ... the comradeship he had for everyone ... [He was] ... a good soldier who had not allowed any of his human feelings to be blunted. He took innumerable risks for the CA and devoted himself wholeheartedly to the task of building it up.'[1]

Mallin's relationship with Connolly was more formal than intimate. Mallin suffered from periodic occurrences of malaria, contracted when serving with the British army in India, which could make him appear intoxicated. Sensitive by nature, he was once offended when his superior accused him of being drunk. It was his regular appearances from mid-1915, at the head of ICA route marches, uniformed and with a revolver often visible in his waistcoat, which first drew him to the attention of the Dublin police. He was fully involved in the force's preparations for the Rising. Diarmuid Lynch considers that had Connolly not fallen into line with the Military Council's plans in January 1916, he would not have been released and, Lynch continues, 'who is so naive as to believe that Mallin would have been permitted to remain at large to lead the ICA into immediate action. The men [Military Council] ... would have found a way to deal with Mallin.'[2] Early in Holy Week, Mallin was present at a drill instruction, when Connolly called members out individually and outlined to each their specific function during the opening stages of the Rising. William Oman claims that on Good Friday, 21 April, Mallin dispatched one of his men to Amiens Street to watch for 'any movements of troops or a big force of police'. When he reported back, Mallin informed him that 'a meeting of the provisional government' was in progress (ICA members were acting as bodyguards) and that the *Aud* had been captured.[3] Months earlier Mallin had assembled an orchestra with just four members, formed to help sustain the morale of the force; it played regularly on Sunday evenings at Liberty Hall. His pianist recalls that on Easter Sunday, 'on the eve of the revolution, we set to our task as usual and played all the night as if it were just a normal night'.[4]

Connolly had given Mallin command of the main ICA body involved in the Rising: it was to occupy St Stephen's Green. At 10 a.m. on Easter Monday morning, clearly disappointed by the turnout, Mallin indicated to James O'Shea: 'We will be fighting in a short time ... and we will have to fight alone.' When O'Shea asked if any of the Volunteers would fight, Mallin replied: 'There is no knowing ... but it will be short and sharp. We will all be dead in a short time.'[5] At 11:45 a.m., 24 April, Mallin set off from Liberty Hall with just thirty-six men (half the number expected) and with the women's units and Fianna boys in support. Countess Markievicz, who was his second-in-command, was busy delivering first-aid equipment, and followed the others later by car. Despite his lack of formal education, Mallin proved himself to be a capable officer during the Rising – typically calm and methodical, respected and trusted by his men. His military experience served him well, but when it came to strategy, he was unimaginative and this was a grave deficiency.

Soon after midday, St Stephen's Green was successfully cleared and occupied and on Mallin's orders, some adjacent properties were taken as outposts; most crucially these included the College of Surgeons, a large, tall, strong fortress-like building in St Stephen's Green West. The main focus of his defensive preparations was on the potential British military threat from the south and east of the Green. Surprisingly, no attempt was made at any stage to seize the Shelborne, Dublin's premier hotel. It dominated virtually the entire park, especially the north side and initially, it was defenceless. The gravity of this tactical blunder soon became tragically evident. Early on Tuesday morning, the building was occupied by one hundred and twenty British troops from Dublin Castle, undetected by rebels, some of whom were entrenched no more than thirty yards away. From 4 a.m., a machine-gun located on the top floor delivered a systematic and withering barrage across the square, mercilessly exposing the inadequacy of the rebels' defences, inflicting casualties and finally compelling Mallin to evacuate his beleaguered forces to the College of Surgeons.[6] In the early morning stillness, Dick Humphries, a Volunteer at the GPO, heard 'a volley of shots ring out with startling distinctiveness',[7] coming from the direction of the Green.

At once, the rebel garrison sought to make the building secure, but for the rest of the week it existed under a veritable state of siege. Although it was solidly built and therefore made an ideal outpost, it was also cold and uncongenial, its large, draughty rooms abounded with cases filled with specimens used for the instruction of students, including jars containing human body parts preserved in liquid. The air was permeated with the smell of formaldehyde. Mallin sought with little positive effect to devise fresh strategies in response to these changed and unforeseen circumstances – by seizing further outposts and even by unsuccessfully attempting to drive the military out of the Shelborne by setting fire to adjacent property. However, he was able to acquire some much needed food supplies and additional manpower from Commandant MacDonagh at Jacob's Biscuit Factory. The newly-arrived Volunteers were at once impressed by the disciplined, regimented, purposeful atmosphere Mallin had imposed at the college. He personally ensured that there was no wanton damage to property; in one case at least he court-martialled a refractory garrison member. He also led by example, fighting with courage and showing impressive skills of marksman-ship.[8]

By Friday, with the conflagration in Sackville Street clearly visible and an all-out British assault on their position thought imminent, Mallin discussed with his officers the feasibility of fighting a way through the military cordon and conducting guerrilla warfare in the hills. During the discussion, O'Briain heard an animated Markievicz expressing a longing for a bayonet or 'some stabbing instrument for action at close quarters', which elicited Mallin's bemused response: 'You are very blood-thirsty.'[9] But at 3:45 p.m. on Saturday, Connolly accepted Pearse's surrender order and appended the specific instruc-tion so that it should apply to the Irish Citizen Army members in the St Stephen's Green command.

Eventually, at 11 a.m. on Sunday, this was delivered to Mallin by Elizabeth O'Farrell acting on behalf of both Pearse and the British military authorities. Mallin first consulted his officers; one of the women present claims to have heard him arguing with the Countess, who initially opposed acceptance. Then he summoned the whole garrison. O'Briain records the astonishment of its mem-bers, 'Surrender! But we had not started yet ... we had all along wait-ed to be attacked.'[10] Mallin recommended acceptance, stating that 'as a soldier he must obey, and as soldiers they must obey also'.[11] One of those present remembered how pale and slight he appeared, and how he had to repeat the surrender order three times. When pressed, he predicted that he would be shot along with the other commandants. Loyally, Markievicz gave him support, saying repeat-edly: 'I trust Connolly.' Volunteer Frank Robbins was struck by 'the atmosphere of awful gloom that had settled over the place ... Men and women who had been gay and light-hearted were now crying.'[12]

At 12:30 p.m., a British officer, Captain de Courcy Wheeler, arrived at the College of Surgeons to take the surrender (Nurse O'Farrell had earlier given Markievicz a 'slip with the directions on how to surrender').[13] Mallin emerged, in uniform, unarmed and carrying a white flag; he saluted the captain, indicated that he was in command and that he and his comrades wished to accept the terms agreed on their behalf. William Oman writes: 'At the appointed hour, we marched out into a double line of troops, ... We proceeded from York St into Stephen's Green, down Grafton St where the mob attempted to attack us. The British officer displayed great courage. He gave the rearguard the order: "About turn, present arms", and he told the crowd that, if they did not get back, he would shoot them. His action frightened off the mob, and we marched in peace down Grafton St.'[14] Mary O'Daly, one of the Cumann na mBan women in the unit, recalls: 'I carried a Red Cross flag as some extraordinary stories were afloat to account for the presence of women among the garrison.'[15] After they had been escorted to Richmond Barracks, DMP detectives identified Mallin and Markievicz and separated them from the others.

Mallin was court-martialled on 5 May, Brigadier Maconchy presiding. The prosecution called three witnesses, including two police constables who gave evidence relating to Mallin's republican involvement during the months prior to the Rising; one of them had witnessed him leading his garrison to the Green on Easter Monday morning. Neither was in a position to provide further information as all DMP members had been withdrawn from the streets a few hours later that day. Captain Wheeler then described the surrender of the St Stephen's Green garrison, and informed the court that Mallin had then declared himself to be its 'Commandant'.[16]

Mallin cross-examined the policemen only and called just one witness for the defence – Lawrence Kettle. He was chief of Dublin Corporation Electricity Department and had been held captive by the rebels throughout Easter week. Though he stated that he had been well treated, he did confirm that the defendant had 'appeared to be in command.' Mallin, in his own statement, made a determined bid to evade the firing squad and in the process gravely distorted the truth. He projected himself as a simple tradesman and band leader who had almost by chance become involved in the ICA and thus in the Rising itself. He sought to exculpate himself from blame by suggesting that he was a mere dupe, obeying orders, ignorant of his leader's insurrectionary plans. He stated: 'I had no commission whatever in the Citizen Army. I was never taken into the confidence of James Connolly. I was under the impression we were going out for manoeuvres on Sunday.' Once aware that a rising was intended, he claimed that he had covertly tried to subvert it, stating: 'I gave explicit orders to the men to make no offensive movements and I prevented them attacking the Shelborne hotel.'[17]

His testimony concerning Countess Markievicz precisely inverted their actual relationship in Easter week. He claimed that she was in command and that, on Easter Monday, she had 'ordered me to take command of the men, as I had been so long associated with them. I felt I could not leave them and from that time I joined the rebellion.'[18] As a consequence, he threatened literally to place her in the firing line. In her own recollections, she emphasised the fact that at St Stephen's Green, Mallin had 'definitely promoted' her to second-in-command.[19] In such extreme circumstances, it is hardly surprising that he should have manoeuvred so desperately to save his life; he had four children and an expectant wife. Perhaps also he believed that had the court accepted his evidence, it would not have executed a woman. During the surrender, when predicting that he would be shot, he had added, 'I question if they will shoot Lizzie' (the Countess's nickname).[20] However, it was a considerable risk to take with a loyal comrade's life, and hardly a chivalrous one.

Nevertheless, Mallin did show magnanimity and grace at the time of his trial. Captain Wheeler records that during the proceedings, the rebel leader had commented on 'how grateful my comrades and myself are for the kindness and consideration which Captain Wheeler has shown to us during this time'.[21] During his garrison's surrender Mallin had earlier given him a walking stick 'as a personal memento'.[22] At Richmond Barracks, he confided to a fellow prisoner: 'taking him all in all, the average Tommy Atkins in not a bad fellow'.[23] In his last letter to his wife he stated: 'I find no fault with the soldiers or police', and admonished her to 'pray for all the souls who fell in this fight, Irish and English.'[24]

The court found Mallin guilty of the main charge – taking 'part in an armed rebellion' – which was punishable by death, but not of the lesser one, attempting to cause civilian disaffection. Neither of the police witnesses claimed to have heard him make a speech and one noted that he was 'friendly with the police'. Next day, 6 May, Maxwell confirmed the sentence. Later, when justifying this decision to Asquith, he stated accurately that Mallin had been second-in-command of the ICA (and associated with it from the outset), commandant of the garrison at St Stephen's Green, where many casualties had occurred, and had led over one hundred armed rebels at the surrender there.[25]

Meanwhile, on the evening of Friday, 5 May, Mallin had been transferred under escort from Richmond Barracks to Kilmainham Gaol with twenty other prisoners. Their route took him past his home in Inchicore and he records seeing 'the dog ... at the door ... the only one of my household that I could cast my longing eyes on'.[26] The rebel group also included Colbert and Ceannt. On the Sunday morning, they attended mass, celebrated by a priest from a neighbouring church. One Volunteer recalls that 'it was an unforgettable scene', adding that he 'did not know Mallin at that time but I remember speaking a few words to him before we separated'.[27] A Cumann na mBan member describes how the women 'were in the gallery and ... saluted the men as they marched out', earning a severe reprimand from the prison authorities as a consequence.[28] Another described how they 'bade them good cheer and kissed hands to them for the last time on this earth' and she noted that Mallin in particular 'looked very sad.'[29]

Certainly, at some point on that Sunday, Mallin heard that Maxwell had confirmed his death sentence. Letters written shortly before his execution suggest his mood was one of resignation and acceptance. He wrote to his parents: 'I tried with others to make Ireland a free nation and failed. Others failed before and paid the price and so must we.' In similar vein he commented to his wife: 'So must Irishmen pay for trying to make Ireland a free nation.' But his correspondence with her also indicates his clear conviction that the Rising would ultimately be vindicated and that his death was, as a consequence, a noble one. He stated: 'I do not believe that our blood has been shed in vain. I believe Ireland will come out greater and grander but she must not forget she is Catholic she must keep the faith ... I am so cold this has been a cruel week [sic].' He concluded: 'I must now Prepare these last few hours must be spent with God alone.' Defiantly and with evident pride, he signed the letter 'Your loving husband Michael Mallin Commandant Stephen's Green Command'.[30]

During Sunday night, Mallin was held in cell eighteen, which was on the ground floor of the central compound at Kilmainham, beside the execution yards; the three other condemned men occupied cells adjacent to his. Father Browne was attending one of them, Sean Heuston, and he records that the sound of 'weeping was intense' coming through the adjoining wall from number eighteen, as Mallin bade a final farewell to his wife, children, sister and brother. His twelve-year-old son, Seamus, recalled that when they reached the prison 'there was a big dark hall; policemen and soldiers all around us. There was hardly a word spoken, and when there was, it was very hushed. We were led through a low doorway on the left hand side, each door exactly like the other. I noticed a light, like a yellow candle-flame, behind a half-opened door and I heard mumbling as if the Rosary was being said.' On joining them soon afterwards, the priest found Mallin 'serene, though very much affected'.[31]

During his final minutes, Mallin was consoled by Father Augustine of the Capuchin priests from Church Street: it was he who led Mallin to the execution yard. Father Albert escorted Heuston and he recalls that while the latter was being prepared to go before the firing squad 'we saw Fr Augustine and Commandant Mallin coming towards us from the cell where they had been. We now proceeded towards the yard where the execution was to take place. On our way we passed a group of soldiers: these I learned afterwards were awaiting Commandant Mallin who was following us.'[32] A Cumann na mBan prisoner records in her diary that during the early morning, she was roused 'as usual by the sound of shots. Such terrible sounds. We pray for their souls ... Lord rest them.'[33] Michael Mallin was executed between 3:45 and 4:05 a.m. on Monday, 8 May 1916.

Trial of Michael Mallin

prisoner number seventy-eight

REFERENCE: PRO WO71/353

DATE: 5 May 1916

LOCATION: Richmond Barracks

JUDGES: Colonel E.W.S.K. Maconchy (President), Lieutenant Colonel
   A.M. Bent, Major F.W. Woodward

CHARGE:

1 'Did an act to wit did take part in an armed rebellion and in the
waging of war against His Majesty the King, such act being o such
a nature as to be calculated to be prejudicial to the Defence to the
Realm and being done with the intention and for the purpose of
assisting the enemy'

2 'Did attempt to cause disaffection among the civilian population
of His Majesty'

PLEA: Not guilty (both charges)

(The members of the court and witnesses were duly sworn in)

VERDICT: Guilty. Death (first charge); not guilty (second charge).

Text of Trial

1st Witness

No. 212C Police Constable, John O'Connell, Dublin Metropolitan
Police states:–

> I know the prisoner Michael Mallin. There is a paper called
> "The Workers Republic" in which it has been stated that
> the prisoner is chief of the Staff of the Citizen Army. I have
> known the prisoner about 9 or 10 months. I have seen him
> marching with the Citizen Army and he has marched with
> James Connolly and the Countess Markievicz and has led
> them in company with James Connolly.

Cross-examined by the prisoner.

> I did not know whether the prisoner was in command or

James Connolly when marching with the Citizen Army. I
never saw him as a drill instructor or a band instructor. I
never heard him make any speech at all. I have only seen it
in the paper that the prisoner was Chief of the Staff of the
Citizen Army.

Examined by the Court.

The Citizen Army and the Irish Volunteers are two distinct
bodies. The Citizen Army is under the control of James
Connolly. There is a slight difference in the uniform of the
two armies.

2nd Witness

No. C128 Police Constable C. Butler Dublin Metropolitan Police
states:–

I know the prisoner now before the Court and have known
him for 6 or 8 months. I have seen him marching with the
Citizen Army wearing the uniform in which he is now
dressed. On one or two occasions he wore a revolver on his
waistbelt. He marched with James Connolly at the head of
the Army and also with the Countess of Markievicz. I saw
him on Easter Monday about 11.50 am he was in front of
Liberty Hall dressed as he is now. He seemed to be busy
generally organising the Citizen Army and there was a large
crowd present.

Cross-examined by the prisoner:–

He led a section across the footbridge as far as I can
remember. He has been on friendly terms with the police
and I know nothing against his character.

Re-examined by the prosecution.

He was going in the direction of St Stephen's Green and
the College of Surgeons when he crossed the footbridge.

3rd Witness

Captain H.E. Wheeler Reserve of officers states:–

I was on duty on 30th April outside the College of
Surgeons. A body of prisoners surrendered to me between
12.30 p.m. and 1 p.m. The prisoner and the Countess of
Markievicz came out of a side door of the College. The
prisoner was carrying a white flag and was unarmed but the
Countess was armed. The prisoner came forward and
saluted and said he wished to surrender and this is the

Countess Markievicz. He surrendered and stated he was the Commandant of the garrison. I took over the garrison which consisted of prisoner, Countess Markievicz, 109 men and 10 women. I found them in the College and they laid down their arms under my directions.

DEFENCE

The prisoner states:–

I am a silk weaver by trade and have been employed by the Transport Union as band instructor. During my instruction of these bands they became part of the Citizen Army and from this I was asked to become a drill instructor. I had no commission whatever in the Citizen Army. I was never taken into the confidence of James Connolly. I was under the impression we were going out for manoeuvres on Sunday but something altered the arrangements and the manoeuvres were postponed till Monday. I had verbal instructions from James Connolly to take 36 men to St. Stephens Green and to report to the Volunteer officer there. Shortly after my arrival at St. Stephens Green the firing started and the Countess of Markievicz ordered me to take command of the men as I had been so long associated with them. I felt I could not leave them and from that time I joined the rebellion. I made it my business to save all officers and civilians who were brought in to Stephens Green. I gave explicit orders to the men to make no offensive movements and I prevented them attacking the Shelborne Hotel.

1st Witness

Mr L.J. Kettle states:–

The prisoner prevented my death by shooting.

I was treated with every possible consideration and also I saw he did the same for any other prisoners who were brought in.

Cross-examined by the prosecution:–

I was taken prisoner on Monday afternoon 24th April and was taken first to Stephens Green and Mallin appeared to be in command. I heard a good deal of firing but actually did not see the firing myself.

On Tuesday morning, I was taken to the College of Surgeons and kept there till Sunday. I could have been released any day during that time but was kept there till Sunday. I was released at the time of surrender and handed over. I heard firing whilst I was at the College. From the sounds it appeared that the firing was coming from the College. I knew the College was being fired at.

The prisoner continuing his statement says:–

I indignantly repudiate any idea of assisting Germany.

James Connolly

Extract from a memorandum entitled 'Short History of rebels on whom it has been necessary to inflict the supreme penalty' sent by General Sir John Maxwell to Herbert Asquith, on 11 May 1916.

JAMES CONNOLLY. (Execution Suspended by Prime Minister's orders)

This man has been a prominent leader in the Larkinite or Citizen Army for years. He was also a prominent supporter of the Sinn Fein movement.

He held the rank of Commandant General of the Dublin Division in the rebel army, and had his headquarters at the G.P.O. from which place he issued orders. On the 24th April he issued and signed a general order to "The officers and soldiers in Dublin of the Irish Republic" stating inter alia "that the armed forces of the Irish Republic had everywhere met the enemy and defeated them." This man was also a signatory to the Declaration of Irish Independence already referred to.

JAMES CONNOLLY WAS BORN IN EDINBURGH in 1868. Like James Larkin, he was brought up in the slums of a British city, the son of Irish parents. Though widely differing in temperament, Larkin and Connolly had much in common. Both were teetotallers, largely self-educated, and were committed revolutionaries, galvanised into political action by the labour movement and drawn through it to Ireland. Connolly first saw Ireland whilst serving briefly with the British army in the 1880s. At the age of twenty-one, he married and settled in Edinburgh, where he worked as a corporation employee. There, he became more deeply immersed in the two creeds that dominated his life – socialism and nationalism. His interest in them was first stimulated through social contacts, and the reading of Marx and other writers, which reinforced the influence of family and personal experience. In 1896 he was invited to become a paid organiser of the Dublin Socialist Society. Though he found the Dublin working class dulled and unresponsive, over the next seven years as an activist and journalist living in the city's slums, he honed his ideas, characteristically fusing together socialist and nationalist principles. He became convinced that there were 'no real nationalists in Ireland outside the Irish Labour movement ... the reconquest of Ireland its aim'.[1]

Despite his formidable political talents, immense written and verbal powers of persuasion and intellectual clarity, Connolly's advanced views made little headway. With a growing family to support, disillusioned and frustrated, he emigrated to the United States in 1903. By the time of his return in 1910, he found the Irish political environment more receptive. He was appointed Irish Transport and General Workers' Union representative in Belfast and helped found the Irish Labour Party. He rose to prominence as a consequence of his union's involvement in the 1913 Dublin lockout (which ended in crippling defeat), and of Larkin's departure for America the following year. He became General Secretary of the ITGWU (Larkin's union) in October 1914 and Commander of the Irish Citizen Army. Liberty Hall was the headquarters of both and became the power base from which Connolly helped revitalise the labour movement.

The Irish Citizen Army had been established in mid-November 1913, to protect workers in clashes with the police, and to provide them with purpose and cohesion in the context of mass unemployment. Connolly described the formation of the force as 'a measure possibly needed for future eventualities arising out of the ferment occasioned by Carsonism in the North';[2] he advised the men to 'drill and train ... as they were doing in Ulster'.[3] Through his ability, energy and determination, Connolly rescued the ICA from terminal decline and welded it into a potent force and potential weapon for his own use – 'a real revolutionary army'. He vetted its officers, determined its structure, imposed a rigid discipline and above all demanded an ideological commitment to revolution and the goal of an independent Irish socialist republic. Given the context – Ireland's small working class, its political conservatism and the strength of catholicism – inevitably its membership was small, just two hundred and twenty in 1916. But it was otherwise superior to the much larger Irish Volunteer Force, in its unity of purpose, its lack of factional and ideological division and in the quality of its training. There was a record of tension between the two bodies; in late 1915, Bulmer Hobson described Connolly's attitude towards the Volunteers as 'one of persistent hostility'.[4]

With the outbreak of war in 1914, Connolly became increasingly committed to fomenting an insurrection against British rule in Ireland. On 9 September he declared: 'Ireland has now a wonderful chance to rid herself of English rule.'[5] He expressed the hope that Ireland's actions 'may yet set the torch to a European conflagration'.[6] Though he hoped for German support (he considered ten thousand German troops would be sufficient), he was quite prepared to proceed without it. His sense of urgency is reflected not only in the content of his writings and speeches, but in his own military preparations with the ICA. He steadily discarded his earlier persona as a labour organiser and agitator and emerged more and more as a military commandant and theorist. Bulmer Hobson said of him that: 'His conversation was full of clichés derived from the early days of the socialist movement in Europe. He told me that the working class was always revolutionary, that Ireland was a powder magazine and all that was neccessary was for someone to apply the match. I replied ... Ireland was a wet bog and that the match would fall into a puddle.'[7] However, already in 1913, the ITGWU's disastrous defeat had made it more difficult for Connolly to sustain a belief in the efficacy of proletarian action. He recognised that the looming prospect of partition – possibly permanent – would weaken still further the Irish working class. He was disillusioned by the failure of international socialism to prevent the onset of war: he had hoped that its outbreak might have been the tocsin for revolution. Though he did see a bright side: watching thousands of Irishmen leaving for the front, he commented to a comrade, 'Would you rather they stayed here to fight us when we come out?'[8]

As an Irish nationalist, Connolly believed that 'England's difficulty [was] Ireland's opportunity' and thought that even if a rising failed it would keep the revolutionary nationalist spirit alive and reawaken the 'soul of the nation'. In August 1915, he stated: 'The Irish Citizen Army in its constitution pledges its members to fight for a Republican Freedom for Ireland. Its members ... believe that at the call of duty they may have to lay down their lives for Ireland, and have so trained themselves that [at its] worst [this] shall constitute the starting point of another glorious tradition.' In February 1916, Connolly declared: 'Deep in the heart of Ireland has sunk the degradation wrought upon its people ... so deep and humiliating that no agency less potent than the red tide of war will ever enable the Irish race to recover its self-respect ... Without the slightest trace of irreverence, but in all due humility as that of mankind before Calvary, it may be truly said: "Without the shedding of blood there is no redemption".'[9] Eoin MacNeill later observed with justification that Connolly 'believed in insurrection for the sake of insurrection'.[10] Hours before his execution Connolly observed: 'The socialists will never understand why I am here. They will forget I am an Irishman.'[11] After his death, Sean O'Casey said of Connolly that he was 'no more an Irish socialist martyr than Robert Emmet ... or Wolfe Tone', and that Liberty Hall had ceased to be 'the headquarters of the Irish labour movement' and became rather the 'centre of Irish national disaffection'.[12] The increasingly strident and impatient statements made by Connolly reflect his fear that the war might end abruptly without its political potential for Ireland having been exploited. His public comments were also intended to stir up the Irish Volunteer rank and file so that they in turn might coerce their leadership into taking action.

The Military Council members, notably Clarke, had long recognised the merits of collaborating with the ICA. By 1916, all were alarmed by the content of Connolly's statements, justifiably fearing that he might act on his own before their own preparations were complete, or might provoke repressive measures by Dublin Castle against the Irish Volunteers. On 19 January 1916, Connolly disappeared from family and friends; he had last been seen leaving Liberty Hall in a taxi, accompanied by two IRB men. He was conducted to a brickworks at Dolphin's Barn and there over the next three days, Pearse, Plunkett and MacDermott disclosed to him their clandestine plans for a rising, and offered an alliance. Connolly was at first described as 'very angry but later became so enthusiastic that the trouble was to persuade him to go home'.[13] An agreement to cooperate was reached; the arrangement suited both parties. Connolly was made a member of the Military Council and, in February, joined the IRB. He informed a close colleague at the time that: 'Things are now going very well with our friends [the Brotherhood].'[14] On 18 April, he disclosed details of the insurrection to his ICA officers, and, sworn to secrecy, gave them precise instructions as to their own specific roles on Easter Sunday.

Connolly had definite ideas on the best strategy to adopt; this clearly influenced the tactics actually adopted during the Rising and was the basis on which he had trained his own small force. He strongly opposed the idea, traditional in Ireland, of conducting a campaign from remote bases in the hills, on the grounds that this was likely to cause the insurgents to lose access to vital supplies. He instead favoured the occupation of towns and cities; he had made a close study of street-fighting techniques. He recommended the occupation of blocks of buildings, with intersecting walls between premises bored through, so that defenders could pass easily from one property to another. By this means, a threatened position could readily be reinforced, and provision could be made for a concealed line of retreat. Connolly regarded pickaxes as an essential item of insurrectionary equipment; he also stressed that care should be taken to ensure each garrison had an adequate supply of food and water. In addition, he urged the necessity of erecting street barricades – to be constructed from any heavy materials available in the area occupied; the purpose was to provide cover for sniper positions and to disrupt the movement of enemy forces.

By the eve of the Rising, Liberty Hall was like a fortress; it was replete with an armoury and for some weeks a large team had been fully employed making bombs on the premises. Connolly had himself been residing there for several weeks. Though he had heard about Casement's arrest, he had gone to bed early on Saturday night (22 April), convinced that 'everything had gone splendidly, that there had not been a single hitch ... perfectly satisfied with the preparations for the insurrection'.[15] The Military Council had told him of their difficulties with MacNeill, but had reassured him that 'it would work out all right'.[16] Connolly was furious therefore when, early on Easter Sunday morning, he heard from his own intelligence sources of MacNeill's countermand order. However, when William Walpole, one of his bodyguards, offered to shoot the Irish Volunteer leader, he violently objected and demanded assurances that he would not do so. He sought also to console disheartened ICA members who complained that 'They [the leadership] will never do anything', by affirming that: 'Things will go on.'[17] Indeed, Mallin (his second-in-command) reported Connolly saying that 'if the Citizen Army had only fifty men mobilised they were going out'.[18] At the crisis meeting of the Military Council held that morning, however, Connolly supported the majority view that the Rising be postponed until next day.

After reaching agreement on this, the council proceeded to appoint Connolly Vice-President of the Irish Republic to be proclaimed next day; his political creed in itself precluded him from the presidency. The members also decided that he should act as Commandant-General, Dublin Division of the Army of the Irish Republic. No one could have disputed his claim to the position and no one more fully vindicated such trust. Over the week that followed Connolly proved himself to be the most effective rebel leader in the Rising. He possessed a steely and well-founded self-belief, and the flexibility to adjust his tactics in response to unexpected military circumstances – not least the unexpected willingness of British troops to deploy artillery and destroy property owned by their own capitalist supporters. Despite his gruff, grave, pugnacious and obstinate persona (one prominent rebel described him as 'very hard to like'), he had a genuine gift for man-management.[19] Partly as a consequence, the Volunteers and ICA by and large successfully overcame the ideological differences, social divisions and personality clashes which had hitherto blighted their relations. After the council had transacted its business on Easter Sunday, Connolly led his garrison on a final route march through the city to St Stephen's Green, returning via Dublin Castle; his purpose was 'to let the British authorities see that they were not acting in concert with the Irish Volunteers'.[20] On their return, he delivered his last public speech, standing appropriately in front of Liberty Hall. In triumph and anticipation, he declared: 'You are under arms. You will not lay down your arms, until you have struck a blow for Ireland!'[21] His spirits were raised by the ruthless realisation of warfare.

Early on Easter Monday morning ICA men and Volunteers began to mobilise at Liberty Hall. There was the constant ebb and flow of officers and section leaders cycling out to round up their men, of scouts being dispatched to scrutinise the military barracks and report back to headquarters, and of arms being taken out of the premises and loaded into cars and trucks. Connolly was at the hub of this frenetic activity, collating the flow of information, issuing final orders, making last minute adjustments to the allocation of men to the various commands. At one point he proudly held aloft the Proclamation, copies of which had just been printed. His own state of mind is not easy to assess. He said to one officer 'Good luck, Sean [Connolly]. We won't meet again.' Famously, he remarked to William O'Brien, a trade union colleague: 'We are going out to be slaughtered.' When asked 'Is there no chance?', he replied, 'None whatsoever.'[22] Perhaps these comments reflect the strains that he must then have been feeling, compounded by the multiple distractions of the morning, and also his own profound disappointment at the inadequacy of the turnout.

At 11:50 a.m., Connolly led the headquarters battalion – just one hundred and fifty men in total – to the GPO. His secretary for the previous five years, Winifred Carney, from Belfast, was the only woman to march with the main body; she was said to be 'plain, strong, determined [and] brusque, like himself.'[23] At the appropriate moment, he gave the order: 'Left turn. Charge!' and the rebels stormed the building. Connolly had a strikingly unsoldierly appearance – his ill-fitting, bottle green uniform did nothing to enhance an unimpressive physique. But it was immediately evident that he was in charge of military operations and that Pearse was nominal Commander-in-Chief. During the week, Connolly proved to be a field commander of exceptional quality, drawing on his British army background, his years as a military theorist, and experience as head of the ICA. Michael Collins said of him: 'I would have followed him through hell';[24] Joe Good described the GPO simply as 'Connolly's building'.[25]

Connolly was in action at once, variously supervising the construction of defences, 'moving from window to window, urging the men to improve their loophole protection', assigning the women to their duties.[26] He broke off briefly to witness Pearse read the

Proclamation, and afterwards grasped his hand and declared: 'Thanks be to God, Pearse, that we have lived to see this day.'[27] He arranged for copies to be posted throughout the area and ordered Sean T. O'Kelly to retrieve flags from Liberty Hall; these were duly unfurled over the building. He was also seen dictating to Carney. One dispatch, which he circulated on Easter Monday – probably his first – was a stirring clarion call to arms. It stated: 'This day the flag of the Irish Republic has been hoisted in Dublin. [Its] armed forces ... have everywhere met the enemy and defeated them, North, South, East and West. This is the greatest day in Irish history and it is you who have made it so.'[28] This was distributed to the other garrisons. Connolly's only major source of irritation was the scale of the looting near the GPO. 'Unless a few of them are shot, you won't stop them,' he declared; but it was a response he shrank from implementing.[29]

Over the next two days, the initiative ineluctably passed to crown forces; a nationwide rising had failed to materialise and British troops were flowing into Dublin virtually unimpeded. The rebel leadership therefore came to anticipate a massed infantry attack with furious hand-to-hand fighting and the likelihood of few survivors. Connolly responded quickly and judiciously to the imminent prospect; he had hoped that the rebels' seizure of buildings in the capital 'would galvanise the country to a general uprising'.[30] He summoned reinforcements from outside the city, and more vulnerable outposts were progressively abandoned. On his orders, the block opposite the GPO (including the Imperial Hotel and Clery's department store) was seized and fortified. The officer commanding was instructed: 'The British must not occupy these buildings.'[31] Similarly, property immediately adjoining the post office (for instance, the Metropole Hotel) was occupied and the position consolidated by boring into adjacent premises. As a result, rebel snipers came to hold an almost impregnable nexus of posts which dominated the approaches from lower Sackville Street and its main intersecting roads. Any frontal British assault would therefore have risked formidable casualties.

Throughout, Connolly constantly monitored and adjusted the disposition of his forces. He was 'tireless ... repeatedly leading sorties ... [to] ... reinforce our positions or establish new ones'.[32] Routinely, he took constant risks with his own safety. One officer relates how he 'insisted on walking into Abbey Street and giving me instructions as to where I should place a barricade'.[33] On another occasion, he dashed into the open street in the direction of the Imperial Hotel in a bid to prevent newly arrived rebel reinforcements from being shot at by their own men. His written orders to his units were concise and comprehensive, indicating the reasons for occupying a property, the likely direction of attack, the location of other Volunteer-held positions nearby, and giving specific instructions – to barricade stairs, to ensure there was adequate food and water for men, to break all glass in windows, and so on.

Though the British cordon around the GPO was tightening, Connolly's spirit seemed indomitable and his attitude eternally optimistic. When Liberty Hall was shelled on Wednesday, he reassured William Pearse – probably successfully – that the British had done it because they were imminently expecting support from Germany for the rebels. But his private feelings were revealed next day when he was overhead speaking to a civilian, anxious to join the garrison. Shaking his head, and talking 'sadly and very quietly', he said, 'Go home while you can, man, but we thank you. Too late now; it's a hopeless cause.'[34] Later that day, 27 April, he was wounded for the second time but on this occasion severely. While returning from establishing outposts in the Liffey Street area, he was struck by rifle fire at fairly close range, above the ankle, shattering both leg bones. Losing blood rapidly, he crawled back to Princes Street and was brought by stretcher from there to the GPO. For a short time he was 'out of action and out of sight', but helped by morphine injections he regained much of his former verve and 'showed that his energy and courage were indefatigable'.[35] Even after his injury, Pearse described him as 'still the guiding brain of our resistance'.[36] He insisted on taking an active part in the battle and next day asked to be placed in a bed with castors which was then located in the front hall of the GPO. Jim Ryan, the medical student who treated him, observed: 'Nothing could conquer the will of this man.'[37]

Meanwhile, during Thursday, a British barrage of incendiaries had generated a fire-storm which engulfed the east side of lower Sackville Street. Early on Friday morning, with no sign of infantry massing, it seemed inevitable that these tactics would be displayed against the GPO itself. Almost certainly the leaders convened, with Connolly in attendance, and agreed that in these circumstances they would evacuate the building. Shortly afterwards, a manifesto dictated by Connolly, was read to the Volunteers; it was intended to express his gratitude to them, acknowledge their courage and bolster their morale. It was to be his last attempt to enthuse an Irish garrison and it was successful. One of those who heard it described it as 'the most amazing thing I witnessed that week ... considering the situation'.[38] The statement claimed: 'Our commandants around us are holding their own,' and continued with some justification: 'The British Army ... behind their artillery and machine guns are afraid to advance to the attack or storm any position held by our forces. The slaughter they suffered in the first two days has totally unnerved them and they dare not attempt again an infantry attack on our positions.' It concluded: 'Never had men or woman a grander cause, never was a cause more grandly served.'[39]

That evening, at 6 p.m., when the wounded were transferred to Jervis Street hospital, Connolly insisted he must remain with his men at the GPO. At 8 p.m. when the whole garrison was evacuated, he was amongst the last to leave, borne on a stretcher, shielded by Miss Carney, and still issuing instructions. When asked how he felt, he retorted: 'Bad, the soldier who did this did a good day's work for the British government.'[40] That night he slept in a room with Pearse and others; appropriately a portrait of Robert Emmet was hanging on one of the walls. Next day at noon, the leaders met at 16 Moore Street and, clustered around Connolly's bed, agreed by a majority vote to seek surrender terms. One of the women he afterwards comforted observed, 'how terribly affected he was by the idea'. When Winifred Carney asked, through her tears, 'Was there no other way?' he responded simply that 'he could not bear to see his brave boys burnt to death'.[41] Whilst being prepared to be brought over to enemy lines − a condition of the agreement reached with Brigadier-General Lowe − Jim Ryan enquired what terms was he expecting the British to offer; in reply, Connolly said that 'the signatories [of the Proclamation] would be shot but the rest of us set free'.[42] The moment he was borne off by four Volunteers towards British lines was regarded by Joe Good as the moment 'the insurrection was over'.[43]

The local officer commanding had been informed of Connolly's injuries; on reaching the British barricade nearby, the bearer party was searched and in due course proceeded with an escort of seventeen soldiers along Parnell Street and Capel Street to the upper yard, Dublin Castle. There, after a short discussion, the prisoner was brought by Red Cross personnel to a small ward in the officers' quarters of the hospital wing. He was still having his wounds dressed when Captain Wheeler arrived from army headquarters and requested that he issue a surrender order to his men along the same lines as Pearse's to the Volunteers. Having read Pearse's statement, Connolly dictated to the officer his own instructions which were appended below it, and he then signed and dated them. These read: 'I agree to these conditions for the men only under my own command in the Moore Street District and ... in the Stephen's Green Command.'[44]

At the castle hospital, Connolly's leg was set. One of the nurses said of the patient: 'No-one could have been more considerate or have given less trouble. All through, his behaviour was that of an idealist.'[45] His family's efforts to visit him were at first unsuccessful. His daughter, Ina, said that when she called on 3 May, she was told by medical staff that he was 'very weak for loss of blood and was not improving'.[46] Meanwhile, on 1 May, Father Aloysius was informed through the military chaplain that Connolly had expressed a wish to see him. He went immediately and heard his confession, and next morning gave him Holy Communion. Connolly was eventually tried on 9 May, probably in the morning (prisoner number ninety). That his court martial should have proceeded, despite his injuries, prompted questions in the Commons afterwards. Laurence Ginnell (an erratic Irish Parliamentary Party MP, who was returned for Sinn Féin in 1918) asked whether the authorities had tried Connolly after the surgeon had reported that he was dying of his wounds and what was 'the precedent for the summary execution of a dying man?' Harold John Tennant, Under Secretary of State for War replied, with justification: 'The medical authorities were consulted and certified that he was in a fit state to undergo his trial.'[47] Two doctors, one of whom was R.F. Tobin, who had responsibility for Connolly's treatment, had informed Maxwell: 'We certify that during the entire period of James Connolly's detention as a patient he has been perfectly rational and in full possession of his faculties. His mental condition has been and is perfectly normal and his mind, memory and understanding entirely unimpaired and that he is fit to undergo trial.'[48] Tobin was personally aware of Connolly's mental sharpness. On asking the prisoner on one occasion, 'Do you want anything?', Connolly had immediately responded, 'Only liberty'. Thus the GOC was able to reassure Asquith that Connolly 'had been reported fit to be tried' and 'would recover under ordinary circumstances in three months'.[49] Maxwell certainly seems to have been anxious that the trial should proceed as quickly as possible. William Wylie recalls a conversation he had with the GOC at this time: '"Who is next on the list?" barked Maxwell. "Connolly, Sir." "Well, I must insist on him being tried." "But he's wounded, Sir," I said. "The court can be convened in hospital," he replied. I again demurred. I forget what I said but it was to the effect that Connolly should not be tried until he was well again. Maxwell didn't reply and the next I heard was that Connolly had been tried and condemned. I don't know who prosecuted.'[50]

Unique amongst the rebels, Connolly's court martial took place in his hospital ward, with the prisoner 'propped up in his bed'; Connolly commented later that the 'strain was very great'.[51] Colonel D. Sapte presided as he did at MacDermott's trial, probably held immediately afterwards on 9 May. Mainly the crown sought to establish that the accused had been in command at the General Post Office, though issues relating to the treatment of prisoners held there were also raised. The prosecution called four witnesses. The first of these was Lieutenant S.L. King, who had already given evidence in the cases of Clarke and of both Pearse brothers. King claimed that whilst held captive at the post office, he had noticed Connolly several times. On one occasion, he said, he saw him 'in uniform and equipped with a revolver ... going across to the Hotel Metropole ... pointing out as if to order a window to be broken ... and fire opened from' it. He stated that though 'very well treated generally by the rebels ... when we were put out of the Post Office, we were told to run for our lives and we were fired on by rebels and 2 of us hit.'[52]

Captain Wheeler, who was called also at MacDermott's trial, told the court of Connolly signing, 'in my presence', Pearse's surrender order; the document was produced as evidence. Lieutenant S.H. Jackson testified that the signature it bore was the same as that on a paper found on John MacBride when he had searched him on 1 May (this was the dispatch issued by the accused on Easter Monday). It too was shown to the judges. The final witness, Lieutenant A.D. Chalmers, had been taken captive at the GPO at noon on Easter Monday and held until the following Friday. He also claimed to have seen Connolly 'giving orders about firing from the Hotel Metropole' and, until 26 April, to have 'heard him give orders for firing on more than one occasion'. He alleged that when the

Rising began he had been 'tied up in the telephone box' for three hours (almost suffocating as a consequence), probably on Connolly's instructions. Under cross-examination, he conceded that 'the rebels did their best for us whilst we were in the Post Office', though unlike King, he made a number of unsubstantiated allegations of mistreatment outside the court.[53]

Connolly questioned two of the prosecution witnesses and when invited to speak read a prepared, handwritten statement. It provides ample evidence that despite his injuries and the strain he was clearly under, there was no diminution in either his mental capacity or alertness. Implicitly, the statement was directed at the Irish people rather than at the three judges gathered at his bedside. Connolly began by stating : 'I do not wish to make any defence except against charges of wanton cruelty to prisoners.' He was dismissive of the 'trifling allegations' made 'in that direction', describing them as 'almost unavoidable incidents' in a 'hurried uprising'. He proceeded by referring to the 'call we [the rebels] ... issued to the people of Ireland', and asserted that it was 'nobler ... in a holier cause that [sic] any call issued to them during this war'. He continued: 'We succeeded in proving that Irishmen are ready to die endeavouring to win for Ireland their national rights ... As long as that remains the case the cause of Irish freedom is safe.' He declared: 'The British government has no right in Ireland ... The presence in any one generation of even a respectable minority of Irishmen ready to die to affirm that truth makes that Government for ever a usurpation.'[54]

The judges found Connolly guilty, and that same day Maxwell confirmed the death sentence they had imposed; he had already indicated to Asquith that if convicted the prisoner must suffer the 'extreme penalty'.[55] He regarded him along with MacDermott as the most culpable of those court-martialled. In justifying his decision, the GOC stated that he had been a 'prominent leader in the ... Citizen Army for years' and a 'prominent supporter of the Sinn Féin movement', that he was a 'signatory to the Declaration of Independence,' had been 'Commandant General of the Dublin Division in the rebel army', and had had his headquarters in the GPO from which he had 'issued orders'.[56] Maxwell also referred to the text of Connolly's Easter Monday dispatch, a copy of which had been found on MacBride. He made no reference to the treatment of prisoners. Despite some controversy on this issue raised in the trials of members of the garrison at the GPO, prisoners appear to have been treated humanely and with consideration whilst held there, with due concern being shown for their safety.

On Sunday afternoon, 7 May, Connolly's wife was informed that she could visit her husband on the following Monday or Tuesday morning. She called on the Tuesday with her eldest daughter, Nora. They were escorted to his ward and found him 'very calm and very cool ... cheerful', and he told them he was 'not suffering much pain'. He spoke of being 'proud of his men' and affirmed that the 'cause cannot die now'. Nora was 'depressed' to hear that he had been court-martialled earlier that day. Fearing the worst, she suggested that 'because he was wounded, he would not be executed', to which he promptly retorted: 'That will have no effect on what they decide to do and that is that.'[57]

On the day following, Connolly was indeed informed that he would face the firing squad at dawn next morning. However, his 'execution [was] suspended by Prime Minister's orders'.[58] When Father Aloysius called with him on the afternoon of 11 May, to give him Holy Communion and hear his confession, his fate was still unclear. The priest enquired before leaving if there was 'any danger of anything happening that night', and was reassured that this was unlikely.[59] But at 9 p.m. Father Aloysius was informed by a British officer who called at Church Street, that his services would be required at the castle at 2 a.m. next morning: he fully understood the cryptic message. At around midnight, military personnel also informed Connolly's wife and daughter that he wished to see them. Nora immediately deduced that her father was to be executed. The journey to the hospital left an indelible impression on her memory; she recalled later 'the horrible smell of burning in O'Connell Street' and that because of a curfew, 'not a soul [was] to be seen, not even a soldier'.[60]

When they arrived at Connolly's room they had to push through a heavy guard of up to two dozen soldiers armed with rifles and bayonets. During their visit Connolly gave Nora a piece of paper 'folded up very tightly' – his court martial statement – and implored her to 'try and get it out' (in court he had requested that a copy of the proceedings be given to his wife and had been directed to make a formal application to Headquarters, Irish Command). Nora continues: 'when I knew that he was going to be executed, I determined to tell him all I knew [the authorities had instructed his family only to discuss personal matters]. I told him of the execution of Patrick

Pearse, and Thomas MacDonagh and all the others. He was silent for a while, I think he thought he was the first to be executed. "Well," he said, "I am glad that I am going with them."' Nora then told him that: 'It had been in the papers that there were to be no more shootings and that it had been stated in the House of Commons.' To which he replied: 'England's promises, Nora, you and I know what they mean.'[61] In fact, whatever reservations Asquith may initially have had about the likely impact of Connolly's execution on Irish opinion, he appears to have been quickly convinced by Maxwell that it should proceed. Earlier that day (11 May) at Westminster, Asquith had said: 'There are two other persons who are under sentenced to death – a sentence which has been confirmed by the General – both of whom signed the Proclamation and took an active part, one of them [Connolly], the most active part of all in the actual rebellion in Dublin ... I do not see my way ... to interfere with the decision of Sir John Maxwell.'[62] Clearly, the rebel leader was right to feel that there was no reason to hope for a reprieve. To the end, he lost none of his capacity for vitriol. When his daughter informed him that: 'P.T. Daly [a former Supreme Council member] was also arrested ... although he was not in the fight', he responded: 'The d---d cowardly skunk. He pretended to be with us to the very last minute and then to save his skin, he stayed out of it.'[63]

At 1 a.m. on 12 May, Father Aloysius was collected from Church Street and brought to Dublin Castle. Once more he heard Connolly's confession and gave him Holy Communion, and just before they left for Kilmainham, he suggested to the prisoner that he should forgive the soldiers who would be responsible for his execution. 'I do, Father,' he replied, 'I respect every man who does his duty.' He was then 'brought down to the [ambulance] car and laid on a stretcher in it'. Father Aloysuis sat with him and on arrival at the prison, he states: 'He [Connolly] was put sitting on a chair and the order was given. They fired and Father Eugene McCarthy who had been in attendance on Sean MacDermott earlier went over and anointed him.'[64] James Connolly was executed in the early hours of 12 May: he was the last of the rebel prisoners to face the firing squad after the Easter Rising.

Trial of James Connolly

prisoner number ninety

REFERENCE: PRO WO71/354

DATE: 9 May 1916

LOCATION: Red Cross Hospital, Dublin Castle

JUDGES: Colonel D. Sapte (President), Lieutenant Colonel A.M. Bent,
       Major F. W. Woodward

CHARGE:

1 'Did an act to wit did take part in an armed rebellion and in the
waging of war against His Majesty the King, such act being o such
a nature as to be calculated to be prejudical to the Defence to the
Realm and being done with the intention and for the purpose of
assisting the enemy'

2 'Did attempt to cause disaffection among the civilian
population of His Majesty'

PLEA: Not Guilty (both charges)

(The members of the court and witnesses were duly sworn in)

VERDICT: Guilty. Death (first charge): Not guilty (second charge)

Text of Trial

SUMMARY OF EVIDENCE

Accused – James Connolly

1st witness for the Prosecution.
2/Lieut. S.L. King 12th Res Battn. R. Innis. Fus. states:–

> In Sackville Street Dublin about 11 a. m on the 25th April
> 1916, I was taken prisoner by the rebels and taken upstairs
> in the General Post Office. There were 2 other officers
> confined in the same room. There were many armed rebels
> in the building. I saw firing from the Hotel Metropole.

> I saw the accused, in uniform and equipped with a revolver
> etc., going across to the Hotel Metropole.

I saw him pointing out as if to order a window to be broken in the Hotel which was done, and fire opened from the window. I saw the accused on 3 or 4 occasions near the General Post Office.

Crossexamined by the accused

I was in the Post Office from 25th to 28th April when I was marched out of it by one of the rebels. We were very well treated generally by the rebels. The window broken gave a good field of fire across Sackville Street. The uniform the accused wore was the green Volunteer uniform with rings on his arm, and a wideawake hat. I cannot remember any feathers in it.

Re-examined by the Prosecution

When we were put out of the Post Office we were told to run for our lives and we were fired on by the rebels, and 2 of us hit. I cannot state whether the British troops were firing at the time.

2nd witness for the prosecution

Captain H.E. de C. Wheeler Res. of officers states:–

I saw the accused, James Connolly, in bed at the Dublin Castle Hospital on the 29th April 1916 between 3 & 4 p.m. I had previously seen the rebel leader P.H. Pearse surrender at the top of Moore Street off Great Britain Street. I produce a document which I brought to the accused from Pearse, which he signed in my presence. (Marked X. signed and attached).

3rd witness for Prosecution.

2/Lieut S.H. Jackson 3/R. Irish Regt. states:–

On the 1st May 1916 I searched the rebel John McBride and found on him the document I produce to the court. It purports to be signed by James Connolly and I consider the signature the same as that shown to me by the Court (signature on document X)

(Document marked Y. signed and attached)

4th Witness for Prosecution.

2/Lieut A.D. Chalmers 14th Royal Fusiliers states:–

About 12.10 p.m on 24th April 1916 I was in the General Post Office Dublin when about 300 armed rebels entered and seized the Post Office and made me prisoner.

I saw the accused present among them. The accused ordered me to be tied up in the telephone box. This was done. I was kept there about 3 hours. One of the rebels came and asked me how I was getting on. I replied I was about suffocated. Apparently the man went to the accused. I then heard the accused say "I don't care a damn what you do with him." The words were obviously concerned with me.

I was kept in the General Post office until 28th April 1916. On the 25th and 26th April from the window of the room I was in, I saw the accused giving orders about firing from the Hotel Metropole. I heard him give orders for firing on more than one occasion.

Cross-examined by the accused.

I think I last saw the accuse on the 26th April. Up to that I had frequently seen him. The rebels did their best for us whilst we were in the Post Office.

The accused was in dark green uniform with a distinctive hat with cock's feathers in it. The distinctive uniform was very noticeable from the other Volunteer uniforms. I saw the accused close while he was in the Post Office. I did not actually hear the accused order me to be tied up in the box. One of the rebels went up to the accused and on his return I was tied up.

DEFENCE

The accused in his defence says:–

I read this written document.

(The document is marked "Z" signed and attached).

The accused desires that a copy of these proceedings shall be given to his wife.

He is directed to make a formal application to Hd. Qrs. Irish Comd.

Document "Z"

I do not wish to make any defence except against charges of wanton cruelty to prisoners. These trifling allegations that have been made in that direction if they record facts that really happened deal only with the almost unavoidable incidents of a hurried uprising, and overthrowing of long established authorities, and no where show evidence of a set purpose to wantonly injure unarmed prisoners.

We went out to break the connection between this country and the British Empire and to establish an Irish Republic.

We believe that the call we thus issued to the people of Ireland was a nobler call in a holier cause that [sic] any call issued to them during this war having any connection with the war.

We succeeded in proving that Irishmen are ready to die endeavouring to win for Ireland their national rights which the British Government has been asking them to die to win for Belgium. As long as that remains the case the cause of Irish freedom is safe. Believing that the British Government has no right in Ireland, never had any right in Ireland, and never can have any right in Ireland, the presence in any one generation of even a respectable minority of Irishmen ready to die to affirm that truth makes that Government for ever a usurpation and a crime against human progress. I personally thank God that I have lived to see the day when thousands of Irishmen and boys, and hundreds of Irish women and girls, were equally ready to affirm that truth and seal it with their lives if necessary.

IRISH REBELLION, MAY 1916

SEAN MAC DIARMADA,
Executed May 7th, 1916.
One of the signatories of the "Irish Republic Proclamation."

Sean MacDermott

Deputy Adjutant General
11 MAY. 1918
NO. 845
Richmond Barracks

JOHN McDERMOTT. (Execution Suspended by Prime Minister's orders)

This man signed the Declaration of Irish Independence.
He was one of the most prominent of the leaders of the Irish
Volunteers and attended at the meetings of the Executive and
Control Councils.

He wrote and sent despatches and mobilization orders
for and to the rebels during the rebellion and he surrendered
with a body of rebels in Sackville Street with whom he had been
operating for the previous week.

Extract from a
memorandum
entitled 'Short
History of rebels on
whom it has been
necessary to inflict
the supreme
penalty' sent by
General Sir John
Maxwell to Herbert
Asquith, on 11 May
1916.

BODLEIAN LIBRARY,
UNIVERSITY OF
OXFORD

Sᴇᴀɴ Mᴀᴄᴅᴇʀᴍᴏᴛᴛ ᴡᴀꜱ ʙᴏʀɴ on 28 February 1884 in Kilyclogher, County Leitrim, the son of a farmer. Aged fifteen, he left home, moving first to Glasgow, then to Belfast, finding varied employment – gardener, tram-conductor, barman. He was initially a constitutional nationalist and a member of the Ancient Order of Hibernians. In 1905, he joined and later helped spread the Dungannon Clubs (a small, openly-recruited organisation, founded in County Tyrone, whose aim was to stimulate nationalist sentiment. It later merged with Sinn Féin). For MacDermott, it proved to be a stepping stone to physical force nationalism and his subsequent single-minded, lifelong commitment to revolution and violence in order to achieve Irish independence. When, in 1906, he joined the IRB, his formidable talent for covert political activity and intrigue rapidly emerged. This was rooted in the force and warmth of his personality, his genius for organisation, his qualities of courage and patience and his innate self-confidence and intelligence – all of which were complemented by his good looks. Mrs S.T. O'Kelly said that MacDermott 'cultivated the art of flattery'.[1] Even Bulmer Hobson, who first met him in 1905 and later became a strong opponent of his political ideas and aspirations, described him as 'lovable'.[2] He continued by stating that MacDermott had been an 'enthusiastic member of the Ancient Order of Hibernians and he never quite got over the habits of intrique and wire-pulling behind the scenes'.[3] Sean Fitzgibbon, who like Hobson opposed the Rising, said of MacDermott that though of 'limited education and ability, he always seemed reasonable. I am satisfied that his reasonableness was a pose to deceive.'[4]

MacDermott became a national organiser for the IRB, eventually managed its paper *Irish Freedom*, joined the Supreme Council and acted as its treasurer. His constant exertions may have contributed to serious illness – he contracted polio in 1912. Though hitherto athletic, it left him crippled, walking uneasily, first with a crutch, and later with a cane. But it affected neither his energy nor his determination.[5]

MacDermott's rise in the IRB was facilitated by his unshakeable partnership in Dublin with his mentor, the veteran Thomas Clarke. Though of contrasting personalities and different generations, they shared an impatient commitment to revolution, dreading that the granting of Home Rule would lead to Ireland's permanent political

assimilation into the United Kingdom. They were also elitists, acting in the belief that they knew what was in the best interests of the
Irish nation and indifferent to the views of the majority. They were
both experts in the art of manipulation and infiltration. Between
1908 and 1912, (cooperating closely with Bulmer Hobson at first),
they revitalised the IRB, moulding it into an effective revolutionary
movement, capable of acting as a dynamic force which would ultimately precipitate the 1916 Rising. They shaped its policies, promoted kindred spirits and excised those they regarded as inimical to
their single insurrectionist goal. Though MacDermott's role in the
future Rising was to be crucial, it has been oddly and almost
uniquely neglected by historians.

Both before and during the First World War, MacDermott repeatedly made clear his motives for supporting an insurrection. For him,
its justification did not rely solely on either the prospects for or the
extent of its military success – though this is what he sought and
helped prepare for in 1916. His essential concern was to revive the
spirit of Irish nationalism, which in his view was then in danger of
extinction. A member of the Volunteer movement in Tralee recalls
an organising tour there by MacDermott in the summer of 1914.
He first addressed the local IVF battalion and then a meeting of the
IRB members on their own, as he 'wished to speak more confiden-
tially than he could to the general body'; he was a highly effective,
often passionate public speaker – on occasion his whole frame, shaking with emotion as he spoke. The 'trend of his remarks' was that
'nationalism as known to Tone and Emmet is almost dead in the
country and a spurious substitute as taught by the Irish
Parliamentary Party exists'. He declared: 'The generation now
growing old is the most decadent nationally since the Norman inva-
sion, and the Irish patriotic spirit will die forever unless a blood sacrifice is made in the next ten years. The spark of nationality left is
the result of the Manchester Martyrs nearly half a century ago and
it would be necessary for some of us to offer ourselves as martyrs if
nothing better can be done to preserve the Irish national spirit and
hand it down unsullied to future generations'[6]

Others record MacDermott as having spoken in similar terms,
with perhaps even greater urgency and force, after the outbreak of
the First World War. Sean Fitzgibbon recalls him saying in the
autumn of 1914 that 'nationality had been living on its capital, the
memory of Allen, Larkin and O'Brien and the Manchester Martyrs,

and the present generation must do something if nationality was to survive'. On another occasion, Fitzgibbon records MacDermott as saying: 'If we hold Ireland for a week, we will save Ireland's soul.'[7] Likewise, Sean MacEntee states that when addressing Volunteers in Dundalk, 16 March 1916, MacDermott 'warned us against letting our opportunity slip away. German armies had shown themselves to be invincible; England and France were being bled to death; Ireland's long-awaited hour was at hand.'[8] Soon afterwards, MacDermott told Desmond Ryan that: 'we must come out before the conclusion of the war'; he feared that a negotiated peace was imminent.[9]

Meanwhile, the prospects for bringing about an insurrection in Ireland had been transformed. Hobson's resignation from the Supreme Council of the IRB in June 1914 confirmed MacDermott and Clarke's domination of the movement. The split within the Irish Volunteers, three months later, prompted by Redmond's speech at Woodenbridge, eased their fears that the force might be emasculated by the Parliamentary Party. It resulted in the emergence of a much smaller, more militant rump which they could more easily infiltrate. Though some of its leaders, notably Eoin MacNeill, opposed a rising, MacDermott and Clarke nonetheless hoped to forge the IVF into a strike force for use in a revolt against English rule at the earliest available opportunity. From its inception, MacDermott had been a member of its governing body and one of its chief promoters nationwide. It was this involvement, as well as his management of *Nationality* (a Sinn Féin paper) from offices in D'Olier Street, Dublin, which first drew him to the attention of DMP detectives.

In mid-1915 MacDermott was imprisoned for sedition; on his release in September, he became a member of the IRB Military Council, formed some months earlier on Clarke's initiative. It was a compact, trusted and dedicated group and the two men ensured that its more other-worldly, romantic nationalist members focussed on the practical steps necessary in preparation for a rising. Its activities were unknown even to the IRB Supreme Council, which in January 1916 received the vague assurance from MacDermott: 'We fight at the earliest date possible.'[10] At the time, the date had probably already been decided on and he was personally involved in the sensitive discussions with James Connolly, which culminated in Connolly becoming the Military Council's sixth member.

MacDermott also played a central role in the Military Council's efforts to deceive MacNeill as to their true intentions. When early on Sunday morning, 23 April, 'physically worn out by the strenuous months of anxiety' and effort, MacDermott heard of MacNeill's countermand order, he was said to be 'writhed in anguish ... He rent the coat of his pyjamas to shreds, crying inconsolably that we were betrayed again', but declaring that 'they should rise if only with pikes and bayonets'.[11] Nonetheless, when hours later he attended a crisis meeting of the Military Council at Liberty Hall, MacDermott opposed Clarke and agreed with its other members that the Rising should be postponed until noon on Easter Monday. He spent that evening at a safe house, under Volunteer protection, issuing dispatches to inform others of the changed arrangements.

Early on Easter Monday morning, MacDermott went to Liberty Hall to help with final preparations and watch anxiously the turnout of Volunteers. At just before noon, because of his lameness, he left with Clarke by car and waited at the corner of Sackville Street and Princes Street for the arrival of the headquarters battalions which had proceeded on foot. After the garrison had occupied the GPO Diarmuid Lynch recalls: 'One of my happiest recollections of Easter week is that of Sean MacDermott and Thomas Clarke sitting on the edge of the mails platform beaming satisfaction and expressing congratulations', amidst the frenetic activity around them.[12] One account states that by then MacDermott 'looked white and prematurely aged by the suspense and tension' of previous months. Most of his comrades, however, were struck by his 'happiness,' his 'joy' that an armed rising was an accomplished fact and that an 'almost absolute degree' of secrecy had been preserved.[13] Volunteer Joe Good noted, if rather enthusiastically, not only MacDermott's enormous cheerfulness, but also his 'almost superhuman vitality', concluding that his 'titanic' performance was comparable to Connolly's over the week that followed.[14]

During the relative calm of the first few days, the Volunteers focussed their energies on making the building secure and on preparations for an anticipated British military assault. MacDermott's own activities then are sporadically recorded. On Monday, acting on instructions from Connolly, he was observed limping onto a wrecked tram and appealing vainly to looters to desist as they were disgracing the struggle for Ireland's freedom. Also that day, both he and Clarke were persuaded by The O'Rahilly to issue orders for the release of Bulmer Hobson: his arrest had been organised by the Military Council three days earlier. Meanwhile, MacDermott had arranged for Jim Ryan, a medical student, to join the Volunteers at the GPO and asked him after his arrival on Tuesday to establish and operate a hospital in the building.[15]

By midweek, the cordon of troops around the GPO was steadily tightening, and their machine-gun and artillery attack was becoming more intense. On Thursday, the east side of Lower Sackville Street had been set ablaze by incendiary bullets and shells. Because of the incapacitating ankle injury sustained by Connolly that day and Plunkett's ill-health, MacDermott (like Clarke) adopted a more assertive role in the actual direction of the battle. He gave instructions on the movement of materials, issued promotions and helped coordinate the efforts of Volunteers engaged in fire-fighting. Diarmuid Lynch states that he did so 'with his usual geniality, thoroughness and imperturbability'.[16] Though dressed in civilian clothes and having no formal military rank, his authority as one of their commanders was recognised by the garrison, due to his high ranking position in the IRB, his membership of the provisional government (he was seen acting as secretary at its meetings) and the respect accorded him by both Pearse and Connolly.

Almost certainly, in the early hours of Friday morning, the rebel leaders held a crisis meeting at which they agreed to evacuate the GPO if it was shelled by British troops or set ablaze by their incendiaries. In preparation, MacDermott ordered the removal of ammunition supplies from the upper floors to a basement extending under Henry Street. Near dawn, he instructed a number of Volunteer units to abandon their outposts so that the men could retreat in greater safety before daybreak. He also indicated to Jim Ryan that he should prepare the wounded for transfer to Jervis Street Hospital. At around noon, he appears to have challenged unsuccessfully Pearse's order to protesting Cumann na mBan members that they should leave the GPO; his concern was that 'in ordering the girls out, we might be ordering them to their immediate deaths' in the context of the gun-battles then taking place.[17] Later, as the fires escalated out of control, he helped fight the flames, supervised the clearance and removal of combustible material and ordered the rebels to withdraw from the Metropole Hotel.[18]

After the evacuation, most of the Volunteers eventually scattered into houses in Moore Street and MacDermott spent that night helping organise the defences of those gathered there. At noon next day, 30 April, he along with the four other members of the provisional government in the garrison met and agreed by majority vote to seek surrender terms 'to prevent the further slaughter of Dublin civilians'. MacDermott fully endorsed the decision. On the previous day, 'for the only time in the whole week he broke down and wept' when passing the body of The O'Rahilly in Sackville Lane.[19] He was also deeply affected by the death of a child, shot accidentally whilst the Volunteers were desperately seeking cover after leaving the GPO. After the leaders had reached their decision, he helped improvise a white flag for Elizabeth O'Farrell, the rebels' intermediary, to carry as she sought to establish contact with the British military command. She notes that: 'he first hung one out of the house [15 Moore Street] to ensure me not being fired at'.[20] She succeeded in her mission. Julia Grenan recalls that before Pearse then left them to meet General Lowe 'sadly and without speaking he shook hands with all at No. 16'. She records that, 'All there, except Sean MacDermott and Willie Pearse, were in tears.'[21] Afterwards, MacDermott arranged for Connolly to be carried over to British lines in fulfilment of the terms agreed.

After leaving his garrison, Pearse met Maxwell and eventually signed a formal surrender order, subsequently ratified by Connolly (then in hospital at Dublin Castle). This was then brought by O'Farrell, with military assistance, to the various rebel outposts. At Moore Street, some of the Volunteers greeted it with open defiance, a predictable reaction, given the extent of their sacrifices especially since the evacuation, their state of exhaustion and the looming prospect of long prison sentences. Peadar Bracken recalls that: 'Everyone ... [was] ... upset ... as it was our intention to work our way to the Four Courts, and then, all for the Dublin Mountains.' Oscar Traynor asked MacDermott: 'Is this what we were brought out for? To go into English dungeons for the rest of our lives?'[22] A number of leaders sought to mollify them including Clarke and Plunkett. Joe Good writes: 'Thank God for MacDermott who was to save our dignity and maybe our necks ... He limped forward leaning on that light cane ... released his astonishing wide smile [and] began to speak with ... total confidence. He was the most powerful personality I ever encountered.' Good regarded his speech as 'the most potent I was privileged to hear ... Yet the words were simple enough.' In essence, MacDermott argued that there was nothing to

be gained by prolonging the conflict. He asked the rebels to consider how many more civilians 'would be butchered' in the streets if
they did not surrender and how much more of 'this beautiful city
[would be] razed'. He praised them for having fought 'a gallant
fight'. which future generations would revere. But he suggested that
now it was their duty to survive and he concluded: 'We who will be
shot will die happy knowing there are plenty of you around who
will finish the job.'[23]

At about 6 p.m., the Volunteers formed up in the street outside,
marched into Sackville Street and on orders from the British officer
commanding, laid down their arms and equipment on the pavement
outside the Gresham Hotel. Soldiers then drew up lists of their
names and addresses; MacDermott and Clarke who were clearly
standing in close proximity appear on the same page. Later at
MacDermott's trial, Lieutenant W.H. Ruxton recorded a conversation he held with him then. According to his testimony, the rebel
leader said to him that he 'would not be able to march far on
account of his leg. I asked him why he could not march. One of the
others told me his leg was paralysed.' No doubt struck both by this
reply and the fact that the prisoner was wearing civilian clothes,
Ruxton recalled that he then 'asked the accused how did you get
caught up in this affair. The accused replied to the effect that he had
his place in the organisation.'[24]

The garrison was escorted to the grassy area at the front of the
Rotunda Hospital and was held there overnight under strict guard.
Winifred Carney recalls that she spread her 'coat and Connolly's
coat ... on the grass and insisted on MacDermott and Plunkett having a little warmth and rest'.[25] At 9 a.m. next morning, the rebels
were marched to Richmond Barracks. Though deprived by soldiers
of his cane, MacDermott was permitted to follow his comrades at
his own pace, supported by two young Volunteers, the group being
kept under constant military supervision. Three-quarters of an hour
after the others, he eventually arrived, 'completely worn out "from
the night's exposure and the fatiguing march and as" pale as death'.[26]
He was nonetheless in high spirits; that evening, he wrote to
Thomas Clarke's wife, Kathleen: 'I never felt so proud of the boys.
It's worth a life of suffering to be with them for one hour.'[27]

When the Volunteers were assembled in the gymnasium next
morning, MacDermott was probably identified as one of the leaders by DMP Detective Daniel Hoey, who was later to give evidence

at his trial. For several years, MacDermott had been conscious of being shadowed by police and even spoke lightly of having his 'favourites'.[28] Whilst being searched at the barracks, one of his own dispatches was discovered in his clothing and was later to be used as evidence against him in court. In any case, he seems from the outset to have regarded his execution as inevitable. Just after the surrender at Moore Street, Jim Ryan had asked him: 'What terms did he think Pearse and Connolly had agreed at Dublin Castle. That the signatories [of the Proclamation] would be shot and the rest of us set free, he thought.'[29] When discussing the same matter at Richmond Barracks, a Volunteer records him making a similar comment: 'Sean Heuston and Con Colbert were shot and they did not sign. Only Connolly and myself of the signatories are left. We will be shot.' His comrade observed that 'he did not seem in the least bit worried'.[30] The reasons for his apparent lack of concern were made clear when he spoke to Desmond Ryan. He told him: 'I am going to be shot. If I am not shot, all this is worthless.'[31] When speaking to another prisoner, MacDermott expanded on these sentiments. He said of the executions (the shots were audible at Richmond Barracks in the early morning stillness): '[they] are our victory. Had they [the British authorities] not shot them, we would be presented as a lot of paltroons who dared challenge the power of England. I'll be shot and I hope I will be'; this had always been one of his most cherished motives for supporting a rising.[32]

Bernard O'Rourke, one of the prisoners held at Richmond Barracks, commented on the 'hopeless muddle here with all the prisoners on their hands ... [They] sent many to England, and released them after a few days of landing'.[33] S.T. O'Kelly claims to have seen MacDermott 'in a group assembled for deportation, with bright muffler, talking eagerly and gaily. They were lined up for inpection by detectives. The inspector stood in front of MacDermott for thirty seconds, then [he] was ordered out of the ranks and marched back to his room in the barracks.'[34]

MacDermott was eventually tried on 9 May (prisoner number ninety-one), his name appearing on the official record as 'Sean MacDairmida' – approximately the form in which he always signed it. Colonel D. Sapte presided. Perhaps reflecting the pressures on Maxwell at the time over the courts martial and the executions, the prosecution called six witnesses (four were called in Connolly's trial the same day – the second highest number of the fourteen trials held in Dublin). The first witness was Detective Hoey, who claimed to have known the defendant for three and a half years. He made reference to MacDermott's record of association with the Irish Volunteer leadership and organisation, especially over the previous twelve months, and his role in producing the newspaper, *Nationality*. Three military officers then gave evidence in turn with regard either to witnessing MacDermott surrender or the dispatch which had been found when he was searched at Richmond Barracks: none of them could confirm that they had seen him armed. Next, a warder from Mountjoy Gaol alleged that he recognised the defendant from his prison service there twelve months earlier; he gave no indication of the nature of the charge which had led to MacDermott's sentence. The court proceedings make reference to a sixth witness being called, Captain de Courcy Wheeler; his testimony, however, is either missing or, more likely, was disallowed by the court as it related to a search of property conducted after the Rising (see MacBride case). Documentary evidence was also produced; a list of rebels compiled by a British officer in Sackville Street after the surrender which included MacDermott's name; a dispatch written by MacDermott and found on his person; and a copy of a newspaper, the *Irish Volunteer*, which made reference to him. The records of his case also contain a copy of the Proclamation, but this was not referred to during the course of the trial.[35]

MacDermott cross-examined four of the witnesses. He probably also made a statement: unique amongst these fifteen texts of proceedings the record appears to be incomplete. But in the section of the final page which is intelligible, the accused seems to be refuting Hoey's evidence, stating: 'I did not attend the weekly meetings of the Irish Volunteers, nor any of their meetings. I sent them their accounts by post.'[36] Dairmuid Lynch noted later that in the period immediately preceding the Rising, MacDermott had become so engrossed in making the necessary preparations that he had then neglected his other duties, including his management of the newspaper *Nationality*.[37]

On 9 May, the court found MacDermott guilty of the main charge (that he did 'take part in armed rebellion ... for the purpose of assisting the enemy'), but perhaps surprisingly, innocent of the lesser one (causing 'disaffection among the civilian population').[38] Without hesitation Maxwell confirmed the death sentence; he had already written to Asquith on 9 May, before the outcome of the trial was known, stating that 'if convicted' both MacDermott and Connolly, 'must suffer the extreme penalty'.[39] In justifying his decision two days later, he asserted: 'This man signed the Declaration of Irish Independence' (MacDermott had assumed that this would be decisive). Maxwell also described MacDermott as 'one of the most prominent of the leaders of the Irish Volunteers ... He wrote and sent despatches and mobilization orders ... And ... surrendered with a body of rebels in Sackville Street with whom he had been operating for the previous week.'[40]

Like his mentor, Thomas Clarke, MacDermott retained a deep sense of bitterness towards Eoin MacNeill, the IVF Chief of Staff, for issuing his countermand order on the eve of the Rising. The timing of Frank Thornton's court martial coincided with MacDermott's; he recalls that afterwards, he was sitting with MacDermott and several other captives on a lawn at the barracks, when MacNeill arrived under military escort. MacNeill approached MacDermott and 'tried to shake hands with him, but Sean turned his back and walked away'. Nonetheless, MacDermott must have been heartened by events later that day. He was marched under guard to Kilmainham with a number of other prisoners; he was still without his walking stick, and as a consequence had to be supported by Harry Boland, one of his comrades at the GPO. Thornton, who was also there, recalls: 'We were marched along the road ... and with every yard there were indications of the changed attitude of the people. The open trams passing by always brought a cheer from somebody, even though rifles were pointed at the offender on very occasion, and old men stood at the street corner and saluted despite being pushed around.' He adds that when they had reached the gaol, MacDermott 'turned around to the three of us, shook hands and said: "I'll be shot and it will be a bad day for Ireland if I am not. You fellows will get an opportunity, even if in years to come, to follow on where we left off."'[41] Before leaving the barracks, he had said to one of the rebels, Joe Sweeny, that 'this generation should be proud of us, and that the blow we had struck would awaken the people to greater effort'.[42]

Asquith acted to delay MacDermott's execution out of concern for the negative impact on Irish public opinion. But whatever initial doubts he may have had, he was quickly convinced by Maxwell that it was justified. He publicly made clear his view that the prisoner should face the firing squad in the Commons, on 10 May. 'The trials by court martial of those who took an active part in the rising in Dublin are practically finished and beyond two sentences which have already been confirmed we have the best reasons for hoping and believing that there may be no further necessity to proceed with the extreme penalty.' Next day, Asquith stated: 'There are two other persons who are under sentence of death − a sentence which has been confirmed by the General − both of whom signed the Proclamation and took an active part ... in the actual rebellion in Dublin ... in these two cases the extreme penalty must be paid'.[43]

MacDermott faced death with total equanimity, fully convinced of the legitimacy of the Rising, and certain of its ultimate significance in helping achieve the goal to which he had dedicated much of his life. He wrote to his sister and brothers on 11 May, reassuring them: 'I am as calm and collected as if I were talking to you all.' He continued:

> I have been tried by Courtmartial and sentenced to death − to die the death of a soldier ... I feel happiness the like of which I never experienced in my life before, and a feeling that I could not describe ... You ought to envy me. The cause for which I die has been rebaptised during the past week by the blood of as good men as ever trod God's earth, and should I not feel justly proud to be numbered amongst them. Before God let me again assure you of how proud and happy I feel. It is not alone for myself so much I feel happy but for the fact that Ireland has produced such men.[44]

In a letter the same day to John Daly, the veteran republican friend of both Clarke and himself, he also stated that he had been 'sentenced to a soldier's death ... I have nothing to say about this only that I look on it as a part of the day's work. We die that the Irish nation may live. Our blood will rebaptise and reinvigorate the old land. Knowing this it is superfluous to say how happy I feel. I know now what I have always felt − that the Irish nation can never die ... posterity will judge us aright from the effects of our action.'[45]

At his request, Phyllis and Mary Ryan (sisters of the medical student, Jim Ryan) stayed with him for several hours from midnight on 11 May. Mary records that 'he talked to us in a way that was in no way sad ... about everything under the sun', asking them in particular what they knew of the Rising in areas other than the GPO. As they left, she writes, he 'just said, "We never thought it would end like this, that this would be the end." Yes, that's all he said,' adding 'although he knew long before that what the end would be for him.'[46] Likewise, Father Browne says of his conversation with the prisoner the night before: 'I ... heard [him] ... review the patient years with no regret.'[47] MacDermott was attended by the Prison Chaplain, Father Eugene McCarthy at 3 a.m. on 12 May; he was executed at 3:45 a.m.

Letter written in Kilmainham Gaol on the day before his execution, by Sean MacDermott, to the veteran Fenian John Daly; Daly himself died on 30 June 1916

NATIONAL MUSEUM OF IRELAND

Trial of John MacDermott
(Sean MacDiarmada)
prisoner number ninety-one

REFERENCE: PRO WO71/344

DATE: 9 May 1916

LOCATION: Richmond Barracks

JUDGES: Colonel D. Sapte, (President), Lieutenant Colonel Bent,
Major F.W. Woodward

CHARGE:

1 'Did an act to wit did take part in an armed rebellion and in the waging of war against His Majesty the King, such act being o such a nature as to be calculated to be prejudical to the Defence to the Realm and being done with the intention and for the purpose of assisting the enemy'

2 'Did attempt to cause disaffection among the civilian population of His Majesty

PLEA: Not guilty (to both charges)

VERDICT: Guilty. Death (first charge); not guilty (second charge).

Text of Trial

SUMMARY OF EVIDENCE

Accused – McDermott

1st Witness for Prosecution
Constable Daniel Hoey – Detective Department Dublin Metropolitan Police says:–

> I have known the accused by the name of John McDermott, or in the Irish form Sean MacDiarmada, for 3^{1}/$_{2}$ years. The accused associated with leaders of the Irish Volunteers, Thomas Clarke, P.H. Pearse, Joseph Plunkett, Frank Fahy, Joe McGuinness, E.J. Duggan, and others. They held executive meetings once a week and General Council meetings once a month at the Hd. Qrs. Irish Volunteers

2 Dawson Street. The accused and those mentioned
attended these meetings. The accused visits an office in
12 D'Olier Street Dublin frequently. It has the name Sean
MacDiarmada on a plate. I have seen some of the others
mentioned visiting there – Thomas J. Clarke had a
tobacconist's shop at 75 (a) Parnell Street. This shop was
frequented by leading members. I have seen the accused
there frequently. I did not see the accused at Liberty Hall,
the headquarters of the General Transport and Workers
Union.

Crossexamined by the accused.

I have only known the accused to associate with Irish
Volunteer leaders during the last 12 months. I have known
him for 3¹/₂ years but at first he did not so associate as far
as I know. I do not know all the objects of the Gaelic
league but I understand the Irish Language is one of them. I
do not know his connection with the Gaelic League, I have
not enquired into it. I have not seen the accused at the Hd.
Qrs. Gaelic league.

The report of the Central Executive meeting of the Irish
Volunteers is published in the "Irish Volunteer", I produce a
copy – (marked X. signed and attached to proceedings). A
paper known as Nationality is published at 12 D'Olier
Street. This is the accused's principal means of livelihood.
There are several offices in 12 D'Olier Street. Clarke's shop
sells papers etc as well as tobacco. He did a good business
there. I have seen the accused visit many public houses and
remain a considerable time.

2nd Lieut W.H. Ruxton 3/Royal Irish Regt. 2nd Witness for
Prosecution states:–

I was on duty in Parnell Street on the 29th April 1916 –
3 parties of rebels, two armed one partially armed with
knives and some ammunition, surrendered. The accused was
one of the two armed parties who surrendered between 6
and 7 pm. The accused spoke to me and said he would not
be able to march far on account of his leg. I asked him why
he could not march. One of the others told me his leg was
paralysed. I asked the accused "How did you get into this
affair". The accused replied to the effect that he had his
place in the organisation. The parties came from the
direction of the General Post Office. They were sent on to
the Rotunda. I am positive the accused is the man I spoke to.

Cross-examined by the accused.

I should imagine there were about 200 men in the accused's party. They were not all armed. I did not see any arms in the accused's possession.

3rd Witness for Prosecution
2nd Lieut. S.A.L. Downing 3/R. Irish Regt. States:–

I was on duty on 29th April 1916 in Sackville Street. I took the names of about 23 of the rebels after they had laid down their arms. I identify the paper as my list (marked Y signed and attached). The accused was in that party and is shown on the list, but I do not know if he actually gave the name.

Crossexamined by the accused.

I did not pay particular attention to the surrender of arms and did not see the accused with any arms.

Lt Col. H.F. Fraser 21st Lancers states:– 4th Witness for Prosecution

I was present in the Richmond Barracks Dublin on the 30th April 1916, and identify the accused as one of those confined there, but not necessarily on that date.

All papers taken from the prisoners on this occasion were handed to me. I identify the paper produced as one of those handed in to me in the gymnasium on that day. (This paper is marked D signed by the President and attached).

Edward Gaunon – Clerk Warden Mountjoy Prison Dublin 5th Witness for Prosecution states:–

I identify the accused as John McDermott who was confined in Mountjoy Prison Dublin in May/June 1915. I produce the cash and property book, in which the accused signed his name Sean McDiarmada on the 26th May 1915. The spelling is the same as on the document D now shown to me. Except for the S, there is a strong resemblance between the signatures.

Cross-examined by the accused

I am not a fluent Irish scholar.

Captain Henry de Courcey Wheeler 6th Witness for Prosecution Res. of officers states:–

On the 7 May 1916 about 6.30 pm I searched

[part of the record is missing]

the voice of a man named McDermott, not the accused, but a man I had not known before. I did not attend the weekly meetings of the Irish Volunteers, nor any of their meetings. I sent them their accounts by post.

List of rebels
who died as a consequence of the Rising
excluding those executed

ADAMS, John Francis	killed in action, St. Stephens Green	25/4/1916	ICA
ALLEN Thomas	killed in action, Four Courts	28/4/1916	IVF
BURKE, William F.	killed in action, Sth Dublin Union	25/4/1916	IVF
BYRNE, Andrew Joseph	died from wounds received at Boland's Bakery	1/5/1916	IVF
BYRNE, James	Jacobs Garrison, killed at home	27/4/1916	IVF
BYRNE, Louis	killed in action, City Hall	24/4/1916	ICA
CARRIGAN, Charles	killed in action near GPO	28/4/1916	IVF
CLARKE, Philip	killed in action, St Stephen's Green	25/4/1916	ICA
CONNOLLY, Seán	killed in action, City Hall	24/4/1916	ICA
CORCORAN, James	killed in action, St Stephen's Green	25/4/1916	ICA
COSGRAVE, Edward	killed in action, GPO	25/4/1916	ICA
COSTELLO, Edward Joseph	died from wounds received at Church St near Four Courts	25/4/1916	N/A
COSTELLO, John	killed while taking despatches from Boland's Bakery to Mount St	26/4/1916	IVF
COYLE, Henry	killed in action, Moore Lane	28/4/1916	IVF
CRENIGAN, John	killed in action, Ashbourne	28/4/1916	IVF
CROMIEN, John	killed in action, Prussia St	25/4/1916	IVF
DARCY, Charles	killed in action, Parliament St	24/4/1916	ICA
DONOLAN, Brendan IVFF	killed in action, Sth Dublin Union	24/4/1916	
DOYLE, Patrick	killed in action, Clanwilliam House	27/4/1916	IVF
DWAN, John	killed in action, Nth King St	27/4/1916	IVF
ENNIS, Edward	killed in action, Bolands Bakery	29/4/1916	IVF

FARRELL, Patrick	killed in action, Nth Brunswick St	29/4/1916	IVF
FOX, James Joseph	killed in action, St Stephen's Green	25/4/1916	ICA
GEOGHEGAN, George	killed in action, City Hall	26/4/1916	ICA
HEALY, John	died from wounds received at Phibsborough.	27/4/1916 Fianna Éireann	
HOWARD, Seán B	died from wounds receved at Church St	29/4/1916 Fianna Éireann	
HURLEY, Seán	killed in action, Church St	27/4/1916	IVF
KEATING, Con	drowned off Ballykissane Pier, County Kerry	21/4/1916	IVF
KEELY, John	died from wounds received, GPO	25/4/1916	IVF
KENT, Richard	from wounds received at Bawnard House, Castle Lyons, Co Cork	4/5/1916	IVF
KEOGH, Gerald	killed in action outside Trinity College	25/4/1916	IVF
McCORMACK, James	killed in action, Beresford Place	26/4/1916	IVF
McDOWELL, Wiliam	killed in action, Sth Dublin Union	24/4/1916	IVF
MACKEN, Francis	killed in action, Moore St	28/4/1916	IVF
MACKEN, Peadar	killed in action, Boland's Bakery	27/4/1916	IVF
MALONE, Michael	killed in action, 25 Northumberland Rd	26/4/1916	IVF
MANNING, Peter Paul	killed in action, Nth Brunswick St	29/4/1916	IVF
MONAGHAN, Charles	drowned off Ballykissane Pier	21/4/1916	IVF
MULVAHILL, Michael	killed in action, Moore Lane	28/4/1916	IVF
MURPHY, Richard	killed in action, Clanwilliam House	26/4/1916	IVF
MURRAY, Daniel	died from wounds received in Camden St	13/5/1916	ICA
O'CARRROLL, Richard	died from wounds received in Camden St	5/5/1916	IVF
O'CONNOR, Patrick	killed in action, O'Connell St	27/4/1916	IVF
O'FLANAGAN, Patrick	killed in action, North King St	29/4/1916	IVF
O'GRADY, John J	died from wounds received at St Stephen's Green	29/4/1916	IVF
THE O'RAHILLY	killed in action, Henry Place	28/4/1916	ICA

O'REILLY, John	killed in action, City Hall	24/4/1916	IVF
O'REILLY, Richard	killed in action, Sth Dublin Union	24/4/1916	IVF
O'REILLY, Thomas	died from wounds received while taking dispatches from City Hall to Liberty Hall	27/4/1916	ICA
RAFFERTY, Thomas	died from wounds received at Ashbourne	29/4/1916	IVF
REYNOLDS, George	killed in action, Clanwilliam House	27/4/1916	IVF
RYAN, Frederick	killed in action, Harcourt St	27/4/1916	ICA
SHEEHAN, Donald	drowned off Ballykissane Pier	21/4/1916	IVF
SHORTIS, Patrick	killed in action, Moore St	28/4/1916	IVF
TRAYNOR, John	killed in action, Sth Dublin Union	24/4/1916	IVF
WALSH, Edward	died from wounds received at Parliament St	25/4/1916	IVF
WALSH, Philip	killed in action, North King St	29/4/1916	IVF
WEAFER, Thomas Joseph	killed in action, O'Connell St	26/4/1916	IVF
WHELAN, Patrick	killed in action, Boland's Bakery	27/4/1916	IVF
WILSON, Peter	killed in action, Mendicity Institution	29/4/1916	IVF

The information contained in this list has been derived from a range of sources

Notes

INTRODUCTION

1 Quoted in account by Bulmer Hobson, NLI MS13170.
2 For Clan na Gael, see PRO HO317/37; see also Michael Foy and Brian Barton, *The Easter Rising* (Sutton Publishing Limited, Stroud, 1999), for a comprehensive survey of the whole period.
3 F.S.L. Lyons, *Ireland since the Famine* (Fontana/Collins, Suffolk, 1982), p. 348.
4 *Ireland Report*, NLI MS130855(5); see also Foy and Barton, pp 13–19.
5 Liam O'Briain to William O'Brien, 15 December 1949, NLI 13978.
6 Account by Frank Robbins, NLI MS10915.
7 Leon Ó Broin, *Dublin Castle and the 1916 Rising: The Story of Sir Matthew Nathan* (Helican, Dublin, 1966), p. 149.
8 Inspector General's Report, dated 15 June 1916, PRO CO904/99.
9 Diary of Easter Week and note, dated 23 May 1916, Midleton Papers, PRO 30/67/31.
10 Diary of Dorothy Stopford, NLI MS 16063.
11 Lyons, p. 364.
12 Diary of Easter Week, Midleton Papers, PRO 30/67/31.
13 Foy and Barton, pp. 42–3.
14 Report by Chalk, 16 March 1916, PRO CO904/23.
15 Inspector General's Report, March 1916, PRO CO904/99.
16 Diary of Henry Hanna, 24 April 1916, TCD MS1066/192.
17 See situation report for 24 April 1916, PRO WO35/69.
18 Comment made in Nathan Papers, MS 360, Bodleian Library, Oxford University.
19 Ibid., MS 476 (4).
20 John J. Reynolds, *A Fragment of 1916 History* (Sinn Féin Press, Dublin, 1919), p. 4.
21 Declan Kiberd, *1916 Rebellion Handbook* (Mourne River Press, Dublin, 1998), p. 25.
22 For report of enquiry, see PRO WO35/67/3.
23 Ibid.
24 Kiberd, p. 23.
25 Maxwell to his wife Louise, 18 May 1916, Maxwell Papers, Princeton University Library, CO583, Box 2/6.
26 Maxwell to Kitchener, Maxwell Papers, Princeton University Library, Box 30/107.
27 Note made repeatedly by Maxwell, PRO WO141/21.
28 Kiberd, p. 24.
29 Undated memorandum (late May 1916) by Sir Edward Troup in PRO WO141/21.
30 County Inspector's Report, June 1916, PRO CO904/100.
31 Maxwell to Asquith, 26 May 1916, Asquith Papers, Bodleian Library, Oxford University, MS 37(12); the description of the rebels as 'heroes, martyrs and clean fighters' is from the Inspector General's Report, August 1916, PRO CO904/100. He was indicating how

they were popularly perceived.
32 Account by Pat Rankin, NLI MS22251.
33 William Smith (District Superintendent), *Report of Work Done by St John's Ambulance Brigade during the Sinn Féin Rebellion, April–May 1916* (John Falconer, Dublin, 1916), passim; see also PRO WO141/22.
34 Descriptions given in the following: E. Mahaffy diary, 24 April 1916, TCD MS2074; Hanna diary, 3 May 1916, TCD MS1066/192; account by Dick Humphries NLI MS18829.
35 Joe Good, *Enchanted by Dreams: the Journal of a Revolutionary* (Brandon, Dingle, 1996), p. 50.
36 Diary of Douglas Hyde, 1 May 1916, TCD MS10343/7.
37 Account by Ismena Rohde, NLI MS15415.
38 Quoted in Foy and Barton, p. 88.
39 Diary of E. Mahaffy, 27 April 1916, TCD MS2074. She was the Provost's daughter at TCD.
40 Account by Michael Kent, NLI MS15292.
41 Diary of John Clarke, 29 April 1916, NLI MS10485.
42 Account by Paddy Holohan, *Capuchin Annual* (1966): p. 188; see also Foy and Barton, pp. 203–8.
43 Account by Oscar Traynor, UCD P150/3655.
44 Account by Dorothy Stopford, NLI MS16063.
45 Maxwell to his wife, 30 April 1916, Maxwell Papers, Princeton University Library, Box 2/6.
46 Diary of E. Mahaffy, 29 April 1916, TCD MS2074; see also Military Court of Enquiry, 19 May 1916, PRO WO141/22.
47 Asquith to King George V, 27 April 1916, PRO CAB 37/146.
48 Kent trial, PRO WO71/356.
49 Account by Robert Holland of events at Marrowbone Lane, Allen Library, Dublin.
50 Account by Piaras Beaslai, in Desmond Ryan, *The Rising: the Complete Story of Easter Week* (Golden Eagle Books, Dublin, 1949), p. 258.
51 Maxwell memorandum, 3 May 1916, PRO WO35/69.
52 Account by Paddy Doyle, Allen Library.
53 Account by Jack Plunkett, NLI MS11397.
54 Beaslai cited in Ryan, p. 259
55 Judge Advocate General's Office to Sir Reginald Brade, Secretary, Army Council, 28 October 1916, PRO WO141/27; lists of names given in PRO WO213/8.
56 Gerard Oram, *Death Sentences Passed by Military Courts of the British Army, 1914–24* (Boutle, London, 1998), p. 13.
57 Undated minute, PRO WO141/27.
58 Quoted in memorandum by Adjutant General, General Sir Neville Macready, 10 January 1917; and undated memorandum by Brade, PRO WO141/27.
59 Law Officers' Judgement, 30 January 1917, Brade memorandum.
60 All quotes from undated memorandum by Brade.
61 Memorandum by Adjutant General, 10 January 1917; also undated memorandum by

Brade, ibid.

62   Law Officers' judgement, 30 January 1917,
     Brade memorandum.
63   Undated memorandum by Brade.
64   P. C. Parr, *The Court Martials of 1798–99* (The
     Irish Historical Press, Kilkenny, 1997), passim.
65   Gerard Oram, *Worthless Men; Race, Eugenics and
     the Death Penalty in the British Army during
     World War I* (Boutle, London, 1998), pp. 72–3.
66   Elizabeth Countess of Fingall, *Countess of
     Fingall, Seventy Years Young: Memories of
     Elizabeth, Countess of Fingall* (Lilliput, Dublin,
     1991), p. 376; see also file on Brigadier-
     General Blackader, PRO WO374/6825 and
     The Times obituary, 5 April 1921.
67   Unpublished memoirs of Brigadier E.W.S.K.
     Maconchy, p. 456, British Army Museum,
     London; also *The Times* obituary, 3 September
     1945.
68   Typescript of unpublished autobiography by
     William Wylie (amended from original
     handwritten version, PRO 30/89/1) PRO
     30/89/2; see also Leon Ó Broin, *W.E. Wylie
     and the Irish Revolution, 1916–21* (Gill and
     Macmillan, Dublin, 1989), passim. Between
     1919–20, Wylie became Adjutant General and
     Attorney General of Ireland, Judge of the
     Supreme Court of Judicature and a
     government legal advisor.
69   Wylie's typescript autobiography.
70   Ibid.
71   Wylie's handwritten autobiography.
72   Wylie's typescript autobiography.
73   Trial of William Pearse, PRO WO71/358.
74   Piaras F. MacLochlainn, *Last Words; Letters and
     Statements of the Leaders Executed after the Rising
     at Easter 1916* (The Stationery Office, Dublin,
     1990), p. 71.
75   Account by Jack Plunkett, NLI MS11397.
76   Trial proceedings in PRO WO71/346, 348,
     350, 352,357.
77   Trial of Thomas Kent, PRO WO71/356.
78   Wylie's handwritten autobiography.
79   Account by Plunkett NLI MS11397. For
     examples of the courts martial of soldiers in
     1916 see PRO WO71/509, the case of Harry
     Farr, and PRO WO71/525, the trials of
     Longshaw and Ingham. General D. Haig
     noted, 21 November 1914, that at that time in
     Field General Courts Martial, 'a complete
     record of all the evidence given before the
     Court has to be recorded in order to
     substantiate any finding of "Guilty"'. He
     advocated that less scrupulous records should
     be kept owing to the difficulty of conducting
     trials at the front (they were often held in
     trenches, men could not easily leave their
     military duties to attend court, stationery was
     not often available, etc, and 'witnesses, owing
     to wounds or death, are frequently not
     forthcoming...'. None of these circumstances
     applied in Ireland at Easter 1916. I am grateful
     to Dr Gerard Oram, of the Open University
     for these references.
80   Quoted in Lyons, p. 348.
81   MacLochlainn, p. 45.
82   Account by Hobson, NLI MS13170.

SIR JOHN MAXWELL

1   Colonel P.J. Hally, 'The Easter Rising in
     Dublin: The Military Aspects, Part II', *The Irish
     Sword*, vol. VII, p. 53.
2   Maxwell to his wife, 8 June 1916, Maxwell
     Papers, Princeton University Library, CO583,
     Box 2/6.
3   Sir George Arthur, *General Sir John Maxwell*
     (Murray, London, 1932), p. 247; also Kitchener
     Papers PRO30/57/55. For overview of British
     government's response to the Rising, see
     Michael Foy and Brian Barton, *The Easter
     Rising* (Sutton Publishing Limited, Stroud,
     1999), pp. 218–44.
4   Leon Ó Broin, *Dublin Castle and the 1916
     Rising: the Story of Sir Matthew Nathan*
     (Helican, Dublin, 1966), p. 145.
5   Asquith to King George V, 27 April 1916,
     PRO CAB 37/146, regarding the Irish
     appointment.
6   Note dated 8 March 1915, PRO30/57/45; the
     predominantly Irish and Catholic Tenth
     Division fought at Suvla Bay, August 1915, and
     sustained heavy losses, before going on to
     Salonika and Palestine.
7   Maxwell to his wife, 28 April 1916, Maxwell
     Papers, Princeton University Library, Box 2/6.
8   Arthur, p. 249.
9   Ibid., p. 256.
10   Ibid., p. 250.
11   Joe Good, *Enchanted by Dreams; the Journal of a
     Revolutionary* (Brandon, Dingle, 1996), p. 63.
12   Maxwell's reports to the War Office, 30 April,
     2 May 1916, PRO WO35/69.
13   Nathan Papers, 29 April 1916, MS 476.
14   Notes by Brigadier-General Lowe, 29 April
     1916, originals at Kilmainham Museum,
     Dublin.
15   Arthur, p. 247.
16   PRO CAB42/12/83A.
17   Cabinet minutes, 28 April 1916, PRO CAB
     42/12, also Cabinet papers in PRO CAB
     37/146.
18   Arthur, pp. 272, 275.
19   Maxwell to his wife, 1 June 1916, Maxwell
     Papers, Princeton University Library, Box 2/6.
20   Maxwell to his wife, 28 April, 4 May 1916,
     Maxwell Papers.
21   Ó Broin, p. 116.
22   Arthur, p. 245.
23   Birrell to Nathan, 3 May 1916, Nathan papers,
     MS 476; also Ó Broin, p. 118.
24   Diary of Dorothy Stopford, 6 May 1916, NLI
     MS16063; see also Ó Broin, p. 183–4.
25   Captain H. Peel to his wife, 27 April, 2 May
     1916, IWM P391.
26   Account by J.W. Roworth, IWM 80/40/1.
27   Account by A.L. Franklin, IWM 93/25/1.
28   Maxwell to his wife, 30 April, 5 July, Maxwell
     Papers, Princeton University Library, Box 2/6.
29   Handwritten autobiography by Wylie, PRO
     30/89/1.
30   Maxwell to his wife, 4 May 1916, Maxwell
     Papers, Princeton University Library, Box 2/6.
     Dr Walsh was the Catholic Archbishop of
     Dublin.
31   Report of Hardinge Commission, PRO
     WO35/69.

32   Maxwell to Unsworth, 14 May 1916, Maxwell Papers, Princeton University Library, Box 2/6.

33   Quotes from letters to his wife, 20 May, 11 June, 2 July, 20 July, 31 July 1916, Maxwell Papers, Princeton University Library, Box 2/6; see also Arthur, p. 265.

34   Memorandum by Maxwell, 13 May 1916, Asquith Papers MS43, Bodleian Library, Oxford University. Maxwell's biographer makes it clear that in the exercise of his military and administrative duties before the First World War in British imperial Africa, Maxwell had been responsible for the execution of a number of disidents and spies and became imbued with a great love of Empire.

35   Order by Maxwell, 3 May 1916, PRO WO35/69.

36   Memorandum by Maxwell, 13 May 1916, Asquith Papers MS43, Bodleian Library, Oxford University.

37   Inspector General's Report, 1 April–31 May 1916, PRO CO904/99.

38   Arthur, p. 264.

39   Account by MacNeill, NLI MS11437. Wylie felt little sympathy for MacNeill. He wrote: 'I felt that MacNeill while avoiding the results of his teaching had done more that anyone else to mislead the youth of the country and had made the rebellion possible', Wylie's typescript autobiography, PRO30/89/2.

40   Ó Broin, p. 130.

41   Parliamentary Debates, Commons, Carson's speeches, 27 April 1916, vol. LXXXI, col. 2511, 3 May, vol. LXXXII, cols. 38–9; Redmond's speeches, 27 April, vol. LXXXI, col. 2512, 3 May, vol. LXXXII, col. 37; Dillon's speech, 11 May, vol. LXXXII, cols. 940, 945, 948, 951.

42   See Declan Kiberd, *1916 Rebellion Handbook* (Mourne River Press, Dublin, 1998), pp. 67–96, for lists of deportees.

43   Order from headquarters, 3 May 1916, PRO WO35/69.

44   Maxwell Order, 5 May 1916, PRO WO35/69.

45   Maxwell Order, 2 May 1916, PRO WO35/69.

46   Account by J.N. Galloway, IWM 87/45/1; also Lieutenant Colonel J.P.W. Jamie, *The 177th Brigade, 1914–18* (W. Thornley, Leicester, 1931), p. 14.

47   Account by E.F. Chapman, IWM 92/3/1.

48   Account by R.A. Pedler, IWM 86/30/1.

49   E.U. Bradbridge, *The 59th Division, 1915–1918* (Wilfrid Edmunds, Chesterfield, 1928), p. 46.

50   Account by H.M. Hughes, IWM P450.

51   Account by Galloway, IWM 87/45/1.

52   Account by J.W. Roworth, IWM 80/40/1.

53   Account by R.A. Pedler, IWM 86/30/1.

54   Lieutenant Colonel Jamie, p. 14.

55   Galloway, IWM 87/45/1.

56   G.I. Edmonds, *2/6 Battalion Sherwood Foresters; Its Part in the Defeat of the Irish Rebellion* (Wilfrid Edmunds, Chesterfield, 1960) p. 58; also account by W.N. Hendey IWM 78/42/1.

57   Lowe to Maxwell, 13, 27 May 1916, Asquith Papers, MS43, Bodleian Library, Oxford University.

58   Lowe to Maxwell, 13 May, Asquith Papers.

59   Cabinet minutes, 27 June 1916, PRO CAB41/37/21.

60   Inspector General's Report, 1 April–31 May 1916, PRO CO904/99.

61   Comment by Samuel, 15 May 1916, PRO CAB 37/147/36.

62   Ó Broin, p. 141; see also Roy Jenkins, *Asquith* (Collins, London, 1964), p. 398.

63   Maxwell to Asquith, 13 May 1916, Asquith Papers, MS43, Bodleian Library, Oxford University.

64   Maxwell's correspondence with Henderson, 12–16 May 1916, NLI MS17233 and with Redmond, NLI MS15206.

65   Maxwell to Redmond, 15 May 1916, NLI MS15206.

66   Maxwell to War Office, 30 May 1916, PRO WO141/19.

67   Leon Ó Broin, *W.E. Wylie and the Irish Revolution 1916–21* (Gill and Macmillan, Dublin, 1989), p. 36.

68   Report by E.N. Sharpe, Prison Matron, 6 September 1916, in PRO CO904/197. Those women who were deported were regarded by Maxwell as highly seditious; Asquith was, however, opposed to it and delayed their transfer, see PRO WO141/19.

69   Order by Maxwell, 14 May 1916, PRO WO35/69.

70   Arthur, p. 257.

71   Report, 23 May 1916, PRO WO32/957; see also NA S12303 for account of applicants to Sankey Committee.

72   'Joe' to John Caffey, 5 May 1916, Asquith Papers, MS43, Bodleian Library, Oxford University.

73   Wylie's typescript autobiography, PRO 30/89/2.

74   Account by Oscar Traynor, UCD P150/3655.

75   Quotes from O'Rourke's correspondence, UCD P1.

76   Undated note by G.W. Rushton, PRO WO35/69.

77   Quoted in Eoin Neeson, *Birth of a Republic* (Prestige Books, Dublin, 1998), pp.175–6.

78   Maxwell to his wife, 9 May 1916, Maxwell Papers, Princeton University Library, Box 2/6.

79   Report to War Office, 5 May 1916, PRO WO35/69.

80   Memorandum by Maxwell, 11 May 1916, Asquith Papers, MS43/26-33, Bodleian Library, Oxford University.

81   Maxwell to Asquith, 10 May 1916, Asquith Papers, MS43, Bodleian Library, Oxford University.

82   Account by Michael Kent, 8 May 1916, NLI MS15292.

83   Account by Jack Plunkett, NLI MS11397; see also Pat Cooke, *A History of Kilmainham Gaol, 1796–1924* (The Stationery Office, Dublin, 1995), passim.

84   Minute circulated by J.R. Young, 2 May 1916, PRO WO35/67/2.

85   Piaras F. MacLochlainn, *Last Words; Letters and Statements of the Leaders Executed after the Rising at Easter 1916* (The Stationery Office, Dublin, 1990), p. 103.

86   Ibid., pp. 115–6.

87   Minute by Young, PRO WO35/67/2.

88   Comment by Maxwell in Ó Broin, p. 139.

Maxwell's observations were perceptive.

89   Minute by Young, PRO WO35/67/2.

90   Father Aloysius, Memories of Easter Week, 1916, Allen Library, Dublin.

91   Bradbridge, p. 43.

92   Colonel Maconchy's unpublished memoirs, British Army Museum, p. 456.

93   Father Aloysius in MacLochlainn, pp. 214–5.

94   See file on Lennon, PRO WO339/13484, passim.

95   MacLochlainn, p. 83.

96   Account by Michael Kent, NLI MS15292.

97   Account by Nora and Lily Connolly, NLI MS13947.

98   Maxwell to his wife, 9 May 1916, Maxwell Papers, Princeton University Library, Box 2/6.

99   Wimborne to Maxwell, 8 May 1916, British Library MS 58372 f53. There was much criticism of both Birrell and Wimborne. Mahaffy said of Wimborne that he had, 'cowered in the safety of the Vice-regal Lodge, unconsidered by soldiers and civilians; doubtless the laughing stock of the Sinn Feiners,' and he thought Birrell 'a vain worthless man, a failure … in his profession and every walk of life … we must despise him,' see Foy and Barton, p. 208.

100 Obscurely dated note, almost certainly 8 May 1916, in Asquith Papers, MS43, Bodleian Library, Oxford University.

101 28 April 1916, PRO CAB42/12/16315.

102 Ó Broin, *Dublin Castle* p. 106; also Lyons, *Ireland since the Famine* (Fontana/Collins, Suffolk, 1982), p. 378.

103 Ó Broin, ibid., p. 130.

104 Asquith to King George V, 6 May 1916, PRO CAB41/37/19.

105 Maxwell to Asquith, 10 May 1916, Asquith Papers MS43, Bodleian Library, Oxford University.

106 Telegram by Kitchener, dated 11 May 1916 at 14:40 P.M., Asquith Papers.

107 Asquith Papers. MS Asquith 43, fol.22.

108 Maxwell to his wife, 12 May 1916, Maxwell Papers, Princeton University Library, Box 2/6.

109 HRH Princess Louise (daughter of King Edward VII) to Kitchener, 12 May 1916, PRO30/57/104; see also memorial by influential persons in Asquith Papers MS43, Bodleian Library, Oxford University.

110 Maxwell to Asquith, 9 May 1916, Asquith Papers.

111 Memorandum by Maxwell, dated 11 May 1916, Asquith Papers, MS43/26–33.

112 Maxwell to his wife, 4 June 1916, Maxwell Papers, Princeton University Library, Box 2/6, and Maxwell to Kitchener, quoted in Arthur, p. 257.

113 Arthur, p. 259.

114 Memorandum by Maxwell, 11 May 1916, Asquith Papers, MS43/26–33, Bodleian Library, Oxford University.

115 De Valera's MI5 file, PRO KV2/514.

116 See PRO HO144/10309/79275. S.T. O'Kelly saw de Valera being led off to Kilmainham after his trial, anticipated he would be executed, and was relieved to hear 'no fusillade next morning'. O'Kelly attributed this to the pressure of liberal opinion and also from the

US. See his account in the *Irish Press*, 15 July 1961.

117 Unsigned minute, 12 August 1916, PRO HO144/10309/79275.

118 Edward Bell to Major Frank Hall, 28 June 1916, PRO KV2/514.

119 See both Wylie's handwritten and typescript versions of his autobiography, PRO30/89/1,2. Wylie clearly overstates the significance of de Valera's reprieve.

120 Petition dated 17 June 1916, PRO HO144/10309/79275.

121 Memorandum by Battiscondie, 20 October 1916, PRO HO144/10309/79275.

122 Report by K. Strath, 29 September 1920, in PRO HO144/1580/316818.

123 Ibid.; see also police files on Markievicz, PRO CO904/209, PRO WO35/207.

124 Kemah to Thompson, 17 December 1920, PRO HO144/1580/316818.

125 Crime Branch records in PRO WO35/207.

126 Ibid.

127 See Inspector General's Report, October 1917, PRO CO904/104.

128 Handwritten account by Nurse O'Farrell, Allen Library. De Courcy Wheeler's daughter, born just before the Rising, was named after Markievicz.

129 Wylie's handwritten autobiography, PRO30/89/1.

130 Mahaffy Diary, 6 May 1916, TCD MS2074.

131 Report of trial, 4 May 1916, PRO HO144/1580/316818.

132 Mahaffy Diary, 30 April, 1 May 1916, TCD MS2074.

133 See trial records, PRO HO114/1580/316818. The outrage expressed by the British government over the execution on 12 October 1915 of the English nurse, Edith Cavell, by Germany, may well have influenced the outcome of Markievicz's case.

134 See Crime Branch Report, PRO CO904/209.

135 Maxwell to Samuel, 8 July 1916, PRO HO144/1580/316818.

136 Crime Branch Report, PRO CO904/209.

137 See courts martial lists, PRO WO213/8.

138 Maxwell to his wife, 2 May 1916, Maxwell Papers, Princeton University Library, Box 2/6. He wrote regarding the trials: 'It is these that tie me by the leg and I can't get away until they are over.'

139 Maxwell to his wife, 23 May 1916, Maxwell Papers.

140 Maxwell to Asquith, 9,10 May 1916, Asquith Papers, MS43, Bodleian Library, Oxford University.

141 Robert Kee, *The Green Flag; A History of Irish Nationalism*, (London, Weidenfield and Nicolson, 1972), p. 577.

142 Wylie's typescript autobiography, PRO30/89/2.

143 Parliamentary Debates, Commons, 27 April 1916, vol. LXXXII, col. 2511; 11 May, vol LXXXII, cols 954, 955, 959.

144 Jenkins, op. cit., p. 398. During his visit, Asquith gained at first hand, some impression of the bitterness being generated by Maxwell's actions in Ireland. Whilst being held at Mountjoy Prison, Frank Thornton recalls: 'We were all marching around the circle one day

when our friend "wait and see" Asquith arrived, and walked into the ring and attempted to shake hands with de Valera but de Valera walked away.' According to Thornton's account, the Prime Minister was similarly spurned by all the prisoners and was finally compelled to beat an undignified retreat – account by Frank Thornton, UCD P67/45.

145 Asquith to Maxwell, 12 May 1916, British Library MS58372 f57.

146 Jenkins, p. 398.

147 Arthur, p. 258.

148 Maxwell to his wife, 18, 30 May 1916, Maxwell Papers, Princeton University Library, Box 2/6.

149 Cabinet conclusions, 26 October 1916, PRO CAB41/37.

150 Account by Plunkett, NLI MS111397.

151 Account by Brennan, NLI MS10915.

152 Account by Bick, 29 May 1916, IWM71/11/2.

153 Inspector General's Report, 1 April–31 May 1916, PRO CO904/99.

154 Inspector General's Report, 10 August 1916, PRO CO904/23; see also his report for April–May 1916, PRO CO904/99.

155 Quoted by Gearoid O'Sullivan, NLI MS15382.

156 Reports in PRO CO904/99,100.

157 Report of speech in County Cork, 14 December 1917, PRO CO904/199.

158 Cabinet conclusions, 19 September, 11 October 1916, PRO CAB41/37.

159 Arthur, p. 268.

160 Ó Broin, *Dublin Castle* p. 143; see also Arthur, p. 275.

161 Arthur, p. 266.

162 Maxwell to his wife, 1 June, 5 July 1916, Maxwell Papers, Princeton University Library, Box 2/6.

163 Arthur, p. 268.

164 Maxwell to his wife, 16 May, 30 May, 19 June, 27 July, 1916, Maxwell Papers, Princeton University Library, Box 2/6; see also Arthur, pp. 266, 268–9.

165 Donal O'Herlihy et al., *To the Cause of Liberality; A History of the O'Connell Schools and the Christian Brothers, North Richmond Street* (Allen Library Project, Dublin, 1995), p. 54.

166 Ibid., p. 53.

167 Ó Broin, *W.E. Wylie and the Irish Revolution*, p. 10.

168 Police reports, PRO CO904/98,99.

169 Cabinet conclusions, 19 September 1916, PRO CAB41/37. It was after discussing Maxwell's reports on the pubic mood in Ireland that the cabinet initially decided not to introduce it, despite a keen awareness amongst ministers of 'the practical difficulty of dealing with the depleted Irish divisions and the growing feeling of resentment in Great Britain at the slackness of Irish recruiting'.

170 Reports in PRO CO904/100,120.

171 Maxwell to his wife, 11 June 1916, Maxwell Papers, Princeton University Library, Box 2/6.

PATRICK PEARSE

1   Ruth Dudley Edwards, *Patrick Pearse: The Triumph of Failure* (Faber and Faber, London,

1979), p. 116; see also Pat Cooke, *Sceal Scoil Eanna: The Story of an Educational Adventure* (Office of Public Works, Dublin, 1986), passim, and Margaret Pearse, 'Patrick and William Pearse', *Capuchin Annual* (1943).

2   F.S.L. Lyons, *Ireland Since the Famine* (London, Fontana, 1986), p. 333. By Christmas 1915, Sean Fitzgibbon felt that Pearse no longer wanted a political settlement in Ireland, *Irish Times*, 19th April 1949.

3   Lyons, p. 334.

4   Ibid., p. 338.

5   Ibid., p. 337.

6   Pearse to John Devoy, 12 August 1914, Allen Library Dublin. Bulmer Hobson describes a conversation with Pearse after the outbreak of war, in which the latter stated: 'I cannot answer your arguments but I feel that we must have an insurrection.' Hobson was somewhat contemptuous of Pearse; see account by Hobson, NLI MS13170.

7   Edwards, pp. 173–4.

8   Pearse Papers in Pearse Museum. When writing his speech, Clarke had advised Pearse to 'make it as hot as hell, throw all discretion to the wind', Edwards, p. 235.

9   Donagh MacDonagh, 'P.H. Pearse', *An Cosantoir*, August 1945.

10   Unpublished autobiography, Pearse Museum.

11   Pearse to legal advisers, 1 May 1916, Asquith Papers MS43, Bodleian Library, Oxford University.

12   Sean Fitzgibbon, *Irish Times*, 19 April 1949.

13   Pearse to Devoy, 12 August 1914, Allen Library.

14   Sean Fitzgibbon, *Irish Times*, 19 April 1949.

15   Michael Foy and Brian Barton, *The Easter Rising* (Sutton Publishing Limited, Stroud, 1999), p. 50.

16   Series of interviews for BBC, NLI MS15015.

17   Account of E Company, Fourth Batallion, NLI MS10915. Most, if not all, the members of the company were ex-pupils.

18   Father Aloysius, Memories of Easter Week, 1916, Allen Library.

19   Edwards, p. 277; see also Foy and Barton, p. 54.

20   Edwards, p. 279.

21   Account by Humphries, NLI MS18829. For summary of events in the GPO, see Foy and Barton, pp. 124–160.

22   Joe Good, *Enchanted by Dreams: The Journal of a Revolutionary* (Brandon, Dingle, 1996), p. 44.

23   Pearse to Devoy, 12 August 1914, Allen Library.

24   All quotes from Desmond Fitzgerald, *Memoirs of Desmond Fitzgerald 1913–16* (Routledge and Kegan Paul, London, 1968), pp. 136, 139, 142, and pp. 132–144, passim. Though born and brought up in England, Fitzgerald had been drawn into republican politics through involvement in the Irish literary movement, and later helped organise the IVF in County Kerry, see MacEntee Papers, UCD P67/17. He was incharge of supplies at the GPO and his son, Garret, went on to become Taoiseách of the Irish Republic.

25   Piaras F. MacLochlainn, *Last Words; Letters and*

Statements of the Leaders Executed after the Rising at Easter 1916 (The Stationery Office, Dublin, 1990), pp. 5–7.

26   Dillon's comments,11 May 1916, Parliamentary Debates, Commons, vol. LXXXII, cols 947, 952.
27   Quoted in Edwards, p. 296.
28   Account by Oscar Traynor, Allen Library
29   MacLochlainn, p. 8.
30   Edwards, p. 296.
31   Account by Humphries, NLI MS18829.
32   Ibid.
33   Tim Healy's comments, 11 May, Parliamentary Debates, Commons, vol. LXXXII, col. 964.
34   M. J. Staines and M. W. Reilly 'The Defence of the GPO', *An tOglac*, 23 January 1926.
35   Good, p. 49.
36   Jim Ryan, 'General Post Office Area', *Capuchin Annual* (1966).
37   Sean MacEntee, *Episode at Easter* (M.H. Gill and Son Ltd., Dublin/Melbourne, 1966), p. 157. MacEntee was from Belfast, the son of a publican; he was a qualified engineer and took up employment in Dundalk, where he helped organise the IVF, see MacEntee Papers, UCD P67/45.
38   Edwards, p. 32.
39   Account by Oscar Traynor, UCD P150/1527; see also Frank Henderson's account of the evacuation NLI MS10915.
40   Good, p. 63.
41   MacLochlainn, p. 12.
42   Pearse to his Mother, 1 May 1916, PRO WO71/345.
43   See account by Nurse O'Farrell, 'The Surrender', *Capuchin Annual*, (1917).
44   Account in papers of J. Loder, IWM 75/80/1.
45.   Foy and Barton, p. 155.
46   Account by Henry de Courcy Wheeler in the magazine, *Irish Life, Record of the Rebellion of 1916*, pp. 26–32. Wheeler had been appointed Staff Captain to Brigadier-General Lowe on 28 April 1916; see also MacLochlainn, p. 14. Like Pearse, de Courcy Wheeler had been called to the Irish Bar; he had studied law at Trinity College, Dublin.
47   MacLochlainn, pp. 15–17.
48   Edwards, p. 312.
49   Ibid., p. 316; see also MacLochlainn, p. 23.
50   Pearse to his Mother, 1 May 1916 PRO WO71/345.
51   MacLochlainn, p. 20.
52   Text of trial, PRO WO71/345.
53   Ibid.
54   Handwritten autobiography by Wylie, PRO 30/89/1.
55   Statement by Pearse, PRO WO71/345.
56   Handwritten autobiography by Wylie, PRO 30/89/1; Wylie had a copy of Emmet's speech in his private papers.
57   Edwards, p. 317.
58   Countess of Fingall, *Seventy Years Young: Memories of Elizabeth, Countess of Fingall*, Lilliput, Dublin, 1991, p. 376.
59   Memorandum by Maxwell, 11 May 1916, Asquith Papers, MS43/26-33, Bodleian Library, Oxford University.
60   Father Aloysius, Memories of Easter Week, Allen Library; see also MacLochlainn, pp.

214–5, and account by Lily O'Brennan, NLI MS15602.
61   Father Aloysius, Memories of Easter Week, Allen Library, Dublin.
62   MacLochlainn, pp. 28–9.
63   Ibid., pp. 32–3.
64   Account by Desmond Ryan, *Irish Press*, 25 April 1961.
65   Certificate of Death by Stanley, PRO WO71/345.
66   MacLochlainn, p. 78. Pearse's cell was subsequently occupied by Eoin MacNeill; see speech by MacNeill, 2 September 1917, report in PRO CO904/209.

THOMAS MacDONAGH

1   Donagh MacDonagh, 'Thomas MacDonagh', *An Cosantoir*, October 1945.
2   Johann Norstedt, *Thomas MacDonagh: A Critical Biography* (University Press of Virginia, Charlottesville, 1980), p. 144. See also Marcus Bourke, 'Thomas MacDonagh's Role in the Plans for the 1916 Rising', *Irish Sword*, no. 8 (1967–8).
3   MacDonagh.
4   Ibid.
5   Comment made in interview for BBC programme in 1966, see transcripts, NLI MS15015.
6   Norstedt, p. 141.
7   Bourke.
8.   Account by Oscar Traynor, UCD P150/1527.
9   See reports by Chalk, 22 March, 19 April 1916, PRO CO904/23. MacNeill was aware that MacDonagh was 'to some extent an intermediary between that section [the IRB in the Volunteer movement] and myself', see Michael Foy and Brian Barton, *The Easter Rising* (Sutton Publishing Limited, Stroud, 1999), p. 36. Bourke, states: 'at last in mid April he [MacDonagh] was taken fully into the confidence of the Military Council'.
10   Austin Clarke, *A Penny in the Clouds: More Memories of Ireland and England* (Routledge and Kegan Paul, London, 1968), p. 25.
11   Bourke.
12   Piaras F. MacLochlainn, *Last Words; Letters and Statements of the Leaders Executed after the Rising at Easter 1916* (The Stationery Office, Dublin, 1990), p 47.
13   Account by Fitzgibbon, *Irish Times* 20 April 1949.
14   MacLochlainn, p. 47.
15   Padraig O'Ceallaigh, 'Jacob's Factory Area', *Capuchin Annual* (1966); see also 'Jacob's and Stephen's Green Area', *Catholic Bulletin*, September 1918. For narrative summary of events at Jacob's, see Foy and Barton, pp. 89–97.
16   Account by Peadar Kearney, TCD MS3560.
17   Account by William Oman, Allen Library.
18   Hyde Diary, 29 April 1916, TCD MS10343/7.
19   Maire Nic Shuibhlaigh, *The Splendid Years* (James Duffy, Dublin, 1955), p. 176.
20   Account by Nurse O'Farrell, 'The Surrender', *Catholic Bulletin*, May 1917.

21 MacLochlainn, p. 60.
22 Father Augustine's account quoted in ibid., p. 51; see also Father Aloysius, Memories of Easter Week 1916, Allen Library, where MacDonagh refers to the peace conference as 'on the point of being summoned'.
23 Father Aloysuis, Memories of Easter Week 1916; also see O'Farrell. Fitzgibbon implies that MacDonagh may have been irked by the fact that Connolly had been appointed Commandant General of the insurgent force in Dublin 'over his head', see Fitzgibbon.
24 MacLochlainn, p. 61; MacDonagh met Lowe at the north-east corner of St Patrick's Park at between 12:00 and 1:00 p.m. and they then talked for up to fifteen minutes in Lowe's car.
25 Ibid., p. 60.
26 Maire Nic Shuibhlaigh, The Splendid Years (Dublin, James Duffy, 1955), p. 184.
27 Peadar Kearney, TCD MS3560.
28 Account by Michael Walker, Allen Library.
29 Peadar Kearney, TCD MS3560.
30 Father Aloysius.
31 Account by Michael Walker, Allen Library.
32 MacLochlainn, p. 48.
33 O'Ceallaigh; see also MacLochlainn, p. 52. O'Ceallaigh states that 'as late as Low Sunday our men fired on and scattered a group of soldiers in St Patrick's Park'.
34 Wylie's typescript autobiography, PRO30/89/2.
35 Trial Proceedings, PRO WO71/346.
36 For Father Augustine's account see MacLochlainn, p. 51.
37 Wylie's handwritten autobiography, PRO 30/89/1.
38 PRO WO71/346.
39 MacLochlainn, p. 62.
40 Ibid., pp. 54–57.
41 Wylie's handwritten autobiography.
42 Maxwell Memorandum, 11 May 1916, Asquith Papers MS43/26-33, Bodleian Library, Oxford University.
43 Quoted in Desmond Ryan, The Rising: The Complete Story of Easter Week (Dublin, Golden Eagle Books, 1949), p. 259.
44 MacLochlainn, p. 61.
45 Wylie's handwritten autobiography.
46 MacLochlainn, p. 63.
47 Father Aloysius; see also MacLochlainn, pp. 214–5.
48 MacLochlainn, pp. 214–5.
49 MacDonagh.

THOMAS CLARKE

1 Desmond Ryan, 'Stevens, Devoy and Clarke', University Review Vol.1 No.12; see also 'Thomas Clarke', Capuchin Annual, (1968): p. 154. Clarke spent part of his childhood in South Africa.
2 Evidence by Head Constable Shea in the Trial Records, PRO HO146/116/A26493; Clarke was charged with 'feloniously conspiring with others unknown to make and levy war, etc, within this realm ... to subvert the constitution ... to overthrow the power of the Queen in Ireland...'
3 Thomas Clarke, Glimpses of an Irish Felon's Prison Life (National Publications Committee, Cork, 1970), pp.12, 14. The prisoner he refers to as going 'mad' whilst at Chatham (where they were treated as 'special men') was Albert George Whitehead. Whitehead was one on those who was tried along with Clarke; he was also given penal servitude for life. See Louis Le Roux, Thomas Clarke and the Irish Freedom Movement (Talbot Press, Dublin, 1936), passim. Clarke was held at Millbank, Chatham and Portland Prisons.
4 Michael Foy and Brian Barton, The Easter Rising, (Sutton Publishing Limited, Stroud, 1999), p. 6; see also Ryan.
5 Donagh MacDonagh, 'Thomas MacDonagh', An Cosantoir, October 1945. Clarke settled first in Limerick and then in Dublin.
6 Sean T. O'Kelly, Irish Press, 8 July 1961.
7 Account by Bulmer Hobson, NLI MS13171.
8 Joe Good, Enchanted by Dreams: the Journal of a Revolutionary (Brandon, Dingle, 1996), p. 64. Good writes that 'there was nothing in his appearance to suggest that he was an old Fenian of the earlier generation'.
9 Le Roux, p. 208, (he informed his wife that 'even Sean MacDermott voted against me'). See also pp. 205–6, 212–3 and Ruth Dudley Edwards, Patrick Pearse: The Triumph of Failure (Faber and Faber, London, 1979), p. 273.
10 Le Roux, pp. 207–8; some Volunteers erroneously believed that Clarke was President of the Republic as his name was first to the Proclamation, and after their release – Christmas 1916 – they were surprised by the elevation of Pearse.
11 Desmond Fitzgerald, Memoirs of Desmond Fitzgerald 1913–'16 (London, Routledge and Kegan Paul, 1968), p. 133; see also accounts by Lynch, NLI MS11128, 34109 (12).
12 Account by Rankin, NLI MS22251.
13 Account by Lynch, NLI MS11128; Good describes him, with Plunkett, 'examining a sheaf of maps and despatches ... smiling a lot', Good, p. 31. For narrative of events at the GPO, see Foy and Barton, pp. 124–60.
14 Sean T. O'Kelly, Irish Press, 3 July 1961. The letter was delivered by S.T. O'Kelly, after he had called at a house in Cabra Park to arrange for the release of Bulmer Hobson.
15 Le Roux, p. 225.
16 Jim Ryan, 'General Post Office Area', Capuchin Annual (1942).
17 Fitzgerald, p. 148.
18 See 'Thomas Clarke', Catholic Bulletin, July 1916.
19 Good, p. 53.
20 Le Roux, pp. 226, 229; see also Good, p. 63.
21 Ryan.
22 Piaras F. MacLochlainn, Last Words; Letters and Statements of the Leaders Executed after the Rising at Easter 1916 (The Stationery Office, Dublin, 1990), p. 39.
23 See handwritten account by Nurse O'Farrell, Allen Library.
24 Good, p. 67.
25 Julia Grenan, 'The Story of the Surrender', Catholic Bulletin, June 1917.
26 MacLochlainn, p. 40.

27   Grenan.
28   MacLochlainn, p. 42.
29   Ibid., p. 42.
30   Edwards, p. 312.
31   Trial Proceedings, PRO WO71/347; see also
     Declan Kiberd, *1916 Rebellion Handbook*
     (Mourne River Press, Dublin, 1998), p. 11.
32   Wylie's handwritten autobiography, PRO
     30/89/1; see also PRO WO71/347.
33   Desmond Ryan, *The Rising: The Complete Story
     of Easter Week* (Golden Eagle Books, Dublin,
     1949),
     p. 258.
34   Maxwell Memorandum, 11 May 1916, Asquith
     Papers, MS43/26-33, Bodleian Library, Oxford
     University.
35   MacDonagh.
36   MacLochlainn, p. 44.
37   Ibid., p. 44.
38   Ibid., pp. 44–5.
39   Kiberd, p. 272; nonetheless, perhaps
     surprisingly, Clarke died intestate, see Le
     Roux, p. 238.

EDWARD DALY

1   'Edmund Daly', *Catholic Bulletin*, July 1916;
     also T. .P Kilfeather, 'Commandant Edward
     Daly', in Colonel J.M. McCarthy (ed.),
     Limerick's Fighting Story (Anvil Books, Tralee,
     ND), passim; see also Helen Litton (ed.),
     *Kathleen Clarke, Revolutionary Woman,
     1879–1972, an Autobiography*, (O'Brien Press,
     Dublin, 1991), passim.
2   See 'A Company, 1st Battalion, Irish
     Republican Army, historical sketch, 1913–23',
     Allen Library. Sean MacDermott wrote to
     Daly's uncle, John Daly, immediately after the
     Howth gun-running to say: 'Ned acted all the
     part of a man today', see Louis Le Roux, *Tom
     Clarke and the Irish Freedom Movement* (Dublin,
     Talbot Press, 1936), p. 140.
3   'A Company, 1st Battalion, Irish Republican
     Army, historical sketch, 1913–23'; see also
     anonymous account of A Company, UCD
     LA9.
4   J.J. Reynolds, 'The Four Courts and North
     King Street Area in 1916', *An tOglac*, 15, 22,
     29 May 1926; see also Paddy Holahan, 'The
     Four Courts Area', *Capuchin Annual*, (1942).
     For an account of the Four Courts during
     Easter week, see Michael Foy and Brian
     Barton, *The Easter Rising* (Sutton Publishing
     Limited, Stroud, 1999), pp. 110–23.
5   *War History of the 6th Batallion, South
     Staffordshire Regiment* (Heinemann, London,
     1921), p. 149.
6   List of those who received first aid at Father
     Matthew Hall, compiled by Chistine
     O'Gorman, dated 29 May 1929, NAI D/T
     S6023. Amongst those treated there was Sean
     Hurley, the brother-in-law of Michael Collins.
     O'Gorman writes: 'When this poor fellow was
     brought into the hall he was dying. No person
     present knew him ... he was dead before he
     reached hospital. He was buried unidentified.'
     With considerable good fortune, he was later
     identified with the aid of a photograph

brought over by a 'London lady friend', who
had come over to Dublin to make enquiries
about him.
7   Piaras F. MacLochlainn, *Last Words; Letters and
     Statements of the Leaders Executed after the Rising
     at Easter 1916* (The Stationery Office, Dublin,
     1990), p. 71.
8   See the magazine, *Pictorial Review of 1916; an
     historically accurate account of events which occurred
     in Easter week* (Dublin, 1966), p. 30.
9   Ignatius Callender, 'Diary of Easter week',
     Dublin Brigade Review (Dublin, 1939).
10   Declan Kiberd, *1916 Rebellion Handbook*
     (Mourne River Press, Dublin, 1998), p. 100;
     see also Reynolds, 15 May, 1926.
11   *Pictorial Review of 1916*; p. 30.
12   Kiberd, p. 25; see also military and police
     reports relating to deaths in North King
     Street, PRO WO141/22, PRO WO35/67/3.
13   Military Reports in North King Street
     Enquiry, 19 May 1916, PRO WO141/22.
14   Daly's comments, PRO WO71/344.
15   Nurse O'Farrell, 'The Surrender', in Roger
     McHugh, *Dublin 1916* (Arlington Books,
     Dublin, 1966), p. 211.
16   Account by Brighid Lyons Thornton, in
     *Curious Journey; an Oral History of Ireland's
     Unfinished Revolution* (Hutchinson, London,
     1982), K. Griffith and E. O'Grady (eds.), p. 77.
17   Piaras Beaslai, 'Edward Daly's Command,
     Easter week 1916' in *Limerick's Fighting Story*,
     p. 146.
18   Diary of John Clarke, entries for 29, 30 April
     1916, NLI MS10485.
19   Beaslai, p. 146.
20   Major General P.J. Hally, 'The Easter Rising in
     Dublin; the Military Aspect, Part 1', *The Irish
     Sword*, (Vol. 7 1966), p. 324.
21   Trial proceedings, PRO WO71/344.
22   Ibid.
23   Maxwell memorandum, 11 May 1916, Asquith
     Papers, MS43/26-33, Bodleian Library, Oxford
     University.
24   MacLochlainn, p. 68.
25   Le Roux, p. 234.
26   MacLochlainn, pp. 68–74. The authorities
     rejected the request for Daly's body, informing
     his family on 4 May 1916, see Le Roux, p.
     237.
27   MacLochlainn, p. 74.
28   See Trial proceedings, PRO WO71/344,347.
     Daly's uncle, the veteran Fenian, John Daly
     (who was also a close friend of Clarke), died
     the following month, on 30 June 1916; see
     Kilfeather, p. 137.

WILLIAM PEARSE

1   Ruth Dudley Edwards, *Patrick Pearse: The
     Triumph of Failure* (Faber and Faber, London,
     1979), pp. 112, 13 and passim; William Pearse
     was universally known to his contemporaries
     as 'Willie'. He was taught by Oliver Shepard at
     the Metropolitan School of Art, and himself
     taught Patrick Touhy at St Enda's.
2   Ibid., p. 166.
3   Ibid., p. 166–7.
4   Account by Tomas King Moylan, NLI

MS9620.

5   Ibid.

6   Edwards, p. 315; see also Piaras F. MacLochlainn, *Last Words; Letters and Statements of the Leaders Executed after the Rising at Easter 1916* (The Stationery Office, Dublin, 1990), pp. 22, 31; Pearse said of his brother William: 'As a boy he was my only playmate, as a man my only intimate friend.'

7   Edwards, p. 320.

8   Bulmer Hobson's comments were made in a BBC interview, 1966; see transcripts NLI MS15015; account by Oscar Traynor, UCD P150/3655.

9   Father Aloysius, Memories of Easter Week 1916, Allen Library.

10 Edwards, p. 264.

11 MacLochlainn, p. 75.

12 Ibid., p. 75. For an account of events at the GPO in Easter week, see Michael Foy and Brian Barton, *The Easter Rising* (Sutton Publishing Limited, Stroud, 1999), pp. 124–60.

13 Sean MacEntee, *Episode at Easter* (Dublin/Melbourne, M.H. Gill and Son Ltd., 1966), p. 150; see also his Papers, UCD P67/1-44.

14 MacLochlainn, p. 77.

15 Ibid., p. 75.

16 Edwards, p. 283.

17 Account by Frank Henderson, NLI MS15015.

18 Desmond Ryan, *The Rising; The Complete Story of Easter Week* (Dublin, Golden Eagle Books, 1949), p. 143.

19 MacLochlainn, p. 163.

20 MacEntee, *Episode at Easter*, p. 163.

21 MacEntee Papers, UCD P67/17/9.

22 Edwards, p. 312.

23 MacEntee, *Episode at Easter*, p. 167.

24 Account by Lily O'Brennan, NLI MS15602.

25 Father Aloysius; see also, MacLochlainn, p. 214.

26 Both accounts in MacLochlainn, pp. 79–80.

27 Trial proceedings, PRO WO71/358.

28 Ibid.

29 See account in Leon Ó Broin, *Dublin Castle and the 1916 Rising: The Story of Sir Matthew Nathan* (Helican, Dublin, 1966), p. 138. He writes: 'Desmond Ryan told the author ... that William Pearse practically condemned himself to death by the exultant attitude he adopted at the court-martial.' See also Edwards, p. 320.

30 PRO WO71/358.

31 Ibid.

32 Correspondence in ibid. A friend said of William on stage that he spoke 'with a sort of inanimate monotone that never suggests manliness', quoted in Edwards, p. 166.

33 Maxwell memorandum, Asquith Papers, MS43/26-33, Bodleian Library, Oxford University.

34 Edwards, pp. 270,320.

35 MacLochlainn, p. 32. Tom Clarke 'felt sure [Ned Daly] would be shot as well as William Pearse'; see Louis Le Roux, *Thomas Clarke and the Irish Freedom Movement* (Talbot Press, Dublin, 1936), p. 234.

36 F.S.L. Lyons, *Ireland since the Famine* (London, Fontana, 1986), p. 377.

37 MacLochlainn, pp. 79–80.

38 Ibid., p. 80.

MICHAEL O'HANRAHAN

1   Father M. O'Flanagan, in Foreward to *Michael O'Hanrahan, Irish Heroines; being a Lecture written during the Winter preceding Easter Week* (The O'Hanrahans, Dublin, 1917).

2   Ibid.

3   'Michael O'Hanrahan', *Catholic Bulletin*, July 1916.

4   Michael O'Hanrahan, *A Swordsman of the Brigade* (Sands Publishing Company, Edinburgh, 1914).

5   O'Flanaghan.

6   Declan Kiberd, *1916 Rebellion Handbook* (Mourne River Press, Dublin, 1998), p. 281.

7   'Michael O'Hanrahan', *Catholic Bulletin*, July 1916.

8   O'Flanaghan.

9   Account by Pat Rankin, NLI MS22251.

10 Intelligence reports, dated 27 February, 7 April, 1916, PRO WO141/27.

11 Maire Nic Shuibhlaigh, *The Splendid Years* (Dublin, James Duffy, 1955), p. 168–9.

12 Ibid., p. 174.

13 Ibid., p. 174. For an account of events at Jacob's in Easter week, see Michael Foy and Brian Barton, *The Easter Rising* (Sutton Publishing Limited, Stroud, 1999), pp. 89–97.

14 Account by Peadar Kearney, TCD MS3560.

15 Foy and Barton, p. 92.

16 Ibid., p. 92.

17 O'Ceallaigh, 'Jacob's Factory Area', *Capuchin Annual*, (1966).

18 Nurse O'Farrell, 'The Surrender', *Catholic Bulletin*, May 1917.

19 O'Ceallaigh.

20 Ibid.

21 Piaras F. MacLochlainn, *Last Words; Letters and Statements of the Leaders Executed after the Rising at Easter 1916* (The Stationery Office, Dublin, 1990), p. 83.

22 O'Flanaghan.

23 Trial proceedings, PRO WO71/357.

24 Maxwell memorandum, 11 May 1916, Asquith Papers MS43/26-33, Bodleian Library, Oxford University.

25 MacLochlainn p. 83.

26 Both quotes in ibid., pp. 84–5.

27 Ibid., p. 84.

28 O'Flanaghan.

29 Ibid.

30 MacLochlainn, pp. 86–7.

31 See list of those court-martialled, PRO WO213/8; O'Hanrahan is cited as 'M O'Haurehan'. See also Gerard Oram, *Death Sentences Passed by Military Courts of the British Army, 1914–24* (Boutle, London, 1998), p. 33.

32 K. Griffith and E. O'Grady, *Curious Journey; An Oral History of Ireland's Unfinished Revolution* (London, Hutchinson, 1982), p. 255.

33 Brade memorandum, undated, PRO WO141/27.

34 Kearney.

35 This phrase was used by the Adjutant General, General Neville Macready, 10 January 1917,

PRO WO141/27.

EAMONN CEANNT

1   Piaras F. MacLochlainn, *Last Words; Letters and Statements of the Leaders Executed after the Rising at Easter 1916* (The Stationery Office, Dublin, 1990), p. 141.
2   Donagh MacDonagh, 'Eamonn Ceannt', *An Cosantoir*, 1946; see also 'Eamonn Ceannt', *Catholic Bulletin*, July 1916.
3   MacDonagh, p. 152.
4   Ceannt Papers, NLI MS13069.
5   Ibid., NLI MS13070.
6   Comment by Bulmer Hobson in BBC interview, NLI MS15015.
7   Ceannt's wife to William O'Brien, 10 December 1949, NLI MS13978.
8   Article by Sean T. O'Kelly, *Irish Press*, 14 July 1961.
9   Maire Nic Shuibhlaigh, *The Splendid Years* (Dublin, James Duffy, 1955), pp. 162–3; see also account by Ceannt's sister, Lily O'Brennan, NLI MS15602 and account by William Oman, Allen Library.
10 O'Brennan, NLI MS15602
11 Account by Robert Holland, Allen Library. For a full account of fighting at the South Dublin Union, see Michael Foy and Brian Barton, *The Easter Rising* (Sutton Publishing Limited, Stroud, 1999), pp. 97–103.
12 'The Fighting in the South Dublin Area', *Catholic Bulletin*, May 1918.
13 Account by Joseph Doolin, NLI MS10915.
14 Account by Peadar Doyle, Allen Library.
15 Article by Sean Fitzgibbon, *Irish Times*, 22 April 1949.
16 Doyle.
17 Father Aloysius, 'Personal Recollections', *Capuchin Annual* (1966).
18 MacLochlainn, p. 176.
19 Doyle.
20 Ibid.
21 Holland.
22 Wylie's unpublished handwritten autobiography, PRO30/89/1.
23 Ceannt's trial proceedings, PRO WO71/348.
24 Doyle.
25 MacLochlainn, p. 134.
26 Diary of Michael Kent, NLI MS15292.
27 PRO WO71/348.
28 Wylie's unpublished typescript autobiography, PRO 30/89/2.
29 Wylie's unpublished handwritten autobiography.
30 PRO WO71/348.
31 MacLochlainn, p. 132; see also trial proceedings, PRO WO71/348.
32 See trial proceedings, PRO WO71/348; Michael Kent refers to his brother putting up a 'great defence', NLI MS15292.
33 Wylie's unpublished handwritten autobiography.
34 Memorandum by Brade, Secretary of the Army Council, undated – but clearly early January 1917, PRO WO141/27.
35 Correspondence relating to trial proceedings,

PRO WO71/348. Corrigan and Corrigan, the family solicitors, wrote to the Judge Advocate-General, 4 April 1917 and received reply, 5 May 1917.
36 Maxwell memorandum, 11 May 1916, Asquith Papers, MS43/26-33, Bodleian Library, Oxford University.
37 MacLochlainn, p. 135.
38 Ceannt said this to his brother, NLI MS15292.
39 Memoirs of a female member of the Marrowbone Lane garrison, NLI MS18556.
40 Ceannt to wife, 8 May 1916 in MacLochlainn, p. 141.
41 Ceannt in his last statement, 7 May 1916, in MacLochlainn, p. 136.
42 Michael Kent's diary.
43 Ibid.
44 MacLochlainn, p. 142.
45 Ibid., p. 136.
46 Michael Kent's diary.
47 PRO WO71/348; see also PRO WO67/2 for dates and times of executions of the Rising's leaders.

JOSEPH PLUNKETT

1   Donal MacDonagh, 'Joseph Plunkett', *An Cosantoir*, November 1945; Grace Plunkett described Joseph as 'very athletic', see her account, NLI MS21598.
2   P. Brennan, 'J. M. Plunkett – the Military Tactician', *An Cosantoir*, November 1987.
3   Ibid.; See also Ruth Dudley Edwards, *Patrick Pearse: The Triumph of Failure* (Faber and Faber, London, 1979), p. 201; see also articles by Geraldine Plunkett on Joseph in NUI *University Review*, vol. 1, nos 11 and 12.
4   Brennan; see also Plunkett's Diary NLI MS17484.
5   Reinhard R. Doerries, *Prelude to the Easter Rising; Sir Roger Casement in Imperial Germany* (Frank Cass, London, 2000), p. 118.
6   'The Ireland Report', Plunkett Papers, NLI MS130855 (5); see also Michael Foy and Brian Barton, *The Easter Rising* (Sutton Publishing Limited, Stroud, 1999), pp. 13–19, and Sean Fitzgibbon, *Irish Times*, 18 April 1949.
7   Doerries, pp. 206–9.
8   Account by William O'Brien, NLI MS13978.
9   Comment in article by Desmond Ryan, *Irish Press*, 27 April, 1961.
10 Quoted in account by Sean Fitzgibbon, *Irish Times*, 19 April 1949.
11 Piaras F. MacLochlainn, *Last Words; Letters and Statements of the Leaders Executed after the Rising at Easter 1916* (The Stationery Office, Dublin, 1990), p. 89.
12 Plunkett Papers, Kilmainham Museum.
13 Account by Grace Plunkett, NLI MS21598.
14 Records of Grace Plunkett's baptism, NLI MS21591.
15 Account by Grace Plunkett, NLI MS21598.
16 MacLochlainn, pp. 92, 95.
17 Joe Good, *Enchanted by Dreams: the Journal of a Revolutionary* (Brandon, Dingle, 1996), p. 65.
18 Grace Plunkett, NLI MS21598.
19 Good, p. 25; see also Foy and Barton, p. 24; according to some accounts, his hair had been

cut very short whilst under medical treatment.

20 Desmond Fitzgerald, *Memoirs of Desmond Fitzgerald*, (London, Routledge and Kegan Paul, 1968), pp. 138,142.

21 Good, p. 31.

22 Account by Humphries, NLI MS18829.

23 Account by Lynch, NLI MS11128.

24 Cormac Turner, 'The Defence of Messrs. Hopkins and Hopkins, O'Connell Street, Dublin', *An tOglac*, 5 June 1926. For a narrative account of events at the GPO in Easter week, see Foy and Barton, pp. 124–60.

25 Plunkett's Army Field Message Book, NLI MS4700.

26 Fitzgerald, *Memoirs of Desmond Fitzgerald*, pp. 139, 141–2; Plunkett speculated that the leaders might well be hung after the collapse of the Rising, p. 149.

27 Good, p. XI

28 Ibid., p. 50.

29 MacLochlainn, p. 91.

30 Good, p. 49.

31 MacLochlainn, p. 91.

32 Ibid., pp. 91–2.

33 Jim Ryan in 'General Post Office Area', *Capuchin Annual*, (1942).

34 Good, pp. 68, 70.

35 Julia Grenan, 'The Story of the Surrender', *Catholic Bulletin*, June 1917.

36 Sean MacEntee, *Episode at Easter* (Dublin/Melbourne, M.H. Gill and Son Ltd., 1966), p. 167; see also MacLochlainn, p. 93.

37 Ibid., p. 94; Grace stayed during Easter week with her sister, Muriel MacDonagh and her two children in Oakley Road, Dublin.

38 Ibid., p. 94.

39 Trial proceedings, PRO WO71/349.

40 Ibid.

41 Ibid.

42 Wylie's handwritten unpublished autobiography, PRO 30/89/1.

43 Maxwell memorandum, 11 May, Asquith Papers, MS43/26-33, Bodleian Library, Oxford University.

44 Account by Grace Plunkett, NLI MS21598.

45 Plunkett Papers, Kilmainham Museum.

46 Account by Father Sebastian, *Catholic Bulletin*, July 1916; Grace found it difficult to understand why, in sharp contrast to herself, Mary Ryan was allowed to stay 'ages and ages' with Sean MacDermott, NLI MS21598.

47 Account by Lynch, NLI MS11128.

48 MacLochlainn, p. 139.

49 See court martial lists, PRO WO213/8; see also Gerard Oram, *Death Sentences Passes by Military Courts of the British Army, 1914–'24* (London, Boutle, 1998), p. 33.

JOHN MacBRIDE

1 Unpublished autobiographical material, MacBride Papers, NLI MS29817; see also Anthony A. Jordan, *Major John MacBride, 1865–1916, MacDonagh & MacBride & Connolly & Pearse* (Westport, Westport Historical Society, 1991), passim and 'John MacBride', *Catholic Bulletin*, August 1916.

2 NLI MS29817.

3 Donal P. McCracken, *The Irish Pro-Boers, 1877–1902* (Perskor, Johannesburg, 1989), p. 169.

4 Ibid., p. 166.

5 NLI MS29817; also McCracken, p. 144, describes him as 'not a polished man'.

6 McCracken, p. 166.

7 Account by Bulmer Hobson, NLI MS13170; Jordan, passim.

8 Ignatius Callender, 'A Diary of Easter Week', *Dublin Brigade Review* (The National Association of old IRA, Dublin, 1939).

9 MacBride's trial proceedings, PRO WO71/350.

10 Piaras F. MacLochlainn, *Last Words; Letters and Statements of the Leaders Executed after the Rising at Easter 1916* (The Stationery Office, Dublin, 1990), p. 99.

11 MacBride's trial proceedings, PRO WO71/350.

12 MacBride Papers, Kilmainham Museum.

13 Maire Nic Shuibhlaigh, *The Splendid Years* (Dublin, James Duffy, 1955), p. 168.

14 Ibid., p. 173; see also Padraig O'Ceallaigh, 'Jacob's Factory Area', *Capuchin Annual* (1966). For a full account of events at Jacob's during Easter week, see Michael Foy and Brian Barton, *The Easter Rising* (Sutton Publishing Limited, Stroud, 1999), pp. 89–97.

15 Account by Peadar Kearney, TCD MS3560.

16 Jordan, p, 119. Father Aloysius' account is less dramatic; he states that MacBride 'said he would not oppose any attempt at surrender'. Account by Father Aloysius, Allen Library.

17 MacLochlainn, p. 100.

18 Foy and Barton, p. 95.

19 Account by Kearney.

20 Ibid.

21 Nic Shuibhlaigh, p. 172.

22 Account by Kearney; see also Foy and Barton, p. 96.

23 Account by Robert Holland, Allen Library.

24 O'Ceallaigh.

25 PRO WO71/350.

26 Wylie's unpublished handwritten autobiography, PRO30/89/1.

27 Ibid.; see also PRO WO71/350.

28 Jordan, p 124. See also Sean T O'Kelly's account, *Irish Press*, 14 July 1961

29 MacLochlainn, p. 100.

30 Wylie's unpublished handwritten autobiography.

31 Maxwell memorandum, 11 May 1916, Asquith Papers, MS43/26-33, Bodleian Library, Oxford University.

32 Robert Kee, *The Green Flag; A History of Irish Nationalism* (Weidenfield and Nicholson, London, 1972), p. 575.

33 Jordan, p. 125.

34 T.B. Lyons, *The Enigma of Tom Kettle; Irish Patriot, Essayist, Poet, British Soldier, 1880–1916* (Glendale Press, Dublin, 1983), p. 294.

35 Jordan, p. 127; see also Crime Branch Special Report on Maud Gonne dated 28 September 1916, PRO CO904/208 and PRO WO71/350.

SEAN HEUSTON

1   Heuston Papers, NLI MS10076.
2   Ibid.; see also Madge Daly, 'Sean Heuston's life and death for Ireland', in *Limerick's Fighting Story*, edited by Colonel J.M. McCarthy (Tralee, undated).
3   Desmond Ryan, *The Rising: The Complete Story of Easter Week* (Dublin, Golden Eagle Books, 1949), p. 109.
4   Notes written by Heuston in Easter week, captured by the troops and used at his court martial, PRO WO71/351.
5   Ignatius Callender, 'A Diary of Easter week 1916', *Dublin Brigade Review* (The National Association of old IRA, Dublin, 1939).
6   Account by Heuston's mother, NLI MS15382.
7   D.A. Chart, *The Story of Dublin* (Dent, London, 1907), p. 272.
8   James Brennan, 'The Mendicity Institution Area', *Capuchin Annual* (1942); see also John McCann, *War by the Irish* (The Kerryman, Tralee, 1946), pp. 63–6 and Michael Foy and Brian Barton, *The Easter Rising* (Sutton Publishing Limited, Stroud, 1999), pp. 112–3, 115, 116.
9   See Heuston's notes captured after the Rising and witness evidence in his trial proceedings, PRO WO71/351; See also Brennan.
10 Heuston's dispatches during the Rising, PRO WO71/351.
11 Brennan; see also T.P. O'Sullivan's account, NLI MS18555.
12 PRO WO71/351; see also John M. Heuston OP, *Headquarters Battalion, Easter Week 1916* (Nationalist Printers, Carlow, 1966), passim.
13 Brennan.
14 PRO WO71/351.
15 Ibid.
16 Ibid.
17 Maxwell memorandum, 11 May 1916, Asquith Papers MS43/26-33, Bodleian Library, Oxford University.
18 Piaras F. MacLochlainn, *Last Words; Letters and Statements of the Leaders Executed after the Rising at Easter 1916* (The Stationery Office, Dublin, 1990), p. 109.
19 Account by Heuston's mother, NLI MS15382.
20 Ibid.
21 NLI MS15047; see also Heuston Papers, Kilmainham Museum.
22 Text of letter, *Capuchin Annual* (1966): p. 306.
23 NLI MS8497.
24 Heuston Papers, Kilmainham Museum.
25 MacLochlainn, pp. 112–3.
26 Ibid., pp. 115–6.
27 Comments made by Sean Harling, a member of Fianna, quoted in K. Griffith and E. O'Grady, *Curious Journey; an Oral History of Ireland's Unfinished Revolution* (London, Hutchinson, 1982), p. 86.
28 Press cuttings, MacEntee Papers, UCD P67/1.

CON COLBERT

1   Account of action at Marrowbone Lane, by Robert Holland, Allen Library.
2   'Con Colbert', *Catholic Bulletin*, July 1916.

3   Account by Holland.
4   Account by Sean Fitzgibbon, *Irish Times*, 19 April 1949.
5   Account by Peadar Doyle, Allen Library.
6   Account by Holland.
7   Ibid.; see also Ruth Dudley Edwards, *Patrick Pearse: The Triumph of Failure* (London, Gollanz, 1977), p. 249.
8   Quotes taken from Holland.
9   Ibid.; for a full narrative of events in this garrison area see Michael Foy and Brian Barton, *The Easter Rising* (Stroud, Sutton Publishing Limited, 1999), pp. 104–9.
10 Both quotes in Holland, op. cit.
11 All quotes in ibid.; see also the memoirs of a female member of the Marrowbone Lane garrison, NLI MS18556.
12 Account by Holland.
13 Memoirs of a female member of the Marrowbone Lane garrison, NLI MS18556.
14 Account by Holland, op. cit.
15 Memoirs of a female member of the Marrowbone Lane garrison, NLI MS18556.
16 Account by Holland.
17 Ibid.
18 Memoirs of a female member of the Marrowbone Lane garrison, NLI MS18556.
19 Account by Peadar Doyle.
20 Account by Holland.
21 Ibid.
22 Trial proceedings, PRO WO71/352.
23 Ibid.
24 Maxwell memorandum, 11 May 1916, Asquith Papers, MS43/26-33, Bodleian Library, Oxford University.
25 Piaras F. MacLochlainn, *Last Words; Letters and Statements of the Leaders Executed after the Rising at Easter 1916* (The Stationery Office, Dublin, 1990), pp. 146–50; see also Colbert's correspondence, NLI MS39093.
26 MacLochlainn, pp. 151, 153.
27 Ibid., p. 153.
28 Account by Holland.
29 Hugh MacNeill, 'Na Fianna Eireann', *An Cosantoir*, April 1944. MacNeill lists John Healy and Sean Howard as the two Fianna boys who died.
30 Parliamentary debates, Commons, 22 May 1916, vol. LXXXII, col. 1807.

THOMAS KENT

1   'Thomas Kent', *Catholic Bulletin*, August 1916; see also *Irish Press*, 23, 25 April 1966, and Kent Papers NLI MS24040.
2   See David Kent's trial records, PRO WO35/68.
3   Ibid.
4   Statements made by RIC, ibid.
5   *Irish Weekly Independent*, 21 January 1954.
6   Liam Ruiseal, 'The Position in Cork', *Capuchin Annual* (1956); see also Jim Ryan, 'General Post Office Area', *Capuchin Annual* (1942) and Foy and Barton, *The Easter Rising* (Sutton Publishing Limited, Stroud, 1999), pp. 27–8.

7   RIC Inspector-General's Report, April 1916,
    PRO CO904/99.
8   *Irish Weekly Independent*, 21 January 1954; see
    also Ruiseal.
9   County Inspector's Report, April 1916, PRO
    CO904/99.
10 Ruiseal.
11 Ibid.
12 County Inspector's Reports, April, May, 1916
    PRO CO904/99,100.
13 This account of the gun-battle at Bawnard
    House is based on the trial records of Thomas
    and David Kent, PRO WO71/356, PRO
    WO35/68.
14 Ibid.; see also Foy and Barton, pp. 215–7.
15 PRO WO71/356; see also *Catholic Bulletin*,
    August 1918, p. 458.
16 Piaras F. MacLochlainn, *Last Words; Letters and
    Statements of the Leaders Executed after the Rising
    at Easter 1916* (The Stationery Office, Dublin,
    1990), p. 155.
17 A.T. Bucknill to W.H. Campbell, 29 May
    1916, PRO WO35/68.
18 Ibid.; see also PRO WO71/356.
19 Ibid.
20 PRO WO35/68.
21 Maxwell to Asquith's secretary, Bonham-
    Carter, 25 May 1916, Asquith Papers, MS37
    (12), Bodleian Library, Oxford University.
22 Maxwell memorandum, 11 May 1916, Asquith
    Papers, MS43/26–33, Bodleian Library,
    Oxford University.
23 Asquith to Maxwell, 12 May 1916, British
    Library, MS58372 f57; see also General W.F.H.
    Stafford, Queenstown garrison, to Irish
    Command Headquarters, 15 May 1916, PRO
    WO35/68. In David Kent's case, he was
    accused on having done 'an act of such a
    nature as to be calculated to be prejudicial to
    the public safety and the defence of the realm,
    with the intention and for the purpose of
    assisting the enemy, in that he ... feloniously
    and with malice aforethought did kill and
    murder one Head Constable Rowe ... [and] ...
    he did aid and abet in armed rebellion and in
    the waging of war against His Majesty'.
24 Parliamentary Debates, Commons, 11 May
    1916, vol. LXXXII, cols 935, 939, 940, 954.
25 MacLochlainn, p. 157. On 10 May 1916, the
    Cork Examiner, which was unsympathetic to
    the Rising, stated: 'Officially announced
    yesterday morning that Thomas Kent was
    sentenced to death. The sentence was carried
    out yesterday morning. William Kent was
    acquitted.' Its issues for 3, 5 May, gave a very
    scant account of the course of events at
    Bawnard House.
26 *Catholic Bulletin*, August 1916, p. 459.

MICHAEL MALLIN

1   All quotes from R.M. Fox, *The History of the
    Irish Citizen Army* (James Duffy, Dublin, 1944),
    pp. 90,92, 96, 167, 178; see also Frank
    Robbins, *Under the Starry Plough; Recollections of
    the Irish Citizen Army* (Academy Press, Dublin,
    1977), passim.
2   Diarmuid Lynch, *The IRB and the 1916*

    Insurrection (Mercier Press, Cork, 1957), p. 73;
    see also Mallin's trial proceedings, PRO
    WO71/353, Robbins, p. 70.
3   Account by William Oman, Allen Library.
4   Account by C. McDowell, NLI MS21560; see
    also Robbins, p. 47.
5   Fox, p. 142.
6   Liam O'Briain, 'The St. Stephen's Green area',
    Capuchin Annual (1966); see also 'St. Stephen's
    Green', *Catholic Bulletin*, 1918. See Michael
    Foy and Brian Barton, *The Easter Rising*
    (Sutton Publishing Limited, Stroud, 1999), pp.
    56–71, for a full account of events in the St
    Stephen's Green and College of Surgeons area
    during Easter week.
7   Account by Dick Humphries, NLI MS18829.
8   O'Briain.
9   Ibid.
10 Ibid.
11 Ibid.
12 Robbins, p. 121; see also Mary O'Daly, 'The
    Women of Easter week', *An tOglac*, 2 April
    1926.
13 Handwritten account by Nurse O'Farrell,
    Allen Library.
14 Account by William Oman, Allen Library.
15 O'Daly.
16 Mallin's trial proceedings, PRO WO71/353.
17 Ibid.
18 Ibid.
19 Countess Markievicz, 'Women in the Fight; a
    Memoir by Countess Markievicz', in Roger
    McHugh, *Dublin 1916* (Dublin, Arlington
    Books, 1966).
20 Account by William Oman, Allen Library.
21 Account by Charles de Courcy Wheeler in
    Irish Life; Record of the Rebellion of 1916,
    (Dublin, 1916); see also his account in *Irish
    Press*, 30 April 1949.
22 *Irish Press*, 30 April 1949.
23 Comment by Liam O'Briain, quoted in Piaras
    F. MacLochlainn, *Last Words; Letters and
    Statements of the Leaders Executed after the Rising
    at Easter 1916* (The Stationery Office, Dublin,
    1990), p. 120.
24 MacLochlainn, p. 122.
25 Maxwell memorandum, 11 May 1916, Asquith
    Papers, MS 43/26–33; see also PRO
    WO71/353.
26 Mallin to his wife in MacLochlainn, p. 122.
27 Account by Maurice Brennan, NLI MS10915.
28 MacLochlainn, p. 151.
29 Memoirs of a female member of the
    Marrowbone Lane garrison, NLI MS18556.
30 Both letters in MacLochlainn, pp. 122–4.
31 Quoted in Foy and Barton, p. 237; see also
    MacLochlainn, p. 127.
32 MacLochlainn, p. 114.
33 Memoirs of a female member of the
    Marrowbone Lane garrison, NLI MS18556.

JAMES CONNOLLY

1   *The Irish Worker*, 30 May 1914. Connolly
    stated, in 1898: 'The two movements of
    revolutionary thought in Ireland, nationalist
    and socialist, are not antagonistic but
    complimentary', quoted in Donagh

MacDonagh, 'James Connolly', *An Cosantoir*, January 1947.

2　History of the Irish Citizen Army, O'Brien Papers, NLI MS15673.

3　Ibid.

4　Account by Bulmer Hobson, NLI MS13170; see also Austin Morgan, *James Connolly; A Political Biography* (Manchester University Press, Manchester, 1988), passim.

5　Article by S.T. O'Kelly, *Irish Press*, 8 July 1961. Connolly made the comment at a meeting of 'advanced' nationalists, held on 9 September 1914.

6　Quoted in William O'Brien, *James Connolly and Easter Week, 1916* (At the Sign of the Three Candles, Dublin, undated). Connolly stated this in the first issue of *The Irish Worker* published after the outbreak of the First World War.

7　Bulmer Hobson, *Ireland: Yesterday and Tomorow* (Tralee, Anvil Books, 1968).

8　Account by C. McDowell, NLI MS21560.

9　Both quotes in MacDonagh.

10　MacNeill quoted in article by Sean Fitzgibbon, *Irish Times*, 19 April 1949.

11　Piaras F. MacLochlainn, *Last Words; Letters and Statements of the Leaders Executed after the Rising at Easter 1916* (The Stationery Office, Dublin, 1990), p. 193.

12　Sean O'Casey, *The Story of the Irish Citizen Army*. (Dublin, Maunsel & Co. Ltd, 1919), pp. 52, 54.

13　Desmond Ryan to William O'Brien, 9 August 1949, NLI MS13978. Connolly stated: 'I have no objection to secret societies, providing you can show me one', quoted in MacDonagh.

14　O'Brien, *James Connolly in Easter Week, 1916*.

15　Article by William O'Brien, *Irish Press*, 2 January 1936.

16　O'Brien, *James Connolly in Easter Week, 1916*.

17　Account by C. McDowell, NLI MS21560; see also account by William O'Brien, NLI MS15673(1).

18　R.M. Fox, *The History of the Irish Citizen Army* (Dublin, James Duffy, 1943), pp. 186–7.

19　Comment by Liam O'Briain in BBC interview given in 1966, NLI MS15015.

20　O'Brien, *James Connolly in Easter Week, 1916*.

21　Margaret Skinnider, *Irish Press*, 9 April 1966; see also account by William Oman, Allen Library.

22　O'Brien, *James Connolly in Easter Week, 1916*, op. cit. For full account of events at the GPO in Easter week, see Michael Foy and Brian Barton, *The Easter Rising* (Sutton Publishing Limited, Stroud, 1999), pp. 124–160.

23　Joe Good, *Enchanted by Dreams: The Journal of a Revolutionary* (Dingle, Brandon Book Publishers Ltd, 1996), op. cit., p. 61. Carney had acted as Connolly's secretary for five years. She had first met him in Belfast, where she was from, through her involvement in the Textile Workers' Union. She arrived in Dublin on 21 April 1916. After the Rising she was deported to Lewes; because of her 'hostile associations, [she was] reasonably suspected of having favoured, promoted and assisted in armed insurrection against His Majesty', see PRO HO144/1457/314179.

24　Ruth Dudley Edwards, *Patrick Pearse: The Triumph of Failure* (Faber and Faber, London, 1979), p. 281–2.

25　Good, p. 36.

26　Ibid., p. 31.

27　MacLochlainn, p. 178.

28　Despatch is included among the papers in Connolly's trial proceedings, PRO WO71/354.

29　Quoted in Foy and Barton, p. 131.

30　Quoted in Desmond Ryan, *Irish Press*, 26 April 1961.

31　Account by Frank Thornton, UCD P67/45.

32　Good, p. 45.

33　Account by Oscar Traynor, UCD P150/3655.

34　Good, p. 45.

35　Ibid., pp. 45, 49.

36　MacLochlainn, p. 11.

37　Jim Ryan, 'General Post Office Area', *Capuchin Annual* (1942); see also Sean MacEntee, *Episode at Easter* (Dublin/Melbourne, M.H. Gill and Son Ltd, 1966), p. 147.

38　Good, p. 50.

39　MacLochlainn, p. 180–2. Frank Thornton states that it was the shells and incendiary bombs that 'beat us in the finish', UCD P67/45.

40　Both quotes in Julia Grenan, 'Story of the Surrender', *Catholic Bulletin*, June 1917.

41　Ibid.

42　Ryan.

43　Good, p. 65.

44　MacLochlainn, p. 185–6. During the preliminary negotiations with the headquarter's garrison, Brigadier-General Lowe had told Nurse O'Farrell to tell Pearse: 'I will not treat with him at all unless he surrenders unconditionally, and that Mr Connolly follows on a stretcher', account by O'Farrell, Allen Library. Initially the British authorities had believed that Pearse was the rebel leader who had been wounded, rather than Connolly.

45　MacLochlainn, p. 185.

46　Ibid., p. 187.

47　Parliamentary Debates, Commons, 30 May 1916, vol. LXXXII, col. 2535.

48　Medical statement in Connolly's trial proceedings, PRO WO71/354.

49　Maxwell to Asquith, 10 May 1916, Asquith Papers, MS43, Bodleian Library, Oxford University. See also Nora Connolly, *Portrait of a Rebel Father* (Talbot Press, Dublin, 1935), p. 320; she describes Tobin as 'a white haired, elderly man'.

50　Wylie's typescript autobiography, PRO30/89/2.

51　MacLochlainn, p. 189.

52　Trial proceedings, PRO WO71/354.

53　Ibid.; see also Declan Kiberd, *1916 Rebellion Handbook* (Dublin, The Mourne River Press, 1998), pp. 9–11.

54　PRO WO71/354.

55　Maxwell to Asquith, 9 May 1916, Asquith Papers, MS43, Bodleian Library, Oxford University.

56　Maxwell memorandum, 11 May 1916, Asquith Papers, MS43/26–33.

57　MacLochlainn, pp. 189–91.

58   Maxwell memorandum, 11 May 1916, Asquith Papers.
59   Father Aloysius, Memories of Easter Week, Allen Library.
60   Account by Nora and Lily Connolly, NLI MS13947.
61   Ibid.
62   Parliamentary Debates, Commons, 11 May 1916, vol. LXXXII, col. 955.
63   Account by Nora and Lily Connolly, NLI MS13947.
64   Father Aloysius.

SEAN MacDERMOTT

1   Mrs S.T. O'Kelly in an interview for the BBC in 1966, NLI MS15015.
2   Bulmer Hobson in an interview for the BBC in 1966, NLI MS15015.
3   Account by Bulmer Hobson, NLI MS13170.
4   Sean Fitzgibbon, Irish Times, 18 April 1949.
5   Donagh MacDonagh, 'Sean MacDiarmada', An Cosantoir, March 1945; see also description of MacDermott, Catholic Bulletin, July 1916.
6   Account by D. O'Sullivan, NLI MS10915; see also S. O'Casey, The Story of the Irish Citizen Army (Maunsel Co. Ltd., Dublin/London, 1919), p. 62. On 18 September 1867, two Fenians were being escorted to the county gaol in Manchester, when the police van containing them was attacked; the prisoners escaped and a policeman was shot dead. In the November following, five men were convicted of his murder and three of them, the 'Manchester Martyrs', hanged – William O'Meara Allen, Michael Larkin and William O'Brien.
7   Articles by Sean Fitzgibbon, Irish Times, 18, 21, April 1949.
8   Sean MacEntee, Episode at Easter, (Dublin /Melbourne, M.H. Gill and Son Ltd, 1966), p. 62.
9   Account by Desmond Ryan, Irish Press, 27 April 1961.
10   Account by Lynch, NLI MS11128.
11   All quotes from Breifne, 1966–7, p. 32.
12   Account by Lynch, MLI MS11128; see also Lynch Papers, NLI MS34109 (12).
13   Lynch quoted in Breifne, p. 34.
14   Joe Good, Enchanted by Dreams: The Journal of a Revolutionary, (Dingle, Brandon Book Publishers Ltd, 1996), pp. VIII, 51. In contrast, Nora Connolly described him as looking 'very pale and tired' on the morning of the Rising, Portrait of a Rebel Father (Talbot Press, Dublin, 1935), p. 294.
15   See Michael Foy and Brian Barton, The Easter Rising (Sutton Publishing Limited, Stroud, 1999), pp. 124–160 for an account of the GPO during Easter week.
16   Breifne, p. 34.

17   Desmond Fitzgerald, Memoirs of Desmond Fitzgerald, 1913–'16, (London, Routledge and Kegan Paul, 1968), p. 151.
18   Account by Oscar Traynor, UCD P150/3655; see also accounts by Lynch, NLI MS11128 and MacEntee, pp. 154–6.
19   Breifne, p. 34.
20   Handwritten account by Nurse O'Farrell, Allen Library.
21   Julia Grenan, 'The Story of the Surrender', Catholic Bulletin, June 1917.
22   Accounts by Traynor, and by Peadar Bracken, Allen Library.
23   Good, p. 68–9; see also account of this incident by Jack Plunkett, NLI MS11397.
24   MacDermott's trial proceedings, PRO WO71/355.
25   Grenan.
26   Breifne, p. 37.
27   Piaras F. MacLochlainn, Last Words; Letters and Statements of the Leaders Executed after the Rising at Easter 1916 (The Stationery Office, Dublin, 1990), p. 165.
28   Breifne, p. 36.
29   Jim Ryan, 'General Post Office Area', Capuchin Annual (1942).
30   MacLochlainn, p. 167.
31   Ryan in BBC interview, April 1966, NLI MS15015.
32   Account by William O'Brien, Irish Press, 11 January 1936.
33   Bernard O'Rourke to his wife, 19 May 1916, UCD P117/9.
34   Account by Sean T. O'Kelly, Irish Press, 14 July 1961.
35   PRO WO71/355.
36   Ibid.
37   Account by Lynch, NLI MS11128.
38   PRO WO71/355.
39   Maxwell to Asquith, 9 May 1916, Asquith Papers, MS43, Bodleian Library, Oxford University.
40   Maxwell memorandum, 11 May 1916, Asquith Papers, MS43/26-33.
41   Account by Frank Thornton, UCD P67/45.
42   Account by Joe Sweeney, NLI MS10915.
43   Parliamentary Debates, Commons, 10, 11 May 1916, cols. 631,955, vol. LXXXII.
44   MacLochlainn, pp. 168–9.
45   Ibid., p. 171.
46   Ibid., p. 172.
47   Ibid., p. 173. It was later reported that MacDermott had asked to see a Capuchin friar, but then stated that he was 'perfectly satisfied' after his meeting with Father MacCarthy; the issue was raised by Irish Nationalist MPs at Westminster, see Parliamentary Debates, Commons, 30 May 1916, vol. LXXXII, col. 2536.

Select bibliography

PRIMARY SOURCES

ALLEN LIBRARY, DUBLIN

Depositions by Father Aloysius, Paddy Daly, Peadar Doyle, Robert Holland, Elizabeth O' Farrell, William Oman and Michael Walker

BODLEIAN LIBRARY, OXFORD

Asquith papers
Nathan papers

BRITISH ARMY MUSEUM, LONDON

Maconchy memoirs

BRITISH LIBRARY, LONDON

Bucknill papers

IMPERIAL WAR MUSEUM, LONDON

P.A. Bick papers
E.F. Chapman papers
A.L. Franklin papers
J.N. Galloway papers
A. Hannant papers
W.N. Hendey papers
H.M. Hughes papers
A.M. Jameson papers
R.A. Pedlar papers
H. Peel papers
J.W. Roworth papers

KILMAINHAM MUSEUM, DUBLIN

Papers and memorabilia belonging to the leaders of the Easter Rising

MILITARY ARCHIVES, CATHAL BRUGHA BARRACKS, DUBLIN

Miscellaneous papers relating to the Rising

NATIONAL LIBRARY OF IRELAND

Papers of the executed leaders
Roger Casement papers
John Clarke diary
Bulmer Hobson papers
Dick Humphries diary
Michael Kent diary
Diarmuid Lynch papers
Eoin MacNeill papers

William O'Brien papers
Florence O'Donoghue papers
Grace Plunkett papers
Jack Plunkett papers
Ismena Rohde diary
Dorothy Stopford diary

PRINCETON UNIVERSITY, NEW JERSEY
Maxwell papers

PUBLIC RECORD OFFICE, LONDON
Kitchener papers
MI5 files
Midleton papers
William Wylie papers
Cabinet papers
Colonial Office papers
Home Office papers
War Office papers

TRINITY COLLEGE, DUBLIN
Henry Hanna diary
Douglas Hyde papers
Peadar Kearney papers
Elsie Mahaffy diary

UNIVERSITY COLLEGE, DUBLIN
Sean MacEntee papers
Bernard O'Rourke papers
Depositions by Frank Thornton and Oscar Traynor

SECONDARY SOURCES

ARTHUR, SIR GEORGE, *General Sir John Maxwell*, London, Murray, 1932

CAULFIELD, MAX, *The Easter Rebellion*, London, New English Library, 1965

DEVOY, JOHN, *Recollections of an Irish Rebel*, New York, Chas. P. Young, 1929

DOERRIES, REINHARD R., *Prelude to the Easter Rising: Sir Roger Casement in Imperial Germany*, London, Frank Cass, 2000

EDWARDS, RUTH DUDLEY, *Patrick Pearse: The Triumph of Failure,* London, Faber and Faber, 1979

FITZGERALD, DESMOND, *Memoirs of Desmond Fitzgerald, 1913–16*, London, Routledge and Kegan Paul, 1968

FOSTER, ROY, *Modern Ireland 1600–1972*, London, Penguin, 1989

FOX, R.M., *The History of the Irish Citizen Army*, Dublin, James Duffy, 1943

FOY, MICHAEL and BARTON, BRIAN, *The Easter Rising*, Stroud, Sutton Publishing Limited, 1999

GOOD, JOE, *Enchanted by Dreams: The Journal of a Revolutionary*, Dingle,

Brandon Book Publishers Ltd, 1996

GRIFFITH, K., and O'GRADY, E., *Curious Journey: An Oral History of Ireland's Unfinished Revolution,* London, Hutchinson, 1982

HOBSON, BULMER, *Ireland: Yesterday and Tomorrow,* Tralee, Anvil Books, 1968

JENKINS, ROY, *Asquith,* London, Collins, 1964

KEE, ROBERT, *The Green Flag: A History of Irish Nationalism,* London, Weidenfield and Nicolson, 1972

KIBERD, DECLAN, *1916 Rebellion Handbook,* Dublin, The Mourne River Press, 1998

LYNCH, DIARMUID, *The IRB and the 1916 Insurrection,* Cork, Mercier Press, 1957

LYONS, F.S.L., *Ireland since the Famine,* London, Fontana, 1986

McCARTHY, COL. J.M., *Limerick's Fighting Story,* Tralee, Anvil Books, undated

MacENTEE, SEAN, *Episode at Easter,* Dublin/Melbourne, M.H. Gill and Son Ltd, 1966

McHUGH, R., *Dublin, 1916,* Dublin, Arlington Books, 1966

MacLOCHLAINN, PIARAS F., *Last Words; Letters and Statements of the Leaders Executed after the Rising at Easter 1916,* Dublin, Stationery Office, 1990

MARTIN, F.X., *Leaders and Men of the Easter Rising,* London, Methuen, 1967

MORGAN, AUSTEN, *James Connolly: A Political Biography,* Manchester, Manchester University Press, 1988

NIC SHUIBHLAIGH, MAIRE, *The Splendid Years,* Dublin, James Duffy, 1955

Ó BROIN, LEON, *Dublin Castle and the 1916 Rising: The Story of Sir Matthew Nathan,* Dublin, Helicon, 1966

–, *W.E. Wylie and the Irish Revolution 1916–21,* Dublin, Gill and Macmillan, 1989

ORAM, GERARD, *Death Sentences passed by Military Courts of the British Army, 1914–24,* London, Boutle, 1998

–, *Worthless Men: Race, Eugenics and the Death Penalty in the British Army during the First World War,* London, Boutle, 1998

REID, B.L., *The Lives of Roger Casement,* New Haven, Yale University Press, 1976

LE ROUX, LOUIS, *Tom Clarke and the Irish Freedom Movement,* Dublin, Talbot Press, 1936

RYAN, DESMOND, *The Rising: The Complete Story of Easter Week,* Dublin, Golden Eagle Books, 1949

SAWYER, R., *Casement,* London, Routledge and Kegan Paul, 1984

STEPHENS, JAMES, *The Insurrection in Dublin,* Gerrards Cross, Colin Smyth, 1978

TAILLON, RUTH, *The Women of 1916,* Belfast, Beyond the Pale Publications, 1996

Index